THE RE-FORMED JESUITS

Joseph M. Becker, S.J.

THE RE-FORMED JESUITS

VOLUME I:
A History of Changes in Jesuit Formation
During the Decade 1965–1975

IGNATIUS PRESS   SAN FRANCISCO

Cover by Roxanne Mei Lum

Cover Photo of Pedro Arrupe, S.J. CNS/KNA

©1992, Ignatius Press, San Francisco
All rights reserved
ISBN 0–89870–402–2
Library of Congress catalogue number 91–76517
Printed in the United States of America

CONTENTS

FIGURES

ACKNOWLEDGMENTS

Thanks must go to Georgetown University for its support of the Jesuit Center for Social Studies while the Center was collecting the evidence of change, evidence involving hundreds of interviews and the ransacking of archives in all parts of the United States. Thanks, too, must go to Xavier University for its support of the Jesuit Center for Religious Studies when the collection of materials was being completed and the results given the form of this book.

I wish there were room to list by name all the interviewees and all the archivists whose generous cooperation was literally essential to the task of amassing the historical evidence. I am especially indebted to Father Robert H. Harvanek, whose experience of the period was unusually wide and deep and who shared that experience (information not evaluation) with me by letter, tape, and telephone.

The early work of collecting and organizing the body of materials was made possible by the cooperation of Mary Lou Drittler and Dr. Genevieve Walsh. The final task of producing a usable manuscript involved the indispensable assistance of Mary V. Byrne and K. Dianne Trainor. Mrs. Trainor prepared the manuscript for the printer and saw it through the press.

Readers of the manuscript in its successive stages—and there were many of these living in various Jesuit provinces—provided valuable assistance in helping me avoid both errors of fact and undue intrusion of personal views. Only the author is responsible for any personal evaluation that may have crept into this history.

9

If history is less than a story it cannot fulfill its social function, while if it is more it competes unnecessarily with other disciplines, speaks in an uncertain voice, and brings confusion rather than guidance.

G. J. Renier

INTRODUCTION

In the decade following the Second Vatican Council, the Jesuit order (the Society of Jesus) underwent a significant internal transformation, probably greater than any it had experienced in its previous four hundred years. There had been abundant instances of great external changes, as when the order was expelled from various countries, or when the entire order was suppressed in 1773 by Pope Clement XI. The order had also made changes in its ministries over the centuries as it accommodated its work to the secular developments about it. In all probability, however, it had never before experienced so great an internal, self-chosen transformation.

The theme of the period covered in this study is sounded in the opening line of the first decree of the Thirty-First General Congregation of the order (1965–66): "In this 'new age' in which the human race now finds itself . . . "[1] It is true, of course, that every age is new and Adam may well have spoken the congregation's opening line to Eve as they left the Garden. In some ages, however, the rate of change picks up and effects more notable transformations in human structures. For the Jesuit order, the 1960s were such a period of accelerated change.

In affecting the largest of the religious orders, the Jesuit experience has significance in itself. It has additional significance as being contained within, and connected with, three broader circles of experience. The Jesuit experience is similar to that of other religious orders in the United States and, indeed, in all regions

---

[1] All citations to the documents of the Thirty-First and Thirty-Second General Congregations are to be found in the 1977 source given in the list of references.

sharing the Western culture. In the absence of detailed histories of the other orders, as is currently the case, this Jesuit narrative may serve to illuminate that larger world. The Jesuit Center for Religious Studies plans to produce similar histories of the other major orders, but until that goal is reached, the present history is usable as a general guide to what has been happening throughout vowed religious life. Though the separate orders differ among themselves, the similarities in their experience have been much greater than the differences.

The Jesuit experience has still wider significance. The Catholic Church herself has been undergoing a profound transformation, a paradigmatic shift, a new way of viewing reality. The transformation of the Jesuits is a part of the total Catholic shift and illustrates nearly all the major changes in the Church. A detailed history like the present one provides a unique window onto that larger scene.

The Jesuit history lies within still another circle of significance: it is part of a major cultural shift in the West. Geoffrey Barraclough and other historians think the shift has been distinctive enough to deserve a separate title; they speak of the shift from "modern history" to "contemporary history". As will be pointed out in a future volume, there is an unmistakable similarity between the general cultural shift that has occurred in the West and the particular changes that have occurred in the Jesuit order. In some instances, there is even a close similarity in timing. For example, the experience of the young Jesuits in their houses of study followed that of the general college population remarkably closely.

Two aspects of the Jesuit shift will be of particular interest to social scientists. First, in the Jesuit order, as in the broader society, the shift has been a Western phenomenon. Though the Jesuit order is worldwide, the changes described here came first and principally to its Western regions, such as Europe, the Americas, and Australia.

Second, the Jesuit experience supplies a measure of the strength of the general cultural shift. It was not to have been expected that the religious orders—with their initial selectivity of candidates, their long period of controlled training (fifteen years in the case of a Jesuit entering from high school), and their relatively secluded lifestyle—would have resonated so closely with the secular culture. The extent to which the Jesuits were affected by the general cultural shift serves as a kind of seismic measure of the strength of that shift.

This history of changes in the Jesuit order comprises two volumes, of which the first covers changes in the formation of Jesuits, while the second covers all other changes, such as those in numbers,[2] vows, dress, community lifestyle, governance, and ministries. Both volumes focus on the decade following Vatican II, roughly the period 1965–75. When, however, events occur shortly before or after this period and are particularly pertinent, they are noted. Changes slowed but did not stop after the period covered by this history; hence, the present state of any situation may be different from the final one described here.

The entire first volume of the history has been allotted to the story of changes in the process of formation because formation is the key to the character of any group. "Formation" imparts the "form" to the body; that is, it determines what the soul, the animating principle, will be. No change is so important as a change in the system of formation.

Furthermore, the changes began in the houses of formation. Contrary to what might have been expected, the first stirrings of adaptation to modernity appeared not in the universities and parishes, which were in direct contact with the "world", but in the (at that time) secluded houses of formation. The explanation of this surprising development is provided in the text.

This history is primarily a narration of events and an identification of causes—both efficient cause (who made the change?) and final cause (why was the change made?). The causes sought in this history are the immediate, measurable, certain causes. Back of these are more profound causes, and back of *these* still more

---

[2] The change in numbers was especially significant, both in itself and in its impact on all the other changes. The number of scholastics, which determines the eventual size of the order, dropped from 10,594 in 1960 to 3,770 in 1975.

profound causes. The more profound the cause, the more significant it is, but it is also likely to be the more speculative and uncertain. This history is "story" in Renier's sense; but it also provides both the fuel and the test of speculation, that is, it provides a detailed, reliable account of what it is that needs to be explained and what will always be the measure of any explanation's worth.

Though the second volume ventures somewhat more into theory regarding causes, neither volume attempts evaluation. Evaluation requires results, especially long-term results, and such data are not yet available. The history, however, is not unconnected with evaluation. Indeed, its whole purpose is to provide the kind of data which will best serve the purposes of evaluation—both the tentative evaluation that is possible now and the more definitive evaluation that will be possible later.

The author is a member of the organization which he is describing. Though this has its dangers, on the whole it is an advantage. As the eminent American anthropologist Clifford Geertz holds, the investigator should be a participant observer, that is, someone who shares the cultural milieu which he seeks to describe.

The author's personal values have inevitably affected his choice of materials and emphases, but I trust that this impact has been kept to the irreducible minimum. By way of approaching that goal, I have submitted the manuscript in its developing stages to many readers who could be expected to detect undue bias.

I have avoided all explicit evaluation and have tried to avoid even implicit evaluation. Indeed, I have refused to let myself even think in those terms, lest it influence my search for the actual events and causes. A great help to this desired neutrality has been the simple fact that I do not have a judgment yet. I readily identify with the attitude expressed by Pedro Arrupe on the occasion of his golden jubilee in the Society (January 15, 1977): "The figure of Abraham has always been for me an inexhaustible source of inspiration. 'Where is the Society heading?' men have asked me. My reply has always been: 'Where God is leading it.' In other words, I do not know."

Perhaps "cautious" would be the most exact term to describe my approach to this history. I am cautious because we have been living through a revolution, and revolutions tend to breed exaggerations. I lived through the revolution in economic science that followed the 1935 publication of Lord Keynes' *General Theory*. It was a genuinely needed revolution but in its early stages developed the inevitable exaggerations that led to Keynes' wry remark: "I am meeting people these days who are much more Keynesian than I am." The revolution of the 1960s is still so recent that I consider it prudent to guard against possible exaggerations. Such an attitude is quite compatible with Arrupe's further remark that "God is leading us toward a new land", and although Arrupe does not know, "He [God] knows where it is."

This history is based almost entirely on primary sources, which include several hundred interviews with people who were active in bringing about the changes. The history is also based, of course, on documents of many kinds: proceedings of meetings, house histories, official published documents, and much correspondence. Some of the documentation is of a confidential nature usually not available until more time has elapsed. Authorities granted an exception in this case because of the perceived need for as much light as possible as soon as possible. The order is still in the process of adjusting to a very complex period of change.

Jesuit participants in the history who later left the order are identified in Appendix 5. There seems to be significance in the fact that some of the leaders in the task of restating Jesuit life themselves later left religious life entirely. The exact nature of that significance probably will be determined variously by various readers; but all who were consulted on this point agreed that it did have significance and should be made a part of the history.

Most unpublished materials in the history, including all interviews, may be found in the files of the Jesuit Center for Religious Studies, or in Jesuit province archives, or in both.

I

GENERATORS OF CHANGE: EARLIER

An understanding of change—or of anything else—requires a knowledge of its causes. Those causes are, of course, themselves effects of prior causes; but history must start somewhere. This history starts with a dozen developments which were notable generators of altered viewpoints and assumptions and thus contributed substantially to the changes in Jesuit formation described in subsequent chapters.

The twelve "generators" reviewed in the first two chapters are numbered consecutively and are divided into developments that came somewhat earlier or somewhat later. The chronological ordering is rough, being affected by considerations other than the merely temporal, but serves our purpose adequately.

1. Vatican Council II (1962–65)

In the Catholic Church, by far the most significant generator of change was the Second Vatican Council, which met in four sessions between 1962 and 1965: October 11–December 8, 1962; September 29–December 4, 1963; September 14–November 21, 1964; and September 14–December 8, 1965. (As indicated below, the two sessions of the Jesuit Thirty-First General Congregation bracketed the last session of the council.)

The tap root of the Second Vatican Council was the newly-elected Pope, John XXIII, elected in 1958. Within three months of his election he decided on a council. It was a decision reached without any preceding investigation and even without any formal consultation with his Curia. Pope John had simply decided that there would be a council—soon.

In some of his later descriptions of how he had reached his decision, he may have overdramatized its inspirational character. For example, he wrote in 1962, in his journal, that when he proposed the council in 1959 in a private conversation with Cardinal Domenico Tardini, his secretary of state, he himself was as surprised by what he was saying as was his hearer (Hebblethwaite 1984, 316). As a matter of fact, however, he had previously, in November and December of 1958, stated the desirability of a council (Hebblethwaite 1984, 308). There can be no doubt, however, that the decision was entirely his own and that in making it he had a strong sense of being moved by the Spirit (Wynn 1988, 103).

Five days after his private conversation with Cardinal Tardini, which was held on January 20, 1959, Pope John publicly announced his decision to call a meeting of Roman cardinals. A period of preparation began that brought to Rome over 800 theologians and experts and covered almost four years.[1]

During the preparatory period, expectations regarding the council were generally low-keyed. In 1975, a decade after the council, *The Critic* had the inspiration for an article entitled "Just Before the Council, Mother". A number of Catholic leaders, twenty of them, were invited to answer the question, "What were your hopes for the Church in 1961?" on the eve of the council. Their expectations ran the gamut from doubtful to hopeful, but no one remotely foresaw what a watershed the council would become ("Just Before the Council, Mother!" 1975, 14–24).

Protestant church historian Martin Marty recalled how in 1961 his publisher suggested that he "take off a year or two to write a

---

[1] Pius XII had considered calling a council and did much preparatory work in the period 1948–50. When he decided against the idea in 1951, results of the work were filed away in the papal archives. This preparatory work, which included many special studies, probably was of assistance to the planners of Vatican II (Wynn 1988, 102).

book on the forthcoming Second Vatican Council". Marty replied: "I am busy. Why spend time on such an unpromising prospect? [The Council] ... is for the bishops who want to rearrange the Church's furniture." The publisher replied: "We checked with Gus [Father Gustave Weigel, S.J.]. He pretty much agrees. Forget the book" (Marty 1975, 49).

Pope John, however, had in mind a unique kind of council. Its principal objective was to be an updating of the Church, an *aggiornamento,* as he styled it. Back of that objective was his conviction that the Catholic Church and the non-Catholic world had been drifting apart, like continental plates. To halt and reverse that drift was a task so immense that no lesser instrument than a general council would suffice.

He never abandoned this initial objective. According to one story, the Pope responded to a visitor's question, "What is the Council really about?" by going over to a window and throwing it open with a single word: "This!" While he probably did not foresee how far the council's momentum would finally carry it, he gave his support, as long as he lived, to the side of innovation. In an opening statement at the beginning of the council he publicly described his official advisors as "prophets of doom" for attempting to hold him to a more cautious course and asserted that "Divine Providence is leading us to a new order of human relations" (Abbott 1966, 712). Where other ecumenical councils were called to put out fires, Vatican II was called to start one.

A clear indication of his openness to change occurred early in the council's deliberations. The preparatory commissions, which had been at work during the years preceding the council, had constructed a series of draft proposals along traditional lines. When these drafts—all of them previously approved by the Pope— were presented to the assembled council members, a group of northern European bishops found them hopelessly out of date— contributing nothing to *aggiornamento*—and demanded that they be completely redone (Rynne 1968, 76–90). At this crucial point, Pope John sided with the advocates of change, directing that the prepared drafts be scrapped in favor of a new start. The first of these face-offs occurred on November 21, 1962, when the draft on Divine Revelation was withdrawn and entrusted to a mixed commission more representative of the council. From this point on, the momentum for change never faltered.

Vatican II differed in significant ways from its twenty predecessors. First, it differed in composition. It had ten times as many members as did the Council of Trent; excepting the ancient councils, it had a greater proportion of non-European members, especially from Asia and Africa; and it had a large group of non-Catholic observers, who had the best seats at the council and full access to all documents and discussions. Vatican II differed also in being the first to carry on its deliberations in the full light of the modern media, omnipresent and insistent.

The greatest difference, however, was in its spirit. The modern historical school emphasizes the personal element in past and present judgments and hence emphasizes the relative and changeable over the absolute and perennial. There was some affinity between this approach to reality and the council's proclaimed objective of *aggiornamento*. The Dominican theologian Edward Schillebeeckx may have found the most revealing description of the new spirit by calling it a shift from the essentialist to the existentialist approach to reality (Schillebeeckx 1963, 10). The application of this philosophical theory to history helps to produce the modern historical consciousness. In this council, modern historical consciousness was clearly at work, especially among the members from northern Europe (Germany, Holland, Belgium), who became the leaders of the innovative wing.

Change poses a special problem for an institution like the Catholic Church, which claims to be an infallible source of permanent truth. In his opening speech to the council, Pope John offered the solution that the council would give old truths "new formulations" (Abbott 1966, 715).[2] Did the Pope's statement mean

[2] "As we shall see, this seemingly innocuous distinction would be pressed to its limits by theologians and bishops both during and after the Council and would have the most far-reaching consequences on the structure of the Church" (McSweeney 1980, 138).

to cover development of doctrine in some sense? If so, in what sense? According to a leading Jesuit theologian, John Courtney Murray, development of doctrine was *the* issue underlying all other issues at the council. The council itself never addressed the issue explicitly and was ambiguous in its actions. It juxtaposed new formulations and traditional ones without indicating how they were to be reconciled. This made it possible after the council for innovators to declare how much had changed and for traditionalists to claim that all the fundamentals remained what they had always been.[3]

While there is room for debate over the nature of the changes flowing from Vatican II, there can be no doubt about their quantity. Through its concrete decrees, touching almost every aspect of Catholic life, and still more through the spirit it engendered, Vatican II became an enormous generator of change. And this applied not only to the Church herself but to all churches and the general culture itself. A decade after the council, writer Will Herberg, a non-Catholic, summed up his impression: "It is, indeed, difficult to find the words sufficiently impressive to convey one's sense of weight and importance of the Second Vatican Council in the ongoing life of the West" (Herberg 1974, 336).

The first and most direct effect of the council was, of course, on the Catholic Church herself.[4] According to British analyst William McSweeney, the impact of the council on the Church "was to carry forward the most fundamental reappraisal of its doctrine,

---

[3] In a 1983 article, John O'Malley recognized the growing number of the latter but held that this attempt at damming the river of change would prove temporary and ineffectual (O'Malley 1983a, 374, 405–406). Father O'Malley sees Vatican II as almost unique among the councils because it represents a "paradigm-shift", which he defines as follows: "By paradigm-shift I mean not merely that some important changes were made in law or rite, but that a new frame of reference came into being that had an across-the-board impact" (O'Malley 1983b, 308).

[4] The council supported four modifications in Church structure that are likely to be generators of continuing innovation. It supported internationalization of the Roman Curia and of the College of Cardinals and establishment of the Synod of Bishops and of national conferences of bishops.

liturgy and relationship to the world in its 2000-year history"
(McSweeney 1980, 135). Schillebeeckx prepared a list of council
actions that he considered to be significant innovations. His list
totaled sixty-eight and covered the liturgy, the Church, revelation,
bishops and priests, the laity, non-Catholics, freedom of conscience,
and religious institutes (Schillebeeckx 1967). When the prelimi-
nary commission on canon law began its work on the revision of
the code, it started by reviewing Vatican II for principles to guide
it. (N.C.R. 1983)[5]

In its instructions to religious orders,[6] the council could hardly
have done anything more explosive. It required each order—male
or female, active or contemplative—to hold a general chapter
with the explicit purpose of examining whether anything in the
order needed to be changed.[7] In the case of the Society of Jesus,
this requirement was met by the order's Thirty-First General
Congregation (G.C. 31), which was held toward the end of the
council and was swept along by the full force of the council's
momentum. (G.C. 31 is described later in this chapter.)

This action of the council moved the burden of proof in religious orders from innovation onto stability. The effect was that of
an earthquake, shaking every part of a religious institution. Even
novices could, and did, question practices of the traditional religious life and ask for evidence that any given practice was better
than an alternative that anyone might propose. Such evidence is
not easily produced. In human relationships truth is usually discerned
not through abstract deduction, as in mathematics, but through
experience painstakingly accumulated over long periods. Since
such evidence is difficult to produce on demand, the shift in the
burden of proof was unsettling in the extreme.

[5] See also McNaspy on the Santa Clara Conference, below, pp. 74–75.

[6] Throughout this history the term "order" is used in its popular sense, as
referring to any religious institute. Canonically, "order" refers only to religious institutes whose members take solemn vows.

[7] This directive was communicated in the conciliar decree Perfectae Caritatis
(1965) and Pope Paul's apostolic letter Ecclesiae Sanctae (1966). For the text of
these two documents, see Flannery 1975, 611–33.

If the proposals for new life patterns had been required to produce the same evidence, they would have encountered the same difficulty. But, in fact, the innovations were not required to bear the burden of proof. On the contrary, they enjoyed the benefit of the doubt. The prevailing mood of *aggiornamento* positively shifted the benefit of the doubt to change. The legitimacy and respectability with which Vatican II invested change was a more powerful force than any of the council's specific decrees.

The effects produced by the council were the greater because they were aided by a kind of gravity. Practically all the changes proposed for the new era were liberating changes. They lessened some obligation here or removed some restriction there, thus enlarging the area of individual freedom. Since mankind is inclined in this direction naturally, the proposals for change were the more easily accepted. The force implied in Virgil's *facilis descensus* was at work.

Partly for these two reasons—the shift in the burden of proof and the abetting force of psychological gravity—changes came quickly and in great quantity, at least in the first decade after the council. The durability, however, of the changes may depend more on other forces, especially those discussed in Volume II of this study. In 1964, Paul VI published a document entitled *Ecclesiam Suam,* in which he declared that no updating of the Church could be effective if it stemmed from archaeism, relativism, naturalism, or immobilism (Jurich 1969, 9).

2. Theological Institutes

Alma College: 1959–62

Some early signs of the changing era began to appear at Alma College, the theologate of the California province, shortly *before*

Vatican II. In the academic year 1959–60 the Alma scholastics proposed a number of innovations. Among those most active in the events of this period were Michael J. Buckley and Robert L. Maloney, respectively first- and second-year theologians at Alma. James Albertson and Albert Jonsen were also very active. Among the faculty, the most helpful were Joseph B. Wall, professor of ascetical theology, and William A. Huesman, dean of the theologate. Without the active support of the dean, none of the proposed innovations could have succeeded.

One proposal was to substitute two seminars for the more traditional "circles" (where one theologian defended a "thesis" against appointed objectors). The first seminar dealt with church-state relations, a lively topic at that time because of the controversy between Msgr. J. C. Fenton, a theologian at Catholic University, and John Courtney Murray, S.J. The seminar accepted Murray's position over Fenton's, thus anticipating Vatican II's "Declaration on Religious Liberty", of which Murray is said to have been the principal author.

A second seminar studied the Constitutions of the Society of Jesus in their historical development. By this seminar the scholastics gained possession of a basic tool for reflecting upon the Society's makeup. The seminar's approach resembled that of the Renaissance: it returned to the distant, classical past (Jesuit origins) in order to study the immediate past and update the present. The scholastics were thus engaged in a formal process of passing judgment, sometimes an adverse judgment, on existing customs. The seminar reached the conclusion, for example, that the universal requirement of hour-long daily meditation was an aberration, that is, not in accord with the letter of the early documents.

Another, and more important, innovation at this time—at Alma— was the institution called "town hall". Held at regular intervals, in the evening, presided over by the dean of the theologate, and open to any students and faculty that cared to attend, the town hall meetings provided an opportunity for the public discussion of common concerns and often produced proposals for changes in the way of doing or considering things. The town hall institutionalized change by moving criticisms of the existing order out of the snack room, where they had been aired for generations, and giving them a quasi-official public forum. The town hall had an automatic twofold effect. First, it stimulated the critical sense in the minds of those scholastics, the majority, who otherwise would have taken things much as they were; this was the "consciousness raising" technique so commonly used in the 1960s. Second, it generated a new form of pressure on superiors to respond publicly to the scholastics acting as a formal group.

Some similarity between the town hall and the more confrontational tactics of the 1960s can be detected. However, the tone of the theologate at this earlier time was by all accounts milder. According to the testimony of both faculty and students, Alma was a happy house in the early 1960s. The incoming scholastics had come from a happy experience in philosophy and regency and found at Alma a faculty of good teachers personally interested in the students. There was none of the bitterness which marked all the theologates later, beginning about 1965. Proposals for change at this early stage reflected a mood of reform rather than of revolution.

Though there seem to be no written records left by the first three town halls, which occurred during the academic year 1959–60, the fourth left a full history. The fourth town hall was a three-day theological institute (September 5–7, 1960) dedicated to "Problems in Jesuit Asceticism". The institute was primarily the creature of the scholastics of Alma College. They conceived the idea, obtained the necessary clearances, chose the topics, secured the speakers, and published the proceedings. When Joseph B. Wall came to summarize the work of the institute, he voiced the obvious question: "Why such an institute now rather than five years earlier?" His answer was as follows:

Because this year, and not five years ago, there were in the community scholastics who were willing to inaugurate this project and to carry it out. This thing happened because the scholastics had the imagination and the will, and above all the

courage to try to bring this about. We had these particular
scholastics this year and not five years ago (Ascetical Institute
1960, 116).

The issues that were to arouse the liveliest interest in the later
years of the decade were already manifest in this 1960 institute. As
noted, for the theme of the institute, the scholastics chose not
dogmatic, scriptural, or liturgical theology, but ascetical theology.
Though one reason for the choice was simply that this field
received little formal attention in the regular theologate courses,
the new dynamics that would distinguish the later 1960s were
undoubtedly at work. For it was in the area of human problems
covered by ascetical theology that the revolution of the 1960s
would produce their most characteristic results.

The choice of topics within this general field also clearly reflected
what were to be the principal issues of the 1960s. For the topics of
the opening two sessions, the scholastics chose "Obedience" and
"The Rule". The choice represented an accurate assessment of
where the first and most critical engagement would have to occur
between tradition and change. The third session dealt with
"Frustration" and thus touched on one of the principal sources of
the demand for change. The fourth session, dealing with "Mobility
and Adaptability", was a discussion of the need for change in
every living organism. The final session, dealing with "The Individual and the Community", was an early example of the discussion which was to agitate the United States Jesuit Assistancy for
the succeeding decade, namely, how to enlarge the creative freedom of the individual.

Though the attitudes and directions expressed during the institute were not as well defined as they became later, they clearly
belonged to the same family. The following examples of some of
the more common issues are extracted from the institute. A major
problem was perceived to be monasticism. (See, for example,
Ascetical Institute 1960, 55, 56, 58, 64, 104.) Several speakers
developed the theme that though Saint Ignatius had deliberately
departed from monasticism later generations of Jesuits had gradually

returned to it. As Clarence J. Wallen, mathematics professor at the Alma theologate, put it: "How many of our men in regency and in the later work of the Society have had to completely overturn the habits of the mind they learned in the novitiate because the novitiate had trained them to be monks rather than Jesuits" (p. 49). One proposal meeting with general approval was to move the houses of formation away from the countryside, which more easily accommodated the monastic form of life, to the cities, preferably to a university campus.[8]

A related criticism was that later members of the order, as compared with early Jesuits, had become conservative. One major cause of this development was said to be the Society's growing involvement with "institutions". (All page references in this paragraph are to Ascetical Institute 1960.) It was also argued that Jesuit asceticism was too "negative" (p. 55) and that there should be more emphasis on developing "warm friendships" (p. 59). As a help to this end, it was suggested that the young Jesuits be allowed "to use each other's first name or nickname" (p. 111). A psychologist attending the institute (Joseph R. Caldwell) maintained that the average Jesuit was not emotionally mature, the result of the training he received. The training was defective in not giving adequate recognition to the importance of feelings and the need to express them (pp. 51–52). Such commentary and proposals became familiar themes in the decade that followed.

Though the institute drew little attention in the California province outside the theologate, it occasioned some local uneasiness. One of the older fathers, not a faculty member, was asked by the Alma rector for an evaluation. In a letter dated September 11,

[8] Father Francis Marien, a faculty member, entered a strong demurrer against the notion that "monasticism" posed a serious danger. "I submit that there is nothing particularly monastic about these regulations and that it could cause serious error to consider them as such. We could go through the Summary [of the Jesuit Constitutions], rule by rule, and ask what is particularly monastic about that?" (p. 36). Marien's viewpoint became a rarity as the decade wore on.

1960, he submitted a long, detailed analysis which included the following:

> There are problems in the Jesuit life, but it does not seem that this type of Institute is either the way to find out these problems or to find solutions to them.... This public method savors of the democratic processes which are foreign to the Society of Jesus. Pope Pius XII warned the last group of Jesuit procurators in Rome that the Society of Jesus must remember that its government is monarchical and not democratic.... Such Town Hall discussions on the difficulties of government, of economics, of literary criticism, etc., might be acceptable and stimulating, but to apply Town Hall methods to the difficulties of Religious Life will not solve those difficulties, but might rather deepen them and spread them more widely to the discomfort of the individual members and to the whole Society.

The issue of obedience attracted so much interest during the 1960 institute that the Alma scholastics arranged for a second institute devoted entirely to this one topic. Entitled "The Meaning of Jesuit Obedience" and held September 4–6, 1961, its speakers included professors of theology, philosophy, and science, along with superiors, administrators, and spiritual directors. Though it came a year later, the second institute actually had fewer characteristics of the later 1960s than the first had. In fact, there is little in this second institute that could not have been said a decade earlier. A spiritual director, writing to the provincial on September 14, 1961, commented: "Like yourself I was somewhat inclined to be pessimistic about it, especially after last year. However, I must admit I was pleasantly surprised."

The same writer observed: "These institutes are not like the Town Hall meetings of the theologians. From what I hear of these [town hall meetings], I am not too enthusiastic about them. The institutes were not given to criticism but to positive doctrine."

In the fall of 1962, the Alma scholastics organized a third ascetical institute, which clearly returned to the more challenging mood of the first one. The third institute was dedicated to the subject of "Jesuit Maturity" and concerned itself with two questions:

What is Jesuit maturity, and what are the means to attain the end thus defined? Answers to these questions were proposed in connection with each stage of the process of formation.

Preparatory to the institute, the scholastics listed questions which the speakers were invited to address (Ascetical Institute 1962, 133). The questions reflect the concerns of the young Jesuit of that early period and anticipate many of the concerns of the later 1960s—for example:

— What are the characteristics of the "good novice"?

— Is he defined by what he is not, that is, not singular, not selfish, not worldly, not immodest, not noisy, etc.?

— Does an unhealthy attitude toward the horrible "particular friendship" tend to influence one's attitude toward true friendship?

— Does the master of novices tend to form novices according to his own subjective attitudes?

— Does Rodriguez [a sixteenth century Jesuit spiritual writer whose three-volume directory was obligatory reading in the novitiate] present a true picture of Jesuit spiritual maturity? Should Rodriguez not be replaced?

— Do superiors sufficiently recognize the fact that the regent has been a Jesuit for 7–10 years and is as old or older than newly ordained diocesan priests? To say nothing of men who are married and already have one or two children?

— Is our abstract methodology, especially in philosophy and theology, fitted for use in concrete situations?

— Does not the strict interpretation of the rule of grades lead to a sterile division, even a caste system, in the conscious life of many communities?

— How can a Jesuit attain and maintain his sense of personal worth to the Society and the Church?

At the institute, psychologist John Evoy of the Oregon province presented a paper describing two undesirable attitudes: (1) self-depreciation, or failure to recognize one's own worth; (2) overdependence on obedience, or failure to recognize one's own ability to make decisions. The opposites of these two attitudes were to absorb the attention of the 1960s. A sense of self-worth and a preference for self-direction were to be encouraged steadily in speeches, papers, and books.

St. Mary's College: 1961

Stimulated by the Alma Institute of 1960, the theologians at St. Mary's College, Kansas, the theologate of the Missouri Province, held a similar institute the following year, 1961. Called the Institute on Jesuit Asceticism, its structure and contents were generally similar to those of the first Alma institute. Its opening session dealt with the familiar problem of obedience, while the second session continued with the related issue of superior-subject relationships. Succeeding sessions dealt with the individual-group tension, and with the apostolic (as distinguished from the monastic) quality of the Jesuit life; the concluding session was on American Jesuit spirituality. The tone of the St. Mary's institute was somewhat more traditional than that of the Alma institute. While the assumption was clearly present that Jesuit asceticism needed reevaluation and probably alteration, the papers and the discussions were not yet marked by the outright advocacy that was to show itself later in the Santa Clara Conference (see below, pp. 69ff.). There was not yet the excitement of expectation that a new era was about to dawn.

Woodstock College: 1962

The theological institute was clearly "in". In 1962, the scholastics at Woodstock, Maryland, the oldest and most prestigious of the theologates, held a three-day session (August 28–30, 1962) entitled "Woodstock Ascetical Institute". The speakers were from various provinces and included Fr. Joseph Wall, the faculty member most active in the original Alma institute.

The scholastics had formulated eight pages of discussion questions to which the speakers and commentators were invited to address themselves. The questions and the program of the institute indicate that the contents were generally similar to those of Alma and St. Mary's. But if the proceedings of the institute were published in some form, no copies found their way into the archives of either Woodstock College or the Maryland province.[9] It is probable, however, that this institute was a close eastern cousin of its western and midwestern predecessors.

Weston College: 1964

Two years later, in March 1964, Weston College, the theologate of the New England province, held an institute with a somewhat different focus. The Weston scholastics produced a three-day institute on the Jesuit theologate (Institute 1964; all page references in this section relate to this work). The papers and discussions were presented under three headings—the academic, spiritual, and social dimensions of the theologate. The concern throughout was with the apostolic efficiency of the training imparted in the theologate. The general conclusion was that the training was inefficient and needed to be changed. The institute's tone combined the academic ferment with the excitement of an imminent revolution.

The first presentation was made by Michael P. Walsh, president of Boston College, and his opening statement could stand as the institute's theme: "Pope John opened the windows in the besieged fortress of the post-Reformation Church" (p. 13). All the speakers addressed their particular topics from this general standpoint. By this time the movement for change had picked up measurable momentum (Vatican Council II was in its third session), and it was

[9] Copies of the program and of the scholastics' questions are in the Center's files. Participants did not recall any other publication. Brief summaries of some of the papers presented at this institute may be found in *Woodstock Letters;* this same article, "Institutes of Spirituality", with a preface by the editor Joseph P. Whelan, similarly summarizes the institutes held at Alma and at St. Mary's (see vol. 93, 1964, pp. 59–90). This article is actually a composite of short reports by more than 30 Jesuits.

taken for granted that alterations would be made over a spectrum whose boundaries were far from clear.

Edward J. Sponga, then president of Scranton University,[10] began his talk on the first day with an anecdote to illustrate the new climate. He recalled that nine years had elapsed between the time he left Woodstock as a student and returned as its rector. He observed that no noticeable changes had taken place in those nine years. "I fitted right back into the field . . . hardly realizing that I had been away for nine years." He continued, "And now it is about nine months since I left theology again, but I have a feeling that within those nine months I have already become obsolete. . . . The pace of change and thought and development has been so rapid that I am already dated" (p. 45). When James E. Coleran was called upon for a summarizing statement at the end of the institute, he made a similar remark: "I would say that when I finished my six years as New England provincial, my education started then. And I'm being re-educated in this new age" (p. 160).

Sponga went on to enunciate the theme of the institute and indeed of the next decade: "The major need of present theological training may be summarized in terms of this: that we are seeking how we can foster relevancy to the modern world" (p. 46). He argued that relevancy required making the life of the religious more like the life of the lay person.

> Is there any wonder that more and more we look here and there for ways to narrow the gap between ourselves and the Christian in the world? . . . As we become more acutely conscious of our difference, we become uneasy with the contrast in our more structured, disciplined, authority-centered lives especially in our years of training, as compared with the world in which the layman lives—a world "marked by freedom and self-direction" (pp. 48–49).[11]

[10] Sponga was made Maryland provincial the following year (1965) and became a leader among the provincials. He was called to Rome as a member of a small group to prepare for G.C. 31.

[11] The phrase after the dash ("marked by freedom and self-direction") was

A second theme was closely related to the first.

The human person cannot be (in some kind of ontological sense) a person today, to the extent that could have been possible not too long ago, without the interaction of other human beings. . . . In such a view, loving God does not mean going away from the fellow, but going deeper into the fellow man where God may be found. Dialogue, then, in its radical sense, is a category of being (p. 50).

In the discussion period, W. Paul Kiley, professor of philosophy at The College of the Holy Cross, said he wanted to underscore Sponga's point, that the changes needed "are not just a matter of technique; but really there is a new dimension of reality that we are dealing with" (p. 59). The deeper significance of Sponga's "relevancy" obviously depends on the extent to which this proposition is or is not true.

The principal address on the second day was by Francis X. Shea, professor of English at Boston College. In his presentation, he supported the Sponga thesis that the churchly world needed to be brought into closer contact with the secular world by being made more like it. He developed three propositions, each having the effect of diminishing traditional differences: (1) the natural is sacred; the natural and the supernatural should not be opposed; (2) the material is good; spirit and body should not be seen in opposition; and (3) all social groups should be democratic; the differences between laity and clergy need to be deemphasized. As part of the process of getting out of the cloister and into the world, he recommended to the scholastics that they read at least two novels per month.

He sounded another note that would be heard frequently in the 1960s. He urged a "sturdy" independence "from institutional support on the one hand, and from overweening concern for institutions on the other"; he warned against valuing "institutional good

---

taken from an article which was alluded to several times in the course of the institute. Entitled "The Freedom of Priests", the article was written by Daniel Callahan and appeared in *Commonweal,* October 18, 1963.

above the personal". It was necessary to "recognize that modern man seeking, as he does, to found his further progress on a personal fulfillment scaled out now to the size of his expanding understanding of himself and his world, will turn away in disgust when he encounters a religious custodian, a janitor of the spirit, who attempts to persuade him that the house rules are the law of Christ." He summarized his message by saying that if there was anything novel in the present time it was an openness toward the human. "*Contemptus mundi,* hatred of the flesh, scorn for the material and temporal—these, at least in their more vigorous articulation, the world will no longer brook, nor should it" (pp. 78–80).

At the end of the discussion that followed his presentation, when asked to summarize again, Shea said:

> I found yesterday as I sat and listened to Father Sponga's talk that everything that I wanted to say was said much more profoundly and more to the point than I said it myself.... Our achievement of holiness, our achievement of divinity now must be something that takes place rather more horizontally than vertically, more materially than spiritually, and more in common than in isolation. At least that's the way I see a great deal of the discussion that has taken place both yesterday and today (pp. 91–92).

The proceedings reflect practically no opposition to the dominant direction. However, there may have been more conflict than appears in the proceedings, because at the end of the day, John R. McCall, professor of psychology at Weston College, called for tolerance: "Some people are ready for this change; some people don't want these changes. Let's basically follow the Ignatian idea of accepting the fact that each person has good will. I think this is terribly important, or no changes will be made" (pp. 92–93). The last phrase implies that the side proposing change is correct; the reason for following "the Ignatian idea" is to open the door to change.

The concluding meeting of the institute was a panel discussion among the theologate deans. During this panel it was revealed that many experimental changes had already begun to be implemented in the theologates. It was repeatedly stated that the method of teaching theology needed to be changed. There was much dissatisfaction with the thesis method because, as one student put it, the scholastics resented having to start with conclusions (p. 152). They wanted to start with questions and to arrive at the possible answers through dialogue. Throughout the institute there were repeated calls for a greater use of discussion, whether to identify theological truth or to influence community lifestyles. A greater use of dialogue was an essential part of the democratization called for in the Shea paper.

As far as one can judge from the proceedings, especially from the discussions, the three most influential figures at the institute were Edward Sponga, Francis Shea, and John McCall. All three left the Society and married.

Other Institutes

Similar institutes, though on a less elaborate scale, were held in other parts of the country, especially in the philosophates. The philosophate in St. Louis, Missouri, for example, held a series of weekend institutes from 1966 to 1969. The last of these meetings dealt with a favorite topic, "Authority and Obedience in the Society of Jesus". Clearly, a general pattern that began in the theologates had quickly spread to the philosophates.

3. General Congregation 31 (1965–66)

Of the various formal steps taken by the Society of Jesus in response to the 1960s' call for modernization, the first in both time and significance was the Thirty-First General Congregation (G.C. 31). Jesuit historian John W. Padberg called it by far the most unusual, the most important, in the history of the Society (Padberg 1974, 74–75). The largest and longest-lasting general congregation, it was also the only one to meet in two separate sessions (May to July 1965, and September to November 1966).

The delegates to this congregation were selected in the traditional way, by the fifty oldest members of each province. Delegates selected by such a "gerontocracy" might have been expected to approach the prospect of change gingerly; and the early stages of the first session did indeed see much opposition to the proposals for renovation. But the longer the congregation stayed in session, the more open to change it became. The thematic chord of the congregation, when it had finally reached its decisions, was struck in the first sentence of its first decree, "In this 'new age' in which the human race now finds itself . . . "

The phrase "new age" is quoted from Vatican Council II, with which G.C. 31 met concurrently; the concurrence was accidental, rather than designed. The General of the order, John Baptist Janssens, died on October 5, 1964, and a congregation had to be called to elect his successor. Vatican II had been in preparation for three years and in session for three additional years before G.C. 31 began. During this six-year period, the Catholic *aggiornamento* had acquired great momentum. In a world of instant communication, the wind sweeping through Pope John's open window had become a gale affecting everything Catholic, including the Jesuit order.

In 1965, in its last session, Vatican II had issued the decree "The Adoption and Renewal of Religious Life" (*Perfectae Caritatis*). This decree contained the sweeping directive: "Constitutions, directories, custom books, books of prayers, of ceremonies and such like, should be properly revised" (Flannery 1975, 613). In this task, the order was to follow democratic methods by providing "ample and free consultation with all the subjects . . . by setting up commissions, by sending out questionnaires, etc.". Likewise, the orders were invited to experiment freely, albeit prudently, and were given the assurance, "Experiments which run counter to common law . . . will be readily authorized by the Holy See as need arises" (p. 625). Nothing better reflects the prevailing climate than this open invitation to "experiment", an invitation extended by the highest authority and accompanied only by the general limitation that the experimentation should be "prudent".

The following year, Pope Paul VI (1963–78) issued detailed instructions for implementing this conciliar decree in his apostolic letter *Ecclesiae Sanctae* published in 1966 between the two sessions of G.C. 31. According to the letter, each religious institute was to summon a special general chapter for the purpose of updating itself.

G.C. 31 began its second session on September 8, 1966. At the opening meeting, Father Pedro Arrupe, who had been elected General in 1965, told its members that they faced "profound, complicated, and immense problems of every sort". He also said that "some call this a period of transition; others, of crisis; others, of revolution; others, of degeneration; others, of imminent chaos." He "stressed that the Congregation must not be over timid" but that "it should say what must be said about our basic principles without fear of offending the younger members of the Society" (Jurich 1969, 16–17).

During this session, as reported by James P. Jurich, a delegate "called on the General to put a stop to certain unfortunate experiments going on in the Society". Jurich reported, further, that the General intervened at this point to say in effect: "Unfortunately, renewal and adaptation are too often carried out today according to the method of *faits accomplis,* something that has ill-fated consequences. This method continues to exist because superiors are pulled in every direction and do not have clear directives coming from the Congregation" (p. 22). Jurich also noted:

The impression that comes out of this first contact [with the members returned after the first session] is the uneasiness that a number of people have with regard to a possible split between generations or between the scholastics and the older fathers. One provincial went so far as to say that he no longer knows which way to turn. The young men threaten to leave the Society if there aren't greater reforms; and twenty-five of the older fathers have signed a letter of protest against all the upheavals already going on; and they are also threatening to leave the Society to go and live with the Carthusians if the Society continues to secularize itself (p. 7).

The most significant development between the two sessions was the congregation's own change of attitude. It shifted from a cautious mood of protecting tradition to an attitude of reevaluating everything. For example, in its first session, the congregation had prepared, and nearly completed, a document entitled "The Conservation and Renovation of Our Institute". At the start of the second session, the congregation rejected the draft completely. Explaining the reasoning, one of the delegates said, "the schema presented to us aims at a fuzzy kind of canonization of everything that comes from the past. Even if the word *renewal* is there, the reality isn't there." The congregation felt that the document did not adequately reflect the papal document *Ecclesiae Sanctae* and its direction: "Those elements are to be considered obsolete which do not constitute the nature and purpose of the institute and which, having lost their meaning and power, are no longer a real help to religious life" (Jurich 1969, 20–21). Accordingly, the congregation voted to send the document back to the commission to have it rewritten. As a midwestern provincial wrote to a friend, "One startling thing that all of us remarked is the extraordinary difference of feeling and mutual acceptance this year in comparison with last year. It has been a long, hard learning process for all of us."

It was in this atmosphere that G.C. 31 reconvened in Rome to begin its second session and to supply answers to the questions raised in the first session. It was a most active congregation, promulgating scores of important decrees.[12] Here it will suffice to note a few decrees that illustrate the most significant force at

---

[12] Brief histories of G.C. 31 may be found in Clancy 1976 and Padberg

work, namely, the congregation's general attitude toward change—
an expectation that a turn in the road had been reached and a
willingness to explore the new region lying ahead.

Prior to G.C. 31, the "substantials" of the Jesuit institute were
carefully listed and were classified as belonging to the first or
second order. Substantials of the first order were untouchable;
indeed, provincial congregations could not even discuss them. But
after obtaining explicit approval of Paul VI (Padberg 1974, 77),
G.C. 31 abrogated the list, decreed that each general congregation
could define the meaning of substantials as need required, and
allowed even provincial congregations to raise questions regarding the substantials (Dec. 4). This action gave the clearest of
signals that G.C. 31 was geared to the possibility of change. In the
"new age", not even the substantials were exempt from review
and possible alteration.

The vows—of poverty, chastity, and obedience—are, of course,
of the essence of the religious state. Many postulata (formal recommendations addressed by provincial congregations or by individuals to the general congregation) requested that studies be made of
the relationship between the vows and modern advances in the
fields of theology and psychology. Accordingly, the congregation
recommended to the General that he authorize a study of chastity
(Dec. 16). It began its statement on obedience by declaring it was
"conscious of the social change in our day which gives rise to a
new awareness of the brotherhood of men and a keener sense of
liberty and personal responsibility" (Dec. 17). The congregation's
consideration of the remaining vow of poverty starts with a
recognition of "the need of adaptation and renewal of the Institute in regard to poverty" (Dec. 18). Thus, with respect even to
the vows, the congregation was prepared to make adjustments in
the light of the new age.

1974. Also, one of the delegates from the French Canadian province wrote a
series of letters to his province describing the work of the congregation as it
developed. Full of concrete, personal details, these letters, transcribed and
edited, may be found in Jurich 1967a, 1967b, and 1969.

Finally, the health of any organization depends on how effectively it selects and trains its members. In this crucial area, the congregation was likewise prepared to make changes, stating, "To ensure that the intellectual formation of Jesuits is ordered to meet the needs of the times the entire *Ratio Studiorum* shall be revised." The congregation also recommended that "experiments" be made and offered the assurance that these ventures in new directions "can depart from the decrees of preceding general congregations as this is necessary" (Dec. 9.15).

The following are examples of the congregation's welcoming attitude toward change (emphasis added):

— "It [the congregation] has determined that the *entire* government of the Society must be adapted to modern necessities and ways of living; that our *whole* training in spirituality and in studies must be changed" (Dec. 2.3).

— Regarding the formation of novices: "*New* experiments . . . ought to be prudently and *boldly* pursued" (Dec. 8.14). "Superiors should provide that the novices . . . have sufficient social contact with contemporaries, both within and *outside* the Society" (Dec. 8.22).

— Regarding the scholastics (mostly Jesuits with vows but not yet ordained): "True dialogue should exist between superiors, professors, and scholastics. It should be possible for *all* to express opinions and make suggestions" (Dec. 9.10). "The scholastics should learn . . . to read critically and use prudently the works . . . of those who have great influence on the *modern* mind" (Dec. 9.47).

— With regard to ministries, the congregation noted a worrisome disproportion "between Jesuit efforts and the results achieved", considered various possible reasons, and concluded that "the *principal* reason is our failure adequately to adapt our ministries to the *changed* conditions of our times" (Dec. 21.1).

— In the formation of scholastics, "the advice of trained *psychologists* should be used when it is necessary" (Dec. 9.5).

— The possible scope of changes is caught in the statement,

"The programs of the *entire* philosophical and theological curriculum shall be revised" (Dec. 9.25).

Two recommendations that had considerable impact were the following: "As far as it is possible, our houses of studies should be built near university centers" (Dec. 9.32); also, "Care should be taken that the number of scholastics in the houses of formation be not too large, so that . . . the discipline may be that of a family" (Dec. 9.9). Other changes could be instanced, such as the abrogation of the requirements to have reading at table and to spend a fixed amount of time in prayer. But the examples given suffice to convey the open spirit of G.C. 31.

The Sacred Congregation for Religious had no difficulty in deciding that G.C. 31 had fulfilled the requirements of the apostolic letter *Ecclesiae Sanctae,* mentioned above. In the decade that followed G.C. 31, Father General Arrupe was often accused of presiding at the dissolution of the traditional Society. He could justly reply that he was only carrying out the mandate of the congregation and reflecting its obvious commitment to a process of modernization.

Indeed, G.C. 31 welcomed *aggiornamento* so enthusiastically that it itself became a powerful generator of successive waves of change. For example, in its Decree 51 it revamped the method of selecting the members of provincial congregations: instead of the fifty oldest in the province automatically going to the congregation, members were to be elected by and from all those with last vows. This change increased the probability of future provincial congregations being younger and more open to change. For another example, in its Decree 22 it directed each province to establish a planning commission to review all ministries and recommend needed adaptations. As a result, there was established in each province a new engine of change, which functioned for years after G.C. 31 ended and poured out a flood of studies and recommendations described in Section 6 of the following chapter.

However, before the congregation ended, Pope Paul VI, who

in *Ecclesiae Sanctae* had directed the religious orders to modernize, expressed his concern that the Jesuits might be modernizing too much or in the wrong ways. Early in the second session of the congregation in 1966, in a private meeting, the Pope gave Father General Arrupe a message to convey to the congregation. The following excerpt, from a contemporary account, alludes to the Pope's second thoughts:

> Thunderbolt at the Congregation! At the beginning of the day's session, Father General took the floor and gave us an important communication. He had seen the Sovereign Pontiff. The Pope had shared with him his desires and wishes with regard to the Society in general and the present Congregation in particular. From the reports coming from the nuncios and apostolic delegates throughout the whole world, the Pope gave the General a sketch of the image which the Society projects at present, and this image needs serious retouching. The Pope did not wish to speak in public, for the press would be able to seize upon his statements and do more harm than good, but he confided fully in the General, commissioning him to communicate to the Congregation the wishes of the Pope. And for a good quarter of an hour, the General exposed for us, point by point, what the Pope had told him. Unfortunately for you and for me, the General ended by asking all of us to keep the content of the Pope's message to the Congregation secret, at least until further notice. I'm losing the biggest scoop of the year ... and so is *Lettres de Rome.* (Jurich 1969, 28)

In the period following G.C. 31, the Society continued to change, and the Pope continued to be uneasy. (See Section 12, dealing with G.C. 32, in the following chapter.)

4. Committee of Spiritual Review (1964–68)

In 1964, the three eastern provinces of Maryland, New York, and Buffalo established a joint committee composed of the spiritual directors of the three novitiates, the three juniorates, and the common philosophate at Shrub Oak. The decision to set up such a committee, made at a meeting of the three provincials in February 1964, antedated by over a year both G.C. 31 and *Perfectae Caritatis,* the Vatican II document directing all religious orders to modernize their constitutions. The committee had been suggested by the General himself as a way of addressing a prolonged history of unrest at Shrub Oak. In responding to the General's wish, the provincials had decided to extend the scope of the committee to include the entire period of spiritual formation—usually seven years at that time—leading up to and including philosophy. They believed that any cure for Shrub Oak would have to include attention to the three novitiates and juniorates which fed Shrub Oak.

This committee represented an early and thorough attempt in the United States Assistancy to modernize the beginning years of Jesuit formation (novitiate, juniorate, philosophate). Starting in July 1964, the committee held thirteen three-day sessions, ending in February 1968. Toward the end, the scope of the committee was enlarged to include the New England province and to cover the entire period of formation; this would include regency (the teaching years before theology), theological studies, and tertianship (a final year of spiritual audit and internship). Membership changed over the committee's life, so that at the last meeting only three of the original members were still in attendance: John J. McMahon, Dominic W. Maruca, and Frederic M. O'Connor. In the course of its work, three of its members experienced difficulty with their own vocations and left the Society. Probably the most active member of the committee was Frederic O'Connor, who arranged the agenda, kept the minutes, and was in more direct contact with the young men at Shrub Oak through his office of spiritual director there. Father O'Connor favored most of the new values and life patterns.

Fortunately, the committee kept full minutes, and its accounts provide a first-hand, detailed, month-by-month account of how Jesuits of that period became aware of emerging problems and gradually and tentatively formulated answers. It will be best to let this source speak for itself through excerpts presented in chronological order. For the most part, the minutes do not identify the authors of the statements. Unless otherwise noted, all page references are to minutes of the session mentioned. The thirteen sessions make up a single source (C.S.R. 1964–68).

The first session (July 1964) selected as its first topic "The Emotions"—a revealing choice. The committee agreed that the new problems being observed among the scholastics were most manifest in the area of the emotions. There was also agreement that the chief emotional change was the intense need of the young men for self-fulfillment through loving relationships (p. 4). A generally perceived result was that among the young men "the word of the group is commanding as much allegiance as the word of the novice master" (p. 5 of the agenda). The committee members obviously disagreed in their evaluation of the new developments. Some stressed the desirability of expressing emotional needs; others were critical of what seemed to them a dangerous reliance on shifting, self-regarding norms.

Obedience was discussed on the second day, a virtue that all agreed was under new pressure. In developing the topic for the committee, Thomas P. Gavigan, a master of novices, reported his impression that "parents, high schools and perhaps Superiors are too permissive". He noticed that, as a result, "when a sign is posted on the bulletin board, the first reaction is not to obey but to criticize it, to ask why. Boys seem to have this attitude when they come into the Novitiate" (pp. 15–16).

On the third day, John J. Heaney described the changes taking place in the interpretation of sacred Scripture and the results on the scholastics. Observing that one of the results can be "a kind of relativism", he explained: "If the young Jesuit sees the Church changing its thoughts on so many matters, how can he hold sacrosanct what is of a lesser order than the Church, scl. [namely], the Society's rules and traditional modes of procedure. The young Jesuit can feel these too are subject to change and therefore need not *now* be adhered to strictly" (p. 20).

In its third session (March 1965) the committee discussed the
changing nature of the Society and of the novitiate. John J.
McMahon, a tertian instructor, reported that

> many of the Tertians feel there is a need for a restatement of the
> purpose of the Society, and hence of the Novitiate. For example,
> they feel that the General Examen should be entirely rewritten
> in the modern idiom, and even much of it dropped completely.
> In their eyes, much of the Examen represents the 16th-century
> ascetical viewpoint which has a dubious value for 20th-century
> man. One Master of Novices tended to agree, noting that, for
> example, the attitude toward relatives and family, readily accepted
> in the 16th century, today seems harsh and unrealistic (p. 8).

One member remarked at this point that he felt the meeting had
here taken a decisive turn. "We have begun to question certain
values, or at least the formulation of certain values, which have
been accepted in the Society since its inception." He then went on
to declare: "Just as there was an old and now a new apologetic for
the Church, so there must be a new apologetic for religious life. It
is no longer enough to simply say Pope Paul VI says this or that.
The argument from authority does not carry that much weight
today" (p. 8).

In its fifth session (July 1965), the committee discussed several
topics that were to become burning issues in the next half-dozen
years. Some members thought that the traditional novitiate and
juniorate did not provide enough "maturing experiences". By that
they meant "experiences such as rebelling against something, learning to control the use of alcohol, the responsibility of caring for
oneself while away from home, and the development of a normal,
Christian relationship with those of the opposite sex" (p. 7).

All recognized that permanent commitment, especially as
expressed in the vows, had become a newly pressing problem.
"They [the scholastics] feel perfectly free to reassess their vocation
from time to time. They feel that their acceptance of the obligation of the vows was a free act on their part and this is the light in
which the matter is looked upon all along. . . . Their commitment

to the Jesuit way of life was made freely and to their way of thinking is not irrevocable" (p. 9).

At Shrub Oak scholastics were being taught a personalist philosophy which held the following:

> . . . a knowledge of Christ is had through a knowledge of oneself and a knowledge of oneself is had through a knowledge of other persons and that therefore a knowledge of Christ is ultimately gotten through one's knowledge of other people. If we come to a knowledge of Christ through a knowledge of other people, the ideal would seem to be to broaden our contacts with other people. This seems to be almost directly opposed to existing situations in our houses of formation and training, where silence prevails at prayer, meals, etc. (pp. 11–12).

On the third day, Thomas E. Henneberry addressed the committee. According to the minutes, "he noted that he saw a marked change in the New York philosophate between 1952, when he was rector of the philosophate at Bellarmine College [Plattsburgh, N.Y.], and 1960, when he became rector at Shrub Oak. Philosophers seemed to have decidedly changed" (p. 17). He added, "They constantly seek personal meaning in things; the fact that someone in authority tells them that something is good for them is not sufficient" (p. 18). The committee assured the rector of Shrub Oak: "The problem seems to exist even before they reach Philosophy, for the idea of accepting things only on one's own experience rather than from authority seems to be present in young men when they enter" (p. 18).

A final item in this July 28 session noted that some of the scholastics at Shrub Oak had begun to claim the right to omit daily Mass: "Some of those who have admitted to not attending Mass daily will say that they do not because it does not have any particular meaning for them" (p. 22).

The sixth session (November 3–5, 1965) was concerned equally with the intellectual and the spiritual formation of the scholastics. The committee agreed unanimously that the five-year period following the novitiate (two years of juniorate and three years of philosophate) should be changed to a single four-year period of collegiate studies. The chairman, John J. McMahon, tertian master of the New York Province, reported that he had asked the opinions of tertian fathers [in tertianship, the final year of Jesuit formation] on the proposed collegiate arrangement. One of the letters written in response to his request was by John Replogle (ordained in 1964):

> I would begin by saying that it is almost the unanimous opinion of the Tertians here that four years at Shrub Oak (or any house of studies, for that matter) would be very difficult for our men. I offer two reasons for this. First, it would be too long a period where there would be no visible sign of progress in the course. For many this would be a serious problem. Second, it would make the community too large. And the difficulties that arise from an oversized community cannot be solved by additional Superiors (although this might help) because the issue here is the distance that arises between the subjects themselves, not that between the Superior and the subject. I feel that the importance of this sense of community has to be given serious consideration (p. 6).

The two reasons assigned are typical of the 1960s, as is also a reason given by Thomas King (ordained in 1964): "Intellectual requirements have changed. A number of courses are no longer strictly necessary; a fluent use of Latin is no longer essential." King also added: "Our generation finds philosophical proofs unconvincing" (p. 7).

The minutes do not make clear the extent to which the committee agreed or disagreed with these reasons, but the committee did unanimously recommend the adoption of a collegiate program with classes in the university (see below, pp. 275ff.), and one member argued that the change would "give the scholastics a sense of doing what their [lay] peers are doing" (p. 10). The last argument reflects a distinctive departure from the longstanding traditional approach.

A previously made change moved the weekly holiday of the scholastics from Thursday to Saturday. Thursday had originally been chosen over Saturday for the reason that was now discounted, namely, to separate the scholastics from the other students. The committee's minutes contain the statement: "Normal college experiences are now missed by our men. With the unified college course, contacts could be made with extern colleges in debating, sports, etc." (p. 11). The committee cautiously approved the idea of a junior year abroad for the scholastics. "The trip abroad may help eliminate the feeling of some of Ours that they would have done better at an extern college; that they missed something" (p. 12). However, some members of the committee must have demurred, because the minutes note the following: "As religious, we must accept some narrowing of experience" (p. 12).

At this session there was much discussion of the mode of government at Shrub Oak. There seemed to be agreement that in the changed climate of the 1960s "The Superior must be able to conduct a dialogue with his community" (p. 14). Throughout the discussion there was emphasis on the need to shift from a structure in which a superior simply communicated his wishes to a structure in which there was wider participation in the decision-making process. Instead of the traditional conferences, the spiritual fathers might do better to use group discussions: "To an image-oriented generation, a movie followed by a group discussion can be very effective" (p. 17). After agreeing that the number of spiritual directors—also called spiritual fathers—should be sufficient so that each director would be responsible for no more than fifty scholastics, the minutes note: "Perhaps the Spiritual Father should not give a triduum to the whole community but only to the group of about fifty assigned to his regular care" (p. 17).

The seventh session (February 22–24, 1966) dealt primarily with problems in the spiritual lives of the scholastics. The committee agreed that one of the roots of the current problem was the general mood of change in the Church:

This is a time of questioning. . . . The Church has newly discovered a true Christianity outside the visible Church. Our approach to philosophy is through the analysis of experience. . . . There is an awareness that the Gospel is not a historical recording of the exact words of Christ, and some, knowing this, feel they have lost contact with him as a reality (p. 2).

The committee noted that scholastics in other parts of the world (outside the West, for example in the Philippines) were still "willing to seek Christ in the Gospel rather than in the existential situation" (p. 2).

The committee noted other changes in the spiritual lives of the scholastics. "They wonder if prayer is a more rewarding locus of encounter with Christ than conversation with others." And "they do not understand the significance of sacrifice or covenant or the need to worship. They look on the Mass only as an action of the community, agape, communion, rather than as Christ's offering to the Father." The committee recognized that a current danger was "fragmentation [of the liturgy] at the whim of individuals" (p. 4).

The committee discussed at length the question "Is compulsory attendance at daily Mass desirable?" The suggestion was made that "Perhaps daily Mass could be presented as an ideal without external regulations. Regulations beget resentments and rebellion" (p. 5). The committee did not make any recommendation but did seem to agree on the following statement: "We should first show [to these scholastics] the intrinsic good in participation at Mass. This should be clear to all. Then the individual's reasons for not going have to be refuted individually" (p. 6).

The committee agreed that there had been a notable decrease in the frequency of the reception of the sacrament of penance. "Some say they don't feel the need for it and wish to make a colloquium of it. . . . The role of the *sacrament* in reconciliation is obscured" (p. 6) [emphasis added]. In discussing difficulties in prayer, the committee noted that some of the difficulties stemmed from changed interpretations of scriptural passages (p. 10). At this session, also, one member voiced the following view:

There are some good things emerging from the changes taking place in the spiritual lives of the scholastics. Spiritual conversation is more frequent. Perhaps silence should be relaxed to promote this conversation. . . . In general, the scholastics do obey the rule, but they continually request certain changes. Perhaps Superiors should investigate whether some rules should be changed. The Spirit may be working in these continual complaints (p. 11).

Repeatedly the committee noted in their discussions that the changed attitudes did not apply to all scholastics but to a group of leaders who were followed by many, though not by all. This observation is applicable to nearly every development described in this history.

In its eighth session (June 14–16, 1966), the committee continued to discuss the regulation of the time of prayer. The committee "noted that the Church herself has cut down the time of prayer, e.g., in liturgy, breviary, etc." (p. 5). In addition, someone observed, "if each person cannot be responsible for his life of prayer, we are admitting that our formation program is a failure" (p. 6). The committee agreed: "If the present General Congregation merely reaffirms the present legislation, most Jesuits will be disappointed, because under the present legislation the general practice of prayer is poor" (p. 7). The committee went on to say that what was needed from the congregation was not another juridical document but a pastoral document on prayer (p. 7). (At this time, G.C. 31 was about to start its second session.)

Most of the rest of the meeting was taken up with the discussion of the annual eight-day retreat. "It is an interesting fact that many postulata to the General Congregation asked for a five-day retreat" (p. 8). There was considerable difference of opinion in the committee; some members favored a retention of traditional requirements, and others favored various relaxations in the requirements. The chief relaxations suggested were in the number of required days and in the method of the retreat, especially in the use of "discussion sessions" (p. 10).

The committee agreed that the Litany of the Saints, the common evening prayer, was no longer viable but was unable to agree on any substitute.

During the ninth session (November 8–10, 1966) the committee discussed the traditional requirements of silence in the scholasticates. One member advanced the argument that it is confusing to the scholastics to have one form of silence in the novitiate and a looser form in later life. He proposed that silence in the novitiate be identical with silence in later Jesuit life (p. 4). Mention was made of a recent Woodstock house retreat during which the traditional silence did not prevail. The reason given for the change was the following: "It is from others and through others that we receive enlightenment and inspiration." Another member stated "Silence must be different today than twenty years ago. A silence that in any way resembles a monastic silence is unreal for the mentality of our men" (p. 5). The committee reached no agreement on whether the rules on silence should be changed.

One committee member commented on the selectivity with which the scholastics read their sources. He noted that they quoted council peritus Karl Rahner, for example, when they wished his support for lines of action they had decided upon; on the other hand, they ignored his writings about eucharistic devotion, which the scholastics regarded as outmoded medievalism.

There was much discussion again of the size of the Shrub Oak community. For the modern scholastic, the community was too large to be acceptable. The comment was made that a single minister (i.e., father minister, second to father rector, whose duties concerned house maintenance, etc.) can not adequately care for 180 scholastics (p. 6).

In the tenth session (February 7–9, 1967), there was much discussion of the decrees of G.C. 31, from which Chairman John McMahon had just returned. There was also considerable discussion of religious obedience, with some members expressing difficulties with aspects of the virtue as traditionally explained (p. 4).

The committee agreed, however, that in listening to the young men, the older men of the provinces should not be overlooked. It seemed to the committee that there was presently a lack of balance in this regard (p. 5).

With the eleventh session (May 31–June 2, 1967), the committee was enlarged to include members from the New England province. It was decided also to extend the scope of the committee to include the total Jesuit formation in all four eastern provinces.

A large part of the committee's work at this session was a discussion of the relationship between psychology and religious life. There began to be evident in discussions more opposition than previously to recent trends in the Society. This may have reflected the presence of a new committee member, William J. Burke of New England, whose criticisms of some Jesuit innovations were later made public.[13]

Some committee members showed concern about certain qualities of the scholastics (pp. 3-4). "There seems to be an increase in effeminacy among candidates. How can authentic virility be instilled?" Other members posed questions: "What are the mechanisms operative in the pressure groups forming to exert influence on superiors?" "Is the young man structurally distrustful of parental authority prior to entrance in our Society? Is this carried over?" "Does the young man really believe that divine providence will utilize the Church and the Society of Jesus as instruments for guiding his life?"

There was recognition, again, that the scholastics were having difficulty with prayer: "They say they just find nothing." "Is the Spirit trying to evoke some different approach to prayer? This question can be asked because the phenomenon is so widespread; the scholastics give up but still are searching" (p. 6). There was also much discussion of the "problem of identity diffusion". Many modern Jesuits, scholastics and priests, were beginning to have a blurred image of the Society (p. 6).

The scholastics saw the decrees of G.C. 31 as a great advance but not enough. "They [the decrees] represent a sign of confidence and give the scholastics hope that this is only a starting point. A certain spirit seems to appeal to the younger men: experiment, dialogue, confrontation" (p. 7).

The twelfth session (November 7-9, 1967) differed markedly

[13] See below, pp. 82-83.

from all the others. Six psychiatrists had been invited to meet with the committee. The agenda for the meeting, prepared as usual by Frederic O'Connor, shows in some detail the topics to be covered by the psychiatrists. The topics included the celibate life, the authority crisis, group dynamics, strictly personal problems, and "guilt".

The list of topics is all the trace the meeting has left. Tapes were made of the meeting, and a report was prepared by a professional secretary. The committee, or its secretary, decided not to have the tapes transcribed and not to publish the report of the professional secretary. The tapes and the report seem to have been lost or destroyed, and no minutes were made of the meeting. Members recall that the meeting was very controversial and that the secretary, Frederic O'Connor, was much opposed to the positions taken by the psychiatrists. Another member of the committee, on the contrary, wrote to one of the psychiatrists soon after the meeting saying that he had derived great benefit from the session. It had restored his confidence in what he had been trying to do: "You men gave us a swift kick in the seat of our spiritual pants and, in effect, told us to get on with it. We had been underestimating our resources and traditional wisdom" (telephone conversation with author).

In the thirteenth session (February 27–29, 1968), the committee devoted its attention to two chief topics, namely, the best way of dealing with postulants and novices and the reasons that so many men were leaving the Society.

The committee recommended a college postulancy program for all applicants. In this program, the applicant would live the life of the ordinary college student but have some regular connection with the Jesuits. It was expected that such a postulancy would "contribute in many ways to his human growth, especially in the area of emotional maturity and a sharpened sense of responsibility". The principal assumption underlying the proposals for new methods of admitting postulants and training novices was that the young men of modern times were slower to mature affectively. The committee's assumption was in obvious agreement with that of

G.C. 31: "Experience has shown . . . that in our own time affective maturity has become more difficult for adolescents" (p. 16). They needed more experience than their predecessors in such problems as "living away from home, independence from family, college-type academic achievement in a non-supportive atmosphere, use of freedom in a relatively unrestricted atmosphere, encountering the female in a more mature context" (p. 8).

On the problem of men leaving the Society, Frederic O'Connor presented an analysis with this conclusion: "Present-day Jesuits do not think of men who leave the Society as defectors, but quite simply rejoice in the fact that they have found their vocation in life" (p. 25). However, this judgment met strong opposition and was modified in the recommendations of the committee to read: "This committee wishes to express its deep concern and genuine interest in the men who once were our fellow Jesuits and have left the Society" (p. 3).

There are no records of further meetings. The thirteenth session seems to have been the last. None of the members can recall when, how, or why the Committee of Spiritual Review ended. Probably a number of factors converged. After four years the committee had covered, sometimes repeatedly, all the major issues involving the formation process. Moreover, the same issues had been thoroughly discussed the previous year (1967) with the participation of all the provincials at a conference at Santa Clara University, whose proceedings had been published in six volumes. Further, the province planning period had begun in 1966, and by this time its various planning bodies were in full operation. Finally, the decision had already been made to close Shrub Oak, whose troubles had been the occasion for the formation of the committee in the first place. The Shrub Oak philosophate actually closed the following year, 1969.

Though the Committee of Spiritual Review begins early, namely, before Vatican II ended or G.C. 31 began, it exemplifies all the major issues that were to occupy the period of modernization. The committee's minutes are unusually full, and they reflect the experience of those who were in actual daily contact with the novices and scholastics. On all counts, these minutes must be rated a rich firsthand historical source. They would have been even more useful if the secretary had identified speakers and if he had included an account of that strange twelfth session.

5. Rockhurst Report (1965)

The story of the Rockhurst Report, which marks the watershed of theologate reform, begins with the decision of the American provincials in 1964 to establish a Commission on Houses of Study in the Jesuit Educational Association. This was part of a reorganization of the entire academic apostolate of the Society—its high schools, its colleges and universities, its houses of formation. In all cases, a principal goal was to achieve a closer integration between the Society and the secular world in which it was working.[14] The Commission on Houses of Study in turn established a Committee on Theologates, composed of the deans and rectors of the schools of theology in the United States and Canada. This committee met at Fordham University in April 1965 and in its turn appointed the Inter-Faculty Program Inquiry, which authored the Rockhurst Report.

In embarking upon the chain of decisions that led to the Rockhurst Report, the provincials and deans were responding not only to the ongoing deliberations of Vatican II and G.C. 31, both in session at the time,[15] but also to numerous earlier and broader proposals for seminary change. A collection of essays on this broader topic includes the following summary of the situation as it existed in 1965:

[14] The full story of this development for the colleges and universities is told in Fitzgerald 1984.

[15] For Vatican II, see its "Decree on Priestly Formation" in Abbott 1966. For G.C. 31, see its Decree no. 9, "The Training of Scholastics Especially in Studies" in *Documents of the Thirty-First and Thirty-Second General Congregations of the Society of Jesus,* The Institute of Jesuit Sources, 1977.

Any given seminary today is at one of three stages: (1) the traditionalists are in the saddle but they face growing discontent among the students, or (2) the institution is in the painful throes of transition, with the students often caught in the "crossfire" between the two "camps," or (3) the "New Breed" of theologians and scripture scholars predominate and are giving the institution new intellectual and spiritual orientations (Lee and Putz 1965, 214).

This situation accounts for the appointment, as stated, of the Committee on Theologates (1964) and is clearly reflected in the committee's decision (1965) to launch the inquiry—they saw an "imperative need". As reported in the minutes of its April 1965 Fordham meeting, the committee reached the following conclusion:

After a lengthy discussion on the imperative need of revising and rejuvenating the theology courses in the scholasticates of North America, the Committee resolved to appoint a special group composed of representatives of the theological faculties of the United States and Canada, to be known as the Inter-Faculty Program Inquiry (Committee on Theologates 1965, 1).

The committee went on to describe the task of the inquiry:

The Inquiry should seek to create the best possible course in theology for the education of Jesuit priests in the American Assistancy. . . . In the not unfounded expectation that both the Second Vatican Council and the 31st G.C. will grant rather wide powers to various regions for the devising of seminary programs best suited to local conditions, it is hoped that the Inquiry will not feel bound by past Church and Society legislation regarding the particulars of seminary training (Committee on Theologates 1965, 2).

The Inter-Faculty Program Inquiry, with twenty-one members present, including the theologate deans, met at Rockhurst College (Kansas City, Missouri) during the week of November 7–13, 1965, and produced the Rockhurst Report (Inter-Faculty Program Inquiry 1966, 335–56; page references in the following paragraphs also refer to this work). At the opening session, held on November 8, the first question raised was whether the meeting was limited by existing ecclesiastical laws. The general consensus was that the "openness" in the relevant decrees of Vatican II and of the Society seemed to warrant going beyond existing documents.

The report was a spare document, consisting chiefly of twenty-seven resolutions and four detailed appendices, which proposed alterations in nearly every aspect of the theology curriculum. The report seemed to be guided by two principles. In the first place, it sought to individualize the course of studies, that is, to fit the curriculum to the differing needs of the individual students. Abandoned were the traditional "tracts", similar for every Jesuit student throughout the world. Requirements were to be in terms of credit hours, as in a university, with "a high proportion of electives" (p. 339), which would include courses cognate to but outside of theology (p. 341) and which could be taken in non-Jesuit or even non-Catholic institutions (p. 344). The report suggested that the fundamental degree, bachelor of divinity, might be attained in two, two and a half, or three years, depending on the individual student (p. 340).

The second and more fundamental guiding principle was that of relevance to the times. At the heart of the report was the conviction that the world had changed greatly since the Council of Trent and that the study of theology needed to change accordingly. The report appealed, in its Resolution 21, to the decree of Vatican II on priestly formation, which states that students of theology should learn the "application of the eternal truths of revelation to the changeable condition of human affairs and their communication in a manner suited to men of our day". The report was also guided by the statement of G.C. 31 that in theology those questions should be emphasized "which have influence at the present time" (p. 341). With only three abstentions and no opposing votes, the group resolved that a modern theologate "demands close contact with a full university complex" (p. 338). The group also resolved that the training should begin with "a course on the religious needs, difficulties, and aspirations of contemporary man, so that the total program of theology may be more evidently relevant" (p. 338).

An article written by Justin J. Kelly, then a student at Woodstock (later to chair the Religious Studies Department at the University of Detroit), analyzed the Rockhurst Report at length and probably reflected the typical view of the report held by the young Jesuits of the period. Kelly concluded that a redefinition of theology "appears to be implicit in the practical measures adopted at Rockhurst. . . . Theology *itself* will be somehow different, and not just the learning process" (Kelly 1966, 361–62). The article noted that the Rockhurst Report opted for a historical approach to theology and concluded that in a historical theology not only the questions would differ over time but also to some extent the answers.

The Rockhurst Report provides several examples of possible curricula. Appendix 2 of the report, covering historical theology, includes a section, "Special History of Christian Ideas", which is largely a history of the councils of the Church. This appendix includes a minority report, however, that finds fault with such an unimaginative approach:

> The topics of SPECIAL HISTORY represent the majority opinions at the caucus, but it does not seem to be the best expression of the principles operative in setting up the area of historical theology, the emphasis being taken away somewhat from the dialectic of creative ideas and put rather on the judgmental decision of the Church. However, it can be 'interpreted' locally as long as the principle of the original motion is saved (Inter-Faculty Program Inquiry 1966, 351).

The opposition between "creative ideas" and "judgmental decision of the Church", with preference given to the former, reflects the dominant mood of the period. Equally characteristic is the expectation that "local interpretation" would offer enough freedom to escape the restriction implicit in the majority report.

As noted in the account of the theological institute held at Weston College in 1964, some experiments were already underway in some of the theologates (see p. 35); but the Rockhurst Report marked the formal and general beginning of the new era in Jesuit theologates. After Rockhurst, the theological scene was transformed. Most of the major recommendations of the report, including that of moving to an urban university location, were soon implemented by Jesuit houses of theology. The details of the transformation are provided in Chapters III, IV, and V.

II

GENERATORS OF CHANGE: LATER

Other generators of change operative during the post-Vatican II period are considered in the present chapter. The seven generators in this second group are somewhat later in time and span roughly a decade, 1965–75. (They are numbered consecutively with the five in Chapter I.)

6. The Planning Period (1966–77)

Survey of the Society of Jesus.

One of the more seminal actions taken by G.C. 31 was its directive that planning commissions be established: "To promote a better choice of ministries and some long-range planning, a commission should be set up as an aid to the provincial and under his authority" (G.C. 31, Dec. 22.1). The planning commissions set up in response to this directive were a power belt between the vision of modernity glimpsed by G.C. 31 and the concrete actions taken by the individual communities, which alone could give the vision actuality. The commissions were stable institutions set up to evaluate existing structures and to update or replace features that were no longer seen to fit the times. Each commission was thus an instrument designed expressly to facilitate change.

The endeavor got underway during G.C. 31 itself, when the

new Father General, Pedro Arrupe, met with all the provincials to discuss the project. In a letter written December 9, 1965, he announced that the project would begin with a general sociological survey of the Society.[1] In March 1966, at a meeting in Rome, it was decided to aim the survey at concrete decisions regarding Jesuit ministries. This crucial decision was reached with full recognition of the serious internal problems then facing the order. The healthiest approach, it was thought, was first to settle on what the order should do for Christ and then to adjust lifestyle and other internal matters to the requirements of the contemporary apostolate. (For some later thoughts on this decision, see pp. 95–96.) In the event, though the emphasis on ministries was maintained throughout the survey, some attention was also directed to internal issues such as the meaning and practice of the vows.

Planning took place at all levels, from the international to the local, and covered almost every aspect of the Society's life. In the United States, the activity occupied three periods. The first period, 1966–70, was devoted to fulfilling the directives of G.C. 31. This period saw the completion of the general survey and the publication of its results in the five-volume work, *General Survey of the Society of Jesus, North American Assistancy* (Biever and Gannon 1969). While not formally a part of the general survey, there were several other planning activities going on at the same time and energized by similar objectives. One of the more important was the Santa Clara Conference (1967), described later in this chapter. The second period, 1971–74, was devoted to preparation for the next general congregation, the thirty-second, which would meet in 1974. This preparation included the vote of the entire Society

---

[1] Directed by the International Survey Commission in Rome, the official title of the project was *Survey of the Society of Jesus.* It is sometimes referred to under the shorter titles *Sociological Survey* or *Society Survey* or simply *General Survey.* A study titled "Survey of the Capabilities and Activities of the Society" was a major part of the *General Survey.* This part is sometimes referred to as the "Roman Questionnaire". The *General Survey* is distinct from, though connected with, a 1967 activity in the United States called *Survey of American Jesuits* and conducted in preparation for the Santa Clara Conference.

on the "Forty-Six Propositions" also described later in this chapter. The third period, which followed after the interruption of G.C. 32, was briefer, less intense, and generally less significant.

In accordance with the instructions issued from Rome, the general survey included four steps: first, a survey of the characteristics and the needs of the region under consideration (here, the North American Assistancy); second, an analysis of the opportunities of the Church in that region, given her resources and limitations; third, a comparison between what the Church was actually doing in the region and what the Church could be doing; and fourth, a survey of Jesuit resources, opportunities, and performance in the region.

While the results of the first three steps are summarized in the first volume of the *General Survey,* the results of the fourth step occupy three volumes: volume 2 presents the data produced by a survey of Jesuit manpower; volume 3 summarizes a number of studies of Jesuit attitudes and values; and volume 4 reviews some of the studies made by individual provinces of their particular ministries. Volume 5 consists of a summary and conclusions.

The general survey served two chief purposes in the United States. Requiring as it did the participation of each province in this Society-wide effort, it resulted in each province having the basic materials needed for its own particular planning; without this requirement, some provinces might have done little or nothing by way of formal planning. Experience with the general survey led most provinces to establish a permanent planning body — called variously "assembly", "congress", "forum", or "committee" — which continued to function after the general survey had been completed. Secondly, the general survey resulted in the compilation of common statistics on the whole assistancy and gave the province some experience in cooperation. This led to a permanent increase in such cooperation after the general survey was completed — for example, in the founding of the National Jesuit Conference in 1972. Other examples of such cooperation were the *National Jesuit News* (1971), more frequent national meetings of the provincials, and an easier transition of men from one province to another.

Province Planning

Activity at the assistancy level was primarily for the sake of planning at the province level, where the data had to be assembled and the operative decisions made. In response to the call of the International Survey Commission in Rome, each of the ten American provinces established some kind of planning body to make a survey of its ministries. Within the format determined by the general survey, each province was free to devise its own planning method. The most widely used method was that adopted by the six provinces of Chicago, Detroit, Maryland, New England, New Orleans, and Oregon; this method is described below, using the example of Chicago. The remaining four provinces (California, Missouri, New York, and Wisconsin) adopted methods that differed from each other as well as from the six-province pattern. A description of all the methods is given in volume 4 of the *General Survey* (Biever and Gannon 1969, 4:13-77).

The planning experience of the Chicago province is selected as an example for several reasons. Chicago (with Detroit) developed the method (borrowing some materials from New England), the largest number of provinces used it, and Father General praised it as a usable model not only in the United States but worldwide: "Indeed, it seems more likely that your pioneering work will not be circumscribed by national boundaries but will eventually penetrate the Society as a whole."[2]

The Chicago Province Planning Program spanned the period 1968-77 and was carried out by two agencies, the congress (1968-69) and the assembly (1970-77).[3]

Structured with the help of the consulting firm of Arthur D. Little, Inc., the planning program proceeded in six phases.[4] In

[2] Letter of Pedro Arrupe to Robert F. Harvanek, S.J. dated May 13, 1969.

[3] The archives of the Chicago province have preserved three full file drawers of materials produced in the course of the planning program. An excellent summary of these materials was prepared in 1977 (Esenther 1977).

[4] Each phase had to be completed before a set time limit. Together, the

Phase I, the communities prepared plans for action through the Chicago Province Congress, a newly established body of elected representatives. The simple phrase "the communities prepared plans" covers innumerable meetings held by the individual communities that produced over 500 pages of proposals and much polarizing controversy. In Phase II, the congress reviewed the plans—over a hundred—and appointed twenty-eight task forces to study them. Together with the congress, these task forces involved about 200 members of the province. In Phase III, the task forces eliminated much material and from the remainder fashioned more specific plans. In Phase IV, the congress acted on the specific plans and made concrete recommendations, 586 of them.[5]

In Phase V, the provincial, Robert F. Harvanek, made his selection from among these recommendations and promulgated his decisions in a document dated April 26, 1969 (Esenther 1977, 129–51). He approved nearly all of the 586 recommendations, rejected a few, and qualified a few others. He stressed that one of the "major effects" of the planning process had been a revitalization of province spirit and an increased willingness to work together for common goals. This effect was "major" because of the disturbed state of the province at the time, when members were leaving in unprecedented numbers and polarization among those remaining was acute. The document noted also that the recommendations were "strongly person-centered" as reflected in (a) the "attraction principle" (which held that institutions must attract Jesuits to work there), (b) the *cura personalis* (an emphasis on the superior's personal care and guidance of individuals), and (c) the separation of the community interests of the Jesuits from the interests of the institutions they served. This separation was characterized as "perhaps the central recommendation of the Planning Program" (Esenther 1977, 136). The provincial also reported

---

first five phases occupied eight months—October 1968 to May 1969—and produced five documents (Biever and Gannon 1969).

[5] Many of these aimed at the establishment of still other generators of change. They asked for more studies and for new programs such as "a spiritual congress", "sensitivity training programs for superiors", and so forth.

that "one of the strongest recommendations at the end of the Congress was the proposal that spiritual and religious renewal be a primary project during the next five years [1970–75]" (Esenther 1977, 141–42). This recommendation bore some fruit the following year in the form of a substantial task force report on spiritual renewal (Chicago Province 1970).[6] Spiritual renewal did not, however, become "a primary project during the next five years".

Phase VI began the work of implementation, which was directed by the Chicago Province Assembly, the successor of the congress, which had been a temporary planning instrument. Part of the plan was a decision to establish a continuing, probably permanent, body to implement the existing plan and carry on future planning. (Other provinces made similar shifts at about this time; for example, the New England "forum" became an "assembly" in 1973.) Like the congress, the assembly was an elected body of about fifty persons (one tenth of the province) whose ongoing function was to assist the provincial in moving the province into the new age.

During the period 1970–77, the assembly held a dozen meetings, records of which provide a detailed account of the successes and failures of this new form of shared government. In its early stages, the assembly was a vigorous body on whose activities the attention of the province was focused. For one reason, the assembly was charged with helping implement all those recommendations made by the province through the congress. Also, the General had just set in process a program of intense self-scrutiny intended to prepare the Society for another general congregation. This new program required each province to begin a fresh series of meetings and complete another set of questionnaires and reports; for example, the province had to respond to the "Forty-Six Propositions" mentioned below in Section 12. All this activity became the assembly's responsibility.

[6] In parts of this report, there surfaced a perception, interesting because so early, that the sweep of change had brought with it some exaggerations needing correction. See, for example, the reports of the task forces on chastity and on obedience (Chicago Province 1970, 60–100).

However, during its later stages, the continued worth of the assembly increasingly came under question. Its task forces had become largely inactive between sessions of the assembly, so that when the assembly met it had no more light than when it last adjourned. Likewise, the communities were paying less and less attention to it and were unwilling to assume the costs of sending their representatives to the meetings. Also, the provincial, Daniel L. Flaherty, reported disappointment that projects he had committed to the assembly remained untouched. At the assembly meeting held in December 1972, the trend committee reported, "we were struck by the general lack of interest expressed in the Assembly, in Province concerns and planning, or in the issues of renewal and adaptation. We came to feel that this disinterest and uninvolvement is itself a significant 'Trend' in the Province." This attitude was common to both the advocates and adversaries of change and appeared at all age levels.

In the end, the regular meetings of the assembly were interrupted by the province meeting to elect delegates to the Thirty-Second General Congregation (G.C. 32) and were never resumed. In April 1979, the provincial announced that the assembly had "seen its day" and would not be reconvened. There seems to have been no protest over its demise.

Was all this planning effective? If so, was it desirable? Apparently, neither question has been approached in a formal way by any of the provinces. The answer to the first question is clearly measurable. It would be necessary only to match plans and recommendations against actual events, looking for evidence of causal connections. An adequate answer to the second question may have to wait until long-term as well as short-term results are available.

In the case of Chicago, objections to the whole planning idea had been faced frankly from the start. In a news release dated July 25, 1969, Provincial Robert F. Harvanek reported:

The obvious objection made was that this is not the Jesuit mode of decision making. Another objection concerned the time-consuming aspects of a self-study. All the men of the province were already fully occupied and overburdened and many felt that they would not have the time and energy to engage in a planning process which was scheduled for completion in a little over six months. But the greatest objection was the feeling that the majority of the men in the province were not knowledgeable and skilled in decision making nor well informed about the issues involved in Jesuit ministries. They felt it would be a decision by amateurs. Some Jesuits even said that the results of the planning program were either fore-ordained by the management group of the province, or would be controlled by it. Consequently it was felt that the self-study would be a waste of time.

At the end of the planning program, both provincials who had been involved judged the effort to have been worthwhile. They gave affirmative answers to both questions: planning had produced effects in the province and the effects were desirable.

In a letter to the province, dated September 8, 1969, Robert F. Harvanek wrote, "Our program yielded a mentality and a process. Both, the mentality and the process, are different from what we have been accustomed to in the Chicago province." In the summary document presented to the General, Harvanek stated,

> As I reviewed the work of the Planning Program . . . I asked myself, "Has any change taken place?" It seemed to me that it had. . . . It has definitely changed our Jesuit goals and purposes, and will gradually change our corporate Jesuit image. . . . There has been a change from the ethos of traditionalism to that of the mission of the Church to the world (Biever and Gannon 1969, 4:117, 120).

On the occasion of the province's golden jubilee in 1978, Provincial Daniel L. Flaherty, in a letter to the province, recounted how he had met with his consultors for two days in June 1977 "to compare our impressions of where we were". The result: "I wish you could have shared those days with us, because the most astounding thing was the unanimity with which we all spontaneously expressed our surprise at 'how far we had come' " (Flaherty 1978, 7).

This description of the Chicago province planning activity is a bare skeleton compared to the three file cases of materials (themselves the boiled-down residue of the full planning process) in the province archives. And of course the Chicago province experience was only a small part of the total planning activity carried out in the assistancy. The New Orleans province, for example, published well over a dozen volumes of planning materials and the California province produced a similar set of volumes.[7] Other provinces published their materials in other forms.

In addition to the activities that left a printed or typed record, there were other activities that left barely a trace. For example, in February 1967 the theologate at St. Mary's, Kansas, held a three-day *Institute on Jesuit Renewal* with the following objective: "To initiate an understanding of the new directives of the Society of Jesus formulated by the 31st General Congregation and to explore their practical implications for the American Jesuit life and work today." The institute was important enough to have seven of the ten provincials in attendance; yet it left no record other than the printed program.

Though no complete list exists of even the published materials, a partial, and substantial, list is provided in the fourth volume of the *General Survey* (Biever and Gannon 1969, 4:195–98). Beginning with this list, an energetic scholar could probably gather most of the materials awaiting discovery in the various province archives. In the total output of the ten provinces, there is scope for a doctoral dissertation in history or sociology. Until such studies are completed, no one will have an adequate picture of this extraordinary, literally unprecedented outburst of intense self-study and experimental gropings for self-renewal.

Though these wide-spreading plans were commonly called "experiments", they lacked two of the essential elements of a genuine experiment. They did not specify in advance measurable

[7] Most of the New Orleans studies were done under the direction of sociologist Albert S. Foley, S.J., and most of the California studies under the direction of sociologist Eugene J. Schallert, S.J.

results by which the success of the experiment would be judged; and no plans were made for formal studies to match actual results with expected results.

7. Santa Clara Conference (August 6–19, 1967)[8]

The Santa Clara Conference had its origin in a decision of the American provincials in 1964 to establish an Institute on the Formation of the Jesuit. At that time, the decision was part of a move to reorganize the Jesuit Educational Association and to rewrite its constitutions. The focus of the provincials' concern was the curriculum of studies for young Jesuits. This institute was their proposed response to a growing number of voices calling for changes in the academic formation of Jesuits. According to these voices, the course of studies should reflect more modern developments, should result in secular degrees, should be somewhat shorter, and should keep the Jesuit in closer contact with his secular counterpart in the university world, preferably by integrating the scholastics with a university campus, both physically and academically.[9]

The institute was not actually established until 1966, when its title became the Conference on the Total Development of the Jesuit Priest; as its title indicates, its objective had widened to include every aspect of Jesuit life during formation. This change in scope reflected an important characteristic of the period: the movement for change kept picking up momentum year by year,

[8] Unless otherwise noted, all references in this section are to *Proceedings of the Conference on the Total Development of the Jesuit Priest,* volumes I through VI, 1967 (S.C.C. 1967).

[9] In the early 1950s, for example, a very lively debate took place over the location of the new philosophate of the New York province—whether it should be established on the campus of Fordham University or out in the country. Though the country won and Shrub Oak was opened in 1955, the debate was intensified rather than stilled by this outcome.

almost month by month. By the time the Santa Clara Conference met, nothing in the process of formation was exempt from possible challenge and alteration. Vatican Council II and General Congregation 31 had contributed greatly to this momentum.

The American provincials, under the chairmanship of Edward J. Sponga, were the chief force determining the existence and the nature of the conference. Early in 1966 they appointed a planning committee of twelve men (Robert J. Henle, James S. Albertson, Thomas V. Bermingham, Richard C. Braun, John P. Foley, Garth L. Hallett, Robert F. Harvanek, Albert A. Lemieux, John R. McCall, John A. McGrail, Carlo A. Weber, and Terrence J. Toland) chaired by Robert J. Henle, at that time academic vice-president of St. Louis University. Of these twelve, four—Albertson, Braun, McCall, and Weber—later left the order. A crucial function of the planning committee was the selection of the remaining members of the conference.

The committee selected forty-eight additional members for the conference, chosen to be as representative as possible of regions, ages, occupations, and grades in the Society. There is no indication whether appointments were made with any attention to "liberal" and "conservative" orientation. Eleven were scholastics appointed from a group nominated by their peers. Of these carefully selected forty-eight, ten later left the order (Bourg, Cardegna, Cooke, DeVault, Fledderman, Milhaven, Malony, Sprague, Vigneau, and Winn).

The selection of sixty delegates to represent 8,000 American Jesuits was obviously a difficult task. Chairman Henle, in his opening address, adverted to the many expressions of dissatisfaction over the composition of the conference. He went on to point out that with only sixty places available (forty-eight after the planning committee had been appointed), there was no possible way to give representation to every viewpoint, let alone every activity, in the Society. He also went on to point out that while the priests were appointed, the scholastics were elected by their fellow scholastics. "The planning committee wanted this very clearly understood [sic] that we had not judged the scholastic representation, that candidates were elected and a final selection made" (S.C.C. 1967, 3:1:8). This concern to protect the scholastic delegates from the taint of appointment by their elders is another significant feature of the tenor of the times.

As finally constituted, the Santa Clara Conference consisted of seventy-two participants: the assistant from Rome (Harold Small), the eleven provincials, and the sixty appointed delegates. Included were four rectors, two directors of novices, two tertian directors, and five spiritual directors in houses of study. (The traditional titles of novice master, tertian master, and spiritual father were systematically avoided by the conference.) Theology had twelve representatives, philosophy six, and psychology two. The two psychologists, both of whom later left the order, exercised an influence greater than their small number might suggest.

In the opening conference, Chairman Henle said, "This is the first conference in which we have attempted to take a full look at the total, integrated, interrelated development, formation, or education of the Jesuit priest" (p. 3:1:5). He went on to explain that the planning committee thought more time was needed to prepare for "the size and dimension of the task we were asked to do" (p. 3:1:6). The provincials, however, insisted on an early date because they felt the need for concrete guidelines leading to prompt action. This felt need is a striking indication of the general tension of the period.

The conference was held on the campus of the University of Santa Clara in California and lasted two weeks, August 6–19, 1967. Its published proceedings are in six volumes (S.C.C. 1967); the first volume contains the statistical results of a survey of American Jesuits, while the last is a collection of background papers. The heart of the conference is contained in the middle four volumes. Of these, the second and third volumes contain the presentation papers prepared in advance for the conference, while the fourth and fifth volumes contain the discussion of these papers. The fifth volume also contains the conference's final recommendations.[10]

---

[10] The reader will be helped to know that the list of participants is given in

In its two weeks of meetings, the conference held twenty-seven sessions. Of these, one was introductory, seventeen were discussions of specific presentation papers, and nine were general discussions, which often were a prolongation of a previous specific discussion. The presentation papers included the three major areas of development—spiritual, academic, and apostolic. In addition, there were papers dealing with the vows. Poverty was discussed specifically under that heading, while obedience was discussed under the heading of "government", and chastity primarily under the heading of "psychological development" with some favorable discussion, especially outside the formal meetings, of the "Third Way".[11] There were also papers devoted to the periods of formation: novitiate, college, regency, theologate, and tertianship. The final paper and session dealt with the issue of commitment.

The scholastic delegates to the conference had held a meeting of their own a month earlier and had prepared a background paper entitled "Scholastics' Statement on the Attitudes, Ideals, and Expectations of Younger Jesuits" (4:149–57). The authors approved of most of the presentation papers but felt "serious misgivings" with regard to some others which seemed to see "the conference chiefly as an effort to bring the younger men to heel" (4:157). Their paper

---

volume 3, part 1, as is also the opening session with its explanation of the origin of the conference. The only statement made by the group of provincials is given in volume 3, part 2. Also note that volume 3, parts 1 and 2 are denoted 3:1 and 3:2 respectively in the page references.

[11] Those who know little else about the Santa Clara Conference remember it as being connected in some fashion with the "Third Way". This was a third lifestyle situated between the married state and the priestly or the religious state. (The term seems to have originated with Teilhard de Chardin who, however, did not believe that the human race had evolved to a position where it could actually live in such a way.) Immediately after the conference, General Arrupe wrote a letter to the whole Society (December 12, 1967) formally stating that the Third Way had no place in the Society of Jesus. As late as 1973, however, *Newsweek* thought the issue topical enough to run an article on it, "Priests Who Date: The Third Way" (issue of December 3). The matter is discussed more at length in Volume II in connection with the vow of celibacy.

stated: "The most urgent concern felt by Scholastics is the need for a more flexible and individualized approach to structures. . . . Patterns of behavior originally designed to foster growth have become in the course of time frozen, immutable, and stifling" (4:150). Then follows a detailed list of changes needed to achieve this "more individualized approach". The paper is a most useful window onto the values that inspired the demands for change in the 1960s. When John R. McCall came to write a paper for the Jesuit Educational Association in 1968, he used the six concrete proposals of the Scholastics' Statement to structure his own presentation.

The delegates received the two volumes of presentation papers and the volume of background papers well in advance of the conference and were expected to have absorbed the contents before assembling. At the meetings, the leader of the group that had produced the paper under consideration would offer a short summary of it. Then, after a respondent or two had spoken briefly, the issue would be thrown open to general discussion.

In the meetings there were some voices counseling caution in making changes, but most called for prompt action. This was to be expected since the conference had been assembled under the explicit rubric of modernizing Jesuit life. Presumably the delegates had been selected for their openness to this task. Living together for two weeks, the delegates reinforced each other, not only in the meetings but also in individual encounters and in small group caucuses outside the meetings; references to such contacts occur frequently in the proceedings. Much as had happened in the Second Vatican Council, momentum grew day by day until at the end the chairman could state, "We recognize that we are in a period of choice and creation like that of Ignatius and his early companions" (3:2:C2).

Toward the end of the conference, the delegates responded to the request of the provincials for specific guidelines by establishing sixteen consensus positions (3:2:C3–73). The positions represented "not total agreement but a majority position" and "on some matters there was and remains a strong difference of opinion"

(3:2:Ciii). This was particularly true of the recommendations made by the committee on prayer, whose chairman was Bernard Cooke (3:2:C58–61).

The Santa Clara Conference is one of the more significant sources of knowledge about Jesuits in the 1960s; if one could have only one source, the choice would certainly fall here. The six volumes of its proceedings, reflecting two weeks of discussion by a representative group of Jesuits in the presence of all the provincials, cover every major issue and reveal every characteristic attitude of the 1960s. Though not yet in full swing by 1967 (that was to take another two years), the movement for reform in the order had by this time developed its basic philosophy, a philosophy which the Santa Clara Conference expressed as adequately as any one source could.

Though the provincials were uneasy about the total impact of the conference and debated whether to publish its proceedings, they finally decided that not to publish might look like censorship and, in the climate of the 1960s, be counterproductive. How much influence did the conference actually exert? Probably only a few read all, or even most, of the six published volumes. Had the *National Jesuit News* been in existence at this time to report on the conference, Santa Clara's impact undoubtedly would have been greater. However, the seventy pages of consensus positions and recommendations were printed separately and sent to every Jesuit in the assistancy. These were probably read more widely. It was to this document, for example, that the novices of Wernersville appealed when in 1968 they drew up a white paper containing their proposals for alterations in the novitiate. Certainly the changes which did occur in the Society of Jesus during the 1960s and 1970s were in accord with the main thrust and, indeed, with most of the specific recommendations of the Santa Clara Conference—regarding the vows, the ministries, and the process of formation.

In any event, the participants in the conference left with a happy feeling of accomplishment, of having given direction for a new age. As Chairman Henle put it in a letter to this writer, "they left in a glow of euphoria." This euphoric mood is reflected in an article written by one of the participants a week after the conference. The article ended with the statement, "One provincial—a man not given to uncontrolled expression—described the two weeks as the 'biggest thing that's happened in my life, and maybe the best service we have given other religious orders in this country'" (McNaspy 1967, 224).

This same article singled out "the special insights of Frs. Carlo A. Weber, John R. McCall, John Giles Milhaven and Frederic O'Connor" (McNaspy 1967, 223). Of these four, the first three later left the Society. In a later, fuller account of the conference, the author includes twenty quotations from participants in the Santa Clara Conference (McNaspy 1968). Of these, eighteen were from men who later left the order. In addition, quotations were included from four men not at the conference; three of these also later left the order. Justin Kelly's report on the conference contained a litany of influential delegates almost identical with that of McNaspy. Kelly adds, "Father Bernard Cooke of Marquette [University] would win my vote as the most impressive single figure among the delegates" (Kelly 1968, 382). Later, Cooke also left the priesthood.

Though the general mood of the conference was an enthusiastic endorsement of "modernizing" Jesuit life, some caution was expressed. Mistakes might be made in shifting from the proven old to the unproven new. These cautions usually took the form of proposals that the transition be treated as an "experiment" whose results should be formally reviewed and evaluated at a definite later date. Thus, Chairman Henle stated in his opening address:

> The planning committee has recommended that in three or four or five years there should be another meeting of this sort dealing with the same problems and that in the interim there should be some kind of continuity between this meeting and the next meeting because of the many experiments and the many developments now going on. . . . We have recommended that this Conference be a starting point for development and that what guidelines we lay down will be subject to review and revision at some future date not too far distant (3:1:6–7).

At the end of the conference, the chairman repeated his call for subsequent evaluation of the Santa Clara recommendations (3:2:C2). The provincials, also, in their final and only address to the conference called for later review of the conference's recommendations. However, if such a review of the conference was ever made, it has left no trace.

Participation by the provincials in the conference had a number of noteworthy characteristics. First, the provincials were clearly the instigating force of the conference, the center from which organizing energy proceeded. Second, they insisted, against the advice of their own planning committee, on having the conference in 1967; in their judgment, the climate of the times permitted no delay. Third, they themselves attended the conference, remaining throughout the two weeks of its deliberations.

In addition, they were mostly silent during the conference.[12] There seem to have been several motives for this stance. They were cautious against shutting off a free expression of views by asserting their authority; they were there primarily to ascertain what the assistancy was thinking and feeling. Also, some had doubts about several propositions developed at the conference and wanted more information. In the meantime, the provincials were reluctant to seem to give support by engaging in the discussion. On the other hand, as two of them later remarked to me, their silence may have seemed to give support to such positions. Probably the outstanding example of this was their silence when the Third Way was under discussion. Henle in a letter to the author recalled that Provincial Sponga complained frequently—in evening sessions when provincials and the chair-

---

[12] Apparent exceptions were Robert Harvanek (Chicago) and Gerald Sheahan (Missouri). Both had been active in the planning of the conference before their appointments to the provincial office. Harvanek was appointed in April 1967, Sheahan in July 1967. Sheahan was head of a task force and spoke in that capacity rather than as provincial, while Harvanek's comments dealt with the Bellarmine Plan, of which he was the chief author. Other than this limited and specialized participation, they followed the general policy of the provincials of not taking an active part in establishing positions.

man met alone—that Henle was too traditional, not innovative enough.

Finally, it is clear that the majority of provincials accepted most of the findings of the conference. In their final letter to the conference they spoke of the "amazingly productive work of the Assistancy conference" and concluded that "it seems obvious that a direction has been set" (3:2:Ci, Cii). That is probably the best summary of the Santa Clara Conference. (Volume II will provide additional information on the conference and its recommendations.)

8. Studies in Jesuit Spirituality

The story of *Studies* begins at Woodstock College, the Maryland-New York theologate. In 1964 and 1965, some Woodstock theologians held discussions on the need to promote the in-depth study of spirituality, especially Jesuit spirituality. The discussions seem to have been stimulated by the same considerations that led to the theological institutes described earlier. The young men believed that traditional spirituality was out of step with modern culture and needed renovation.

The discussions eventually led to the establishment of the Bea Institute at Fordham University in 1967 and to further proposals submitted to the provincials at their annual meeting at Ponce, Puerto Rico, in May 1968. The provincials were asked to expand the work of the Bea Institute. In the discussion, Robert F. Harvanek, the Chicago provincial, proposed an alternative that had some similarity to the earlier thought of James J. Doyle (Chicago) and George E. Ganss (Missouri). Harvanek proposed that something be established, on a trial basis, along the lines of a Jesuit seminar. This proposal would have several advantages. It would be free of the requirements that go with university affiliation; it would not require the assignment of full-time men, an important consideration to provincials already feeling the pinch of limited manpower; it would partially meet the recommendation of the General that the provincials establish a think tank to help them resolve emerging problems; and it could be focused on the study of Jesuit spirituality. This proposal appealed to the provincials, was given more precise form at a meeting of the central-region provincials in June 1968, and came into existence in the fall of that year.

The American Assistancy Seminar on Jesuit Spirituality held its first meeting at Florissant, Missouri, in November 1968. It consisted of eleven members under the chairmanship of George E. Ganss. Eventually, it was decided to appoint members for terms (usually three years) so as not unduly to burden its members, all of whom had other full-time responsibilities, and to ensure a constant supply of new blood. The members decided, with the approval of the provincials, to publish the work of the seminar in a series of brochures to be called *Studies in the Spirituality of Jesuits.* These studies, averaging four or five each year, were to be written by the members of the seminar and by other scholars recruited through the seminar. The chairman of the seminar, George Ganss, was to be editor.

In the first issue of *Studies,* John Edwards stated the purpose of the seminar: "To do research in depth in the spirituality of Ignatius and in the historical development of Jesuit spirituality, and also to draw upon all modern sources." This issue also explained the policy that would guide *Studies:*

> In the present era of rapid change, there are various books, periodicals, and newspapers which provide a voice for those who sponsor opinions and causes, some of which are too radical or unproven. In the effort to maintain a proper and helpful balance, we should try to make sure that an opportunity to be heard is given also to those who are very much concerned about genuine Christian tradition, and about the Jesuit tradition within it (Edwards 1969, vi–vii).

In this policy statement, some emphasis should probably be accorded the word *balance.* Because by this time the movement for reform had picked up considerable momentum, the seminar was concerned to provide a scholarly, deliberate voice to accompany, and where necessary moderate, the multitude of more hurried voices calling for change in nearly every area of Jesuit life. The original membership of the seminar, selected by the provincials with the help of the chairman from a long list of candidates, included a novice director, a tertian director, and six professional theologians.

The issues to which the seminar early turned its attention were those occupying the forefront of Jesuit interest. Similar to the issues filling the Jesuit newspapers (see below), they were treated on a more scholarly level. The very first article concerned the question of maintaining Jesuit identity in a period of unprecedented change. Several early articles dealt with the general problem of balancing the values of continuity and change (vol. 1, no. 1, and vol. 4, no. 4). Another early article (vol. 2, no. 1) dealt with the issue so frequently debated in the 1960s, the tension between the institution and the person. A symposium of three writers, including the editor, discussed the delicate problem of "Thinking with the Church" (vol. 7, no. 1). The topic of "Faith and Justice", a distinctive contribution of G.C. 32, was analyzed in volume 7, number 4, and volume 9, number 4. The change that commanded more attention than any other, the precipitous drop in the number of Jesuits, was discussed at length (vol. 3, nos. 2 and 3; vol. 9, nos. 1 and 2). These are only a few examples of a long list of pressing issues. For a serious discussion of major Jesuit concerns in that period, one cannot do better than turn to the *Studies.* As time went on, the topics became less controversial, less rooted in currently pressing issues, and, one would gather from community conversation, somewhat less faithfully read.

The seminar undoubtedly played its part as a generator of change, contributing to the general mood of entering a "new era". Its respectability made its impact the greater, especially among those inclined to dismiss the shriller cries for change heard in community meetings or set forth in Jesuit newspapers. While more balanced than some other discussions of the disputed issues, the articles in *Studies* clearly favored the general movement of the Society towards *aggiornamento.*

A note on the *Woodstock Letters:* while recording the appearance of new Jesuit publications in the 1960s, the disappearance of one venerable magazine should be noted. The *Woodstock Letters,* begun in 1872, suspended publication after its fall issue of 1969 (vol. 98, no. 4). In the several preceding years, *Woodstock Letters* had begun to depart somewhat from its traditional emphasis on Jesuit history and to carry discussions of current issues not unlike those that were to occupy *Studies.* (*Studies* began in the year the *Letters* ended.)

High on the list of reasons for dropping the magazine was the move of the theologate from Woodstock, Maryland, to New York City. At Woodstock the magazine had its own printing press and an assured source of cheap Jesuit labor. It was estimated that expenses in New York would be four times greater, and there was no assurance that the scholastic theologians would be available as needed. They were scattered among widely separated residences, and history, in the 1960s, was not in high repute among the young.

The members of the seminar, along with a few others, protested the closing of the *Letters,* but on the whole the magazine ended with surprisingly little public attention, certainly much less that its importance warranted. It was simply lost amid all the other changes.

9. Jesuit Newspapers (1971–)

Among the more colorful developments during this period of change were the Jesuit newspapers—three of them, all founded in 1971. The New England province led the way with the *SJNEws,* which began in February 1971 and continued until June 1975.[13]

---

[13] In the fall of 1970 the New England province planning office, headed by William R. Callahan, raised the question of starting a new kind of province newsletter. At a meeting held at Loyola House in December, the decision was reached to launch a province newspaper. In addition to the planning office staff, five Jesuits were present at the December meeting: Charles Connolly, Thomas M. Curran, Paul Kenney, Michael O'Connell, James Powers.

The Oregon province followed with the *General Exchange,* which began in November 1971 and continued until the spring of 1981. An assistancy-wide paper, the *National Jesuit News,* was launched in December 1971 and has continued up to the present. All three were monthlies with the declared objective to advance Jesuit unity, an objective that reflected the deep polarization felt in the Society at that time.[14]

The newspapers are a prime historical source. For one who did not live through the period—or who has forgotten it—the newspapers are the best single witness of that history. All the major events are to be found there, month after month, recounted with their original intensity and vivid detail.

The newspapers did more than mirror events; they influenced them. They became themselves significant generators of change. By their very nature as newspapers they focused on the new. In the competition for space, familiar activities lost out to the unusual, especially to proposals to do things differently or to alter values. The wide coverage of the papers meant that a new lifestyle, a new ministry, or a new emphasis adopted anywhere was immediately brought to the attention of Jesuits everywhere. The newspapers contributed significantly to creating a climate of change.

The *National Jesuit News* was launched in conjunction with the National Leadership Conference held by the provincials at Inisfada, New York, November 1–5, 1971. As part of their decision to give the Jesuit apostolate in the United States a more national character, the provincials authorized a national newspaper. The editor, Thomas M. Curran, gave the following explanation of the paper's origin.

> Vol. 1, No. 1 of the *Jesuit National News.* Where did it come from? From those wonderful folks who used to give you permissions—the Provincials of the Assistancy. Their motive? They need widespread grass-roots help from Jesuits all over the country, and they are hoping that a paper will be a vehicle not

[14] For example, the first issue of the first newspaper, the *SJNEws,* described its function thus: "It should be informative, exciting, fun, but, most of all, unifying" ([February 1971]: 4).

only of information about their activities but of input and ideas
from those who will be most vitally affected by whatever process
they develop for national leadership, the troops of the U.S.

Each Jesuit was thus being urged to use the columns of the
newspaper to participate in a process of change. Such a formal
invitation, backed by such a costly enterprise, a national newspaper,
was itself a potent generator of change.

By encouraging debate on nearly every topic and providing a
public forum for it, the paper inevitably had some influence on
the mode of governance, making it more democratic. The paper
provided a means whereby unaffiliated individuals could bring
pressure to bear on the decision-making process. Strong controversy was especially prominent in the first few years, and letters to
the editor sometimes filled several pages.

For example, the first issue of the *National Jesuit News* (December
1971) featured a front-page picture of the provincials gathered for
concelebrated Mass. Except for the principal celebrant, none of
the provincials wore any vestments or even clerical garb. In the
next few issues protests poured in from readers. Then, later letters
condemned the writers of the first batch. Without the newspaper,
this point of friction would have remained local and minor; with
the newspaper it became national and prominent. Given the differences developing among Jesuits in almost every area of religious
life, with new differences emerging almost every month, the
newspaper functioned like a forced draft of air passing over glow-
ing coals and fanning them into a blaze.

Another example occurred in the first issue (February 1971) of
the New England paper, *SJNEws*. Editor Curran chose to publish
a letter written to the General, Pedro Arrupe, by William J.
Burke, who had been elected to represent the New England
province at a meeting to be held in Rome. Burke's letter (June 21,
1970) was his required official report on the state of the New
England province and was not intended for publication. The
report was sharply critical of nearly all the new developments in
the province. Publication of the letter set off a storm of debate—

over its substance and over the propriety of making it public. The New England provincial, William Guindon, thereupon wrote a long report to the General (September 22, 1970) that presented a completely different picture of the state of the province. The spectacle of the official elected to represent the province being formally contradicted by the official appointed to govern the province illustrates sharply the polarization marking that period.

Examples of controversy could be multiplied. In a letter to the editor of the *National Jesuit News,* Vincent P. McCorry, who for many years had written the weekly column "The Word" for the Jesuit magazine *America,* could write with measured bitterness that his mother, the Society, was being raped; another writer could offer the black-humor correction that his mother had not been raped but had gone off with another man. In his letter Father McCorry said he had written an article for *America* proposing that the polarized groups split up the resources of the Society and go their separate ways.[15] Likewise, an early innovation of the *National Jesuit News* drew many letters of strong opposition. The paper began to run a regular column "about the activities of those who have left our midst" (February 1971 issue, p. 5). Critics objected that this was to give a public stamp of approval to a new attitude that was questioning permanent commitment. And so forth.

The intensity of the controversies diminished in later years, especially after G.C. 32, which for all practical purposes decided the outcome of the debate by confirming the decrees of G.C. 31 and supporting the administration of Pedro Arrupe. Another development making for lessened controversy was a change in editors. Thomas M. Curran had been editor of both the *SJNEws* and the *National Jesuit News.* A competent journalist (he had been

---

[15] *America* did not publish the article. In his letter, McCorry says he did not expect publication. For anyone who might surmise that McCorry was joking—as one reader of the manuscript did—he should read the entire letter, which contains McCorry's thought of leaving the Society and ends with the reflection "the shadows lengthen, and that night begins for which there will be no dawn."

editing two local secular papers at the time he was put in charge of
the Jesuit papers), he encouraged controversy on most aspects of
Jesuit life. When he left the order in 1972, he was replaced first by
the team of Joseph M. McFarlane and James Hietter and then, on
the national paper, by Daniel L. Flaherty and Robert J. Bueter.
Under these editors, the tone of the paper became definitely less
controversial.

Did the national paper reach its objective of unifying Jesuits?
The answer is arguable. James L. Connor, provincial of the Maryland province, wrote on March 30, 1972 to all the members of his
province deploring the disunity being caused by the paper. The
editor in reply said that until the differences were brought out
into the open there was no hope of healing them.[16] Whether or
not the newspaper wrought any healing, it did make clear, in a
way that could not have been done otherwise, what was the
actual Jesuit situation.

10. Group Dynamics

The group dynamics movement, which began to attract attention
in the early 1950s, touched Jesuits in a variety of ways, one of
which was the Better World Retreat. Beginning about 1952, the
Italian Jesuit Riccardo Lombardi developed a unique retreat by
applying the principles of group dynamics to the Ignatian Spiritual Exercises.[17] He believed that the Exercises needed to be
adapted to the changed modern world. It was essential to the
Lombardi retreat that it be made by a group functioning precisely
as a group, with constant interaction among the retreatants. It was
conducted by a team consisting of Jesuits and lay persons, including a woman. Most of the hours of the retreat were spent in

---

[16] In this same issue, an editorial written by Curran's successor reminds the
reader what a remarkable feat Curran and his minuscule staff had performed in
launching the paper.

[17] Lombardi n.d.

dialogue. Children's games, including a kind of hockey with brooms and a balloon, helped to lessen reserve and promote easy exchanges. Members of the group were encouraged to be open to one another and not be shy about expressing their personal reflections and feelings in the midst of the group. Most Jesuits found the process novel, some found it dubious.

The Lombardi retreat acquired the name of Better World Retreat in 1958 and was brought to the United States under this title in the late 1960s. John M. Comey, S.J., who was active in the movement, was encouraged by the American provincials to offer the retreat to Jesuits. The provincials hoped that prayerful dialogue might bring some healing to a bitterly divided Society. According to Comey's recollection,[18] a Better World Retreat for Jesuits was conducted in eight of the ten provinces (the exceptions were Maryland and New Orleans).[19]

Did the Better World Retreat achieve its goal of uniting the polarized Jesuits of that period? The retreat probably did little to resolve the intellectual differences separating the two sides, for the differences had theological and philosophical roots too deep to be reached by a brief, emotional dialogue. However, the experience of a retreat did help to lessen suspicion and bitterness. At the end of the retreat, each side was able to grant more easily the sincerity and good will of the other side.

The Better World Retreat was a generator of change for several reasons. First, it represented something new at the heart of Jesuit life. Jesuits were invited to substitute it for their customary Ignatian retreat, at least on a one-time basis, and the reason given was that the changed situation required something new. Given the crucial

[18] When the Better World Retreat movement lost its momentum in the United States in the late 1970s, its records became scattered and seem to have been lost.

[19] I myself made two such retreats, one in Chicago in 1969 and one at North Andover, Massachusetts in 1970. I made the first retreat because my provincial, Robert F. Harvanek, was urging all members of the province to do so. I made the second retreat because I felt my suspicions of the first retreat had prevented me from giving it a fair chance.

place of the Ignatian Exercises in Jesuit life, this change sanctioned
by the provincial had special significance. If the Ignatian retreat
could change, what could not? Second, a predilection for change
was inherent in the entire structure of the Better World Retreat.
Most of the characteristic techniques used were alien to the tastes
of the traditionalists. Talk instead of silence, secular garb even at
the shared liturgies, and the strong exhortations to give expression
to feelings. According to the Lombardi retreat, the supreme asceticism was the dialogue itself, that is the opening of oneself to the
possibility that one's convictions are wrong. Though in principle
this asceticism applied to both sides, the implication was unmistakable that it was needed chiefly by the traditionalists, who had to
be opened up to the possibility of change. The net impact of the
Better World Retreat was to strengthen the impression that change
was "in". For some it seems to have been a liberating experience, a
kind of conversion from traditional to new ways of the Spirit.

Group dynamics played an additional role in the form of encounter groups, training sessions, communication workshops, and so
forth. Some of these were by and for Jesuits only, while others
merely had some Jesuits among the participants. All were characterized by an emphasis on the individual and his feelings and by a
reliance on process rather than on objective, structured norms.

One of the earlier and larger of Jesuit-sponsored experiments in
group dynamics was held at Alma College (California) in February 1967. The psychologist Carl Rogers and his team of nine
travelled to Alma to conduct a three-day workshop for the Jesuit
community, at no financial cost to the community. The arrangements seem to have been made by Robert J. Willis, a student of
Rogers and at that time a Jesuit. All but ten members of the
community elected to participate in this workshop, which took
the place of the regular spring triduum (three-day retreat). After
the workshop the rector of the community (Joseph J. Farraher)
judged that some of the scholastics had been damaged by the
experiment. "They were in extreme agitation following this
experience." Nevertheless, he believed that for the community as
a whole it had been a profitable experience—once. When some of

the scholastics suggested a repetition in 1968, the dean of the theologate refused permission. When some of this community were interviewed seven years later, their evaluations varied, from very favorable to seeing the experience as a dangerous solvent of religious life.

At Woodstock, during 1969, when the community was planning to move to a new life in New York, Dean Robert E. O'Brien made some use of group dynamics over a period of about a year. He was searching for a way of coping with divisions in the community that threatened to become explosive. Some faculty and students were convinced that the new era required basic changes in the nature of theology and the method of theologizing; they also held that the individual student should be allowed a creative role in shaping such changes. Other faculty and students doubted the soundness of some of the new values and counseled a more cautious approach to experiments. Often, the divisions were bitter. The dean hoped that exposure to group dynamics would improve communications and would result in both sides, but especially the traditionalists, becoming more "open".

The Woodstock experience with group dynamics, under the direction of Frederick F. Flach, M.D., head of Creative Catalysts, Inc., proceeded in four phases. The first or trial phase was simply a meeting of Woodstock's curriculum committee, composed of faculty and students, which was held on March 21, 1969, with Dr. Flach present as facilitator. The reaction to this meeting was generally favorable, and the dean proceeded to the second phase, which was a twenty-four hour program conducted by five members of Creative Catalysts, Inc. for the Woodstock faculty at Cape May, New Jersey, in June 1969. This second experience also seems to have been judged satisfactory, for it was followed three months later by the third phase.

The third phase was a meeting held over the weekend of September 26–28, 1969 at Manresa, Maryland. The meeting was conducted by four staff members of Creative Catalysts, Inc. for a group of sixteen, including four faculty members, selected by Dean O'Brien. By this time, about half of the Woodstock community had moved to New York, while the remainder was still at Woodstock in Maryland. The weekend meeting had representatives from both communities, plus two second-year regents (teachers) from New York high schools.[20]

The general reaction of the participants was favorable, with most comments emphasizing the pleasantness of the experience and the release from argumentative tension "as we played games and let down our hair". Two members commented, however, that while they enjoyed the experience they thought the crucial problem was not so much communication (the only problem the group dynamics instrument was designed to address) as it was real disagreement on substantive issues.

The fourth use of Creative Catalysts, Inc. occurred on November 17, 1969. Felix F. Cardegna, rector of the New York Woodstock community, invited all the members of the community to attend an evening-long session with three members of the Creative Catalysts staff acting as facilitators. The purpose of the evening was to discuss "a number of specific issues dividing the community—such as poverty, liturgy, community, lifestyle, et cetera". Available records give no indication of how many of the community accepted the invitation to attend the meeting or what its results were.

Dr. Flach urged that the services of his organization be used more widely—indeed, for the entire Jesuit order. (He probably meant the entire New York province.) This recommendation seems not to have been followed, for there is no record of any further relationship between Woodstock and Creative Catalysts, Inc. One consideration probably was the cost of the services. The four very limited uses made of the services had cost about $5,000,

[20] In addition to Dean O'Brien, the sixteen were John Brubaker (NY), Robert Carter (NY), Robert Cummings (NY), James Dolan (NY), Gerald Fogarty (MD), John Healy (NY), John Langan (Detroit), J. Giles Milhaven (NY), Peter Neary (New York), Peter O'Brien (NY), Vincent Quayle (NY), Joseph Roccasalvo (NY), Peter (Philip) Rossi (NY), Peter Schineller (NY), Robert Springer (MD), and Robert Stump (NY). Of the sixteen, eleven left the order (see Appendix 5).

and even this cost represented a substantial discount from the usual fees.

The most ambitious use of group dynamics occurred in the New England province, which invited Robert Willis to conduct several workshops for the members of the province during the summer and fall of 1970. A large number of New England Jesuits attended one or other of these sessions. Commended by the provincial, William Guindon, but severely criticized by William J. Burke in the Procurators' Report mentioned earlier, the workshops attracted many letters of appreciation in the *SJNEws*. (Willis was also involved in a minor way in a workshop conducted in Rome for a group of new provincials assembled to receive some general orientation.)

Many Jesuits experimented individually with group dynamics in situations too numerous to be recorded. Two experiences which I myself had were probably fairly typical. One was a communications workshop promoted by the Center for Spiritual Growth (Wernersville, Pennsylvania) and conducted by a St. Louis team consisting of a layman, a former nun, and an (unidentified) priest. I also attended a sensitivity session at the College of Notre Dame (Baltimore) which sought "the intensification of interpersonal relations through the experience of music". This group was under the direction of a team of four young men and women connected with the University of Chicago. I found both experiences interesting, even entertaining, but not particularly useful. One of my clear impressions was that I was being urged to adopt ways of acting, with their implied values, different from those traditional ways in which I had been trained as a Jesuit. The chief differences involved a shift in emphasis from impersonal observation to involvement, from the rationally derived to experience. The query was always "What do I *feel* about this?" Also the norm of choice was not some objective, unchanging value but was simply the perceived effect on the individual's life here and now: "What value does it have for *me*?"

Among the more colorful centers of group dynamics was the Esalen Institute in California. In an article on Esalen, *Time* magazine noted the presence of a Jesuit priest, Paul Hilsdale of the California province. When Hilsdale later left the order, he said that after the liberating experience of Esalen he found religious life too narrow to be endured.

At the Chicago province scholasticate in North Aurora, Illinois, some of the scholastics (philosophers and theologians) were taking courses at the Illinois Psychiatric Institute. In 1967, they went to the rector, Robert Murray, with the suggestion that the community be offered the opportunity of experiencing a session of group dynamics. He agreed and engaged a Dr. Issl for this purpose. After a trial session arranged for fifteen scholastics was judged successful, the rector contracted for two faculty sessions and encouraged faculty members to participate. As usual, reactions to the experience were diverse. Some praised it for its power to "open up" people, while others condemned it as substituting doubtful psychology for traditional religious values.

The Missouri philosophate (Fusz Memorial in St. Louis) made considerable use of the T-group[21] technique during 1967–68. Under the direction of Fathers E. J. Merz and E. T. Foote, about two thirds of the community engaged in T-group activity at some time during this period, and many engaged in it almost continuously. The directors gradually changed their evaluation from enthusiastic expectation to caution and apprehension as some of the young men seemed to be damaged by the experience. Lack of trained leaders was a major difficulty. Superiors gradually came to discourage the activity, which practically disappeared after 1968. (See below, p. 317.)

[21] T-group is a shortened form of "training group", which according to Webster is "a group under the leadership of a trainer who seeks to develop self-awareness and sensitivity to others by verbalizing feelings uninhibitedly at group sessions".

11. Roman Policy

In all probability, the *aggiornamento* inaugurated by Vatican II was reflected in the appointment of ecclesiastical authorities. The most direct and efficient method to achieve the objectives of the new era would have been to appoint bishops and religious superiors who shared the new values. It may be worthwhile to take notice of some evidence pointing in that direction.

After the council, Rome seems to have adopted a definite policy of appointing bishops more open to change. This policy began at least as early as 1973 with the appointment of Belgian Archbishop Jean Jadot as Apostolic Delegate to the United States. Jadot favored the selection of bishops younger and more open to change. Within a decade, the "Jadot bishops", as they came to be called, accounted for about half of all the active bishops in the country (Hyer 1983, B-4).[22]

Speaking of Jesuits during the period 1965–75, the historian Thomas H. Clancy (himself a provincial appointed during that period) records a similar change in the Society. "Actually in the previous decade the whole process of choosing superiors had changed. Many veteran superiors found themselves ill-equipped to handle the new problems and challenges of religious life. In some provinces a whole new cadre of local superiors had to be recruited" (Clancy 1976, 249).

One such instance of Roman policy occurred in the appointment of a provincial. In this case, the *terna* (a list of three candidates) for provincial was returned by Rome twice because no one of the three nominees was thought to be sufficiently open to change. When a man so qualified was finally added, he was the one selected and appointed. He lived up to the expectations of the General, becoming one of the more active provincials in promoting change.[23] It is difficult to judge how general this Roman

[22] For Jadot's later history, see "The Selection of Bishops" in *America*, (August 25, 1984): 70.
[23] In forming his curia, he appointed two young Jesuits who after very active careers in promoting changes were separated from the order.

policy was, but to the extent that it influenced appointments—especially of provincials, rectors, and novice masters—it would have been a potent generator of change.

G.C. 33 was composed largely of the generation of the 1960s, including superiors appointed since Vatican II. By 1983, the older generation, still significantly represented in G.C. 31 and 32, had died or retired or at any rate moved out of positions of influence. The newest generation, which is showing many characteristics different from those of the 1960s, had, of course, not yet reached the age in the Society that would allow them to participate in G.C. 33. Depending on the date of the next congregation, they may begin to appear as a distinct influence in G.C. 34 or G.C. 35.

12. General Congregation 32 (1974–75)

Coming at the very end of the period under consideration, the Thirty-Second Congregation is significant for our purpose chiefly for what it has to say about the decade just concluded. Ten years into the "new age" announced by G.C. 31, G.C. 32 had the opportunity to approve or disapprove the recent course of legislation. There is no doubt what G.C. 32 chose to do: it confirmed its predecessor in the most positive manner. After G.C. 32, it was clear that the new path opened by G.C. 31 represented not a temporary jog in the road but a relatively stable change in direction.

As described earlier, the new direction had been accompanied by deep divisions within the order and was much questioned. A detailed and balanced analysis of the situation was made on September 27, 1970, when Father General Arrupe opened the congregation of procurators (elected representatives of the provinces who meet between general congregations) with an extended "Account of the State of the Society". In this account he viewed the many problems that faced the Society and that explained his obvious desire for another congregation.[24] He began by observing that when G.C. 31 elected to modernize the order, it necessarily opened the door to many dangers, four especially: (1) "many tensions will necessarily arise"; (2) there may be "some defections from the Society"; (3) some mistakes will likely be made; (4) the "final issue" of the whole attempt might be failure. He went on to indicate that some of these dangers had already materialized. He noted that in the Society "crises concerning the faith . . . are becoming more marked day by day." He reported also: "Others are troubled by the pervasive secularization whereby one assumes more fully day by day the right of self-government in opposition to the norms and statutes which express sacred or religious order." Finally, he observed: "Others who do not go so far have doubts concerning our identity as Jesuits."

He then reviewed the state of the Society in relation to the vows, to prayer, and to the Vicar of Christ. Under each heading he listed gains and losses, but in each instance he devoted more space and emphasis to the losses. Though it is clear from the total allocution that he had no intention of turning back from the new adventure he did think that enough problems had arisen to require another general congregation. He was speaking only four years after the previous one.

In the United States Assistancy, concrete details of the overall situation described in the General's address can be found in the Jesuit newspapers. Though the papers did not begin until 1971, and thus missed five or six years of unrest, the issues and struggles they narrate are essentially the same as those in the earlier years. The Burke/Guindon controversy (pp. 82–83) illustrates the kind of stories of Jesuit disarray that were pouring in on the General since G.C. 31. Some Jesuits held that the changes amounted to a loss of identity (Ganss 1976, 7–8). A few left the order for this reason, while others stated that they would not have become Jesuits if

---

[24] The following quotations are all from this address ("Father General's First Allocution, Congregation of Procurators, Rome, September 27, 1970").

they had known how the order would change.[25] There was considerable criticism of the General, Pedro Arrupe, for countenancing the changes, many of which were made on local initiative. An extreme instance of dissatisfaction surfaced in Spain, where a sizable group sought permission from the Holy See to establish a separate branch within the order, where they could continue the traditional lifestyle and train their own novices.[26] At the urging of the General, the Pope denied the petition. The papacy also, however, felt deep uneasiness over some aspects of the situation. Additional indications of papal dissatisfaction are listed at the end of this section (pp. 98–100).

When the General and procurators had completed their meeting in the fall of 1970, the General announced their joint conclusion that "a new General Congregation ought to be held within a few years because of the problems of contemporary change" (*Documents* 1977, 345). They also agreed that it should not be convoked immediately. According to the Constitutions, the General must convoke a congregation not later than eighteen months after the procurators decide that there should be a congregation. Eighteen months was felt to be an inadequate time for preparation — given the task of adjusting the ministries of the Society to the modern world, given also the task of healing the painful divisions within the order. The General was encouraged to begin the work of preparation at once and when this work was sufficiently advanced to announce a general congregation.

Though the congregation would not be formally summoned until September 8, 1973, and would not begin deliberations until December 2, 1974, preparations began early in 1971. The General appointed a preparatory commission of six members under the presidency of Jean-Yves Calvez, who in turn appointed thirty task forces to organize the immense work of renewal the General envisioned (*Documents* 1977, 346). Arrupe was convinced that

---

[25] I encountered a half-dozen of the latter in my own limited experience and heard of others.

[26] A somewhat similar proposal was put forward in the United States Assistancy (p. 98).

what was needed could not be accomplished simply by enacting decrees. What was needed was nothing less than an internal renewal of the very soul of the order. Too much emphasis cannot be given to this perception; it is a prime explanatory factor of much that was done during the four years of preparation. It explains, for example, the insistence of the General that work not be confined to the central commission or to the task forces but that it enlist the active participation of each assistancy, each province, and each individual community. The planning period treated elsewhere in this chapter includes the period of preparation for G.C. 32. There is no doubt that G.C. 32 was preceded by the most thorough preparation of any congregation in the history of the Society.

According to Father Calvez, the focus of the work shifted somewhat during the four years of preparation. Beginning with a clear emphasis on the internal problems of the order, by 1973 the focus had shifted to apostolic choices, and by 1974 this had taken the more precise form of concern about "promotion of justice" (Calvez 1975–76, 947). Calvez records that Pope Paul VI wrote to the General on September 15, 1973 to urge that the work of preparation focus on religious conversion in order to recover the spiritual force of the original Society (p. 940). Calvez himself remarks that as time went on attention was turned more, "perhaps too much", to other questions (p. 941).

The New England *SJNEws,* in its issue of December 1974, presented an expression of views regarding the forthcoming G.C. 32. Karl Rahner put all his emphasis on "the spirit of the times" which required more flexibility, because of greater uncertainty, and therefore more pluralism than Jesuits were accustomed to in the past — though in the Society there had always been room for differences. John L. Swain, a former Vicar General, summed up his hope for G.C. 32 in the word "clarification". He hoped the congregation would establish some guidelines to indicate the limits of "pluralism" in theological and moral matters, in liturgical observances, and in lifestyles.

Joseph McFarlane, editor of the paper at this time, wrote a long editorial entitled "Search for Unity". In it he recognizes that there have always been differences in the Society but thinks that the current differences are not only wider but much deeper, stemming from differences in philosophy and theology and core values. The acceptance of some necessary pluralism and a recommendation of guidelines may get the Society through a transitional period but "is not the basis for a lasting solution to the problems of unity". He hopes "that one of the chief results of G.C. 32 will be a unified result of the best brains of the Jesuit order to labor together with all men of good will to get to the roots of our worldwide confusion today."

Many of the postulates—requests for action—addressed to the congregation concerned formation. Cecil McGarry, in charge of formation for the entire Society, summarized the tenor of the postulates as follows:

> There is widespread concern about a lowering of standards in our academic formation, about the unity and solidity of doctrine, about the influence of apostolic experiments on the life of study, about the sufficiency of the time being devoted to the study of philosophy and theology and about its seriousness, about the effects of many of the new elements in formation not only on the unity and coherence of formation itself but on the unity of the Society as a whole; and concern was expressed about the prevalence of special studies in subjects that might be considered peripheral to the priestly ministry (Ganss 1976, 100).

When the multitudinous task forces had completed most of their work, the Preparatory Commission for the General Congregation collected their conclusions into "Forty-Six Propositions", which it distributed to all the provinces for comments (Preparatory Commission 1972). The following year it published a synopsis of the provinces' reactions to the propositions (Preparatory Commission 1973). These two documents, much too voluminous to be presented here, even in condensed form, provide a panoramic view of the principal issues facing the coming congregation and the variety of positions already developing on each issue.

G.C. 32 enacted a number of important decrees.[27] For example, it settled some long-standing problems with regard to poverty. It also issued a call to combine justice with faith. Despite the vagueness of the call—the congregation twice refused to define either term—it was appealed to very frequently thereafter to justify efforts, often carried out in new ways, to improve the lot of the impoverished masses. Nevertheless, the congregation's chief claim to be considered among the generators of change was its firm, unqualified endorsement of G.C. 31 and the administration of Pedro Arrupe. Its Introductory Decree proceeds immediately to the main point, making clear that the congregation was called into existence precisely to judge the changes inaugurated by G.C. 31 and promptly announcing that judgment: "The 32nd General Congregation makes its own and confirms all of the declarations and dispositions of the 31st General Congregation.... The documents of the preceding Congregation accurately and faithfully express the genuine spirit and tradition of the Society . . . and superiors are directed to see to their ever fuller implementation" (G.C. 32, Dec. 1.2). Given the extraordinary length and thoroughness of the preparation for G.C. 32 and the extent to which even the local communities were drawn into that work, the congregation's confirmation of G.C. 31 must be accorded great weight.

Cecil McGarry does note, however, that in the area of formation G.C. 32 felt the need to do some balancing. Without disowning the new direction taken by G.C. 31, the congregation placed it in a broader context:

> The opening of the 31st Congregation towards a formation that laid more importance on the development of the individual and his personal gifts, and on education to responsibility and freedom, is reaffirmed; but this reaffirmation is made within the context of the Society as a body consecrated to mission under the

[27] A one hundred–page narrative analysis of G.C. 32 was written by one of its American participants, John W. Padberg, for *Studies in the Spirituality of Jesuits* (Padberg 1983). See also the doctoral dissertation, "Making the Jesuits More Modern" (Faase 1976), which describes in great detail the actions of G.C. 32.

direction of obedience. There is a new harmony here, a new balance which it was clear from both the postulates and the interventions during the Congregation was called for (Ganss 1976, 112).

During the congregation, Father General Arrupe addressed the congregation on the subject of his relations with the Pope. Donald Campion, editor of the *G.C. Bulletin,* reported the talk as follows:

Father General is not aware of any differences of judgment on his part from the pope's on any basic question. If such ever existed, he would have no difficulty in making any needed change so that he could work together with the pope more easily and effectively. From all this can be seen that those rumors, which circulate both within and outside the Society, about an alleged opposition between the pope and Father General are false (Campion 1975, 4).

The judgment of the papacy on the changed Society was not unqualifiedly approving. Already during G.C. 31, in the second session, Pope Paul VI had spoken privately but strongly to the General about developments in the Society that he considered undesirable (p. 42). The years following G.C. 31 saw a series of papal admonitions that questioned the wisdom of some of the changes, or at least the way they were being carried out. Pope Paul VI sent admonitory messages to the General, in his own name or through his secretary of state, Cardinal J. Villot, on the following dates: March 26, 1970; April 18, 1972; February 15, 1973; September 13, 1973; December 3, 1974; February 15, 1975; and May 2, 1975. All of these contained some expression of unease over recent developments in the Society.[28]

In his opening address to the congregation the Pope said he felt "trepidation" when reviewing the state of the Society and mentioned such problems as "systematic doubt, uncertainty about one's identity, desire for change, independence, and individualism". He described

[28] *The Pope and the Jesuits* (Hitchcock 1984) supplies a long list of Jesuit actions that might have contributed to this papal disquiet. The author's sources are mostly newspapers and magazines.

the recent period: "Certainly, it is a crisis of suffering, and perhaps of growth. . . . " His choice of "certainly" for the one statement and "perhaps" for the other may reflect an ambiguity he perceived in the events of the 1960s. He went on, "Certain regrettable actions, which would make one doubt whether the man were still a member of the Society, have happened much too frequently and are pointed out to us from many sides, especially from bishops of dioceses; and they exercise a sad influence on the clergy, on other religious, and on the Catholic laity (*Documents* 1977, 519–29). In a personal letter addressed to Father Arrupe and dated February 15, 1975, the Pope put the question bluntly: "Is the Church able to have faith in you?" (p. 540).

At the end of the congregation, the uneasiness of Pope Paul VI was not entirely alleviated. He took the unusual step of withholding the congregation's decrees from publication for two months while he reviewed them. When he did release them, it was with a letter from Cardinal Villot (May 2, 1975), which stated: "From an examination of the decrees, it appears that well-known circumstances prevented the General Congregation from achieving all that His Holiness had expected from this important event, and for which, at different times and in various ways, he gave some paternal suggestions" (*Documents* 1977, 545). The letter provided an appendix to which "reference should always be made" when interpreting the congregation's decrees. The appendix renewed the Pope's warnings against excessive immersion "in the temporal order", and against abuse of the freedom to differ from the teachings of the Magisterium (p. 547–48).

This clouded ending of G.C. 32 may have forecast certain events of the 1980s, especially the unprecedented action of John Paul II when he prevented the order from electing a successor to the ailing Arrupe and instead appointed (in October 1981) Father Paolo Dezza as his personal delegate to administer the order, a situation which lasted for almost two years and seems to have involved some misunderstanding on both sides.

Arrupe's successor, elected in 1983, was Peter-Hans Kolvenbach. Interviewed by the National Catholic News Service on October

29, 1984, the new General was asked how he would assess the history of strained relations with the Vatican. He replied:

> I think that we should be very clear on this point. The Holy See knows that the 26,000 Jesuits are also men, with all their richness, with all their weaknesses, with all their possibilities, and with all their limitations. Maybe the problem a few years ago was that the weaknesses did not arouse a reaction from the apostolic body of the society. There was some silence on a lot of positions and situations which certainly were not according to the spirit of our society and at the service of the Church. And the problem was that the society did not react to it.
>
> Now what happened after the papal intervention, thanks to Father Dezza and Father Pittau, is that the society began to react as an apostolic body on those weaknesses. It does not mean that today every Jesuit is an angel. But if there are weaknesses, if there are errors, now the society says, "this is an error, this is a weakness."

G.C. 33 was a short congregation (September 9–October 25, 1983) which falls outside our period of interest and in any case did little more than elect a new general on the first ballot. As in every reform movement, a certain satiety with change had set in and there was a general desire for a period of tranquility and stability. The expectations of some who had opposed many of the changes — that the congregation following the papal intervention would see some repudiation of the "new era" — were, to say the least, unrealistic. The generation that was responsible for G.C. 31 and G.C. 32 was, in good part, still in place at G.C. 33.

III

THE THEOLOGATES:
RELOCATION AND CONSOLIDATION

Introduction

The story of the changes in the Jesuit order starts with changes in Jesuit formation because formation is the most critical area. What happens in formation, the heart of this study, determines the character of the order's life. In turn, the story of changes in formation starts not with the novitiate, as might seem logical, but with the theologate[1] because that is where changes first appeared— preceding not only the novitiate but even, surprisingly enough, the universities.

Several factors explain why changes appeared earliest in the theologates. First of all, the theologians were normally older than Jesuits in the earlier stages of formation (novices, juniors, philosophers, regents). They would have been in the Society for about a decade and would have felt more competent than the younger members to pass judgment on the order as they had come to know it. They felt they not only could but should thus judge the pattern of their formation. They were being told by the new psychology that seminarians were immature for their age because they were kept in leading strings for too long.[2] Averaging about thirty years of age, the theologians were convinced that the road to maturity involved their making more decisions for themselves. As

---

[1] *Theologate* is a Jesuit term. One must go to the unabridged dictionary to find it, but there it is defined as a place where Jesuits study theology.

[2] For example, see Lee and Putz 1965, 270, 277.

they often observed in the discussions that marked the period, their peers outside the Society were married men supporting families and holding responsible positions. The prevailing mood among these men—a mood set by leaders, as usual, but spreading rapidly to the majority—was one of "taking charge".

Since the reform tended to come from below, it might have originated with Jesuits even younger than the theologians. The younger men were, after all, closer to the new times. It is probably true that in this sense they were more "modern" than the theologians, and this is one of the reasons that the firestorm of change, once kindled, swept through the other stages of formation so swiftly. But it must be remembered that the theologians also belonged to modernity. The men who occupied the theologates in the mid-1960s had entered the order in the mid-1950s, about the time that the novices began to be "different" (see Chapter VI, especially pp. 201–4). The potentiality for change had been there from the beginning, at least among the leaders. The time between their entrance into the Society and their entrance into the theologate was a time of incuba- tion. The theologians of the 1960s emerged from contemporary eggs.

The regents were almost as old as the theologians, and they were out working in "the world". For both reasons, change might have been expected to start with them. In their case, however, some offsetting factors were at work. In moving from the philoso- phate into the schools, the regents were moving from a more to a less confining situation; at least for a time they were likely to feel satisfied. The theologians, on the contrary, had made the opposite move—from the less to the more confining situation.

Furthermore, the regents were scattered (only a handful were in any one school) whereas the theologians were massed together in one community. Sociologists have observed that the development of a critical mass is essential to a successful revolution.

Finally, the regents were busy—most of them very busy, indeed— with pressing, practical affairs. The relative leisure enjoyed by the theologians provided more congenial ground for hatching new ideas. Throughout the changes of the 1960s, academe played a leading role.

An academic development, in fact, contributed to the independence of the men coming to the theologate at this time. Many of them had already done advanced work in specialized fields. For example, at Woodstock College in 1967, out of 188 theologians, 140 had master's degrees and eighteen had doctorates. Their degrees covered twenty-three different fields. Thus, the men were coming to theology already experienced in graduate work, some of it done at the most prestigious universities in the country. They came with their own independent norms and were less inclined than formerly to accept the traditional theologate as a given.

Change among the theologians preceded change even among members of the order working in Jesuit universities. This is a surprising relationship and a significant one. Since at this time the theologians were living in rural locations and under traditional rules that restricted them largely to the seminary world, while Jesuits in the universities were presumably in daily contact with the forces shaping the new times, it might have been expected that change would show itself earliest among the university communities. But this was not the case. In the late 1960s, the houses of study were so far advanced that it was common to hear university Jesuits say, "What in the world is happening to the houses of formation?" For example, when Richard A. Blake was assigned to live at Loyola University in Chicago after ordination at Woodstock in 1969, he recalled the experience as "going back in time".

Among the reasons was age, but this time the relationship is reversed. The theologians were younger than the university faculty members. As has been said, the revolution came mainly from below—partly from the younger faculty, who supplied the ideas of the reform, but especially from the students, who carried them into action. The influence of youth was particularly noticeable in the change in lifestyles. The changes in dress, for example, appeared among the young theologians well before they were adopted by Jesuits in the universities. An incident connected with Woodstock College and Georgetown University illustrates the relationship. Two Woodstock theologians had come into the city of Washington to see a doctor and then had gone to the university for dinner with the Jesuit community. They were dressed in secular attire, completely, while the members of the university community were still wearing the cassock. During the recreation period after dinner, one of the older priests took the two theologians over to the rector and announced, "These are Jesuits!"

Another reason that change came early in the theologates is to be found in theology itself. In a theologate one studies theology, and in theology a flood of changes was taking place as young professors returned from their training in Europe, as a new era in theology seemed to be ratified by Vatican II, and as the recommendations of the Rockhurst Report (Chapter I) presaged basic structural alterations in the theologates themselves. Since theology touches the heart of a religious order, the changes here reverberated in every corner of the order's life. Because many of the changes were aimed at modulating traditional understandings, especially in Scripture, their impact was inevitably disturbing.[3] A groundswell was at work, causing many structures to tremble. The theologians were exposed to this influence each day, all day. The very fabric of their daily lives kept them in steady, constant contact with this, the most revolutionary development of the period.

At St. Mary's, Kansas, some students had an early and regular introduction to contemporary theology. Faculty member Gerald F. Van Ackeren began the periodical *Theology Digest* in 1952. As its title indicates, this magazine—at first, a house organ, but later sold to the public—digested current theological articles. Van Ackeren's primary objective in starting the enterprise was to educate the students by introducing them to current, modern trends. Six committees of scholastics were formed to cover six different areas of current theological writing. By this activity, the scholastics

---

[3] For example, Joseph J. DeVault began teaching the new Scripture at West Baden in 1957. At Christmas time, when the fourth-year theologians took their demythologized version of the infancy narratives into the surrounding parishes, they caused an uproar, and the local pastor of one parish, a Jesuit, formally protested to DeVault and forbade any more Jesuits to come into his parish.

were exposed to a theology quite distinct from the traditional treatises that were being studied in class.[4]

Changes among the theologians not only preceded the other stages of formation, they also influenced them. The theologians provided a model for their younger brothers; they also provided advice. They injected themselves into the debate on how the development of the younger Jesuits should proceed. Using their own experience as examples of how novices and scholastics should *not* be formed, they offered advice to rectors, deans, and masters of novices.[5] To some extent, they also directed their advice to the novices and scholastics themselves, for the old "rules of separation" had ceased to apply and theologians could on occasion have direct contact with their younger brethren.

Relocation

During this period, the theologates underwent three chief changes: in their academic structure, in their physical location, and in their lifestyle. While the academic changes may prove to be the most significant in the long run, at the time of their occurrence changes in location and lifestyle were certainly the most dramatic and traumatic. Although all three changes took place at roughly the same time and were interrelated, their stories can be told more clearly by treating them separately. The present chapter deals with the relocation and consolidation of the theologates.

---

[4] The faculty was divided on the desirability of this new enterprise. Some saw the fundamentals being neglected in favor of these "more relevant" currents of thought.

[5] For example, Anthony Meyer and William Sneck, while students at Woodstock, traveled to the Maryland novitiate at Wernersville, Pennsylvania, and spent several days expounding their idea of what a modern novitiate should be like. Or again, the California theologians at Alma composed a questionnaire which they administered to cooperating regents in an effort to influence the course of formation. There are many other examples of theologians volunteering advice and urging action in this area.

Starting with five theologates located in the country, the United States Assistancy ended with two urban theologates, one on each coast. Figure 1 shows this experience.

Old Issue

Long before the 1960s, the relative merits of rural and urban locations had often been debated.[6] A century earlier, during the 1860s, Father General Peter Beckx sent Felix Sopranis as an official visitor to the United States to arrange for the construction of the first common house of studies. The visitor clearly favored the country while the General just as clearly favored the city. In response to the visitor's various proposals for a rural location, the General replied by suggesting that the visitor consult more broadly and continue the search for a suitable location closer to one of the Jesuit colleges, such as Georgetown or Fordham. When the General finally approved the choice of Woodstock, Maryland, it was partly because "it was less than an hour's journey from the Provincial's residence [and] had very good rail connections with a large city" (S.C.C. 1967, 4:200).

Woodstock College was formally opened on September 23, 1869, an event of which historian Gilbert J. Garraghan says, "No more decisive turning-point in the story of Jesuit development in America is chronicled than the opening-day of Woodstock College" (Garraghan 1983, 1:645). In less than a decade the wisdom of its rural location was being questioned. In 1875, the Maryland provincial, Joseph Keller, was proposing to the General that the theologate be moved to Georgetown, while in 1878 Bishop James O'Connor of Nebraska was urging its removal to Philadelphia (S.C.C. 1967, 4:203-5). In the early 1890s, several proposals were

[6] For a brief history of the very early Jesuit formation experiences, see two background papers prepared for the Santa Clara Conference, one by James Hennesy, S.J., and the other by John Daley, S.J. (S.C.C. 1967, 4:162–213).

Figure I

LOCATION OF THE THEOLOGATES

Province	Established	Place	Moved to	Ended**
Maryland	1869	Woodstock, MD	→ New York, NY, 1969	1973
Missouri	1899	St. Louis, MO	→ St. Mary's, KS, 1931 → St. Louis, MO, 1967	1973
New England	1927*	Weston, MA	→ Cambridge, MA, 1969	
California	1934	Alma, CA	→ Berkeley, CA, 1969	
Chicago	1939*	West Baden, IN	→ N. Aurora, IL, 1964 → Chicago, IL, 1970	1980

*New England opened its philosophate at Weston in 1922; Chicago opened its philosophate at West Baden in 1934.
**The date the ending was officially announced. Each theologate remained in partial operation during a short period following the announcement.

made to move the scholastics either to Georgetown or to Fordham
because, among other reasons, "It was very difficult to form the
scholastics 'in the woods' when afterwards they were to be in,
though not of, the world" (p. 210–11).

The move from Woodstock to New York almost took place
sixty years earlier than the actual move. On August 27, 1907, the
Maryland provincial, Joseph F. Hanselman, wrote to James Cardi-
nal Gibbons in Baltimore, "A few weeks ago our Very Rev.
General [Wernz] in Rome sent me word that he had decided to
transfer our scholasticate from Woodstock to Fordham, New
York."[7] Property had been purchased at Yonkers, New York,
and given the name Woodstock-on-the-Hudson. Though the prop-
erty was first used as a novitiate, the question of moving Woodstock
College to Yonkers was raised again shortly after World War II.
One last illustration of this recurring issue: shortly before Vatican
II, Fr. Edward Bunn, president of Georgetown University, pro-
posed that the Woodstock theologate be moved to Georgetown
University.

On the other coast there was a similar history of repeated
debates over the desirability of relocating the theologate. In 1946,
for example, when Alma College had decided to construct a new
library, proposals were made to relocate the theologate first, lest
the construction of a new building bind them more closely to the
old site. At that time the house consultors were already describing
the relocation debate as "an old issue".

Exactly the same question was raised a decade later, in 1956,
when Alma had to expand to accommodate the growing number
of theologians. Committees were formed, studies were made, and
all the traditional arguments were developed for and against
remaining in the country. John T. Curran, a member of the
faculty, argued that it probably had been a mistake to locate at
Alma originally because it was contrary to the general practice of
the Society. "Ordinarily our theologates have been located either

---

[7] Archives of the New York province. The archives contain no further
record of how and why this decision was reversed.

in large cities or in university towns: Naples, Louvain, Rome, Lyons, Frankfurt, Dublin, Montreal, Mexico City, Bogota, Buenos Aires, Maestricht, Barcelona, Granada, Innsbruck."[8] The list could have included the second oldest theologate in the United States Assistancy, that founded by the original Missouri province on the campus of St. Louis University in 1899.

Values Involved

The rural-urban debate over the location of the theologates turned chiefly on economic, academic, and ascetical considerations. Economics functioned as a limiting factor, while academic and ascetical values provided the positive goals. The relative influence exercised by each of the three varied with the situation.

Economic considerations always played an important part in the choice of location, especially in the earlier years when the resources of the nation and of the Jesuits were scarcer. The country usually offered lower costs and, if there were a farm connected with the seminary, an additional source of income.[9] In 1931, the theologate of the Missouri province was already in the city and on a university campus (St. Louis) but was moved out into the country (St. Mary's, Kansas) because the growing number of scholastics required additional facilities somewhere and buildings were standing vacant at St. Mary's, a boarding school which had closed. Likewise, when in 1934 the growing Chicago province opened a new house of studies, it chose West Baden, Indiana, largely because the buildings and extensive grounds were available as an outright gift.

By the end of the 1960s, economic considerations were beginning to work in the opposite direction. The theologate plants

---

[8] The Alma files covering this period are quite full and provide one of the better sources of Jesuit discussion of the issue. See also S.C.C. 1967, 4:182.

[9] In the original choice of Woodstock, shortly after the ravages of the Civil War, the reason urged in favor of location in the country was an assured source of food.

were aging—especially Woodstock and St. Mary's—and were in need of extensive renovation. Given the general decision to move eventually, the economic argument was very persuasive to move sooner rather than later. Also, since the number of scholastics was dropping rapidly at this time and the theologates expected reduced enrollments, the continued maintenance of the existing large plants was uneconomical. Moreover, given an uncertain future, the city offered needed flexibility. In the city, apartments and small houses could be bought or rented as necessary, and they could be added to or disposed of to meet changing needs.

Since a theologate is a school, academic considerations always weighed heavily in the choice of location. Academic needs dictated opposite strategies at the earlier and at the later stages. In the very early days, before there was any common house of studies, the theologians were housed at Georgetown and St. Louis colleges. At both places, they were expected to carry a teaching load while studying theology. As in all mission situations, the work to be done exceeded resources and what had been allowed as a temporary expedient threatened to become a permanent pattern. The General in Rome was concerned over the resulting inadequate education received by the young men and repeatedly urged the establishment of a house of studies sufficiently separated from the colleges to protect the scholastics from this double burden.

Those who favored a rural location argued that in the country the scholastics would be shielded not only from the work imposed by the colleges but also from the distractions offered by the city. In the country there would be nothing to do but study. Throughout most of the life of the rural theologates, this was the way they actually functioned. Distractions were understood to include not only entertainments but also the active ministry. Students were allowed the barest minimum of such ministry, while faculty members were warned from time to time—by rector or provincial— that their chief task was to teach and to be available to the students.

In the mid-1960s, following upon Vatican II, the weight of argument shifted, and contrary considerations were urged. Theology should be less abstract and philosophical, more concrete and applied—more pastoral, more balanced—than it had been. To achieve this goal, the students should have contact with the active ministry and be in the "real" world, that is, in the cities. Also, a growing number of students were coming to the theologate with advanced degrees in fields other than theology. Opportunities for such students to keep abreast of developments in their respective fields were more available in cities or in university towns.

Because theology was such a rapidly developing field, the faculty felt the need to stay in close touch with other theological centers. The younger faculty, especially, and those trained at non-Jesuit universities voiced their need to have easy access to their peers, not only those in other seminaries but also those in universities.

The new emphasis on ecumenism provided additional arguments for moving out of the all-Jesuit environment of the country. This consideration was voiced repeatedly in the ongoing discussion. For example, the Santa Clara Conference (1967), attended by all the provincials, included in its consensus positions the following: "Non-Catholic professors should regularly be invited to lecture or teach in fields of their special competence. Regular ecumenical contact between Jesuit students and non-Catholic students is to be considered normal. Theology should be studied in a university environment, where the goals can be better achieved" (S.C.C. 1967, 3:2:C27).[10]

A third reason advanced for relocation was ascetical. A religious order is marked by a particular *ascesis,* a systematic lifestyle designed to bring its members to Christian perfection. Since ascetical values touch the very heart of religious life, it is understandable that these values entered into the debate over where to locate houses of formation. The change in ascetical values accompanying the 1960s was a significant factor in the shift from country to city. Where the traditional interpretation

---

[10] A fuller account of academic changes and their rationale is provided in the following chapter.

of asceticism favored the country, the new interpretation favored the city.

Traditional asceticism sought deliverance from the world, the flesh, and one's self, a goal reflected in the great religious vows of poverty, chastity, and obedience. The seclusion of the country offered certain advantages in attaining this goal during the period of formation. It provided a degree of automatic physical separation from the allurements and distractions of the city, and it facilitated supervision and control by superiors. That superiors generally shared this ascetical view is clear from the lifestyle they prescribed for the theologates (see Chapter V, pp. 162–65).

In the post-Vatican II world, this view of religious life was labeled "monastic" and rejected as a deviation from true Jesuit spirituality. It will be recalled that the institutes held at the theologates constituted one of the earliest manifestations of the new era. With a sure instinct for getting to the core of the matter, the young men chose ascetical theology as the theme of their institutes. The charge of monasticism developed at the Alma ascetical institute was typical of the time, while the qualification voiced by Father Marien was a rare exception (p. 27, footnote 8). The argument was regularly made that Jesuits should spend their years of formation in the urban environment in which they would later live and work.[11]

Maturity, a value mentioned almost as often as relevance, provided another argument for leaving the rural environment. Modern psychology was emphasizing that maturation required not protection but exposure. At Alma's third ascetical institute, which dealt with Jesuit maturity, Daniel J. O'Hanlon argued for a move to a secular campus primarily for this reason, for exposure. While his argument was debated and distinguished, it seemed in general to be accepted (Ascetical Institute 1962, 67–72). An additional

---

[11] Traditional asceticism took the opposite view: to work efficiently in the world later, the young Jesuit needed the "desert experience" first. To work efficiently with sticky taffy, the cook needed first to cover his fingers with butter.

ascetical reason frequently mentioned for locating in the city was the opportunity of contacting the urban poor.[12]

As described later, the theologates changed their lifestyles very much during their last few years in the country. This change increased the likelihood of moving insofar as it qualified the pattern of values that had supported the choice of a country location in the first place. The changes in lifestyle also provide a measure of the importance of ascetical values: Woodstock would eventually lose out in the competition for continued existence chiefly because of its changed lifestyle.

At all times, whether the theologates were in the country or in the city, there were individuals who liked the existing situation and individuals who disliked it. The proportions varied over time, but the differences were always there. Among the students most satisfied with the countryside were those who combined scholastic ability with outdoor tastes. They appreciated the opportunity for undisturbed study in the field that was central to their lives. Indeed, they would have welcomed more time than was available, especially for reading in the fields of Scripture and history, where the regular courses were least adequate. They saw the all-Jesuit classes as a gain, enabling them to move faster and more surely toward their specific goals. For recreation, they were happy with athletic games and outings. Finally, if their ascetical values were in the traditional mold, they were all the more likely to be satisfied with the existing situation.

Among the students who found the country unsatisfactory were both activists and scholars. The activists wanted only enough theology to allow them to do pastoral work and found the four quiet years in the country both tedious and confining. Some scholars wanted wider contact with the non-Catholic theological

---

[12] At Woodstock College, it was argued in a community meeting that New York City should be preferred to New Haven (Yale) because in New Haven there were only ten thousand blacks, while in New York there were over a million. John Courtney Murray, who favored the option of moving to Yale University, expostulated, "How many blacks are needed to provide the Scholastics with a 'pastoral experience'?"

world, while those with advanced degrees in secular fields found it difficult to maintain an adequate relation with their specialty. If they were not the athletic-outdoors type, they missed the entertainments and cultural opportunities offered by the city. The all-Jesuit classes were seen as a loss, separating them from the "real" world. If their ascetical values were more new than old, they were the more likely to feel dissatisfied with the country.

At Alma College in 1964, the California provincial polled the scholastics on their preference: stay at Alma or move to Berkeley? Only about a dozen preferred to stay. At Weston, Massachusetts, according to the minister, about thirty-five or forty would have preferred to stay.

Among the faculty there were always those who settled down easily in the rural situation and concentrated for the most part on the quiet tasks of teaching and guiding their charges toward the goal of the priesthood. Among those with more scholarly ambitions, some found the rural situation at least not a major hindrance. At Woodstock, for example, professors such as John Courtney Murray, Gustave Weigel, Walter Burghardt, Avery Dulles, and others managed to exercise a national, even an international, influence. Most, however, especially the younger faculty and those whose degrees had been obtained outside the traditional centers, experienced a growing dissatisfaction with their separation from the non-Jesuit university world. Activists among the faculty sought wider activities than were available in the country—sometimes to an extent that brought reminders, by rector or provincial, that their main task was to teach and to be available to the scholastics. Finally, faculty members who were active in changing the content and form of seminary teaching (see Chapter IV) tended to be active also in working for a change of location, for the new academic values could be better attained in a university situation.

At Woodstock some of the community urged that options less drastic than relocation be explored—for example, further developing the already significant number of contacts outside the college. As early as 1961, for example, the Woodstock house history records for January and February lectures at the college by Robert McAfee

Brown of Union Theological Seminary, Father Gerard Sloyan of Catholic University, Philip Herrera, the President of the Inter-American Development Bank, and author and publisher Frank Sheed. During the same short period, the college hosted weekend visits by ten students from Yale University and by sixty students from St. Francis Xavier High School, in New York. At the same time, the college was exporting; in Baltimore John Courtney Murray was carrying on a weekly T.V. discussion with Sheed and Ward editor Philip Scharper, and the scholastics were presenting a play on television. During this period, also, members of the house published half a dozen articles. The rest of 1961 showed similar activities.

Also, beginning with the term of Rector Edward Sponga (1957–63), the scholastics were given increased freedom to leave the seminary for work in their respective specialized fields. Much the same situation obtained at the other theologates, and the same argument was used for exploring less drastic options before deciding that complete removal was the only possibility.

Probably a minority of the scholastics liked the existing situation very much, another minority disliked it very much, and the majority had no strong opinion about it. The existing situation had perdured for generations; presumably it would continue. The crucial change was a change in mood. As one scholastic described it in an interview, "All of a sudden, the possibility of doing something different presented itself as a concrete option. It was like starting a fire in a dry forest; the idea of moving spread with a rush and a roar." The Alma faculty member who had warned that just talking about a change in location was likely to be disturbing was a prophet. At West Baden in 1962, the idea of moving was distant and little discussed. By early 1964, superiors were saying the scholastics were so aroused that there could be no peace in the house until the theologate moved. The actual move of West Baden to North Aurora in that year tended to increase the pressure in the other theologates.

By 1968, at Weston College, President Robert White was saying that the school might not be able to open in the fall if it were still at Weston.[13] As J. A. Devenny, the dean of Weston, said in an interview, "The leaders of change were not certain that they were making the right changes but they were certain that they ought to experiment."

Father General Pedro Arrupe insisted as a condition for his approval of relocation that there be a consensus among the faculty. While never unanimous, a substantial majority in each theologate approved the respective moves. Reports to the General were at pains to point out that those who were carrying the bulk of the teaching burden were predominantly in favor of relocation. While the faculty supplied the initial impetus and worked out the practical plans for moving, it was the scholastics who provided the momentum and hurried the decision-making process along to its conclusion.

Vatican II and G.C. 31 were among the principal precipitators of the new mood. Both favored the association of houses of study with universities—the council more generally in *Optatam Totius,* its decree on priestly formation (Abbott 1966, 453), the congregation more explicitly: "Indeed, let there be concern, as far as it is possible, that our houses of study be built near university centers" (Dec. 9.32). Proposals to relocate at urban and university centers could thus claim the sanction of the highest authorities. The approval voiced by both council (Abbott 1966, 341–66) and congregation (Dec. 9.12) for ecumenical ventures was also appealed to as a reason for moving to a non-Jesuit university setting.

Shortly after the council and congregation, the Rockhurst Report (1965), authored by the deans and the leading faculty representatives of all the American and Canadian theologates, summed up the official theologate mind in the following resolution: "Adequate implementation of the proposed program, especially in its graduate phase, demands close contact with a full university complex to insure a proper range of offerings" (Inter-Faculty Program Inquiry 1966, 338). This resolution received almost unanimous approval; there were no negative votes and only three abstentions.

[13] Interview with John F. Broderick, May 3, 1975.

Site Selections

General Considerations

The theologates had two decisions to make: whether to move and where to move. Though the first decision was the more important, it actually received less study than did the choice of site, which generated a procession of committees and task forces, each of which produced stacks of reports.[14] The difference is understandable: the first decision turned mostly on general values, but the second required detailed investigation of numerous concrete situations.

The choice of site involved an early decision whether to move to the campus of a Jesuit university. All the theologates explored this possibility at least briefly; all except the Missouri theologate rejected it. Two reasons were advanced in favor of linking a theologate to a Jesuit university. It was argued, first, that the added faculty, library, and students would help strengthen a Jesuit institution. The theologates responded that this was not their primary objective or obligation; one theologate committee observed wryly that the university would like to have the faculty and library without the students. It was also argued that being a part of a Jesuit institution would facilitate Jesuit control of faculty and curriculum in what was, after all, a house of Jesuit formation. The General, Pedro Arrupe, repeatedly sought assurance on this latter point in connection with proposals to move to non-Catholic campuses. For example, in writing to the California provincial, John F. X. Connolly, on September 14, 1967, the General said, "I wish to inform YR [Your Reverence] that I have approved the

[14] The bulk of these are in the archives of the five provinces involved. Copies of some are in the Center's files. The theologate of the Upper Canada (the English-speaking) province experienced relocation problems paralleling those of the American provinces. After moving out of the city of Toronto to the suburbs (Willowdale) in 1961, it left Willowdale and returned to Toronto in 1975. (See the *National Jesuit News* [December 1976]:2.)

petition of the Alma Theologate to relocate in Berkeley under two conditions. First, provided our theologate would enjoy full autonomy in the education and formation of our theologians."[15]

Two chief reasons were also advanced for choosing an affiliation other than a Jesuit university. It was argued, first of all, that this option would provide greater resources of faculty and library with a wider variety of courses from which to choose. This would benefit both faculty and students. It would be a particular advantage for those doing research—in theology or in other fields. A second consideration was probably even more influential. The Church was seen as having inhabited a Catholic ghetto since Trent, and Vatican II was understood as a call to emerge into the full secular world. The same values that dictated a move into the city were operative in reaching the decision to move to a non-Jesuit, even a non-Catholic, site.[16] The dangers involved in leaving a controlled Jesuit environment were recognized but were deliberately accepted as the price of becoming part of the contemporary world. The various faculty memos written at the time are eloquent on this point. This reaching out to the world was understood not only, or even primarily, as a mission effort to influence that world; the arguments rather stressed the need to be influenced by that world.

[15] The second condition was "Provided Dr. Dillinberger of the GTU can secure Foundation assistance to help finance the transfer". Eventually the move was made even though the anticipated aid did not materialize. Most of the theologates had the experience of receiving more promises of assistance in moving than were eventually realized.

[16] A few years earlier (1966), the assistancy's social science center, then known as the Institute of Social Order, was moved from St. Louis to Boston—not to the campus of Boston College, which was anxious to have the center, but to a site in Cambridge adjoining Harvard University in order to have closer relations with the non-Jesuit world.

Particular Sites

The decision made by four of the theologates not to go to a Jesuit campus left them with many options. Each made its final choice in its own individual way, but all ended by joining, with varying degrees of closeness, a group of divinity schools comprising various denominations, with some connection to a secular university.

1. *Chicago Province.* The theologate of the Chicago province,[17] which moved twice, was the first and the last to move. It was the first to move from the countryside (1964) and the last to move to an urban campus (1970). (See Figure 1.) The first move, made under stringent economic pressure, was from West Baden, Indiana to North Aurora, Illinois, some forty miles west of Chicago. North Aurora was in commuting range of Chicago; the theologate there represented a kind of halfway house that was never thought of as permanent. Plans to locate on a university campus were under discussion at least as early as 1967, and a definite decision to move—somewhere—was made in 1968.

In a letter to the General dated October 31, 1969, the Chicago provincial, Robert F. Harvanek, said that the move out of North Aurora should be made as soon as possible. One reason was that it was an expensive place to maintain: the philosophers had already left it for a collegiate program at the University of Detroit (see below, p. 281), while the theologians were becoming fewer in number. A second reason was the "restlessness of the scholastics", a characteristic mentioned as a significant pressure in all the theologate moves. The first two years at North Aurora had been a kind of honeymoon for the scholastics, who were greatly pleased with the change. But the restlessness started up again in anticipation of the prospective move and as the word spread that all the other

---

[17] Like the others, this theologate went by several names. Its original legal title was West Baden University (incorporated in the state of Indiana). Its ecclesiastical title was College of St. Robert Bellarmine. It also went by the title of Bellarmine School of Theology of Loyola University. Finally, it was also called the Jesuit School of Theology in Chicago, Divinity School of Loyola University.

theologates were preparing to move to an urban university campus with ecumenical possibilities.

Task forces were established to select the next and permanent site. The first task force made its report to the Province Congress in 1968 and, while recognizing that the desired data were incomplete, recommended that the school, known as the Bellarmine School of Theology (B.S.T.), move to the vicinity of Loyola University so as to become an operative part of that university. It was recognized even at this early date that if the move were made to the South Side of Chicago, an alternative site, the theologate would not be an official part of the University of Chicago. In the end, none of the theologates actually became an official part of the non-Jesuit university into whose milieu the theologate moved.

A second task force reported in March 1969, after a great deal of additional work. The report listed eight general criteria according to which the site should be selected and then proceeded to apply these criteria to seventeen alternatives. The seventeen included such interesting opportunities as becoming part of the University of Notre Dame where President Theodore Hesburgh had extended an urgent invitation, or joining with the Chicago archdiocesan seminary (at Mundelein, Illinois) in a move to Loyola University. Cardinal Cody of Chicago looked favorably on this alternative, and there is the possibility that if it had been chosen, a Jesuit theologate would still be operating in the Chicago area.

Another alternative was to "become the divinity school of Loyola University", as the Missouri theologate had become the divinity school of St. Louis University. This alternative was rejected because it failed to meet four of the general criteria:

— B.S.T. would have difficulty in remaining an academic unit which maintains its own institutional identity and autonomy (criterion 5);
— B.S.T. would have difficulty in remaining strongly Jesuit-oriented as an institution which maintains its Jesuit character (criterion 6);
— B.S.T. would expand so rapidly that its Jesuit character

would be lost and quality education might be weakened (criterion 7); and

— B.S.T. would be so constituted that the versatility, flexibility, and openness to experimentation would be restricted by local and national agencies outside the Society (criterion 8).

The report also mentioned "the implications of the separate incorporation of our Jesuit communities and the possible increase in lay control of Catholic universities". Presumably, the "implications" were seen as diminishing the advantages of moving to a (currently) Jesuit campus.

The work of the task forces was summarized in a long report presented by Robert E. Murray, president of Bellarmine, to the province consultors at their meeting of July 1, 1969 (Murray 1969). Coming after Alma, Weston, and Woodstock had completed their deliberations and thus able to draw on their work, this Chicago report is probably the best single explanation of the choice made by four of the theologates—to move to a cluster of seminaries in the vicinity ("milieu") of a secular university.

The report develops eight reasons for the choice, namely, to move the Chicago province theologate to the Hyde Park area of Chicago in some association with the Lutheran Seminary resident there and somewhat adjacent to the University of Chicago. It also lists ten objections to the choice and provides replies to the objections. Relocation at Loyola University was the chief alternative to the recommended choice. This alternative, besides being explicitly addressed, clearly influenced the way the eight reasons were developed.

The first reason was the "need for interseminary cooperation". The American Association of Theology Schools had concluded that a modern seminary must have a faculty of at least ninety in order to provide an adequate theological education. Since no one seminary could supply such a faculty, it was necessary to join a "cluster". Reason No. 2 was "the milieu of the University of Chicago". The report made clear that it was not "speaking of any academic affiliation with the university as such" but of "the very

atmosphere which one breathes in the environs of the University
of Chicago". Reason No. 3 was the abundance of "supervised
pastoral training and pastoral opportunities".

The next two reasons reflect a new view of governance in the
Society. In the future it would be necessary to "attract" Jesuit
faculty and students. Bellarmine would be able to compete with
Alma, Weston, and Woodstock in attracting Jesuit faculty (Reason
No. 4) and students (Reason No. 5) only if it were in the area of
the University of Chicago. Reason No. 6 adverted explicitly to
Loyola University and argued that Loyola and the province would
ultimately be better served if Jesuits, on whom Loyola and the
province depended, were theologically trained in the superior
environment of the cluster.

The next two reasons are particularly revealing as reflecting the
new view of the Church in the world. Reason No. 7 dealt with
"continuing education" for the older men seeking to review and
update their theology. As compared with Loyola University, the
milieu of the University of Chicago would be better for these men
because "if these men were asked to retheologize just within the
ordinary context of a Jesuit community, they would take too
much for granted; they would never challenge what the best
theologians were challenging." That is, the modern task is not
only to learn what authority is teaching but also to learn how to
challenge as theologians are challenging.

Reason No. 8 extended this view to the whole enterprise; it
dealt with "theologizing in a context fully open to the contemporary world". The report argued, "We can no longer afford to
educate our future priests exclusively in a Roman-Catholic, Jesuit
surrounding. It can no longer be a question of educating Jesuits
apart from the world and then sending them into the world."
Otherwise, "the challenges and problems and frustrations and
temptations will prove too great if they have been overprotected
during their years of formation." To the objection that the perseverance record was better under the old system than under the
new, the reply was made that the total situation was changed and
old experience no longer provided guidance.

On the basis of this report, the Chicago province consultors voted five to one to move to the South Side of Chicago, a conclusion strongly supported by Provincial Robert F. Harvanek and by most of the faculty of theology. However, according to the Dean Michael Montague in his January 27, 1970, letter to the provincial, there were at least nine faculty members who "were willing but uneasy about the move to Hyde Park". He added, "I think they will all go, but they don't like it."[18]

In the October letter mentioned above, Harvanek explained to the General that this decision was made "with awareness that not all of our theologates might be able to continue, but that the next five years should clarify which should continue and which should not". When the General approved the decision, the provincials of the Chicago and Detroit provinces (Harvanek and Walter L. Farrell) announced it in a joint letter dated January 12, 1970. The actual move of the Bellarmine School of Theology to Hyde Park in Chicago was made in the summer of 1970, when it became a functioning member of the Chicago Cluster of Theological Schools.

2. *Missouri Province.* The theologate of the Missouri province was the second to move and the first to locate on a university campus. Like West Baden, St. Mary's had to choose either to invest heavily in repairs to its facility in rural Kansas or to move. The fact that West Baden had moved three years previously made it easier for St. Mary's to take similar action. In the fall of 1967, the theologate went back to the place from which it had started, St. Louis University in St. Louis, Missouri.

Earlier there had been considerable discussion, apparently initiated by St. Louis, of a "supertheologate". The proposal was to close Bellarmine at North Aurora and use the theologate at St. Louis to serve the entire central region, comprising five provinces (Chicago, Detroit, Missouri, Wisconsin, and New Orleans). St. Louis University was to become a prestigious theological center

---

[18] A minority report had argued at considerable length that the theologate should move, not to the University of Chicago but to Loyola University. A copy of this report is in the Center's files.

for research and for training Jesuits, other religious orders, and laypeople. There was some talk of St. Louis University raising a million dollars to float the enterprise. According to Robert Harvanek, the presidents of the colleges of the central region approved of the plan, perhaps expecting that this would release funds and faculty for their own institutions. The provincials of the central region disapproved, however, and they decided to maintain both theologates, at least for the time being.

When the Missouri theologate moved from St. Mary's to St. Louis, it became the divinity school of St. Louis University. Its objective gradually expanded from the formation of Jesuit priests to the "theological apostolate", that is, to the tasks of developing the science of theology in the university world and communicating that science to a wider audience. Here, as in the other theologates, some tension developed between the religious order and the university in achieving simultaneously the narrower and the wider goal.

3. *California Province.* Alma, the California theologate, also had a number of options. One was the University of San Francisco (U.S.F.), which made a strong bid to have the theologate relocate on its campus. The university saw the move as the first step toward establishing itself as a major Catholic presence on the West Coast. At a final meeting, a group consisting of representatives from U.S.F., Alma, other province ministries, and the provincial's staff expressed their preference between U.S.F. and "Berkeley". "Berkeley" signified a consortium of divinity schools in the area of Berkeley, California, known as G.T.U. (Graduate Theological Union) and loosely associated with the University of California. The vote was 26 to 7 in favor of Berkeley, a recommendation that the General accepted. The theologians left Alma on September 30, 1969, and began to occupy houses in Berkeley that same day.

4. *New England Province.* New England's Weston was not under as much external pressure as the other theologates. Its plant was not as old, and it was in suburban Boston rather than truly in the country. Nevertheless, it began to consider relocation at about the same time as the other theologates, and the faculty completed

several lengthy studies. By 1967 the New England provincial was formally asking permission from the General to move to Cambridge, Massachusetts, and establish closer relations with a cluster of divinity schools known as Boston Theological Institute (B.T.I.). A small experimental community was set up in Cambridge in 1967, permission for the school as a whole to move was granted in 1968, and the actual move occurred in 1969.

Though relocation to the campus of Boston College had been discussed, this option seems not to have been pursued very far. There was also some discussion of establishing a single theologate for the entire East Coast, but that proposal, too, died quickly. When, in 1967, Woodstock seemed to have accepted an invitation to move to Yale (New Haven, Connecticut; see below, p. 126), Weston expressed some concern, because New Haven was in the New England province. Representatives of Weston attended several meetings, including one in Rome, at which the prospective move of Woodstock into the New England province was considered. At one point, there was some talk of Weston joining Woodstock at Yale.

As in the other theologates, the faculty of Weston was divided on the choice of site. Most of the younger members, who were carrying the bulk of the teaching load, favored immediate relocation at Cambridge, but at least a half dozen of the faculty remained opposed. During the period of study and decision making, those opposed to the move were sometimes excluded from the discussion by the device of having a dinner outside the house where the leaders of the movement ("the cabal" as their opponents called them) could meet alone. The most active among the leaders seem to have been George W. MacRae and Robert P. White.

When in 1968 the General gave permission to move, he attached the condition that a review of the new situation be made in "three or four years" and a report be sent to Rome. When this review was made in 1971, under the chairmanship of Ladislas Orsy, it did not attempt to answer the question whether it would have been wiser to remain at Weston. The evaluation looked at the current situation and concluded that the new Weston theologate was in excellent condition and had great promise (Committee for Evaluation 1971).

Though there had been serious thought of selling Weston as early as 1966 (a prospective buyer had presented himself), the buildings and some of the surrounding property were in fact retained to be used for a retreat center and a Jesuit retirement home. Weston was the only theologate property that continued in Jesuit use.

5. *Maryland Province.* In Maryland, an early discussion of relocating Woodstock occurred in 1964, when a house consultors' meeting recognized that a great deal of expensive renovation would have to be undertaken or the theologate would have to move. This conclusion was reported at a province consultors' meeting held March 3, 1964. In a subsequent letter, Provincial John M. Daley described this news as a "bombshell" and appointed the Woodstock rector, Michael Maher, as chairman of a committee to examine the problem during 1964.[19] Because a move to Georgetown University was one of the options being considered, the committee included Brian A. McGrath, a dean of Georgetown. This committee never met.

Also in 1964, the Yale Divinity School, feeling the same ecumenical stirrings that were alive in all the seminaries, decided to invite some Catholic group to establish itself at Yale. After a year of investigation, Yale chose Woodstock College as the most promising candidate and in February 1966 extended a formal invitation to come to New Haven. The Woodstock faculty examined the invitation at great length and pronounced it very good. The Yale proposal included a housing provision and whatever degree of integration Woodstock desired with both the divinity school and Yale University. The faculty voted almost unanimously to accept the invitation. At a meeting in Plattsburgh, New York, in

---

[19] In 1964, an engineering firm was retained to estimate the relative costs of renovation and relocation. In early 1965, the firm reported that complete modernization would cost about $1.3 million, while relocation in Washington, D.C. would cost about $14 million (House Consultor's Diary, Woodstock College, February 14, 1965).

1967, the four provincials (Maryland, New York, Buffalo, New England) apparently approved the faculty's vote to accept the Yale invitation— though there is some indication that New England was not fully in accord with this view and felt apprehension over another Jesuit theologate locating in the New England province. In August 1967, the *New York Times* carried the story that Woodstock College had definitely decided to relocate at Yale.

Thereafter, the story is not clear but seems to have developed somewhat as follows. Christopher F. Mooney, head of the department of theology at Fordham University, had an ambitious vision of a theological enterprise to be called International Center for Religious Research. He wrote and perhaps journeyed to Rome to plead the greater values of New York over New Haven and the desirability of making Woodstock a key part of the proposed I.C.R.R. Fordham University was to be an essential part of this enterprise, and Woodstock was to have a close affiliation with Fordham. His cause seems to have been given some support by the General's assistant, Vincent T. O'Keefe, a former president of Fordham University. It is possible, also, that the apprehension felt by New England over a second theologate in the province was communicated to Rome. At any rate, word came back from Rome to delay making a final decision on the Yale invitation until the New York possibilities had been examined more thoroughly. On September 2, 1967, the *New York Times* carried another story, this one quoting Father O'Keefe to the effect that the unanimous vote of the Woodstock faculty in favor of Yale was not decisive and that a move to New York City was still possible.

On September 29, 1967, representatives from Columbia University, Fordham University, Union Theological, and the Morningside Heights Corporation visited Woodstock and made two presentations—one to the faculty and a few students in the afternoon and another to the entire community in the evening.

Some time in 1968, two representatives of the Woodstock faculty, Avery Dulles and Thomas E. Ambrogi, journeyed to New York to explore what advantages the cluster of divinity schools and Columbia University in Morningside Heights had to offer. The two were much impressed and so reported back to the faculty. Influenced by the presentation of the two scouts sent to explore the promised land, and probably also influenced by the negative reaction of Rome to the Yale offer,[20] the Woodstock faculty seems to have shifted in its attitude and to have chosen to move to New York—but to Morningside Heights, not to Fordham.[21]

Available records and memories of those most clearly associated with the move do not suffice to support a more assured statement of how the shift occurred. The withdrawal of the decision to go to Yale in favor of moving to New York City remains a somewhat obscure event awaiting the work of later historians. Among the factors to be considered are the respective roles of the New York and Maryland provincials. Since the Maryland provincial was at this time preparing to leave the Society, he may have left the field more open to the influence of the New York provincial than would otherwise have been the case.

At every stage, there were differing viewpoints among the faculty—both as to whether to move at all and, when that was decided, where to move. In the light of Woodstock's eventual fate, the selection of site may have been the crucial decision. Had Woodstock elected to stay with its original choice of Yale, it might still be in existence today.

A small experimental group moved from Maryland to New York in early 1969, and the rest followed later that year. Woodstock established close relationships with a number of divinity schools in the area, especially Union Theological Seminary. However, some of the promise of the move to New York City was blunted by the unusual events of the late 1960s. The student revolt at Columbia University brought a change in the university's top administrators, some of whom had been the most interested in

[20] See the later letter of the Woodstock administrator to the General, quoted on pp. 133–34.

[21] In an earlier faculty memorandum defending the choice of Yale over Fordham, Woodstock had articulated the argument, later used also by Chicago, that Jesuit institutions would ultimately be better off if the young Jesuits were trained elsewhere, thus avoiding inbreeding.

bringing Woodstock to New York. Also, student activism in the other divinity schools eclipsed for the time being interest in new academic plans. On the whole, Morningside Heights around 1970 was a most difficult environment in which to build a new academic and religious structure.

Consolidation

The consolidation of the theologates took place in two stages—as they were reduced from five to three and then to two. The story of the first stage begins and ends with Woodstock College.

In 1970, soon after establishing itself in New York City, Woodstock College set up a planning group of seventeen persons to determine how to take full advantage of its new opportunities.[22] Between May 15 and July 3, 1970, this group met during four weekends at Shrub Oak. In the course of its work, the group found itself making increasing use of the distinction between a seminary devoted primarily to teaching candidates for the priesthood and a theological center engaged in research, perhaps graduate teaching, and certainly ecumenical activities on a large scale. The function of the first was described as "theological formation" while that of the second was said to be "the theological apostolate".

The planning group recommended that Woodstock choose the second as its primary function. Among the theologates, Woodstock was seen as best situated to develop such a theological apostolate, and since the other four schools would suffice to handle the dwindling number of scholastics in the assistancy, Woodstock could safely divest itself of the burden of teaching seminarians in

[22] The planning group consisted of the two provincials (Maryland and New York), the president, dean, and rector of Woodstock College, two trustees of the college, two faculty members, two students, the vicar-general of the New York Archdiocese, two members of the consulting firm of Arthur D. Little, Inc., and three other lay persons. This planning group set up no fewer than fourteen separate task forces to study the available options.

order to become a center for high-level theologizing. This recommendation accorded with the vision of Woodstock's president, Christopher Mooney, who earlier had proposed an ambitious theological enterprise for New York City (p. 127).

Though some of the Woodstock faculty were not pleased with the recommendation, the provincials of Maryland and New York thought it deserved serious consideration. It was the kind of theologizing ministry the General had praised in speaking to the 1970 Congregation of Procurators. They were reluctant, however, to make a decision — either for or against the proposal — without consulting the rest of the assistancy. Such a change in Woodstock would have implications for the other four theologates and therefore for all ten provinces. Moreover, a trend had begun toward more assistancy-wide collaboration. An assistancy study of the theologate issue could be a part of that larger movement.

At the next meeting of the provincials, in October 1971, the New York and Maryland provincials proposed that the newly structured Jesuit Conference undertake to study the whole "theologate question".[23] The proposal was approved for a number of reasons: (1) under the existing arrangement, five provinces bore a disproportionate part of the burden of providing theological formation, and some adjustment was desirable; (2) the decline in the numbers of Jesuits, both faculty and students, indicated a need for some consolidation, that is, the elimination of one or more of the theologates; and (3) the attractive but difficult distinction between theological formation and the still nebulous notion of theological apostolate needed thorough analysis. As a start on the proposed study, the provincials appointed Walter L. Farrell to be secretary of formation in the Jesuit Conference, with instructions to prepare the materials the provincials would need for their decision.[24]

[23] At this time, 1971, the Jesuit Conference board consisted of the ten provincials and an executive secretary, John V. O'Connor, S.J.

[24] Father Farrell visited the five theologates and prepared a detailed report on each. These five documents are a valuable account of how each institution was operating at the beginning of the evaluation.

The study of the "theologate question" continued through the rest of 1971 and into June of 1972.[25] The work involved many meetings and produced many reports. At their meeting in St. Louis (December 1971), the provincials produced the "Fordyce Statement", named for the house in which they met. This statement described the kind of formation desired and by which they proposed to evaluate the theologates. At this meeting they also agreed to visit personally each of the theologates. All the provincials did so, in two teams of five, during the spring of 1972. Each provincial prepared a report on each theologate and circulated his report to the other provincials.

In June 1972, the provincials met for a week at the Jesuit retreat house in Round Hill, Massachusetts, and, using the formal Ignatian discernment process,[26] arrived at three decisions: (1) to reduce the theologates to three in number; (2) to provide assistancy sponsorship of the three theologates chosen; and (3) to choose as the three surviving theologates Berkeley, Bellarmine, and Woodstock. At this meeting only six of the ten provincials, a bare majority, were in favor of maintaining Woodstock. Shortly after returning home from the meeting, one changed his mind, leaving Woodstock with only five provincials favoring its survival. The three decisions were submitted to the General for his acceptance, rejection, or modification. To allow the General full freedom of action, the provincials refrained from giving any publicity to their recommendations.

In July 1972, the General responded, praising the discernment process followed by the provincials. He did not accept the third decision as final but asked for more information about Woodstock, especially whether it could improve its community life situation.

---

[25] A five-page summary of the steps taken by the provincials between early 1970 and the end of 1972 was prepared by James L. Connor, provincial of the Maryland province, and presented to the Woodstock faculty on January 8, 1973. It is one of the more valuable sources for this period. Another fairly full summary may be found in the April 1973 issue of *SJNEws,* pages 10 and 11.

[26] In this process, they made use of the services of a facilitator, Father Jules Toner, who was a former master of novices and the author of a monograph explaining the process (Toner 1974).

The next two months (August and September 1972) were a period of further reflection on the June decision. The provincials met in Chicago in August and expressed some uneasiness with their earlier deliberations. They agreed that the presidents, rectors, and deans of the theologates and the directors of formation should be invited to express their opinions on the previous decisions. Accordingly, the formation and theologate people met several times in various groupings during the period of August to October. They recommended that the names of the three theologates selected in June continue to be withheld from publication. This suggestion came from Weston and St. Louis, the two theologates designated for elimination. At the August meeting, Woodstock voted against this motion of "secrecy". The group as a whole, however, recognized that to divulge the names of the three at this point would be to make it a self-fulfilling prophecy. Those institutions designated for elimination would find it almost impossible to continue their normal functioning, especially their relationships with other groups.

In September 1972, the St. Louis and Weston theologates wrote to the General presenting reasons why they should be continued as Jesuit seminaries. In September, also, the administrators of Woodstock met several times with the provincials and formation directors of the Maryland and New York provinces and prepared a letter to the General explaining that any inadequacies which might have been noted in the Woodstock lifestyle could and would be corrected. During this same month, there was a substantial amount of feedback to the provincials from all those connected with the theologates. The directors of formation in the ten provinces were especially active in making their views known to the respective provincials. Many of their comments were unfavorable to Woodstock.

In October 1972, the provincials met in Rome to review their June decision in the light of new insights and materials and to work with the staff of the Jesuit Curia. The most important action taken was deciding to give priority to the formation dimension of the theologate question. Thus, if Theologate A were judged better for formation and Theologate B were judged better for the theological apostolate, A would likely be chosen over B. It was understood that degrees of difference between the theologates would be important, but a degree of advantage in formation would weigh more than the same degree of advantage in the theological apostolate. In other words, the provincials were primarily concerned with the task of forming their men for the priesthood. In another, less disturbed period, they might have had the energy, time, and resources to concern themselves also with the more complex and still nebulous vision of a great, central powerhouse for theologizing.

The discernment process in Rome resulted in the reaffirmation of two of the June conclusions: the five theologates should be reduced to three, and these three should be an assistancy responsibility. There was a change, however, in the selection of which three were to survive. After spelling out for themselves what they meant by a "good formation program", the provincials constructed a detailed grid of criteria and used this to evaluate each theologate.[27] Their final selection included Berkeley (ten provincials), Weston (nine provincials) and Bellarmine (eight provincials). Woodstock was preferred by only two of the provincials.

During November 1972 officials of Woodstock met with the General and also addressed several letters to him. One of these, dated November 9 and signed by the rector, president, dean, and chairman of the board of trustees,[28] referred to the events of 1967, when the Woodstock faculty had voted to accept Yale's invitation:

> Woodstock could have gone to New Haven and set itself up within the shadow of Yale University. Yet you yourself, Father General, called on Woodstock to consider and eventually face the possibilities and challenges of New York City. Instead of the quieter realms of a university enclave, Woodstock was asked to place itself boldly within an urban situation. It was asked not to

[27] In retrospect, the Maryland provincial, James L. Connor, judged that once the provincials had accepted this somewhat mechanical measure, the fate of Woodstock was sealed.

[28] Respectively, William J. Byron, Christopher F. Mooney, Bartholomew J. Collopy, and Donald R. Campion.

bolster and cushion itself with cluster arrangements or link itself to lesser schools, but simply to take on the challenge of Union and Columbia. In these last few years of move and transition no other theologate has been asked to do this. The question now is whether Woodstock, having accepted this mandate, is to be closed after two brief years here, and closed because of priorities which bypass the original mandate it received from the Society.

In December, Robert Mitchell, the New York provincial, and Walter Farrell, president and executive secretary of the Jesuit Conference, spent five days in Rome with the General reviewing the entire process by which the theologate question had been handled. On December 23, the General announced his acceptance of the provincials' decision to maintain Berkeley, Bellarmine, and Weston, all to be under assistancy sponsorship. The public announcement was made the following month, January 1973.

The most surprising aspect of the process was, of course, the elimination of Woodstock, the oldest and most prestigious of Jesuit theologates. There is general agreement among those closely involved in the decision-making process that the reason for the elimination of Woodstock was its more open lifestyle.[29] The directors of formation were especially concerned with the Woodstock lifestyle, and some said they would advise their provincials not to send scholastics to that theologate even if it were chosen to survive. In the previous year, five of the New York scholastics had requested that they be sent not to their own theologate, Woodstock, but to Willowdale, the theologate of the English-speaking Canadian province, giving as their reason their apprehension about

---

[29] Indeed, the General said explicitly, "for it was on formation that Woodstock was not chosen as a theologate" (letter of Pedro Arrupe to James L. Connor, S.J., March 3, 1973). In a previous letter to John V. O'Connor, executive secretary of the Jesuit Conference, of July 27, 1972, the General had said, "Definite attention should be given to finding more effective means to develop Jesuit community at Woodstock." Both letters may be found in *SJNEws* (April 1973): 10, 11.

Woodstock's lifestyle. Also in 1971, several Maryland province scholastics asked to go to Weston rather than to Woodstock, giving the same reason. The provincials themselves, of course, all spent some time living at Woodstock and had the opportunity to form their own impressions. Their written reports contain such comments as the following: "The concern for formation is merely nominal for some of the faculty" and "A general impression: would it not be hard [in the Woodstock environment] for some to survive religiously?"[30]

The General, Pedro Arrupe, was genuinely interested in the advancement of the theological apostolate, preferably through the establishment of a high-level, influential center of theological reflection. In his letter of December 23, 1972, to the American provincials, he wrote, "This is a work that is close to my heart and central to the work of the Church. It should involve the three theologates, our university departments of theology, and other theological endeavors. It may even call for some further development in the form of a theological center." In his meeting with the Woodstock representatives in Rome in March 1973, he reiterated his interest and encouraged the American provincials, especially the two immediately connected with Woodstock, to begin such a center. Ironically, he was in effect approving the recommendation of Woodstock's own 1970 planning group with which this whole inquiry into the theologate question had begun.

At its first meeting (January 23–25, 1973) the Jesuit Conference Committee on Theologates addressed the question of a theological center. Recognizing the "urgency in this matter while Woodstock is still in place on Morningside Heights", the committee resolved unanimously to recommend to the provincials that they decide on the possibility and location of such a center "in the near future".

The majority of the provincials proved unwilling to embark on

[30] From the Summary of the comments the provincials prepared for one another following the March 1–3 and April 10–12, 1972 visits to Woodstock.

an assistancy-sponsored theological center.[31] Had the proposal been made ten years earlier, it might have met with a better reception. But it came at the worst possible time: when departures of priests from the order—including the rector and several faculty members of Woodstock College—had reached unprecedented heights; when the number of scholastics was shrinking rapidly, with no end to the decline in sight; when the inflow of novices had slowed to a trickle; and when the time and energies of the provincials were strained to their utmost by all the other changes described in this history. They were reluctant to embark on one more enterprise that was shadowy in form, uncertain of success, but certain to entail a considerable investment of dwindling resources.

Thereupon, the two provinces of Maryland and New York proceeded to act on their own, albeit on a smaller scale than had been envisioned in 1970. The most pressing problem was the housing of the very valuable Woodstock library. Fordham University in New York and Catholic University in Washington, D.C., made bids for it but were unable to provide adequate space and funds. Other universities, some non-Jesuit,[32] also entered bids. The offer of Georgetown University was judged the best and was gratefully accepted by the harried provincials.

The Woodstock Theological Center followed the library, rather than the other way around. The center began gradually on a small scale, with only two of the original Woodstock faculty on its staff. These were Walter Burghardt and Avery Dulles, who were by that time on the faculty of Catholic University and hence already in the city. Their connection with the center, never full time, was later reduced to research associates as the center acquired full-time

[31] It may be noted that in 1973 the assistancy responded to the General's invitation by establishing the Jesuit Council for Theological Reflection (J.C.T.R.). This was simply a board that met once a year to disburse research funds to individual scholars who had submitted proposals. For various reasons, the J.C.T.R. was discontinued in February 1979.

[32] Yale offered space for the library and also for a theological center to be staffed by some (six to eight) of the then Woodstock faculty.

members. Thus the final contribution of the original Woodstock consisted only of its name and its library. The further story of the Woodstock Center falls outside the limits of the present history.

When the three theologates were approved for continuance (December 1972) it was with the condition that they be reevaluated after five years. Planning for evaluation began in the fall of 1977. An evaluation committee of four Jesuits and one nun was set up to prepare the materials the provincials would need for their evaluation and decision.

The evaluation process involved three steps: (1) a self-evaluation by each of the theologates based on a statement it prepared of its "mission and goals"; (2) a visit to each theologate by the evaluation team; (3) a visit to each theologate by each provincial. The amount of work that went into the evaluation process, described in detail in successive issues of the *National Jesuit News,* was impressive.[33]

In June 1979, the provincials assembled to sum up their individual evaluations and make their joint decision. There were two Roman participants at this meeting, the North American assistant, Gerald Sheahan, and the Society's general assistant for formation, Cecil McGarry. The provincials decided that all three of the theologates should continue to function for the time being but gave a number of directives for a more effective operation and warned that eventually one or more of the three might have to be closed.

A year later (June 1980) the provincials assembled at Spokane, with the General in attendance. At the end of their meeting, they announced that the Jesuit School of Theology at Chicago (J.S.T.C., formerly B.S.T.) would be discontinued. Three chief reasons were given for this decision. First, despite the Jesuit Conference subsidy and its own fund-raising efforts, J.S.T.C. had continued to experi-

[33] A detailed account of the planning and decision process is carried in the following issues of the *National Jesuit News:* October and November 1978; March and June 1979; June 1980. For almost twenty years the provincials were involved in one major study project after another. This is one reason that provincial staffs grew in size.

ence severe financial difficulties, which seemed likely to persist and increase. Second, the school had experienced serious problems in recruiting key staff in its ministry programs and in some other areas considered to be among J.S.T.C.'s strongest and most distinctive. Finally, there was a notable and continuing drop in enrollment, especially among Jesuit students. Of the twenty-five persons enrolled for the fall 1981 term, only two were Jesuits. There were only about thirty Jesuits coming into theology in the whole assistancy, hardly enough to require three theologates.

After 1980, the story of Jesuit theological formation is limited to the two coasts: the Weston School of Theology in Massachusetts and the Jesuit School of Theology at Berkeley in California. Both schools had begun to stress the function of theological apostolate in addition to the traditional function of formation. To reflect the new orientation, they had been using the title of theological center or school of theology in preference to the old title of theologate. Though the provincials appreciated the values inherent in this wider function, they insisted that the formation of Jesuits be retained as the chief function, or at least that the traditional Jesuit formation not be imperiled by an enterprise that included a majority of non-Jesuits. As time went on, the two schools developed somewhat different characteristics, while the board of provincials developed tighter controls over both of them. The story of these later developments falls outside our scope, but its main outline is provided by the sources listed in footnote 33.

IV

THE THEOLOGATES: ACADEMIC

Introduction

In addition to changing their locations, the theologates made substantial changes in their academic character. In general, these changes worked to diminish the differences between the Jesuit and the American systems of education and thus to integrate the Jesuit system with the culture in which it was to function. This general trend had begun long before, proceeding by gradual steps. In the 1920s, for example, the Jesuit course of studies in most of the provinces, while remaining substantively unchanged, began to be assigned course titles and credit points.[1] Or again, by the 1960s many men were working on advanced degrees in secular fields and while in the theologate were progressively allowed more latitude in keeping up with their specialties.[2] In 1966, the American provincials reported to Rome that scholasticate faculties had been discussing course reform "intensively" since at least 1962. Also, in the early 1960s, before Rockhurst, some of the theologates

---

[1] Thus, when I came to apply for admission to graduate economics at Columbia University in the 1940s, I was able to present a long transcript of credits covering thirteen years that had earned me four degrees. They were nominally earned at St. Louis University, though I had attended only a half dozen courses on the campus of that university.

[2] In January 1961, the dean of Alma was reporting to the California provincial regarding the practice at other theologates of allowing the students to leave the theologate during the summer to study elsewhere. The percentage of students having such permission in 1960 were as follows: St. Mary's 73%; West Baden, 38%; Woodstock, 17%.

had established academic councils on which, for the first time, students were represented.

But the great change came with the Rockhurst Report in 1965; this was the watershed marking the academic transformation of the theologate (see above, pp. 55–59). The near unanimity of the authors of the report, who included the deans of all the theologates, the generally solid support of the provincials, and the encouraging attitude of the Roman authorities toward "experimentation", all meant that the report's resolutions would not go unheeded. Though the exact nature of the changes and their timing varied among the theologates, all five schools embarked on a major transformation shortly after the report was published. They changed faculty, students, curriculum, and degrees. They changed their method of teaching and to some extent the content of what was being taught.

To grasp the significance of the changes it is necessary to see them against the background of the situation they replaced. For one who was educated in the traditional system, the comparison is automatic; others, however, may find a brief description of the replaced system helpful.

In the traditional system, almost the entire academic effort was directed to imparting book knowledge. Some, but relatively little, time was allotted to the pastoral side of the priesthood, to field work. The young men who were beginning the study of theology had just completed three years of teaching, mostly in high schools, and were presumed to have learned the basics of dealing with people. The theologate did, however, train the seminarians in offering the Holy Sacrifice, in administering the sacraments (especially in hearing confessions), and in preaching. Further pastoral training, especially in directing retreats, was provided later during the year-long tertianship program.

The academic purpose of the theologate was to communicate as much of the vast field of theology and associated disciplines as could be learned in four years of undistracted study. The body of knowledge to be communicated was in the form of propositions (not questions, but answers) whose truth was agreed upon beforehand and sanctioned by authority. The students were expected to understand the answers and to integrate them into their lives—a goal achieved in varying degrees, of course, by students of varying abilities. Whatever the degree of understanding, or lack of it, the answers had to be known well enough to be given back in written and oral examinations. The course was designed to make of the priest a reliable pipeline through which truth, admittedly at different levels of confidence, could flow effectively from the highest authorities to the people in the pews. Priests generally spoke with one voice. This uniformity applied to doctrinal, liturgical, moral, and pastoral theology.

Theology served as a kind of final cause for the whole course of Jesuit studies. Taking up a position within theology, superiors arranged the preceding ten years of formation with a view to preparing the young Jesuit to do theology successfully. Though each step in the total program had its own goal and justification, each was also governed by its expected contribution to the study of theology. It was chiefly theology that bound the long course of studies into a unity, and provincials felt that one of their most important tasks was to staff the theologates properly.[3]

In the traditional theologate, well over half of the academic effort was directed to dogma—the Church's teaching on revelation, on herself, and on God in himself and in his relation to creation, sin, and redemption. Dogma was taught in the form of tracts, consisting of a series of propositions stated in thesis form. The same tracts were studied by everybody, and attendance at all classes was obligatory. The tracts supplied the matter for examinations, which were both written and oral. Since the latter were conducted by a panel of the faculty, the extent to which "house doctrine" was taught in the privacy of a classroom became part of the public forum. The tracts, the examinations, and in some cases

[3] Reflecting this dominant position of the theologate was the custom at Woodstock whereby the faculty met at the end of the year and made recommendations to the provincial on the best disposition of the men leaving the house.

the mandated textbooks provided effective controls for use by authorities.

The degree of this control should not be exaggerated. It was far from complete. From my own experience, I can recall one course on revelation (*De Revelatione*) where, without any change in course description or in textbook, a change of professors changed the course substantially. I recall another course in which the professor announced the official, Rome-designated textbook on the first day of class and never referred to it again. In still another course, where the professor disliked the assigned textbook, he would spend thirty-five minutes of each class explaining the "adversary" doctrine and then spend the remaining fifteen minutes "refuting" the adversary and thus providing the students with their only exposition of the house doctrine. Nevertheless, there was, on the whole, significantly more uniformity and control in the traditional system than in the system inaugurated by the Rockhurst Report.

The traditional theologate of the United States Assistancy was a completely Jesuit enterprise; its essential goal was not a degree but ordination. All the professors and all the students were Jesuits. The school was entirely under the control of religious superiors, followed norms established in canon law, and awarded degrees that were ecclesiastical—for example, the licentiate degree. There was no provision for organized student participation in academic decisions. Students found awaiting them a complete program of courses, class times, study times. The school and the religious community were closely entwined, with everyone—students, teachers, administrators—living and working on the same campus. The language used, both in the classroom and for textbooks, was Latin. That in brief outline was the traditional theologate. The new theologate differed in almost every respect.

Changes in Structure

The theologates differed from one another in many ways, and within each theologate further changes continued to be made, especially during the first decade following Rockhurst. It would not be practical to attempt a catalogue of all the changes that occurred. Even if the task were practicable, it would be tedious and not particularly useful for our purpose. It will be more useful to identify the basic trend of the changes, with some particular attention paid to the two theologates which eventually survived — the Weston School of Theology on the East Coast and the Jesuit School of Theology at Berkeley on the West Coast.

General Developments

Following the recommendations of the Rockhurst Report, the theologates generally divided the study of theology into four areas — biblical, historical, systematic (dogma), and moral/pastoral — and allotted roughly the same amount of time to each area. Systematic theology thus lost the dominance it had enjoyed formerly when it occupied the larger part of the total course and its cycle established the pattern of classes to which the other areas had to adjust. At West Baden, for example, the students formerly had been instructed, when they started theology, that twenty-five hours of private study were expected of them each week, of which fifteen were to be devoted to dogma, leaving ten hours to be divided among all the other subjects.[4]

The biblical and historical areas were the chief gainers.[5] Underlying this shift in emphasis was a changed perception of the theological task. The planners of the new structure wanted the study of Scripture to precede, or at least to accompany, the study

---

[4] Minutes of annual meeting of theologate deans, 1962.
[5] Biblical studies had begun a renaissance in the theologates during the previous decade. Rockhurst amplified and solidified this trend.

of dogma so that from the very beginning theology would have a predominantly biblical rather than philosophical orientation. They also wanted the student to have the opportunity to participate actively in the exegetical process of deriving doctrine from text, rather than simply accumulating texts—the so-called manual method—to fit a preformed doctrine stated in a thesis.

Underlying the increased time allotted to the historical area was an understanding of theology as a developing (and therefore changing) reality to be individually appropriated, rather than as a completed reality always the same and the same for all. The historical emphasis was not understood primarily as the study of "Church history", that is, of events in the life of the Church. It was characterized, rather, by an insistence that doctrine be studied in its historical context and by an acceptance of the consequence that as context changed, doctrine changed—at least in formulation and possibly as a genuine development of doctrine (see pp. 20–21; 57). While the degree of acceptable change was not specified, the favored option was clearly for freedom to adapt— for "creative ideas" rather than for the "judgmental decision of the Church" (see p. 58).

Pastoral and moral theology also gained space in the new structure, with the increase in pastoral theology especially marked. At Berkeley, for example, the units required in field education increased from zero in 1964 to six in 1970 to sixteen by 1974. At Weston, the 1974 catalogue included the following requirement: "Every student's program should include at least one full year of supervised field education." Underlying this development, two perceptions seemed to be at work. The description in Vatican II of the official Church as servant easily led to the conclusion that the seminarian would better absorb the theology he was studying if simultaneously he had the direct experience of using that knowledge to help others. There was also an epistemological perception at work, namely, that real knowledge cannot be completely abstract but must have a substantial experiential content. The Jesuit theologian Karl Rahner was frequently quoted in support of this approach.

Class hours were cut greatly. For example, whereas 130 hours had been devoted to the treatise on the Incarnation at West Baden, after the move to North Aurora fewer than fifty hours were devoted to this subject. The pattern of class attendance also underwent adjustment as the overall academic structure was modified. Traditionally, in the all-Jesuit milieu, with community life inextricably entwined with academic life, attendance had been required at all classes, as at any other community exercise, and in principle any absence was to be reported by the class beadle (a kind of class secretary who served as intermediary between the professor and the class). In practice, there was always some degree of freedom, and on occasion the degree could be considerable, as I recall from an experience in my own fourth year of theology (1940) at St. Mary's, Kansas. At that time, though the doctrine of the "Mystical Body of Christ" was much in the current literature, we had never touched on it in any of our classes. Since I was then in my last year of theology, I concluded that if I was to learn anything about the matter, I would have to study it privately. I thereupon absented myself from all classes and read Mystical Body for ten hours a day for three weeks—beginning with the Fathers of the Church and working up to modern journals. Then I went to the dean, Aloysius Kemper, and reported what I had done. Though uneasy—indeed shocked—over such an exhibition of independence, he issued no punishment or even reprimand. He granted that at age thirty-two and with twenty-six years of experience in the classroom, on one side of the desk or the other, I was probably competent to make such a choice and that in fact my choice had probably been wise—that is, I had learned more in my private study than if I had attended class.

As I recall, there was always some student pressure to reduce the number of classes. Over the years, this pressure gradually increased, especially when students began arriving at the theologate with advanced degrees earned at major universities and hence with experience in the reduced-class pattern of graduate work. In the late 1960s, this pressure, like all other movements for enlarged individual freedom, took on sudden, explosive force. In two of the theologates a small group of students presented formal demands to the dean and at least among themselves spoke of a "strike" against class requirements. According to John L'Heureux, a scholastic at Woodstock, classes were officially made optional beginning in September 1964 (L'Heureux 1967, 115). This would have been the decision of Terrence Toland, the Woodstock dean. Weston officially adopted a policy of optional classes the following year. Many of the younger faculty were also in favor of loosening the requirements for class attendance.

After the Rockhurst Report, especially, many changes were made in this area. As usual, there were differences among the theologates. For example, at the 1967 meeting of the theologate deans, Bellarmine (Chicago) reported that only students beyond first year and only those who had an 8.5 average grade could elect not to attend class—and then only if the professor agreed. At Weston, on the other hand, all students were free to absent themselves from any class, whether or not the professor approved.

Some courses, even though still required, became notable for the empty seats in the classroom. The professors of these courses reacted variously. Some changed their presentation to suit the new student tastes. Some continued unchanged, and there were occasionally disputes over low grades or failures assigned to nonattending students. Some professors requested and received a change in assignment. The more "progressive" among the faculty were not unhappy to see this pressure put on their colleagues, and superiors also generally seemed to accept it as inevitable.

The academic revision of the theologate had to recognize and harmonize two distinctions. The first was the distinction between a seminary and other educational institutions. While attempting to integrate the Jesuit theologate more closely with the general American educational system, the revisionists had to keep in mind that a theologate is a seminary and a seminary has a character all its own. As one proponent of this view expressed it, "Spiritual formation is a heroic enterprise, so precious that many other lesser goals must be forsworn in order to achieve it. Spiritual formation is . . . an esoteric type of life which demands a controlled environment" (Wagoner 1966, 94). This viewpoint also appeared in an intervention by Lawrence Cardinal Sheehan (Baltimore) when Vatican II was preparing its Decree on Priestly Formation. After recalling that the priest is a mediator, he went on to say, "This mediation has a twofold direction: toward God and toward men. In my opinion, the Godward movement is too sparsely treated in the schema, which results in its being excessively anthropocentric" (Yzermans 1967, 479). The schema was later modified.[6]

A cognate form of this same tension appeared in the personal attitudes of individual scholastics toward the work of the school and is described by a theologate dean in a letter of January 1957:

> I note a mounting use among the theologians of the phrase 'I simply want to be a good priest.' This carries the implication that for this all that is needed is a catechetical minimum of doctrine and a collection of pastoral techniques. It amounts to resistance to anything that is seriously academic. I know from other Jesuit theologates that this attitude is not peculiar to [us]."

The other distinction was between undergraduate and graduate work. At what level did a theologate function? This question caused some confusion for a time. The typical first-year Jesuit theologian was close to thirty years of age, with at least seventeen years of schooling; on the other hand, he was just starting his formal study of the field. The eventual solution was to consider the first two years of work to be undergraduate and the last two to be graduate.

For a few years after Rockhurst there was considerable controversy in some theologates over the requirement that everyone take the comprehensive examinations.

Gradually this issue disappeared as the schools (Weston and Berkeley) continued to insist on the comprehensives as a condition

---

[6] Vatican II changed the previous system, in which during four years a seminarian worked for the baccalaureate and licentiate together. In the new arrangement, the first three years were devoted to the attainment of the baccalaureate. Two additional years were then used for attaining the licentiate by those destined for work in theology. Those destined for pastoral work took only one additional year, during which pastoral theology received the emphasis.

for obtaining the basic master of divinity (M.Div.) degree and as the Society made its mind clear that competence in theology would continue to be an ordinary condition for ordination.[7]

For almost a decade following Rockhurst there was some confusion about how long the theological course should be. Whereas formerly the degrees granted were ecclesiastical, with requirements set by Rome, the degrees were now civil, with requirements set by the American Association of Theology Schools (A.A.T.S.). There was some uncertainty how the two systems were to be related. The Roman system specified years of theology, but in the new system of credit hours, what was a "year"? Also, there was a new flexibility in defining what could be counted as "theology".[8] For both reasons, there arose the possibility of achieving the basic degree—called originally bachelor of divinity, and later master of divinity—in less than the traditional four years.

The possibility was welcomed. Since G.C. 31 there had been an effort to shorten the traditional course and leave more time for acquiring the newly important secular degrees. The Santa Clara Conference generated a number of proposals aimed at shortening the total course (S.C.C. 1967, 2:1:232ff.). A program of pretheologate theology was proposed in the Rockhurst Report and most fully developed by the Chicago province under the title of the "Bellarmine Plan". It aimed at granting enough theology credits in the novitiate and subsequent years to enable the average scholastic to arrive at the theologate with the equivalent of a full year of theology already completed. Rockhurst led to proposals by some scholastics for a personal shortening of the course. For example, at Woodstock three scholastics were able to accumulate all the needed credits in two years and asked for early comprehensive examina-

---

[7] The requirements for the profession (i.e., the religious profession of those Jesuits who followed the honors course successfully) formerly met by the *ad gradum* examination, were met in the case of most students by a combination of the comprehensive examination and whatever examination was given at the end of the fourth year of theology.

[8] See, for example, Resolution 21 of the Rockhurst Report (Inter-Faculty Program Inquiry 1966, 341).

tions and ordination. At Berkeley, one scholastic was able to present a feasible plan whereby he could gain all the requisite credits and be ordained in a year and a half; he wanted to get on to his doctoral work in psychology.[9]

The situation was complicated by the Jesuit privilege of being ordained after only three years of theology, instead of after the four years specified in canon law. Traditionally, this caused no problem because everyone continued at the seminary for a fourth year. In the new situation, with the basic theological degree and ordination both attainable at the end of three years, the fourth year began to splinter badly. In some theologates during the decade following Rockhurst, the majority of the newly ordained left the seminary at the end of their third year—to study theology elsewhere, even at non-Catholic schools, or to do "field" work, or to study subjects, such as psychology and economics, only remotely connected with theology, or simply to begin their life's work. Some simply did not want to study any more abstract theology; they found it uninteresting and felt that their work would not require it.

The General was writing worried letters to provincials asking about the fourth year of theology and getting vague answers in return. When Father Paolo Dezza, one of the general assistants to Pedro Arrupe, was interviewed in 1973, he expressed concern over what seemed to be happening—that the Jesuits were settling for a minimum of three years of theology at the time that Rome was seeking to increase the general requirement for all priests to five years. This led to difficulties; for example, in the Philadelphia archdiocese of John Cardinal Krol, faculties were granted only to priests with at least four years of theology. One young Jesuit priest who had, as he thought, finished with theology, decided to return to Weston for a fourth year because he wished to work in Philadelphia. It was about a decade after Rockhurst before con-

[9] Such proposals ran into insuperable difficulties in the form of Roman requirements. Also, there was a judgment on the part of local authorities that the "assimilation" of theology required an unbroken period of study longer than one and a half or two years.

trols were reestablished and most Jesuits were doing a fourth year of genuine theology.

As the system gradually developed, a master of divinity (M. Div.) degree was usually granted at the end of three years and a master of theology (Th. M.) degree at the end of four years. Alternately, however, the fourth year might be used to gain some kind of ministerial degree or to pursue other studies germane to theology. The M. Div. degree was clearly something less than the traditional licentiate (named for an academic degree ranking below that of doctor given by some European universities), and even the Th. M., though closer, did not have the precise specifications set down for the licentiate. Though a student was normally expected to achieve the M. Div. degree before ordination—or at least before leaving the theologate—provincials occasionally allowed men to be ordained and leave the theologate without attaining the degree.

In the background of some of the discussions was a difference of opinion about the importance of theology as a part of a Jesuit's education. Some felt that in the modern world, with its proliferation of specialized fields of knowledge, there was not the same space as formerly for specifically clerical studies. The issue is posed neatly in a bit of dialogue during a meeting of novice directors in Rome.[10] (The term *brother* used in the passage below is one of three grades recognized in the Society of Jesus—namely, of professed [priest], coadjutor priest, and brother. A brother is not on track to become a priest, and his training ordinarily omits professional studies in philosophy and theology.)

> Father Charles Murphy: Margaret Mead speaks positively of celibacy for professionals because of the amount of time they must devote to their profession. Young men sometimes feel that clerical studies take them away from their specialty. If we could get away from the notion of the Brother as a second-class citizen, a lot of young men might become Brothers.

[10] The quoted statements are on page 33 of the minutes of this meeting, held April 5–8, 1970.

> Father John English: Because of the apostolic vocation of the
> Society, theology is very important. If highly talented Brothers
> took theology, they would not feel second class. On the other
> hand, if highly-trained specialists in the Society do not have
> theology, the Society loses its apostolic character.

Sometimes the issue took the form of a proposal to establish a new
"grade" in the Society, that of "perpetual scholastic"—a Jesuit
who is not, and will not be, a priest and yet is not a brother. The
Holy See has indicated that it would not look favorably on such a
proposal.

Particular Changes

A characteristic change that marked this period was the increased
scope for student participation in governance. Beginning informally
in the early 1960s, it gradually grew more formal. An academic
council with student representatives on it seems to have appeared
first at Alma, the California theologate, but soon spread to all the
others. At St. Mary's, Kansas, an informal group began to function about 1962. Started on the initiative of some of the scholastics,
its meetings were a kind of party to which the faculty was invited.
Gradually, it became a formal institution. Such a formal council
was established also at Woodstock, Maryland, at the start of the
1967 academic year. By the time the theologates had moved to
their new locations, these councils were in full operation. Administrators saw student participation as desirable in the fluid situation
of the 1960s and 1970s, when so many experiments were being
tried.

The students were not reluctant to offer their ideas. They
produced long, detailed analyses of desired curricular changes.
While not necessarily accepting the dictum of their secular coun-
terparts that no one over thirty was to be trusted, they saw
the post-Vatican II world as the age of young ideas. At Bellarmine (Chicago) the first-year theologians, even before com-

pleting their first semester of study, produced a long paper detailing their recommendations for changes in the existing program. They argued as follows: "We live in an age of accelerating change, an age in which every tradition and institution is being forced to radically question and redefine its very identity." They also anticipated any objection based on their youth: "We are mature men who have already dedicated ten years of our lives toward becoming Jesuit priests. We think we have, at least, as good a picture of what we need as Jesuit priests as those had who set up the area programs two years ago."[11] In 1970, a scholastic at Woodstock in New York, when asked by his provincial what he thought of the new theologate, wrote that he—along with other scholastics— was "looking for humble faculty members who treat me as a sort of equal or collaborator, and *with* whom I can help push back the frontiers of theological insight."

The all-Jesuit character of the theologate gradually changed for both faculty and students. Women and non-Catholics were added to the theologate faculty; and of course the faculties of the consortium schools, all of which were open to the scholastics, were predominantly non-Catholic. A Berkeley bulletin for 1972 illustrated the ecumenical advantages of the cluster by reporting the situation of a Baptist professor who had eleven years of missionary experience in the Far East and who teamed with an ascetical theologian from Jesuit School of Theology at Berkeley (J.S.T.B.) to conduct a course on prayer. The Jesuit faculty members themselves began to exhibit a wider variety of degrees than formerly, with fewer degrees coming from the traditional Roman sources and more from non-Catholic universities.

The students attending classes in the Jesuit school now included non-Jesuits; indeed, in some theologate classes more than half the

[11] The Bellarmine Theology Council, which included four scholastic representatives (one elected from each year), approved many of the proposed changes, such as the one to diminish the proportion of required courses and increase the proportion of electives.

students were non-Jesuits.[12] The reaction of the scholastics to this
new situation was mixed. Contact with persons of other theological backgrounds was enriching and stimulating. On the other
hand, the non-Jesuit students frequently lacked the Jesuits' maturity (the scholastics were older than the average consortium student)
and regularly lacked the scholastics' training in philosophy. There
were instances of scholastics forming a small group under a Jesuit
tutor in order to move faster and with more depth than could be
done in the ordinary class.

The opportunity to take a course under a specially qualified
non-Jesuit professor was appreciated but had to be balanced against
the advantage of their being better prepared for the all-important
comprehensive examinations if they took the courses taught by
the Jesuits, who would be on their examining board. According
to John W. Padberg (Weston president, 1975–85), there was a
tendency among the Jesuit scholastics of the 1980s to stay within
the Jesuit family, despite his exhortations to broaden their experience. Much earlier (January 1971), the situation at the Bellarmine
School of Theology (B.S.T.) in Chicago was described by its
rector, in a letter to the provincial, as follows:

> Of the tremendous number of educational, religious and cul-
> tural resources the various relocation documents cite as constitu-
> tive of the attractiveness of Hyde Park for a seminary location,
> many are completely unknown to most of the members of the
> community; few loom large in the life of anyone at B.S.T. A
> substantial number of our men spend most leisure time in their
> own Commons, watching T.V. or chatting, cozy and fairly
> unconcerned about the neighborhood, the university situation,
> even the Cluster activities.

Another view, shared by some faculty and students alike, was
that the early "milieu" expectations had been unrealistic. The
average student found his time largely absorbed in getting an

[12] Many of these students were women, especially in the 1970s, when
activist groups fanned the expectation that women might soon be admitted to
ordination. The proportion of women decreased in the 1980s.

adequate grasp of the basic subject matter in the immense field of theology.

The uniformity that had previously characterized Jesuit theological education disappeared in the new structure. The solid "tracts" of matter formerly studied by all Jesuits dissolved into the hundreds of courses available in the schools of the consortium. Ten years after the Rockhurst Report, when only Weston and Berkeley remained. Weston's 1974 bulletin specified the division of credit hours among the four areas and described the material on which the student must stand examination, but it did not require any particular course by way of preparation. Berkeley's bulletin of the same year distinguished between "core" and "elective" courses, but about one third of the courses were elective and even core requirements could be satisfied by various courses, some of them taught outside the Jesuit theologate. Berkeley also permitted students to elect either a basic core curriculum or a modular program with a minimum of course work and a maximum of study on one's own. In general, theology was being studied much as it would be at a university. The difference between seminary and secular college was being steadily diminished.

A characteristic development of the new period was the appearance of highly individualized ways of "doing theology". Two resolutions of the Rockhurst Report had prepared the way for this development: "A high proportion of electives should be incorporated into the four-year program (Resolution 10)." "Not all of the matter to be included in either comprehensive or course examinations need be presented in lectures, seminars, or other types of formal instruction (Resolution 17)" (Inter-Faculty Program Inquiry 1966, 339–40).

The students were not slow to avail themselves of the opportunity to personalize their contact with theology: the following examples—out of many—are taken from Woodstock College.

Five scholastics in their second year of regency proposed (1966) that when their time came in another year to begin the study of theology, they should be allowed to set up their own small community in New York City and take all their theology courses at Fordham University and Union Theological. Though this proposal was eventually rejected by Provincial Edward Sponga, it is significant as illustrating how widespread was the mood, even among regents, to change the traditional theologate and to substitute a larger degree of self-determination.

Three scholastics in 1967 asked to set up a small community in Baltimore where they would, while engaging in some local social work, complete their theological studies (fourth year) under the distant direction of the faculty at Woodstock. This proposal was strongly supported by faculty member Giles Milhaven and was finally approved by Provincial Sponga.

In 1969, numerous special programs were proposed. In one, a half dozen scholastics led by David Hollenbach approached faculty member Avery Dulles with the proposal that their second year of dogmatic theology consist of reading under his direction. They carried out this proposal when the theologate moved to New York. It was somewhat traditional in the sense that they worked as a unified group, with all doing the same readings at the same time and holding regular tutorial meetings. Everybody connected with this experiment, including the mentor, expressed great satisfaction with it.

Another group beginning in the fall of 1969 was known as the "Experimental Eight". Consisting of eight second-year theologians under the leadership of faculty member Giles Milhaven, it encapsulated much that was most distinctive of the new approach to the study of theology. If principles appear most clearly in strong cases, this group may be taken as a prime example of the new forces at work. Its story is told in some detail in Appendix 1.

At this same time, a group of four students who had just completed their first year of theology proposed to "spend two or more years on the Rosebud Sioux Reservation in South Dakota". Along with devoting time to "explicit theological study", they would involve themselves in the lives of the Indian people. They proposed "that a board of priests and theologians and members of the Indian people be set up to assist the group in their theological reflection and ultimately to approve the group for priestly ordination." They would thus be better prepared to aid "the developments of the people on the Rosebud Reservation". Back of this proposal was the conviction, often voiced at that time, that preparation for the priesthood should be as much ministerial as academic or more so. Superiors considered the proposal but rejected it on the score that there was no practical way for the students to do even minimally adequate "theological reflection" while on the reservation. (The complete proposal, of several pages, is in the Center's files.)

Another student proposed to spend his second year of theology in the study of four authors (Augustine, Newman, Ignatius, and Kierkegaard) under the direction of four different Woodstock tutors. This proposal was approved and carried through. During his third year, this same student lived and worked at *America* while completing what few credits he still needed for the M. Div. degree. Another second-year theologian proposed to spend a semester in El Salvador "to investigate and evaluate the theology of liberation". This proposal, which was approved and carried out, was considered to be the equivalent of two three-credit courses.

A permanent committee consisting of three faculty members and three students was set up to examine all "exceptional programs", as they came to be called, and to make recommendations to Dean Robert O'Brien, who described the committee's function "as being the focus of community consensus on new academic modes of theological education". In their report of May 2, 1970, the committee expressed general approval of these "new academic modes" but also voiced a strong caution: "The basic problem is that a student can complete the regular three-year program leading to the B.D. [bachelor of divinity] at Woodstock without necessarily being asked to reflect upon certain fundamental areas (e.g., Christology, Trinity, Ecclesiology) of theological concern."

Earlier (February 26, 1970), the chairman of the department of sacred Scripture had written to Dean O'Brien to say, "Thinking simply in terms of my own discipline, I have very definite reservations about 'do-it-yourself theology.'" In a memo dated October

8, 1971, the new dean, F. X. Winters, spelled out more clearly the regulations applying to students in exceptional programs. These students, like all others, were required to take the comprehensive examinations; they could not fulfill more than thirty credits (out of the total of seventy-two) by exceptional programs; and they had to take for credit all courses "presently required in the departments".

When the theologates were a completely Jesuit enterprise, composed only of Jesuits and conferring ecclesiastical degrees, they were governed directly by the Jesuit provincials. However, after undergoing the various structural changes previously described, their relationship to the provincials was less direct and less clear. For example, when Woodstock College moved to New York, and a board of trustees, including non-Jesuits, had been appointed, a Jesuit lawyer, Charles M. Whelan, warned the provincials that according to the law of the state of New York the trustees could not take orders from anyone outside the board itself. Eventually, after the theologates had been reduced to two, and various governing arrangements had been tried, the provincials settled on the following structure in 1984.

For each theologate, a board of members was established which owned the institution and had ultimate authority. This board consisted of the ten provincials and the president of the Jesuit Conference. The board of members appointed a board of directors for Weston (in Massachusetts) and a board of trustees for Berkeley (in California) which were responsible for the actual management of the respective theologates. The board of directors and the board of trustees consisted of the board of members and the president and rector of the local theologate. In practice, the control of the provincials was complete. They selected the terna (three-man list) for the rector, who was appointed by the General; they selected the president, after ascertaining that their choice had the approval of the General; and they selected the Jesuit members of the faculty.

The above is a description of the civil, or legal, structure. The ecclesiastical structure was different: the chancellor was the General, the vice chancellor was the local provincial, and the president was the same man who was president in the civil structure.

Changes in Content

The theologates changed not only their structure but also the content of their teaching. Such a change is difficult to document for a number of reasons. The content of courses cannot be judged simply from course titles and descriptions; it is necessary to attend classes, examine assignments, and interview students and teachers. With hundreds of different courses available, many of them taught by non-Jesuits, a wide-ranging, in-depth study would be required to ascertain the details of the changes in content that occurred in this period.

A few leaves in the wind indicate the general direction of the changes. First, the oath against modernism, required of theology professors each year, was dropped by the Sacred Congregation for the Doctrine of the Faith in 1967. Second, there is the comment of a Woodstock professor who described the unwillingness of students "to accept as serious the faculty's questions bearing on intra-Catholic, confessional issues". Third, among their reasons for objecting to the *ad gradum* examination (the final examination concluding theological studies for Jesuits following the so-called long or honors course) the students at Woodstock voiced their suspicion that the main purpose of the examination was to test their orthodoxy. Fourth, a criticism of the traditional course of theology voiced at the Santa Clara Conference implied by contrast the directions the new theology planned to take. The criticism ran as follows: "This theology has traditionally been scholastic, always metaphysical . . . rarely biblical . . . almost never historical. It centered in ideas and abstractions, rather than in persons and things" (S.C.C. 1967, 2:1:340). Fifth, according to James J. Doyle of the Chicago province, Bernard Cooke visited the theologate at St. Mary's and in the course of a lecture said that as long as he was head of the department of theology at Marquette University, he would never hire a graduate of St. Mary's College. They were being trained, he said, in a theology that was of no use in the contemporary world. Sixth, an article by Justin Kelly on the Rockhurst Report stressed the need to change the topics dealt with in theology. The following are three examples:

> Fundamental to the whole concept of a 'historical' theology is the intention to treat certain past ideas *as historical,* i.e., as past, no longer current. . . .
>
> The first questions raised by the contemporary Christian as he confronts the doctrine of the Incarnate Word, for example, are not likely to be about the modes of predication of divine and human attributes with respect to the person of Christ, nor about whether Christ has a human *esse* or possessed sanctifying grace in addition to 'substantial sanctity.' His questions are more likely to concern the meaning and credibility of the Incarnation, the place of Christ in man's history and evolution, the relation between Christ and human culture, etc. . . .
>
> But the theologian of today, raised in a pluralistic environment, intensely aware of the relativity of ideas and institutions, approaches theology with a challenged and often troubled faith. He has much more basic needs than his predecessor of earlier times; above all, he needs a viable understanding of the essential truths of Christianity, one which answers *his* problems, and fits in with his knowledge of the world and modern life. Theology for him must be not a superstructure but a foundation, a personally appropriated understanding which he needs—sometimes desperately needs—simply to make sense out of his personal religious life and his apostolic vocation (Kelly 1966, 362–68).

Since the author was himself at that time a theology student, his observations were the more likely to mirror the attitudes of his fellows.

One description of the theologate changes was provided by Howland Sanks in a 1984 article. Sanks was in an advantageous position to document such changes because he had been either a student or a professor of theology since 1963 and at the time of the article was dean of the Jesuit School of Theology at Berkeley. Yet when he comes to document the changes in *content,* he explains the difficulty of the task and asks the reader to be content with a single illustration. It is an excellent illustration, drawn from the field of ecclesiology, where many significant—and controversial—changes have occurred.[13] Sanks juxtaposes the summary statement used for the final examination at Alma College in 1963 and the one used at J.S.T.B. in 1983 (Sanks 1984, 490–91). The 1963 syllabus read as follows:

> The deposit of divine revelation is guarded by, and authentically and infallibly interpreted by, Christ's Church, which has been instituted as a true society both hierarchical and perpetual. At the head of this Church Jesus Christ has placed Peter and his successors, who have a primacy of jurisdiction over the universal Church. The successors of Peter in this primacy are, by divine right, the Roman Pontiffs—a fact proved both by the absence of other claimants and by positive historical evidence. When the Roman Pontiffs speak *ex cathedra,* they possess the infallibility that the Divine Redeemer willed his Church to have in defining faith and morals. The Church is Christ's mystical body, of which the Holy Spirit is the vivifying soul.[14]

The 1983 syllabus read as follows:

> (1) How does the community of faith which is the Church come to self-understanding in a situation of pluralism within the Christian community and in relation to other religions or other worldviews? (2) In what sense does the Church as primordial sacrament express herself primarily in the proclamation of the Word and celebration of the Eucharist? (3) How did the biblical images of election, covenant, people of God, body of Christ, and creation of the outpoured Spirit form the consciousness of the primitive Church as the true Israel? (4) What is the role of

---

[13] Preparatory to the Extraordinary Synod of Bishops called in 1985, over one hundred national hierarchies submitted their evaluation of events since Vatican II. The Vatican summary of these responses, in *The Progress* of November 28, 1985, included the heading "Ecclesiology: The Heart of the Crisis".

[14] In place of the original Latin, I have provided a literal English translation.

Sacred Scripture in the formation and development of the Church? What is the significance of the canon? (5) How did the emergence of offices and structures both express and transform the understanding of the Church, especially in the tension between conciliarism and papal authority and, more recently, in the development of papal infallibility? (6) Since Vatican II used the word "Church" to refer to both the local community and a universal reality, how is the mission of the Church to the world to be understood? How is this mission affected by the diversity of cultures in the world? (7) How is Mary considered to be model of the Church (cf. Vatican II, *Dogmatic Constitution on the Church,* Chapter 8)? (8) Within the Church what is the function and relationship of ordained and non-ordained ministries? (9) What is the role, function, and content of the Church's teaching authority on such questions as human rights, economic interdependency, world hunger, and disarmament?

Where the first syllabus consisted of positive propositions which were stated in technical terms hammered out over the centuries and which the student was required to prove, the second consisted of questions, stated in less technical language, which the student was invited to discuss, perhaps with room for differences of opinion. Where the first carried the implication that its propositions have always been and always will be true as stated, the second implied historical development, both past and future. Where the statements in the first syllabus are completely unacceptable to non-Catholic Christians and result in separating Catholics from all other Christians, the questions of the second syllabus invite ecumenical discussion, leave room for degrees of meaning, and open the possibility of some accommodation. In general, the new situation was marked by more historical relativity, with room for more pluralism and ecumenism, and by a diminished authority assigned to the hierarchy. It was also marked by a desire to bring the Good News from its sheltered Catholic environs out into the total world, whatever the risk, and allow that world to play a part in developing the form of the message.

V

THE THEOLOGATES: LIFESTYLE

Description of Changes

Lifestyle changes have great significance, for a religious order is essentially a "way of life" in which the individual religious vows to live according to the order's constitutions and rules. A change in an order's way of life is a change close to its heart. Lifestyle is taken here in its widest sense, so as to include all aspects of the theologate not touched on in the preceding descriptions of location and academics. Though some of the changes described were minor in themselves, others were substantial, and all of them had the importance of symbols (inculcating values) and of tools (shaping the individual by their daily, even hourly, pressure).

Predominant among the determinants of the traditional lifestyle was the prescribed daily order. For generations in the United States Assistancy, the daily order in houses of formation had remained stable. The entire house started the day together with a rising bell at 5:00 or 5:30. After a first visit to the Blessed Sacrament, there followed an hour of meditation. An official visitor (usually a brother) saw to it that everyone was out of bed, and another visitor (a scholastic) saw to it that everyone was at prayer. At the end of meditation, all assembled in the chapel for the community Mass, which, with a period of thanksgiving, occupied about forty-five minutes. Then followed breakfast, which was taken in silence. Individuals were free to leave breakfast when they finished, and they normally stopped for a brief chapel visit.

At least up to 1960, dinner, the main meal, was usually at noon, with supper in the evening. Both were sit-down meals served by the scholastics, and the community entered and left the refectory together. During both meals someone read aloud from a book, usually a work of history or biography. The meals began and ended with common prayer and were followed by a chapel visit.

The reading at table was an important channel of communication within the order. For example, it provided the opportunity to hear letters addressed by the General or provincial to the Society or province. More important, once each month the reading consisted of the Rules of the Summary (a collection of key passages from the Jesuit Constitutions), the Common Rules (more detailed and changeable guidelines for Jesuit lifestyle), and Saint Ignatius' Letter on Obedience. This monthly public recitation gave the materials a strong social sanction that tended to produce automatic acceptance. Also, the continuous repetition throughout a lifetime imprinted whole passages indelibly on the group psyche. A common heritage owned by all, a single phrase or even a single word would be understood by everyone in its total context. This common heritage was intergenerational, for each generation had heard the identical rules read out monthly throughout their entire Jesuit lives.

Most of the day was taken up with classes, which all the students were expected to attend, and with study. There was a general rule, less strictly enforced in the later stages of formation, that silence was to be observed outside of times of recreation. There were two periods of common recreation—after dinner and after supper—usable for conversation, or reading the few, selected parts of the newspaper (sports and some national events) that were available, or pursuing group activities—such as choir practice, making Christmas decorations, or rehearsing a play. There was another period of recreation in midafternoon, which the scholastics were expected to use for walks and outdoor games. The work week was broken up by two holidays conveniently spaced at Thursday and Sunday.

A minimum of three hours of prayer was prescribed. In addition to an hour of meditation, there were the forty-five minutes allotted for Mass, a quarter of an hour for the noon examen (review of conscience), and a half hour at night for the evening examen and preparation of the morning's meditation. In addition, the scholastics who were ordained read the Divine Office (Liturgy of the Hours), which before Vatican II took about an hour. The other scholastics were expected to read some spiritual book for a period each day. The community also assembled daily, usually just before dinner, for the common recitation of the litany of the saints.

Each semester was punctuated by a triduum, a three-day period of prayer during which the scholastics attended a spiritual conference each day; the triduum ended with a public renovation of vows. During the triduum classes continued, but recreation was suspended. Once a year, the scholastics made an eight-day community retreat, a time devoted totally to silence and prayer under the direction of a retreat director.

The scholastics spent their summer vacations together at a villa, a place separate from the seminary. In correspondence with Rome, superiors described the villa as an instrument of province unity because it provided the best opportunity for the scholastics to grow to know each other. During this vacation period, the prayer requirements held, but most other aspects of life were relaxed. In some provinces, the scholastics returned to the seminary after villa for summer classes. In other provinces, the scholastics were at villa nearly the entire summer and had some classes there.[1]

Contacts with the outside world were minimal. During the school year, the scholastics generally left the seminary only for health reasons, to visit a doctor or a hospital. The fourth-year theologians, recently ordained, were permitted occasionally to exercise the priestly ministry outside the seminary, but permission for travel to a library, for example, or to a meeting of a learned society was not easily obtained.

Newspapers and magazines were available only to a very lim-

---

[1] I recall acquiring a dozen undergraduate credits in economics during villas by means of reading courses.

ited and controlled extent. Radio (later, television) gradually became available, but only in community and always under closely controlled conditions. Films were beginning to make their appearance, but only when provided by the seminary, at the seminary, on special occasions. The community furnished some of its own entertainment: the large number of scholastics provided abundant talent for skits, plays, and musicals.

Modes of address were formal. Superiors and faculty were addressed by their last names, with proper title. Among themselves, the scholastics were permitted the use of first names, but in formal situations, such as class, they were expected to refer to a fellow scholastic as "Mr. Smith". Outgoing mail was deposited in the superior's box unsealed, and incoming mail was delivered opened. This was the general rule; actual practice varied from place to place and from time to time.

However, by the end of the 1960s, little of the traditional lifestyle remained.[2] A pattern of living that had been followed for generations—sometimes even for centuries—had largely disappeared over the course of three to four years. The timing of the changes and the order in which they came about varied somewhat among the theologates, but the final result was the same—most traces of the previous lifestyle had been obliterated.

The changes with the most obvious impact were the disappearance of silence and of the Jesuit habit. These two had enveloped the seminary twenty-four hours a day with an atmosphere unmistakably eschatological, marking it off from ordinary forms of life. They disappeared by steps but at a rapid pace. As they disappeared,

[2] For those who never knew the former lifestyle, an alternative experience is available in the collaborative work of two unusual people, John LaFarge, S.J. and Margaret Bourke-White (*A Report on the American Jesuits,* published in 1956 by Farrar, Strauss, and Cudahy). His text and her photos recreate the old life about as effectively as it can be done. For seminarians in general, a useful description of the old (Tridentine) and the new seminary may be found in Lee and Putz 1965 (x–xi). All the most characteristic criticisms of the traditional seminary system are to be found in Stafford Poole, C. M., New York: Herder and Herder, 1965.

the atmosphere altered and other changes became easier, more connatural.

In the new lifestyle there were no obligatory times for rising or retiring; each individual was free in this respect. There were no assigned times for individual prayer and, of course, no supervision of such prayer. Community prayer went through a few transformations but soon disappeared entirely. For example, other prayer forms were substituted for the litanies; but attendance was not required and the new forms proved to have no more attraction than the old. Community Mass, formerly early in the day, was moved to various later times but never attracted large numbers. In place of the community Mass, multiple Masses began to make their appearances. These were offered for small groups, in side chapels or other rooms, at times convenient to the particular groups and often with individually designed liturgical modes.

Opinions about these individualized liturgies varied greatly. At Weston, one faculty member wrote that it was necessary "to obtain permission for broad experimentation in the liturgy. . . . Otherwise the scholastics will grow with a very limited vision of ceremonial forms, prayer and music." But another faculty member wrote, "The disadvantages of regular coffee-table liturgies for our young men, who become more and more distanced from formal worship, have not yet been, I maintain, sufficiently appreciated by Superiors."[3] Some scholastics began to change their previous custom of automatic daily Mass to what seemed to them a healthier custom of attending Mass when they felt a need for it.

The community retreat was discontinued in favor of the directed retreat, an arrangement whereby the individual makes a retreat under a personal director at a time and place most suitable to the individual. In place of community conferences in the chapel, superiors attempted to provide more adequate individual spiritual direction.

---

[3] Such differences in opinion were not necessarily a function of age. The first opinion was that of a man ordained in 1937, whereas the second was that of a man ordained in 1964.

The substitution of buffet meals for the formerly served meals was a key alteration. Other changes automatically followed on this one. For example, since people entered and left the refectory at different times, community prayer before, during, or after meals became impossible. Reading at table, including the monthly reading of the rules and the promulgation of official letters and notices, had to be dropped. The special reading during the time of retreat and of triduum also had to be dropped. The periods of common recreation which formerly followed the noon and evening meals, while they did not disappear completely, changed their nature, becoming more scattered and individualistic, but still attracted only a few.

Outdoor recreation, especially in the form of games, was also affected, because people differed in their schedules and personal preferences. Also, on non-class days, many more than previously left the seminary to engage in various individual ministries.

The common vacation villa was used by diminishing numbers and then was abolished as more and more of the students obtained permission to leave the seminary during the summer to attend school at some outside college. The custom was inaugurated of giving each scholastic a sum of money sufficient to cover two weeks of vacation.[4]

The door to the outside world opened more widely. Students were very much freer to leave the house for academic, ministerial, and even entertainment purposes. They also began to spend their Christmas holidays at home, like other college students. And the door swung in both directions. Nonseminary people came into the house for a variety of purposes—to lecture, to socialize, to plan "actions" (protests of various sorts). At Woodstock, for example, a dozen young men and women might come for dinner and remain until two in the morning planning the next antiwar

---

[4] At Woodstock, for example, each was given $300. A group might combine their allotments and rent a cottage on the ocean for two weeks. Or individuals might go to a New York Jesuit house for two weeks of city entertainment.

protest. The house automobiles were increased in number and became much more available to the students. Also, some individually controlled autos made their appearance. A fourth-year father might undertake to help in a neighboring parish and find himself in control of an automobile put at his disposal by the pastor.

The plays and musicals formerly produced by the scholastics disappeared because there were fewer students to participate, as more of them were engaged in ministries outside the seminary, and because alternative entertainments were more available. Access to novels, magazines, television, and films gradually increased until eventually there were no effective external limitations. Each man became responsible for his own lifestyle.

Formal cloister (as approved by Rome) was removed gradually from various parts of the house, and actual cloister, as observed in practice, was removed even further. All modes of address became informal; students addressed even their professors and religious superiors by their first names. Mail gradually began to be delivered and received sealed, the stages of the change varying from house to house.

All these changes took place while the theologates were still in their country locations; for that reason the metamorphosis was the more striking. It was as though in an unchanged structure a completely different tribe of creatures began to live. They looked different (no cassock), they sounded different (no silence), and they acted differently in almost every way. Once the theologates moved into the cities, the single large community split into numerous small groups, and the variety of lifestyles multiplied, for each group was free to set its own style. Some cooked their own meals, others did not; some developed a community liturgy, others did not; some had many visitors and few community meetings, others followed the opposite pattern; and so forth. In some places, the rector invited each group to write a description of its lifestyle and made these descriptions available to incoming scholastics so that they could choose, or at least indicate a preference for, a particular group. Though the superior ultimately made the assignment, in doing so he gave considerable weight to expressed preferences.[5]

Causes of Change

The lifestyle changes were given direction chiefly by changed values, especially by the greatly increased emphasis on individual and secular values. Individualism affected lifestyle in at least two ways. In the first place, because the individual was unique, no one lifestyle could fit everyone. The more this aspect of the individual Jesuit was emphasized, the more unacceptable was the notion that all Jesuits could be molded by a fixed body of rules making for a common lifestyle. All aspects of life — recreation, education, clothing — had to be adapted to the unique needs, abilities, and tastes of the individual. The ideal of a common pattern to which all were to be conformed was rejected as oppressive.

Individualism exercised an even greater influence through modern psychology, which taught that maturity was reached only by taking full responsibility for oneself. Though the doctrine was not new, its interpretation and emphasis were. The new emphasis led to an unease with the very notion of formation. The Santa Clara Conference (Chapter II), for example, which originally planned to deal with the "total formation of the Jesuit priest", came under immediate criticism and hastily changed its title to the "total development of the Jesuit priest". A healthy psyche resulted not from passive conformity to a preexisting pattern but from active responsibility for creating one's own pattern.

The scholastics were acquainted with — or at least quoted from — psychologists like Erik Erikson and Lawrence Kohlberg and their

[5] Before the Chicago theologate made its move from North Aurora to the city, a "Community Life Planning Committee" prepared a questionnaire to help determine groupings in the apartments. The last item on the one-page questionnaire was "The people (by name) I would *absolutely not want* [Italics in the original] to live with are: . . . "

theories of stages of human development. The young men often observed that at thirty years of age Jesuits should be beyond the stage of accepting values and lifestyles on the authority of others. They began to feel an unease with the traditional notion of a "religious way of life" to which one submitted precisely in order to develop according to a preestablished pattern. They tended to wince at the ancient adage, "Keep the Rule and the Rule will keep you." To a proposition like "Silence, as prescribed by the rule, is good for the Jesuit scholastic", their reaction was likely to be, "Is silence (substitute any other traditional practice, such as daily Mass) good for *me*? And is it good for me not yesterday or tomorrow but *today?*"

This view of psychological maturity could deepen, and hence strengthen, a scholastic's observance of the rule; but in most cases, the first effect probably was to diminish observance. This was the more likely to happen to the extent that the rule involved some hardship; the force of gravity usually worked against observing the rule. Thus, when the automatic braking blocks of house discipline were removed, the whole edifice started to slide. Though this individualistic norm ("What does rule X do for me now?") no doubt had an epistemological root, the psychological argument for the norm was the one that was regularly advanced. The mature man decides for himself how best to combine prayer and television, studies and active ministry, obedience and initiative, and so of all other human decisions.

The other major influence accounting for changes in lifestyles was the enhanced status of the secular (see Volume II). This influence was operative at three levels—theological, pragmatic, and psychological.

On the theological level, there was a new emphasis on the sacredness of the secular and a growing reluctance to concede any intrinsic superiority to the religious way of life over the secular. The terms *sacred* and *secular* often were used in quotes to reflect a judgment that both terms needed redefinition so as to remove any suggestion of an intrinsic difference between them. The young Jesuits were unwilling to adopt a lifestyle that might imply a belief in some intrinsic superiority of the religious life. In practice, this meant exchanging their specific religious lifestyle for the general, or common, secular lifestyle. They felt especially uneasy with any marks of esteem accorded on the basis of status in an institution; the only root of true value was the existential activity of the individual.

On the pragmatic level, there was a growing judgment that if the Christian message were to be acceptable to the world, its messengers should not come from, and certainly not live in, a ghetto. The young Jesuits argued insistently that they should dress and recreate and go to school the way their secular peers did. Apostolic effectiveness demanded that Christ's messengers be "in" the world. This very respectable, and therefore potent, consideration was advanced often.

The influence exerted on lifestyles by psychology was perhaps the most potent of all. The humanistic psychology that developed in the late 1950s (Volume II discusses this in more detail) included a judgment that the traditional religious lifestyle ran a serious danger of being a psychologically deprived life, at least in comparison with the fuller, richer life available in the world. This is one of the principal conclusions of the psychological study of American priests commissioned by the bishops and carried out by Eugene Kennedy, himself a priest at that time. After finding that a disproportionate number of priests were "immature", the study stated that the immaturity was the result of "policies such as the removal of seminarians from ordinary developmental educational and social experiences" (Kennedy and Heckler 1972, 16) and offered the following remedy: "The basic therapy for this type of problem is the opportunity and encouragement for a deeper and freer participation in life itself" (ibid.).[6]

This theme was repeated over and over again in the theologates. At Woodstock College, for example, in 1967, a student committee submitted a report on "Student Difficulties". Among these difficul-

---

[6] The study was reviewed by the non-Catholic sociologist, Samuel Z. Klausner, who faulted it severely on professional grounds (Klausner 1976, 112–13).

ties was a feeling among the students that they had "regressed" when they left the "rich experience" offered by regency and came to the theologate, "quiet, rural, and without rich experience". There was an implied solution in the finding: "Many handle this difficulty by ... developing a social life and seeking rich experiences outside of the college campus" (Students 1967, 3).

Characteristics of Change

The course of change, while generally similar among the theologates, was not identical. For example, Alma antedated the other theologates in establishing the first community council—a particularly significant change because it became the formal instrument of further change. In connection with their early moves to the cities of North Aurora and St. Louis, the Chicago and Missouri theologates pioneered some changes, such as the flow of students to the local university, with consequent alterations in house customs. Of Woodstock it can be said in general that more changes began there slightly earlier and were carried further than at any other theologate.

The course of change at all the theologates exhibited three characteristics, closely linked and mutually reinforcing. In the first place, the changes were not planned. They were not carried out according to some grand blueprint. When I asked Felix Cardegna, who was rector at Woodstock College during all its major changes, whether he had such a blueprint, he replied, "On the contrary, the changes occurred in unforeseen fashion. The process was like pulling out one brick in the wall, which loosened others, which loosened still others, until the entire wall came tumbling down."

Though I interviewed hundreds of persons within five years of the changes in lifestyle, and though these persons had been intimately connected with the changes, their recall was vague about the dates, stages, and methods of the transformations. This is in itself an indication that the changes did not take place in the traditional manner. Previously, even a small change in lifestyle at a house of formation would go to the provincial, who would most likely discuss it with his consultors before rendering a decision. Any change would be reflected in a written record (indeed in several records, such as the minister and beadle's diaries), would stem from an identifiable authority, and would have a definite date attached to it.

The changes of the 1960s were of another sort altogether. They were not being ordered by the General or by the provincials but tended to come from below. This was a second characteristic of the period. Almost always the change would begin with a proposal by the religious subject (student or faculty) and very often would actually have been put into practice in a minor way without any authorization, by way of experiment. This was a major inversion of the traditional order, which was strictly monarchical: superiors and the official consultors, all appointed by Rome, made the decisions about house order and simply informed the community.

The fact that the scholastics at the various theologates were in touch with one another as never before accelerated the change. A frequent complaint encountered during this period was that the young men were running up large bills of unauthorized long-distance phone calls directed to other scholasticates. As a result, a change achieved in one theologate very quickly appeared as a change demanded in other theologates, supported by the strong argument that theologate X had already moved in this direction.

A third characteristic of the changes was that they tended to be brought about by exerting pressure on superiors through direct action. The young men applied some of the techniques they were already using to influence the decisions of civil authorities. A desired change might simply be begun by a few leaders and then adopted by growing numbers. There would be no attempt to hide their actions. When challenged by superiors, they expressed willingness to discuss the matter as reasonable men.

Superiors reacted in various ways. Higher superiors generally began by insisting that the rules and customs be followed and urged local superiors to be firm. Local superiors generally attempted to comply but found themselves weakened and finally defeated by a combination of forces. They had to contend with a general spirit of uncertainty. G.C. 31, following the lead of Vatican II, clearly invited "experimentation" leading to "modernization" of religious life, thus subtly shifting the burden of proof from the proposers of change to the defenders of tradition. A greater impact on structural stability can scarcely be imagined. A strong, universal, unmistakable atmosphere developed that change was "in".

Rectors and especially ministers experienced the truth of the principle that one man can command large numbers only to the extent that the large numbers are willing to obey. When some local superiors attempted to enforce existing laws exactly, such tension was created that superiors had to be removed for their own health as well as for the peace of the house. Other local superiors, finding that they could not count on the kind of strong support from higher superiors needed in such an unusual situation, simply did what they deemed possible and let the river of change flow along. When notable numbers began to ignore a given rule and were not effectively corrected, others cited the legal principle that an unenforced law is no law and questioned whether the law still applied. Community officials repeatedly mentioned this situation in their letters to the provincial and to the General and said they could not in conscience require scholastics to assume the unpopular role of opposing the general trend when superiors themselves took no decisive action.

Many, probably most, higher superiors were uneasy over the pace and the manner of changes. The following excerpts from a February 1967 statement of Edward J. Sponga, provincial of the Maryland province, illustrates this apprehension:

> An experimentation that does not feed back into some kind of system of analysis and evaluation seems to me to have very little positive worth, and there are many negative dimensions affecting the whole outlook of law, it seems to me. . . . Litanies and regular Sunday Benediction should not have been dropped without Provincial permission at least. There seems to be in general

an experimentation without reference to higher authorities. . . .
The experiential, the spontaneous has dominated too exclusively,
and the reflective, the contemplative, and the communal discernment have been neglected. In looking at the dynamics of the
thing, one hopes that the latter will return to temper the former,
but one is never sure . . .

Examples of Change

The following examples of lifestyle changes in the theologates
may contribute concreteness to the general description given above.
The examples, which could be extended almost indefinitely, follow a loose topical order, within which specific instances are
arranged generally by date. But both forms of ordering—by type
and time—are quite rough. Moreover, a single example sometimes
illustrates more than one topic.

The examples do not cover all aspects of the period. They are
meant to perform only the one function of illustrating *changes.*
Neither are the examples adequate for the task of evaluation. To
the extent that some of the examples reflect a negative evaluation,
this can be explained by the fact that people calling attention to a
given change were usually doing so because they were puzzled or
disturbed by the change. "Viewing with alarm" usually wins a
wider press than "All is normal."

A Different, Disturbed Era

To get a feeling for historical development, it may help to begin
by viewing developments at one place (Woodstock College) through
the eyes of one person (the provincial) as he makes his annual
visitation of the college. As early as January 1960 (therefore reflecting
an even earlier period), the provincial was remarking in his report
to the General that "the young men coming to the Society in the

postwar period are a different breed." He goes on to say that this causes difficulties for superiors.

In his visitation of 1962, the provincial reports a change in the community which he describes as "a certain free and easy spirit and a definite lack of silence in the house". He notes that some in the community criticize the rector for not being strong enough in his dealing with "the so-called modern scholastic". They want the rector to use the "do-it-because-I-say-so" method. He reports that the rector "has found from his experience that this does not produce the results desired". The provincial ends his report recognizing "the very complex individual who enters the Society these days".

In his 1963 visitation, the provincial reports that "on any given morning it would seem that some fifty of the community are not present at the morning visit at the proper time." He notes an almost complete disappearance of silence and the difficulty of doing anything about it. He links this up with "the independent and democratic streak or spirit about which I spoke to Your Paternity on my visit to Rome". He concludes with this general portrait: "I find the young men immature, and while claiming and desiring to be strongly individual, they seem to me to need very much to lean on each other. In general, they are restless in this generation as I find them and quite impatient with the generations which preceded them. . . . Superiors are constantly being subjected to the pressure of this questioning generation."

The provincial reports in his March 1964 visitation that "religious discipline, as measured according to the customary norms, is but fair at best." He is concerned even more by a growing change in the spirit of poverty. He thought he had perceived this change a couple of years ago and now, he says, he is certain of it. He comments also on "the great size of the house", and says that this "makes it next to impossible for Father Rector and Father Minister to know with any degree of accuracy what the spiritual and religious practice of any individual is." In this same report, he quotes the minister as saying that it is not unusual for him (the minister) to correct a scholastic and to have the man then discuss with him whether or not father minister should have corrected him.

In 1965, a new provincial comments on the spiritual conferences given by the new rector of Woodstock College: "Father Rector's governing is certainly a spiritual one, and in his talks he constantly inculcates the need for basically measuring up to the demands of the religious life, or getting out and not going through a pretense, or through a halfhearted living, of the requirements of our vows. He is respected for his honesty and his firmness in this matter." (In the next several years, both provincial and rector acted on this principle and left the order.)

Indications of an era that was generally different, and disturbed, are to be found in the other theologates, also. At Alma in January 1962 one of the older professors told the provincial:

> The dean makes many changes on the basis that other theologates are making such modifications in traditional practices. Faculty meetings have been multiplied and the scope of these meetings embraces much that was customarily taken up by consultors meetings. The turmoil is unending, and one is inclined to believe that until the present generation came on the scene nothing was done correctly in our house of formation.

At about the same time, another man wrote: "The Rector refuses no request of scholastics. Groups of scholastics have been permitted to go to Santa Clara for plays, debates, et cetera; to attend lectures by Protestant ministers, to visit and attend classes at some non-Catholic seminaries, et cetera. Such radical departures from the traditional discipline at Alma is beyond my understanding."

In 1962 at Alma a priest reported, "Nearly all the changes in lifestyle that are made or proposed are in the direction of a more pleasant life. Each new mode is easier than the old mode. A frequent reason given for the change is that other houses in the Assistancy are following such a new mode." In the following year (1963) this same member remarked that most of the changes were

> doing away with one of the most forming and sobering influences of religious life, namely daily order, and adherence to our

sacred customs. This, it seems to me, can have bad effects and serious consequences regarding the attitudes of our young men towards recollection, mortification, the spirit of prayer during the day, and so forth. It also increases restlessness, and creates many needs that had long ago been given up.

A Scripture professor who came to Alma in 1959 recalled that conditions were very pleasant in the early 1960s. There was much discussion of new things, including Vatican II, but no bitterness and no confrontation. Then, in the mid-1960s, classes came to Alma that had an entirely different spirit. Their members took violent exception to whatever displeased them.

In 1967 one of the community at Alma wrote: "I am sure that the more vocal scholastics do not speak for all. I see some scholastics in counseling who do not agree but who are afraid to speak up. I think there is a tyranny here in reverse." In the same year, another priest wrote: "This past year, including the past six months, has been a somewhat disturbed and agitated period. From what I could gather, the same is true elsewhere; but up until this scholastic year (1966–67) we seem to have been spared."

In November 1964, Father George Klubertanz of St. Louis University attended a meeting at North Aurora and reported back with some surprise that at North Aurora the short form of grace in English was said at all meals. He also noted that there was no rule of silence for the period between the end of litanies and the beginning of supper or between the end of supper and the beginning of recreation. At this time, the St. Mary's theologate had not yet moved to the St. Louis campus, and Father Klubertanz was acquainted only with the traditional lifestyle which still prevailed in the philosophate there.

Weston in 1965 was described as follows. Reporting to the provincial, the dean noted, "House discipline in the theologate is almost nonexistent.... Perhaps the foot must be put down; perhaps a more liberal program should be thought out. In any case, the present chaos should not continue." Another community member reported:

THE THEOLOGATES: LIFESTYLE 179

The religious spirit and discipline of the community as such is not at all healthy . . . though the number of individuals who cause this unhappy state are certainly a minority. We have a community with many good and devoted religious — who are finding it more and more difficult to remain good and devoted in an atmosphere of almost total permissiveness.

At the same time, the New England provincial was writing to the General as follows: "With the variety of ideas being propounded today in so many Catholic circles, control of training in the seminary is becoming more and more difficult. The situation at Weston College is no exception to this general condition." In the same letter the provincial reported: "Teams of Fathers have been visiting various houses in the Province to talk over with the various communities their observations on life in our scholasticates. . . . The rector of Weston has had no difficulty in dealing with the philosophers, who are very docile and observant. With the theologians, he has had to exercise a great deal of patience."

In a 1967 letter, an official of Bellarmine School of Theology wrote:

Having spent some time within the past year at other scholasticates (for example, Shrub Oak, Woodstock, Fusz) I see that the problems and difficulties and unrest and disorder that may seem to be present at Bellarmine are in no way peculiar to Bellarmine. In fact, these are far, far less at Bellarmine than elsewhere — and I attribute this in large extent to the administration we have here.

In 1968 at Alma College a community member noted that many men were getting psychotherapy and that there were disturbing signs of an inability to make up one's mind about ordination. "More and more I hear it said that a man has decided to be ordained and to see how it goes. If he is unhappy, he will give it up later." The same writer also said, "Many scholastics feel lonely, abandoned, looked down upon by less observant scholastics."

During his years at Woodstock College (1963–66), John L'Heureux kept a diary which he later published. One entry reports, "In January of 1964, the theologians put on a musical comedy called

'Tender Is the Knight' which was a slamming satire on education, venerable societies, some four hundred years old, tradition,
pomposity, everything." The most frequent refrain was the reason
repeatedly given for existing customs: "We have always done it
this way" (L'Heureux 1967, 39). In February 1964, L'Heureux
comments: "Again and again I am struck by the moral miracle of
the Church in general and of the Society of Jesus in particular.
Here are all these brilliant men giving their lives freely, nothing
withheld, to a Church which from the fifth century has ruthlessly
crushed initiative, intelligence, enterprise" (L'Heureux 1967, 56).

Prayer Life

The liturgy was the subject of a town hall meeting at Alma in
October of 1961. Throughout the discussion, the need for variety
was emphasized. The speakers did not want the Mass, or any other
prayer, to be handled the same way each day. Typical of the thrust
of the discussion was the following remark: "The litany should
not be said every evening at the same time. Even a variation of the
time would help remove the dead weight of monotony." This
theme, the need for variety, marked all the developments in prayer
and the liturgy during the 1960s.

In 1961 at Alma one of the officials reported that the scholastics
no longer remained in the chapel during the short period between
the end of Mass and the beginning of breakfast. Though the rule
had not been changed, most of them had started another custom.
They left the chapel and stood about talking until the refectory was
opened for breakfast. Another report in January 1963 noted: "The
practice of visiting the Blessed Sacrament is rapidly disappearing."

At its meeting of October 6, 1967, the Alma Community
Council recommended the following: "That there be no regularly
scheduled community prayer. When suitable occasions arise, such
as the eve of major peace talks or events of this nature, prayer
should be held ten minutes before the evening meal." The rector
did not accept the recommendation but arranged, instead, to have

a bell rung at 5:50 P.M. each day with some reading of Scripture at that time. This attempt at community prayer was so poorly attended that it was eventually dropped.

Another development noted in all the theologates is described by one of the officials of Weston College in 1966. He was concerned over the tendency of scholastics to absolve themselves of any spiritual exercise of which they can say, "I don't get anything out of it." He thinks, however, that this problem must be handled individually by the spiritual directors: "Mere general preaching on the point could lead to no results or to unfortunate results." This acute observation reflects one of the more characteristic attitudes of the period—a reluctance, and often a refusal, to accept authoritative general directions.

The Alma Community Council made various recommendations over several years to change the customs at mealtime. In 1968, the council recommended that the community abandon the served dinner in favor of buffet style. The rector is reported as saying that he "would not consider it because there is no realistic way of having the community assemble in the Chapel for community prayer after buffet meals." The report went on to explain, "We have been told by the General and Provincial to have community prayer, and Father Rector interprets this to mean benediction on Sundays and some form of community prayer in the Chapel after sit-down dinners." (Actually, a few months later, in 1969, Alma followed the other theologates in changing to a buffet dinner.)

At Alma in 1969 a priest noted, "There is a large falling off of the recitation of the Breviary. There is a revulsion in quite a few against the practice of formal prayer such as meditation and examen."

At Bellarmine (Chicago) in 1971, the rector described some of the young men as having an attitude toward prayer which worried him:

They talk of the "conversation model" of prayer as one with which they are uncomfortable. They quote theologians like Rahner and Metz as supporting a view of prayer quite different, in which "conversation" has no necessary place. On questioning them about what prayer is for them, I get answers like "reflection" or "thinking about God theologically" which leave me uneasy. But these men will say that my categories are just not the ones they use, and that theirs are equally valid for them. They are extremely bright, very well read and highly articulate.

Throughout this period, the liturgy was the focus of continuous controversy. In 1967, a member of Bellarmine School of Theology (North Aurora) reported: "There have been liturgical problems here for some time. I refer primarily to the unauthorized variations in celebrations of the Eucharist by the fourth-year fathers. It is an extremely difficult problem to face—both because of certain unclarities in principle and because of the impossibility (and undesirability) of policing."

At Woodstock in 1966, L'Heureux notes in his diary: "Jake's experimental Mass is a thing of wonder. I finally attended it this morning and I must say I'm converted to belief in the true Jake.... Imagine making the Mass once again meaningful to people. Exciting" (L'Heureux 1967, 227). "Jake" was James Empereur, a fourth-year father, who was asked by the rector later in the year to moderate his experiments for the sake of other, larger changes the rector was attempting to negotiate for the college. The liturgical experiments were increasing the already strong wind of criticism directed against Woodstock on the score of lifestyle.

In the fall of 1967 at Alma the liturgical committee recommended against fixed times for Masses, preferring small group meetings related to specific occasions. Most of the occasions illustrated were secular events of importance rather than the traditional holy days. The committee recommended: "Some kind of Mass board will be set up so the members of the Alma community will know where and when Masses are being celebrated.... This is not an attempt to regulate, but simply an informational help." The liturgical committee quoted the Santa Clara Conference (1967) as its chief authority for its recommendations.

In his 1968 visitation of Weston College, the provincial reported,

"For liturgical services, they [the scholastics] have no great interest in a large community Mass but prefer to attend small group Masses in various house Chapels."

At Berkeley in 1973, the local bishop wrote to the California provincial to protest various liturgical irregularities occurring at the theologate. The provincial instructed the rector of Berkeley to bring all unauthorized liturgical experiments to a halt. The rector replied that he could, of course, do it but that it would have to be done by means which would destroy his effectiveness with the scholastics in all other areas. In the upshot, word went out to the young men to pursue experiments prudently, that is, quietly.

All the theologates at one time or another asked the local bishop to designate them as official liturgical experimental centers. I do not know the results of these requests.

In 1965, the community retreat at Weston was given in the traditional manner and seems to have gone very well. But in 1967 at Alma, attendance at the community retreat, which was being given in the traditional manner, dwindled as the days went on until it was practically zero.

The retreat of the 1968 Woodstock ordination class differed from the customary retreat in several respects. Three members of the class, uncertain of future developments, made a retreat ahead of time at a Trappist monastery. They also made the regular retreat, which took place away from the Woodstock campus at the Manresa Retreat House, and expressed themselves glad that they had made a previous one. During the retreat, there was little or no silence. Some of the retreatants were smoking marijuana. Four lay persons, two men and two women, were invited to address the ordinands; they dealt chiefly with controversial social issues. Coincidentally, the retreat was held the week that Martin Luther King was assassinated, and a number of the retreatants went into Washington to see what they could do about the resulting civil disturbance. The retreat master, who had been selected by the class, was perceived by the retreatants as being himself disturbed in his vocation. He left the order the next year as did about half of the 1968 ordination class.

Governance and Authority

In 1963 at Alma one of the younger faculty proposed that the refectory reading include an article in which an atheist set forth his reasons for his position. When the faculty member was overruled by the superior, he "went public" by circulating a questionnaire among the faculty, asking whether they approved of the superior's decision. One of the older members of the community judged this "impudent, in view of the action by the superior".

At Weston in 1965, the provincial reported that among the theologians "there seems to be an excess of permissiveness"; and in 1966 he said, "what has to be watched carefully is that a less observant minority does not . . . create an atmosphere of almost total permissiveness." In 1966, the General wrote to all the provincials expressing "concern about the introduction in some provinces and houses of new practices with regard to religious discipline without [his] prior authorization." One provincial replied, "It does not seem to me that any special changes have been introduced anywhere without prior contact with Rome." "Special changes" were not identified, but this province had changed as much as any.

In his visitation of Weston College in 1966, the provincial reported that some scholastics "had the attitude that regulations are not 'promulgated' unless they had been consulted before the regulation was announced, or that there should be a discussion meeting with the authority issuing the regulation in order to talk over its reasonableness."

In 1966 at Weston the father minister wrote to the provincial and listed many external violations of existing regulations: "Faults of this sort are now almost never corrected, and even some of the most sincere and observant scholastics begin to question whether there really is not some kind of tacit permission for what externally appear to be clear violations of poverty, obedience, or the Church's law."

At Alma in 1966 a faculty member noted, "There is much 'questioning' on the part of the scholastics in things relating to religious obedience and religious discipline." In 1969 this same member wrote, "I sense at times a radical questioning on the part of the scholastics about the meaning of religious obedience." The significant term is *questioning;* authority was not merely being disobeyed, it was being questioned in principle.

The rector's address to the Weston community in the spring of 1966 reflected the acceptance of a principle that characterized the period: "Superiors are endeavoring to apply norms of discipline in such a way that personal responsibility, self-mastery and maturing are developed."

In the fall of 1967, Alma inaugurated its community council whose purpose was to provide a channel whereby the community, especially the scholastics, could participate in the ordering of community life, at least on a consultative basis. The other theologates had similar councils for the same purpose. Each theologate also had an academic council whose function was, as its title indicates, the structuring of the academic life of the theologate. To some, the important body was the community council, while to others the academic council was by far the more significant. Both, of course, represented democratic forms of governance that had not previously existed.

A formerly important tool of governance, the beadle's diary, disappeared from the theologates at varying dates in 1967. At Alma, the beadle's diary carries the following notation for May 18th: "It was decided by community vote to abolish the office of beadle and the subbeadle and try a student council." (David Sprague was thereupon elected student body president.) This marked the end of the beadle's diary. At Weston the diary was ended more casually. The beadle came in to see the rector one morning and asked him, as the diary records, whether the tradition of keeping the diary made any sense. After a brief conversation, they both decided that it did not—and that was the last entry in the diary. A practice that had been observed for generations and that had been one of the chief structural determinants of daily life (when any doubt arose as to whether something could or should be done, the first step was to consult the beadle's diary) was abandoned that simply.

In early 1967 three theologates (Alma, St. Mary's, and Weston) made identical, and unusual, requests of their respective provincials. Each of them asked that when the provincial came on his annual visitation he meet with the scholastics as a group and that the scholastics be allowed to set the agenda for the meeting. There is no indication that either the Missouri or New England provincial acceded to the request. The California provincial, however, did meet with the theologians as a group and allowed them to set the agenda. They prepared very carefully for the meeting, assigning specific topics to designated members of their group. The plans for the meeting were detailed, including provision for following up whatever direction the discussion might take.

At the opening meeting, the first speaker began with the pronouncement that the scholastics simply did not trust the provincial. According to one of the scholastics who had arranged the session, the provincial replied, "Then I see no point in having this meeting at all." He started to walk off the platform, stopped at the edge for reflection, turned back, and said, "I will hear you out."

At this point, according to one of the organizers, "We knew we had him." The beadle's diary reports that there were three "open sessions" on February 16, 18, and 20. According to the same source, the three sessions covered the topics of communication, consensus, fear, consultation, delegation of authority, social apostolate, and, especially, "the Berkeley question" (that is, whether to leave Alma and move to Berkeley).

The scholastics set forth what concrete actions they would be looking for as indications that their proposals were taken seriously. The provincial was on the stage, and on the carpet, the whole time. The confrontation was, as usual, conceived and managed by a small group of leaders, was supported by most of the scholastics, but was also criticized by some as not compatible with the Society's form of governance. On the last day of the visitation, there was a concelebrated Mass at which the beadle, on behalf of the community, presented the provincial with a Jerusalem Bible signed by each member of the community. The provincial had tears in his eyes, while the community applauded for eight straight minutes.

In 1967 the theologians at Woodstock College achieved notice in eastern newspapers by picketing the dedication of the National Shrine of the Immaculate Conception, to which the United States Assistancy had contributed $500,000. A busload of scholastics made the trip down from Woodstock to the District of Columbia to carry out the picketing. While the provincial, rector, and Woodstock choir were inside the shrine helping to dedicate it, the pickets were outside with signs that said the money would have been better spent on the poor.[7] They ignored the disapproval of their rector but did obey the direct order of the provincial to disperse. The shrine "action" was one of many public protests led by Woodstock activists.

In January 1968, thirty-nine Jesuits at Alma College publicly supported the Immaculate Heart Sisters in the changes they wanted to make in their lifestyle. These changes had been forbidden by James Francis Cardinal McIntyre, archbishop of Los Angeles.

There were a number of instances in the theologates where men left and married without getting proper clearances and hence were married outside the Church. Fellow Jesuits attended such marriages without feeling the need to obtain permission. When in some cases they were questioned by a superior, they replied that they were responding to a clear demand of Christian charity and felt old enough to make such decisions on their own. In one case in St. Louis, where transportation costs to Oregon were beyond their means, four of them asked the rector for the funds and, when he refused permission, went to the provincial, who granted it.

In 1968, the Woodstock dining room was the scene of an incident that clearly revealed the growing independence individuals were feeling in relation to the institution. One of the scholas-

---

[7] In November of 1966, a group of Bellarmine theologians wrote an open letter of protest concerning the proposed construction of the Schott faculty building at Xavier University in Cincinnati. They considered the appointments of the new building to be contrary to the spirit of poverty. Appealing to the General, they held up construction for about a year. (This "action" is described more fully in Volume II.)

tics had two guests for dinner, a young man and a young woman. On the buffet table was a large bowl of fruit salad, sufficient for the entire community, which contained some grapes. At this time the farm workers in California were urging a boycott of grapes. When the two guests expressed displeasure at seeing the grapes, their host told them to follow their consciences. Whereupon they rose, took the whole bowl of fruit out into the kitchen, and dumped it into the garbage, bringing back the empty bowl. If there were any repercussions of the incident, no record of them has been left.

One characteristic of governance in this period is pointedly described in a 1967 letter of the dean at Bellarmine: "Father Minister is on the point of moving in certain areas; but he and all officials have to be very careful in dealing with the young men since it takes very little to turn them against one and thus all effectiveness is lost." This reflects the same caution voiced above (see pp. 176, 181, 183).

At Bellarmine in 1967 a revealing discussion occurred of the principles by which modern governance should itself be governed. A group of scholastics prepared the following proposition:

> In 1967, the concepts of "formation," "direction" and "leadership" need redefinition. The functions these terms indicate no longer can be truly viewed as the responsibility of a few (for example, superior, spiritual father, faculty member); especially if these few are, because of accepted social structures, viewed by the scholastics as outside the group with whom they cooperate and spend most of their hours. More and more these functions are seen to be effects of close community cooperation, and each member of the community has the responsibility of cooperating in bringing about these effects from maximal community life. The reality of formation, direction and leadership is seen today as best achieved in small heterogeneous groups in which each member makes important contributions, largely in proportion to the differences of his unique experience, training, ideals, earned and recognized authority (e.g., from proven learning, happiness, effectiveness in the apostolate).

One of the faculty reported to the provincial his evaluation of this proposition:

> Thus all aspects of the community situation are to be open to continuous questioning by everyone. Answers to these questions are to be supplied, not by experienced and appointed superiors, but by "natural leaders" who emerge from the "analysis" of the situation. In the community discussions during which the "analysis" takes place, verbal ability counts for much in establishing leadership. This reads like a prescription of continuous unrest and the allocation of considerable time and energy to internal problems. The natural urge of the younger members of any group to assert themselves and escape from the control of the older established members of the group is much strengthened. Also the value of verbal skills in relation to the value of wisdom is much increased.

Varia

The ancient custom of religious silence was seriously questioned. At the 1960 Alma Institute (Ascetical Institute 1960), one scholastic advanced the proposition that the familial aspects of the Society are more important than its institutional aspects. By way of illustration, he said it could be more important to exhibit friendship with one's religious brothers than to keep silence in the halls. In 1963, a community member reported that silence at Alma was "gradually disappearing".

At his visitation of Weston College in 1965, the provincial reported: "It seems that sometimes 'sociability' and 'togetherness' almost exclude such elements as silence or the observance of grades among theologians and philosophers." At the same time at Weston a community member wrote, "Silence is less and less observed. On one occasion indignation was expressed by some of the scholastics when Father Rector stopped to ask for silence after grace." In 1967 at Bellarmine (North Aurora), the dean inquired of the provincial, "Is the 'rule of silence' still in effect here or is it now a 'rule of quiet' so that others are not disturbed?" At Alma in 1967, the community council voted that talking should be allowed at breakfast. The rector did not, however, accept this recommendation until a year later, in October 1968.

The increased importance of humanistic psychology was evident everywhere. The following examples are taken from the Weston experience, but similar developments occurred at all the theologates. Humanistic psychology made its presence felt most clearly in the number of scholastics asking for professional, psychiatric care, but it also appears in the ubiquity of psychological terminology, such as, "interpersonal confrontation and support" or "the personal maturing processes of the individual achieved on the level of dialogue and communication". The *SJNEws* for February 1973 reports that at Weston "Group Dynamics are available three nights a week for those who believe they can profit from these experiences of personal interaction. This type of experience has provided good opportunities for growth in personal freedom and confidence." The minutes of the New England province consultors (October 13, 1970) record, "The Consultors expressed an overall judgment of opposition to a proposal from Father General that each Jesuit scholastic in the third year of theology have a psychiatric conference and evaluation."[8]

After the West Baden theologate moved to North Aurora, the infirmarian reported fewer men using tranquilizers and also fewer seeing psychiatrists. He attributed this to the change in location and the changed (more relaxed) daily order at the new location. The same phenomenon was reported at the California, Missouri, and New England theologates after their change in location.

In the spring of 1966, Woodstock issued a formal policy allowing the clerical suit (instead of the cassock) to be worn to class, to meals, and to community prayer. If there were ever a formal policy on the use of secular clothes on these occasions, it has

---

[8] They agreed that the growing number of men leaving the priesthood shortly after ordination represented a serious problem, but they did not think that psychiatry had the answer.

escaped the memory of those involved and has left no trace in the files. At all the theologates the shift to secular attire seems to have been a gradual process of erosion: a few would begin the practice, perhaps on returning from outside the seminary, a few more would imitate the practice, and soon it would be acceptable. As late as 1968, however, the "Norms for Community Life" at Bellarmine (North Aurora) specified that "when outside the house, our formal and semiformal dress is clerical clothing. Until it is otherwise determined by the Provincial, permission is to be obtained to wear a tie."[9]

Changes in dress were among the more significant of lifestyle changes; but since considerable space is devoted to this subject in Volume II, further examples may be omitted.

All the theologates gradually lifted cloister from various parts of the house. This action by Alma came relatively late: "The Alma Community Council at its meeting of April 9, 1968 voted to open various parts of the house and grounds to non-Jesuits." Weston had modified cloister the year before and Woodstock even earlier.

The rush of change did not proceed entirely unquestioned. For example, in the spring of 1964 the General wrote to express his concern about the use of television at St. Mary's College. He said the practice did not agree with the approved norms and "the religious and academic life is certain to be hindered by such misuse." However, such protests by superiors only partially and temporarily delayed the opening of the theologates to the world.

A final aspect of changed life in the theologates should be at least mentioned here. This was the unprecedented number of men leaving the Society. While not a facet of lifestyle in the same sense as the other changes, the phenomenon did have a pervasive influence on the quality of life in the theologates. The young men all

[9] The norms were issued in a four-page document in February of 1968. The rector issued them in the morning and then left the house for the day. On his return, there were already a dozen notes from the scholastics under his door. The notes were polite but sharp explanations why his norms represented a vote of "no confidence" in the maturity of the scholastics and their ability to shape their own lives.

report the disturbance they felt, while superiors report uncertainty about how far they could prudently go in enforcing traditional lifestyles.

Published data show departures by province, not by house. Since men from more than one province may be living in a given house, the data by province do not adequately reflect the full psychological impact of departures on a particular community. Figure 2 shows departures (both faculty and students) from Woodstock College over the years 1965–73.[10] The period when the outflow was greatest was that between 1969 and 1972. A student entering Woodstock in 1969 would have seen nearly forty members of his community leave during his time at the college;[11] and these were not novices but long-term members who had been in formation on the average for at least ten years. This was perhaps the most significant of lifestyle changes, the change in commitment.

[10] The table reflects the experience only of those from the Maryland and New York provinces. Since there were a few men, both faculty and students, from other provinces living at Woodstock in these years, the table may understate slightly the total number of departures from Woodstock.

[11] In addition, he would have been aware of others with whom he had lived at Woodstock who had completed their work at the college but gone to their first assignment and then had left shortly afterward.

Figure 2

MEN AT WOODSTOCK COLLEGE LEAVING THE SOCIETY BY
YEAR OF DEPARTURE

Year	Maryland	New York	Total
1965	2	5	7
1966	2	4	6
1967	2	3	5
1968	1	4	5
1969	5	10	15
1970	4	5	9
1971	1	6	7
1972	2	6	8
1973	2	2	4

Source: Files of the Maryland and New York provinces.

VI

THE NOVITIATES:
PRINCIPLES AND STRUCTURE

Traditional Novitiate

The novitiate has the unique importance that attaches to all beginnings. The novitiate is the entrance gate, the screening process, which serves to admit only those who show a solid potential of becoming members of the order. It also provides the basic mold of values into which the rest of the long years of training are to be poured.[1] Generally referred to as "probation" and "formation" (G.C. 31, Dec. 8.12), these two functions of the novitiate do not refer to separate goals to be attained by separate means. They are rather the twin goals of all the activities of the novitiate. Each activity is expected to make its contribution to both the testing and forming of the novice. At the end of two years, the candidate makes his permanent decision to enter the order and the order agrees to accept him. (Actually, though the individual commits himself irrevocably to the order by his first vows at the end of the novitiate, the order does not fully commit itself until some fifteen or more years later at the end of the total formation period, when the individual Jesuit pronounces his final vows.)

The Constitutions have much to say about the admission and formation of novices. The chief prescriptions describe a number of "experiments" or "experiences" which all novices are to undergo

---

[1] As the wagon trains set off for the far west from St. Louis, their drivers were told, "Pick your rut carefully; you will be in it for the next thousand miles."

(Ganss 1970, 65–70). These experiences include making the full, month-long Spiritual Exercises of Saint Ignatius, working in a hospital (a very different sort of place than the modern institution bearing the same name), making a pilgrimage, teaching catechism, and performing chores about the house.

There were three objectives to be attained by these experiences: to exercise the novice in self-abnegation, to test him in circumstances when he was on his own responsibility, and to train him from the very beginning to serve others. Though the Jesuits are an apostolic or active order, the emphasis in these experiments was less on the importance of the work than on the formation of the novice in such ascetical virtues as poverty, obedience, and the acceptance of humiliations. For example, the objective of the Spiritual Exercises, as the title states, was "to conquer oneself". The work in the hospital was to enable the novice "the more to lower and humble himself". A pilgrimage was undertaken to introduce the novice to "begging from door to door" and to accustom him to "discomfort in food and lodging". The catechism was to be taught to children and people who are *rudiores* (the uneducated, belonging to the lower social classes). The work about the house was to be "in various low and humble offices".

The Constitutions made it clear, also, that the novices were to be introduced to a radical change of life. For example:

> Since communications from friends or relatives, whether oral or written, generally tend to disturb rather than help those who attend to the spiritual life, especially in the beginning, the candidates should be asked whether they will be content not to communicate with such persons and not to receive or write letters, unless the superior judges otherwise in some cases; also whether, during all the time they will be in the house, they will be willing to have all their letters seen, both those which are written to them and those which they send, thus leaving to him who holds this charge the care of delivering them or not, as he will judge to be more expedient in our Lord (Ganss 1970, p. 94).

(Unless otherwise indicated, all references in this section are to Ganss 1970.) Another prescription taught the lesson of separation even more dramatically. The novice was to be reminded of the gospel text "He who does not hate his father and mother and even his own life, cannot be my disciple" and of the "holy counsel that they should adopt the habit of saying, not that they have parents or brothers, but that they had them, showing thus that they do not have what they gave up in order to have Christ in place of all things" (p. 95). A similar ascetical value was taught in the following prescription:

> For the candidate's greater progress in his spiritual life and especially for his greater lowliness and humility, he should be asked whether he will be willing to have all his errors and defects and anything else which will be noticed or known about him, manifested to his superiors by anyone who knows them outside of confession; and further, whether he along with all the others will be willing to aid in correcting and being corrected, by manifesting one another with due love and charity, to help one another more in the spiritual life, especially when this will be requested of him by the superior who has charge of them for the greater glory of God (p. 95).

The values reflected in these passages and others like them (for example, p. 107, paragraph 101) underlay the rationale of the traditional novitiate. Its objectives had some similarity, *mutatis mutandis,* to the objectives of the boot camp of the U.S. Marines: (1) wean the recruits away from their previous lives; (2) weed out those who find the new life too hard; (3) exercise them in subordinating their personal wishes to the needs of the group, largely through the exercise of authority; (4) achieve the bonding experienced by those who have endured together. In the 1960s and 1970s, when the other branches of the armed services introduced changes generally similar to the changes made in the Jesuit order, the Marines maintained their distinctive toughness.

The traditional novitiate emphasized the so-called desert experience, after the examples of John the Baptist and Jesus and Saul, who prepared for their active ministries by first retiring to the desert. Back of this emphasis was the conviction that of the two dangers facing the members of the "active" orders—that of belonging too much or not enough to the world—in the long run worldliness was the greater danger, the more likely cause of personal shipwreck and diminished apostolic efficiency. The answering strategy was to sink the roots of the desert experience so deeply that they would continue to bear fruit for the rest of the Jesuit's life, even when he was living a life which in its externals bore no resemblance to the novitiate. It was hoped that by thus beginning with a life of more-than-ordinary prayer and mortification—especially these two—the Jesuit's whole later life would be similarly marked.

Central to the traditional novitiate was the strategy of gradualness. The Jesuit, destined for immersion in the secular world, was to start with almost complete detachment from that world, and then, step by step, reenter it to work successfully in it. After the desert experience of the novitiate, he spent the next two years in the juniorate, which might be the same house as the novitiate but in a separate wing, where he followed a very different life. He was engaged full time in secular studies and had more personal responsibility for the allocation of his time. The next three years found him completely removed from the novitiate environs in another house of formation called the philosophate, engaged in the study of philosophy and science and with still more personal responsibility for the allocation of his time.[2]

During the next three years he was completely immersed in the active life. In these years of regency, he taught full time, usually in a high school, and acted as a moderator for many of the school activities: athletics, newspaper, yearbook, students' and parents' clubs, and so forth. He was back in touch with all the usual secular books, magazines, and entertainments. While he was still some-

---

[2] Three of the philosophates were on or immediately adjacent to college campuses: that of the Missouri and Wisconsin provinces, in St. Louis, Missouri; that of the California and Oregon provinces, in Spokane, Washington; and that of the New Orleans province, in Mobile, Alabama. My own philosophate years (1931–33) were spent on the campus of St. Louis University, where I attended many classes with the non-Jesuit university students.

what more supervised than were those who had completed the course of formation, on the whole this period was a very effective test of the solidity of his sacral, eschatological values. He learned a great deal about himself and the strengths and weaknesses of his previous seven years of formation.

The next four years took the now not-so-young Jesuit back to studies and seclusion, to life in the theologate. These years offered the opportunity to strengthen any weaknesses disclosed by the preceding active years of regency.

The final year, tertianship, saw a return to novitiate life. The men, now in their thirties, withdrew from the active world for almost a year to deepen, or to restore, values inculcated in the novitiate. Starting with a repetition of the thirty-day retreat, the core of Jesuit life, the tertianship was equivalently another novitiate—hence its name of "tertianship", the third year of noviceship. The special significance that belongs to first and last places in a series attaches to the double novitiate experience in the total course of Jesuit formation.

In the time of Saint Ignatius, the details of novice formation varied over time and from place to place, but as the number of novices increased and experience was gained, the pattern of forma-tion stabilized. It had acquired all its principal permanent features by the time of the Second General Congregation (1565), which decreed that separate novitiate houses be established (a decision made by Ignatius though he did not live to carry it out) and that the two years of novitiate be devoted not to studies but to mortifi-cation and growth in spiritual perfection.

Continuity

After the suppression of the order (1773) and its restoration in the United States (1804), the dominant concern of the refounding Jesuits was to affirm the continuity between the old and the new Society. Robert Molyneaux, first superior of the restored Society in Maryland, wrote to the English novice master, Charles Plowden, to ask his help in starting the Maryland novitiate. In his reply, Father Plowden gave the time order he had introduced in England, making it clear that his main concern was to restore the daily order that he himself had known before the suppression. The order is shown in Figure 3. This traditional order was introduced in the United States and remained substantially unchanged until the early 1960s.

During the early years, when the United States was mission land to the Jesuits, practice sometimes lagged behind prescription. Novices, for example, were sometimes used in the hard-pressed schools. The prescriptions, however, remained in force—with the General constantly urging their implementation—and in modern times seemed to have been faithfully observed. In my own novitiate (St. Stanislaus, Missouri), for example, the daily order differed from the Plowden order only in minor details. We rose at 5:00 A.M. instead of 4:30 A.M., and we read Rodriguez after, instead of before, breakfast; but otherwise our daily order was practically identical with that used by the presuppression Society for centuries in forming Jesuits.

New Novitiate: Beginnings

Seeds of Change

General Congregation 31 clearly encouraged changes in the traditional novitiate, as may be seen in the following excerpts from the congregation's Decree 8. Article 12 lays down a basic principle: "For any spiritual pedagogy to be fruitful, it has to be adapted to those for whom it is meant to be used. . . . Throughout the indications set forth in the following chapters, this continued quest for adaptation is always presumed." Since it was generally understood that the character of "those for whom it is meant" had changed, this basic principle clearly envisaged corresponding changes in

Figure 3

NOVITIATE DAILY ORDER: THE ENGLISH NOVITIATE, 1806

4:30 Rise; morning visit

5:00 Meditation

6:00 Reflection; make beds

6:30 Mass

7:00 Rodriguez

7:30 Breakfast

7:45 Exhortation, recapitulated by novices in companies

8:30 Manual work

9:30 Study

11:00 Learning by heart

11:30 *ad libitum* [free time]

11:45 Examen

12:00 Dinner

12:30 Visit; recreation

1:45 Visit; *ad libitum*

2:30 Conference; or catechism or Tones [public speaking]

3:00 Manual work

4:00 Spiritual reading

4:30 *Imitation of Christ;* points [for meditation]

4:45 Meditation

5:15 Reflection; visit with vocal prayers

5:30 Rosary; *ad libitum*

6:30 Supper

7:00 Recreation

8:00 Litanies; points

8:30 Examen

8:45 *De Profundis;* retire

Source: *Woodstock Letters* 1956, 85:179.
Note: "Visit" refers to a visit to the Blessed Sacrament.

structures. The use of the term *indications* in place of *ordinations* or *rules* may also be significant.

Article 13 recognizes a need for "adapting the instructions given by St. Ignatius to our own times and having recourse when necessary to the recommendations of men skilled in psychology". Article 14 states "New experiments . . . ought to be prudently and boldly pursued." Article 19 warns: "A further necessity is that the novitiate's way of life be not so rigidly determined that the novices, lacking in all initiative, can hardly ever practice spiritual discernment." Article 22 states: "Although entrance into the novitiate should entail a real separation from the life previously led in the world . . . [the novices] should have sufficient social contact with their contemporaries (both within and outside the Society)." While the subordinate clause leaves the text of the Constitutions (see p. 195) in force, the main clause shifts the emphasis and clearly invites change. Article 23 specifies that "care must be taken to prevent the novitiate's being so remote from reality that novices' difficulties are there overlooked rather than solved." Taken in conjunction with its other invitations to effect changes in the system of formation (see, for example, pp. 40–41), G.C. 31 clearly belongs among the causes of the radical transformation made in the traditional novitiate.

Even before the congregation, however, there had been indications of a new era beginning. Three masters of novices, who had each occupied this position for many years, were asked by this writer if there had come a time when the novices had begun to be "different". Taking down old catalogues and reviewing the lists of novices year by year, all three separately came to the same conclusion— along about 1957 or 1958, the novices had begun to be a "different breed". Different in what way? They were more independent in their thinking, less willing to follow tradition, more likely to challenge authority.[3]

---

[3] When the same question was posed to two school teachers who had

There are other indications of this early change. For example, in 1966, in preparation for the Santa Clara Conference, the Alma theologians administered a questionnaire to the men in the first three years of theology asking them about their formation experience. One of the main conclusions referred to the novitiate: "The novitiate must be radically changed in concept if it is to cease being the regent's first and most serious obstacle to adjustment and happiness in his work in the Society." The men who supplied this conclusion would have been novices in the mid-1950s.

In June 1962, a young priest of the Detroit province wrote to his provincial after a visit to West Baden, "There is among the first-year philosophers at Baden a rather deep antipathy" toward their novitiate experience. These young men would have been novices in 1957 and 1958. In reply, the Detroit provincial wrote, "There is a decided difference in the young men of today and the young men of a few years ago."

Vincent J. O'Flaherty was a spiritual advisor at Fusz Memorial, the philosophate of the Missouri province, during the years 1961 through 1964. During this period, he found the same deep antipathy among the Missouri philosophers toward their novitiate experience at St. Stanislaus. When he was later appointed master of novices at St. Stanislaus, this experience influenced him greatly in deciding to make changes in the novitiate. (See Chapter VIII for other early indicators of change.)

Another, and unusually enlightening, example of this same perception—that young men coming to the novitiate were different beginning in the mid-fifties—is provided by the 1967 Santa Clara Conference (S.C.C. 1967, 2:1:132–33). J. Gordon Moreland, a spiritual director at the philosophate at Mt. St. Michael's and

---

taught first- and second-graders for many years, they returned substantially the same answer. They recalled clearly that the children they taught had begun to be different, in the sense that they had become more independent and less inclined to accept the teacher's word—whether as to facts or as to values. Attitudes that surface this early are clearly the result of some widespread cultural causes.

later to become the first of the new-type directors of novices in the Oregon province, prepared a paper for the conference in which he described a core group of scholastics covering about five years—the last two years of regency and the first three years of theology. He saw this group as marked by a confrontational insistence on change in almost all existing patterns of formation.[4] He recognized that the group had representatives both before and after itself, but he judged that these five years marked the core of the new breed. Since Moreland was writing in 1967, the beginning of this group, the third-year theologians, would have come to the novitiate about 1954, and the concluding cohort would have come to the novitiate about 1959.

Moreland noted that the young men coming behind this core group were different again, and he added the observation that his generation felt more at ease with these youngest Jesuits than with the core group. This same observation was voiced repeatedly in interviews I conducted all around the assistancy in 1974. (In a 1987 letter to the Chicago province, Provincial Robert A. Wild had occasion to distinguish not two, but three, groups of Jesuits: the pre-Vatican II group; his own group, the sixties people; the group who entered after the battles of the sixties had been won and who in their peacefulness felt more at home with their old grandparents than with their feisty parents.)

Early in 1962, the rector of St. Andrew's (a New York province novitiate) described for the provincial a small group of juniors with the following characteristics: a conflict between personal development and submission to authority; criticism of superiors; hypersensitivity to correction; a demand for greater exercise of personal initiative so that they should not be restricted by a schema of regulations that have been drawn up to cover their activities; a desire that they be consulted about the details of house discipline; a demand that the religious life be adapted ("a favorite word of theirs") to modern conditions of living. This latter

---

[4] He also saw them as marked by a romantic idealism and by a tendency to substitute natural for supernatural values.

characteristic, the rector reported, regularly took the form of characterizing the approach to perfection by way of mortification and self-denial as "negative and out of touch with the times". These characteristics, which became clearer and commoner later at Shrub Oak (the philosophate), belonged to men who had been novices before 1960.[5]

Another example, from the same source, that novices coming in during the 1950s showed signs of being a "new breed" is the following: of the 34 entering the novitiate in 1958, 23 (68%) eventually left the Society; of the 33 entering in 1959, 28 (85%) eventually left.[6] These are significantly higher ratios than had prevailed traditionally. Similarly, of the 1969 ordination class at Woodstock, over half left the order. These would have been novices in the mid-1950s and may have been different from the beginning.

Even before G.C. 31, the traditional novitiate was showing signs of serious strain. According to Donald J. Hinfey, socius (administrative assistant) to the master of novices at St. Andrew's, New York in 1965, the traditional novitiate was unchanged, "but it was not working". In an interview, he recalled some of the signs of "not working". (1) The thirty-day retreat did not seem to take with the novices, they simply turned off parts of it. (2) They were not talking easily to the master of novices nor to the socius. (3) They simply could not take anything like a public correction. (4) There seemed to be aspects of the life that they were not fully accepting because they could not believe in them; yet they were not sure enough in their own minds to reject them and hence had a feeling of guilt. They were confused. (5) All authority figures were suspect. (6) He also recalled a great dependence among the

[5] Apropos also is the remark of the then rector of Shrub Oak in 1960 (p. 46). The change he was describing would have occurred sometime before 1960.

[6] These data were contained in an unsigned, undated (probably about 1974) report in the Poughkeepsie files. I have not checked their accuracy, and of course a later survey might have shown an even higher rate of leaving. For similar data from other provinces and years, see Volume II.

novices on their peers; "they might as well have gone about wearing a sign reading 'don't reject me.'"

Brady/Plattsburgh

Not only individual novices but also at least two novitiates exhibited clear signs of a new era well before G.C. 31. The earliest was the New York province novitiate at Plattsburgh. This was the province's second novitiate, in addition to St. Andrew's at Poughkeepsie. Andrew Brady was appointed master of novices at Plattsburgh in 1955, which opened that year with forty novices but expanded to sixty the following year, when Plattsburgh received a contingent of New England Province novices from Shadowbrook, which had just burned down.

Plattsburgh was a new novitiate in several ways. It began in a newly acquired building, a former summer hotel, which provided private rooms for all the novices. A juniorate was established at the same time with an almost entirely new faculty. The rule of separation between juniors and novices was less strictly observed than usual because they were all in one building, rather than in separate buildings or in separate wings of one building.

Andrew Brady did not attempt to model Plattsburgh on the old New York province novitiate at Poughkeepsie. While he accepted most of the traditional house arrangements, simply because they were already in place, his general approach was not to do something because it was traditional but to do that which seemed to fit the current situation. For example, in 1956, he abandoned the formal titles by which novices traditionally addressed each other and directed his novices to use first names. He did this without discussing it with the rector, William J. Gleason, who had been master of novices at Poughkeepsie. There was a confrontation between master and rector, but the change perdured. Thus, while the juniors, who were the former novices of the rector, were held to the traditional rule, the novices could enjoy their new freedom—in the same house.

On some of his day-long business trips, for example into Canada, Father Brady would take three or four of the novices with him. On the return journey, all would stop for dinner, which included drinks. No junior had this experience. The three volumes of Rodriguez were still read by every novice, but only once; upon completing one reading, the novice was free to choose works from a modern spiritual library which the master had collected.

These and many similar small changes were significant primarily as reflecting a changed novitiate spirit, a spirit emanating from the master himself. In an interview with Father Brady, I asked him what made him different from the traditional master of novices. After some thought, he mentioned two experiences. One was the seven years (1947–54) spent as a teacher and student counselor at Le Moyne College; this gave him a feeling for what did and did not work with modern youth. The other was a year (1954–55) spent in Rome studying ascetical theology. This experience introduced him to the new trends in theology and to many European Jesuits whose values reflected those of the theologians—chiefly from France, Germany, and the Netherlands—later to be influential in Vatican II.

Besides the two explanatory factors adduced by Father Brady, two other factors may have been operative. In describing the values that guided him, Father Brady used some of the language of the new humanistic psychology which had begun to flourish in the 1950s. He wanted the novices to establish their identity; to get in touch with their feelings; to be open and at ease with other persons, including women; to value interpersonal affectivity; and to exhibit more spontaneity and initiative than the traditional system produced. The new psychology could very well have been one of the forces shaping the master and his novitiate.

In addition to these external influences, there was the internal influence of Andrew Brady's own personality. By temperament, he was open, direct, concrete, innovative, self-assured. These personal qualities undoubtedly influenced the way he reacted to the three external experiences and constituted a fourth reason why the Brady novitiate was different.

That not all the novitiates changed at the same time or in the same way is illustrated by the following incident. When Shadow-brook burned (1956), some of its novices were sent to Plattsburgh, some to St. Andrew's (New York), and some to Wernersville (Maryland). When they returned to a rebuilt Shadowbrook as juniors, they reported different experiences, which they memorialized in a play. Those who had been to Plattsburgh came on stage dressed in jaunty summer suits, with straw hats and canes. Those who had been to St. Andrew's entered dressed in traditional cassocks, with hands clasped and eyes cast down. Those who had been to Wernersville were depicted as falling between the two extremes.

This distinctive Plattsburgh flavor seemed to have perdured. When the Plattsburgh juniorate closed in 1964, about twenty of its members were transferred to Shadowbrook. In 1965, a community member at Shadowbrook wrote to the New England provincial, "Many of the Buffalo Juniors [from the Plattsburgh novitiate] stressed fraternal charity as opposed to religious observance (I believe that it is a false idea of charity), while the New England Juniors put more stress on religious observance. This has caused some friction in the Juniorate."

Predovich/Colombiere

The Predovich/Colombiere novitiate, while not as early as the Brady/Plattsburgh novitiate, was still well before the others. In 1963, Nicholas A. Predovich was appointed master of novices at Colombiere College in Michigan by the Detroit provincial, John A. McGrail, who was fully aware that Predovich disapproved of the traditional novitiate and if appointed would make changes in it. As Predovich remembered events, the provincial told him to do what he had to do.

In the Predovich novitiate, the cassock was required only in the chapel and dining hall—these two places at the insistence of the provincial, for here the whole community would be assembled, all in cassock, and the novices could not be allowed to be *that* different. The reading of Rodriguez was not required at all. Times for rising and retiring became flexible, the custom of a visitor (to see that the novices were at their prescribed prayer) was dropped, and neither incoming nor outgoing mail was monitored. Along with other changes, the ban on smoking was lifted, and the "experiments", especially those outside the novitiate, were given much more emphasis. To bring about his changes, Father Predovich used methods that would become characteristic of the 1960s, such as confrontation and a liberal use of *epieikeia* (the judgment that a given law is not applicable in the existing situation), mostly of the radical, Thomistic type (see p. 372).

When asked to explain why he saw things differently from many of his predecessors and contemporaries, Father Predovich listed three causes, all of which were also active in the case of Father Brady. One was the years he had spent in teaching theology to college students, an experience which convinced him that the traditional content and method of religious formation needed renovation.[7] Another cause was his two years of graduate theology at Woodstock College; this experience supplied him with some of the new theology he felt was needed. Still another cause was his experience with modern, "third-force" psychology (see pp. 249–52), which he had begun to know in the philosophate and which eventually exerted a strong influence on him.

Because the Predovich/Colombiere experiment was the first fully changed novitiate and because it exemplifies so many of the characteristic features of the 1960s, it is described more fully in Appendix 2. In this connection, the paper presented by Father Predovich at the Santa Clara Conference in 1967 should also be mentioned. In this lengthy analysis entitled "The Jesuit Novitiate— Past, Present, Future", based on three years of actual experience as

---

[7] By contrast, at least two of the novice masters in the mid-1960s had never worked outside a house of formation. Probably always a disadvantage, this limited experience posed a special handicap during a period of rapid change.

novice director, the author develops fully his rationale for the modern novitiate (S.C.C. 1967, 2:1:96–125).[8]

This prominence given to the Predovich novitiate should not be understood as implying that it was either typical or normative. On the contrary, it was at the extreme end of the spectrum and as such was not acceptable to most of the other novice directors, not even to those who likewise were introducing major changes into their novitiates. However, precisely because it was early and extreme, it provides the clearest example of the beginning of a new era.

In the later 1960s there was a marked trend toward changing the masters and other officials in the novitiates. The changes were all in the direction of bringing in more "liberal" people. In one case, the change was complete, involving not only the master, but also the socius, the rector and the minister of the community, and even a couple of priests and brothers in the community who were opposed to the new ways.

As mentioned earlier, the novitiate and the juniorate usually formed two parts of one community. If the two changed at different rates, as they tended to do in a period of rapid and general change, frictions within the community developed. In most cases, the juniorate tended to reflect the new values before the novitiate. For example, at the Sheridan (Oregon) novitiate, the novice master, Francis Mueller, often protested about the lax example the juniors in the house were giving his novices. Occasionally, the process was reversed, with the novices enjoying more freedom than the juniors. This occurred in at least three novitiates: at Plattsburgh under Brady, at Colombiere under Predovich, and to a lesser extent at Grand Coteau under John H. Edwards.

---

[8] A committee of four was appointed to assist Father Predovich in the preparation of his paper and to help guide discussion of it at the conference. Of the four, two (Richard Braun and Carroll Bourg) left religious life and the priesthood soon afterwards.

Committee of Spiritual Review

In 1964, the New York provincial, John McGinty, asked the Committee of Spiritual Review (see Chapter I) to reflect on how the traditional novitiate might be improved. His request stemmed from the unrest at St. Andrew's, the New York novitiate. Accordingly, at its third session (March 1965), the committee discussed the purpose of the novitiate and what changes might be advisable in its program of studies and experiments. John J. McMahon, a tertian master, reported that

> many of the Tertians feel that there is a need for a restatement of the purpose of the Society, and hence of the Novitiate. For example, they feel that the General Examen should be entirely rewritten in the modern idiom, and even much of it dropped completely. In their eyes, much of the Examen represents the 16th century ascetical viewpoint which has a dubious value for 20th century man (C.S.R. 1964–68, 3:8).

The minutes go on to record: "One Master of Novices tended to agree, noting that, for example, the attitude toward relatives and family, readily accepted in the 16th century, today seems harsh and unrealistic" (ibid.).

Concretely, the committee agreed that more stress should be accorded the experiments, more space should be made for studies, and the daily order should be less detailed, leaving more room for individual initiative. One master of novices, however, reminded the committee that "St. Ignatius was not primarily interested in the social apostolate aspect of the Experiments; rather he was interested in their ascetical aspect, i.e., as he conceived them as a testing in humility and in abnegation" (p. 3:12).

At about the same time (late 1964), one of the eastern provincials was writing to Vicar General John L. Swain and describing the novitiate situation as part of a general development that demanded change. It is an excellent illustration of how superiors were gradually becoming aware of and responding to the new era. Though the letter speaks of the changes underway as affecting "incidentals", a very different novitiate is clearly envisaged:

> There are difficulties and tensions occasioned in part by a different type of boy who is being received into the Society at the present time. The mentality encountered in the Theologate several years ago [1961], and last year [1963] at the Philosophate is now present both in the Juniorate and in the Novitiate. The boys accepted over the last four years [1960–64] are highly intelligent, and for this we must thank God, but by this fact they are more dissatisfied with pointless courses in the Novitiate and inadequate challenge during the juniorate. Also, they come from an atmosphere where there has been a great deal of independence, open criticism of practically everything, and the demand for change, which to some extent has been accelerated by the [Vatican II] Council. In a good number of cases home conditions have been poor; in some instances parents are separated and the boys have psychological problems.
>
> Now it seems apparent that some variations in the incidentals of traditional daily order must be made. This is being done at the present time, with special reference to the daily order, the program of studies, the matter covered in conferences and catecheses, the forms of recreation and the trials.

Wernersville White Paper

In 1967, the novices at Wernersville, the Maryland novitiate, produced a "white paper" presenting their views on what a modern novitiate should be. Edited by nineteen-year-old James J. Conn, the paper consisted of the reports of a half dozen task forces, each dealing with a particular aspect of novitiate life. "The idea of writing this group of papers had its genesis among the second-year novices during the long retreat."[9] The master of novices, Dominic Maruca, gave permission for the project; the socius

---

[9] The quoted material in this section comes from the reports of the task forces and from the editor's covering letter to Provincial Edward J. Sponga dated November 19, 1967.

followed its progress; and at two general meetings all the novices had an opportunity to discuss the first drafts of the task forces and to vote on the final drafts. An average of twenty-five (out of forty) voted favorably on the final drafts.

One task force dealt with spiritual formation. It first described the traditional theory, namely, "that asceticism in little things (e.g., schedule, attire, recreation, entertainment, outside contact, etc.) prepares us for asceticism in greater affairs". The paper granted that "this theory may have been effective in the past" but believed it was no longer applicable. "Today's generation of novices, because of their background, have [sic] difficulty deriving profit from structured means which have no obvious connection with their end." The paper recommended that more areas of the novitiate life be "left to the individual's discernment after consultation with the superior." These areas should include "arrangement of spiritual duties, type and frequency of outside apostolic activity, type and scope of reading, entertainment and recreation, engagement in social and cultural activity, visits and correspondence, scheduling of time".

Another task force dealt with community attitudes and had much to say about the relationships between novices and superiors. The desirable relationship was described as one of "mutuality" to be achieved largely by "dialogue". A major obstacle to such a relationship was declared to be the attitude on the part of superiors that a traditional set of rules must be enforced. "Because the superior is seen as the champion of the status quo, he appears to be on the 'other side' and the result is not dialogue, but a debate of opposing forces." Furthermore, the traditional office of superior no longer sufficed to meet modern needs: "An experienced psychologist should be made available for group as well as individual consultation."

A task force dealing with studies in the novitiate argued vigorously that since the Maryland province had embarked on a five-year program calculated to produce a college degree, even in the case of those who entered directly from high school, studies in the modern novitiate would have to be accorded more—much more—importance than they had enjoyed in the traditional novitiate.[10]

A task force dealing with social developments stated, "We must recognize that the social position of the religious in the Church and in society as a whole has changed radically" and warned that without more contact with the outside world "the novice's identity and vocation as a celibate religious remain largely an abstraction until after his vows to this life have been made." The paper made three recommendations: "(1) a wider range of reading materials (secular journals, social and natural sciences, art); (2)... allowing novices to visit other houses in the province for short periods; and (3) more films, contemporary music, and greater attendance at lectures, plays, concerts, and other cultural and social functions outside the novitiate."

In an appendix, the white paper made two additional observations that were characteristic of the period. (1) "Novices and superiors should have great respect for the personal talents, interests, and tastes of each individual member of the community" and should not "expect each novice to fit into a preconceived mold". (2) After stating that the community "must create an atmosphere of confidence and peace in which the novice can discern his vocation", the paper made the not atypical recommendation: "Deep personal relationships between novices should help create this atmosphere of peace."

In submitting their paper, the novices were like underclassmen advising the faculty on how a college should properly be conducted.[11] Underlying this precocious action seems to be the

[10] In the Midwest, this goal was normally met even in the author's time. I entered the order in 1926, from high school, and by 1931 had earned an A.B. degree. This was normal procedure in the traditional system, involving no special effort.

[11] The novices themselves were conscious of the incongruity; the task force on spiritual formation included the remark "Beginners in the spiritual life ought to comment on 'spiritual formation' with great humility, recognizing that especially in this area their lack of experience might be an impediment to their insight."

assumption that in a time of general change the young have better, or at least more workable, values than their elders. The assumption would seem to find some validation in the similarity between their recommendations and the general direction which all the novitiates eventually took. The novices, of course, had the guidance of such earlier discussions as those of Santa Clara Conference, to which, as a matter of fact, they appealed at one point in their paper.

Twenty years later, in 1987, when James Conn was director of planning at Fordham University, he was asked how the editor of the white paper now looked on those days. He replied, in a letter to the author:

> In retrospect, I am very grateful for the traditional formation I received from Father Maruca at Wernersville. Of special value were his emphasis on the scholarly tradition in the Society and his intimate and extensive acquaintance with various dimensions of Christian spirituality. Change in the regimen was inevitable, but I am ironically pleased that I missed the big wave, even if I helped to provoke its coming.

Rationale

The new novitiate differed from the traditional novitiate in both objectives and, especially, methods. As to objectives, while both new and old novitiates could accept the phrase *contemplative in action* as a description of the ideal Jesuit and a definition of objective, they understood the phrase somewhat differently. In the new novitiate, the kind of prayer implicit in the term *contemplative* made less use of a vertical, conversational relationship to "God up there" and more use of a horizontal relationship which found God in all things by dealing with all things, especially with persons. The second term of the phrase, *action*, was not changed in definition, but it did become a larger part of the whole, both in the sense of occupying more of the novice's time and in the sense of being accorded more weight.

The most obvious changes introduced in the new novitiate

were those in method. Basic to all these changes was the decision to abandon the technique of gradualness. From the beginning, the novice was to be introduced to the kind of Jesuit life he would be leading permanently after the temporary process of formation was completed. The minutes of the fifth session (July 26–28, 1965) of the Committee of Spiritual Review reported the following:

> A few of the members present expressed the opinion that the novitiate and juniorate could provide more in the way of maturing experiences. Experiences such as rebelling against something, learning to control the use of alcohol, the responsibility of caring for oneself while away from home, and the development of a normal Christian relationship with those of the opposite sex were among those being considered (C.S.R. 1964–68, 5:7).

That the report limited these opinions to "a few of the members present" may be significant. It was recognized that this method would expose the still unformed novice to danger, but the risk was accepted as furthering both the probation and the formation of the novice. Tempted thus more severely, unsuitable candidates would be revealed more quickly and surely.[12] Moreover, a novice formed in an atmosphere of freedom, and hence of individual responsibility, would develop a character of real strength, one not dependent on the protective atmosphere of the novitiate. (When Thomas F. Walsh was novice director at Poughkeepsie and Syracuse [1967–73], he made considerable use of the principles expounded in a work by Carl Rogers, *Freedom to Learn.*)

In 1973, when he had been the California novice director for two years, Leo P. Rock addressed a sixteen-page report to the province explaining what the new novitiate was all about. Entitled "What We Do and Why" and written in response to the many

---

[12] In the third session (March 1–3, 1965) of the Committee of Spiritual Review, Dominic Maruca, a master of novices, "noted that according to Father Polanco Saint Ignatius used the Experiments with some reserve. He did not bother to send good, fervent novices on pilgrimage or to the hospitals because experience showed that their fervor led them to exhaust themselves. Rather he used these, particularly the pilgrimage, with those who were already half out of the Society as a kind of final test" (p. 12).

accusations leveled against the novitiate, the report is one of the better explanations of the new rationale. It reflects most of the characteristic emphases of the period, as the following examples illustrate. The novices must be put in positions where they can be tempted, make mistakes, and learn from their mistakes (Rock 1973, 4; the remaining page references in this section relate to this work). In one form or another "the basic problem" has been a "negative self-concept" (p. 5). The novitiate life should be similar to Jesuit life after the novitiate: "It seems pointless and uneconomical for men to learn to live in a way that will simply have to be unlearned when they leave the novitiate" (p. 6). Flexibility in a novice is essential because in the modern world endless change is inescapable: "The novices have to learn to live with an insecurity that their predecessors did not have to face" (p. 7). Finally, the young men who come to the novitiate nowadays are simply *different*. Even communication with them must be different; what they say, the director must decode, and what he says to them, he must encode. Rock further states, "I *must* importantly rely on the young for advice because they, in fact, best understand the world of the young" (p. 13).

The report closed (Rock 1973, 15, 16) with two significant observations. First, Rock identifies the ultimate test of what he has been doing: "The final verdict on the value of what is being done now at Montecito [the novitiate] will be the men themselves who come to priesthood and live their Jesuit lives. The final verdict, then, will be in only long after I have departed the scene."[13] Then he ventures an evaluation: "Because of them [the novices] I have no fear about the future of the Society of Jesus. They are better men than I ever was or ever will be."

----

[13] "Many people visited Father Pedro Arrupe, former General of the Society of Jesus, during his last days, his last hours, including some 'representing [his] 12 years of novice classes (from which, someone recalled, no one who took vows had ever left the Society)'" (Flaherty et al. 1991, p. 7).

Novitiate Location

Much the same considerations—economic, academic, and ascetical—
were operative in the relocation of the novitiates as in the relocation
of the theologates. The economic consideration carried exceptional weight in the case of the novitiates for several reasons. In
the first place, the drop in the number of novices was greater, both
absolutely and relatively, than the drop in any other stage of
formation. Moreover, since the novitiates were not shared houses
of formation, as were the theologates, but each province had its
own novitiate, the decline in numbers left each province with
very few novices. Finally, a change was occurring in the relationship of the novitiate to the juniorate. Traditionally, each novitiate
was paired with the juniorate, roughly the same size. A common
arrangement was to house the novices in one wing, the juniors in
another, and to place common facilities, such as chapel and dining
room, in a connecting building. When the new collegiate program was inaugurated (Chapter VIII), and the juniors moved away,
the already diminished community was halved. The economic
logic of the total situation was compelling: some change would
have to be made either in the location of the novitiate or in the use
of the novitiate property.

Academic considerations also advised some change in location.
As the white paper of the Wernersville novices argued, to achieve
the goal of a college degree in five years, the novices, most of
whom had entered from high school, would have to acquire at
least a year's college credits during the two years of novitiate. So
either the novitiate staff would have to be augmented, or the
novices would have to attend courses outside the novitiate. For
many reasons, including the dwindling number of novices, the
latter seemed the more practical choice, a choice that could best be
implemented by relocating the novitiate near a college campus.

The decision to relocate was motivated also by the belief expressed
in many places—for example, repeatedly at the Santa Clara
Conference—that the Society had fallen into "monasticism", from
which it had to be extricated. A move from the quiet country into

the bustling city would be a first step in that direction. All the reasons advanced for the lifestyle changes described in Chapter VII also supported the proposal to move the novitiate into closer contact with the occupations, interests, and entertainments of what were termed "real" people. Proponents of relocation could quote G.C. 31 (Dec. 8.22): "Superiors should provide that the novices . . . have sufficient social contact with their contemporaries, both within *and outside* the Society" (emphasis supplied).[14]

As may be seen in Figure 4, all but three of the novitiates chose to change their locations. The three exceptions were in the provinces of Maryland, New Orleans, and California.

In March 1965, the Maryland novices had been given the opportunity to express their views on the question of location. The great majority, nearly all, preferred to remain in their beautiful and extensive location at Wernersville, Pennsylvania. A few years later, however, the province reached a formal decision, approved by the General, to relocate. After spending a year searching for a suitable new home, the province had second thoughts and decided to keep the novitiate at Wernersville. It was found that the novices, who in the new system were out of the novitiate at least half the time anyway, needed a quiet time in the country between their exacting experiments in the cities. A flourishing spiritual center, mostly for retreats, was established to make use of the property not needed for the novitiate.

(In July 1990 Father James A. Devereux, the Maryland provincial, announced the closing of the novitiate at Wernersville effective in

---

[14] On the other hand, Father General Arrupe showed concern for maintaining a balance. In a letter of March 11, 1970, to Father Charles McDermott, vice provincial of the Missouri province, the General wrote that there should be a significant degree of solitude for the novices, not only during their retreats but during the entire course of the novitiate. He added, "This idea or prescription you will find phrased in *Renovationis Causam,* numbers 2 and 25, II; hence, it is far more than the law of the Society." *Renovationis Causam* contains papal prescriptions for the renewal of religious orders.

the fall of 1991. Once again there were second thoughts. His successor, Edward Glynn, shortly after taking office [September 1990] announced that the novitiate would remain at Wernersville, pending time for a discussion of the problem with the other eastern provincials.)

The California province had grown so fast that a division of the province was contemplated. As a first step, a second novitiate was opened; this was at Montecito near Santa Barbara, a lovely spot close to the ocean, some 250 miles south of the original novitiate at Los Gatos. When the number of novices dwindled, the first adjustment was to close the Los Gatos novitiate, which became a retreat center, a retirement home, and the provincial residence, and to concentrate all California novices at Santa Barbara (1963).

Then followed a lively debate whether to close Santa Barbara also and relocate the novitiate somewhere closer to the poor or to a college. The final decision resembled that of Maryland: continue to house the novices at the rural location but send them out much more often than formerly. Later, in 1981, a separate house was opened at Menlo Park in Los Angeles, which the first-year novices (and staff) occupied from January to May and there devoted themselves, four afternoons each week, to work with the poor and the sick.

The New Orleans province also seriously considered relocation. At one time, in the mid-1960s, the master of novices, Robert Rimes, sent a letter of inquiry around the province asking opinions on the matter. The answers were generally in the negative. In the end, the province elected to keep the novitiate at Grand Coteau while sending the novices out on more and longer experiments and employing the unused facilities for a spiritual center.

Figure 4

LOCATION OF NOVITIATES 1965–75

Province	Located (in 1965)	Moved	Masters of Novices
California	Los Gatos and Santa Barbara, CA	The two novitiates were combined at Santa Barbara in 1968[a]	R. Drendel (1963–67), J. McAnulty (1968–71), L. Rock (1971–74)
Chicago	Milford, OH	North Aurora, IL (1969)	R. Murphy (1958–68), P. Robb (1968–70)
Detroit	Clarkston, MI	Clarkston, MI (1970), Berkley, MI (1971)[b]	N. Predovich (1963–68), J. Toner (1969–72), F. Houdek (1972–78)
Maryland	Wernersville, PA		D. Maruca (1964–68), G. Aschenbrenner (1968–78)
Missouri	Florissant, MO	Kansas City, MO (1970)[c], Denver, CO (1975)	C. Hunter (1956–66), V. O'Flaherty (1966–73), E. O'Brien (1973–82)
New England	Lenox, MA	Weston, MA (1970), Boston, MA (1971)	T. O'Callaghan (1960–67), R. Bertrand (1967–72), D. Lewis (1973–75)

New Orleans	Grand Coteau, LA		
New York[d]	Poughkeepsie, NY	Syracuse, NY (1969)	R. Rimes (1965–75)
			M. Neylon (1955–67)
			T. Walsh (1967–73)
			D. Hinfey (1973–77)
			F. Mueller (1962–68)
			G. Moreland (1968–75)
			J. Sheehan (1956–66)
			J. Sheets (1966–67)
			C. Murphy (1967–70)
			J. Hoff (1970–75)
Oregon	Sheridan, OR	Portland, OR (Jan. 1974)	
Wisconsin	St. Bonifacius, MN	St. Paul, MN (1970)	

[a] During the period covered by the table, the masters of novices at Los Gatos, the original novitiate, were J. Kelly (1964–67) and J. McAnulty (1967).

[b] The Chicago novitiate was closed and the novices sent first to Colombiere College in Clarkston, Michigan and, later, to Berkley, Michigan, both in the Detroit province.

[c] The first-year novices went, for a short time (a few months in 1970), to Clarkston.

[d] The Buffalo province was set up separately from New York in 1960 but was reunited with New York in 1968. A second novitiate established in 1954 by the New York province at Plattsburgh, New York, functioned as the novitiate of the Buffalo province until 1967, when it was closed. The masters of novices at Plattsburgh were Andrew Brady (1955–61), Francis Courneen (1962), James Demske (1963–66), and R. C. Braun (1966–67).

Relocated Novitiates

The Chicago province moved its novitiate four times in two years. The major move was in 1969.[15] Its nine novices, who would have rattled around in the cavernous reaches of Milford (the juniors were also leaving to be part of the new collegiate program), were moved to North Aurora, Illinois, and became part of the theologate/philosophate community there. Since the numbers of both theologians and philosophers were shrinking, there was ample room for newcomers. When North Aurora was closed in 1970, the handful of novices were temporarily housed at Holy Family parish in Chicago.

In June of 1970, the provincials of Chicago, Detroit, and Missouri agreed to establish a joint novitiate at Colombiere College, then the novitiate of the Detroit province. A year later, Colombiere was closed as a novitiate, and the Chicago province joined the Detroit province in moving novices to Loyola House at Berkley, Michigan, just outside the city of Detroit. (The Wisconsin province had declined participation in the merger because of its recent decision to move its novices near the campus of St. Thomas College in St. Paul, Minnesota.)

Colombiere, opened in 1959 in Clarkston, Michigan, was the original novitiate of the Detroit province.[16] It was a large, beautiful location that by 1970 had only six novices and had already lost its juniors to the collegiate program recently established at the University of Detroit. When, in 1971, the novices moved to their new home in Berkley, Michigan, Colombiere remained operative as a Jesuit retirement home and a spiritual renewal center.

---

[15] A dozen years before, the province had so many novices that it had to send some to Florissant, the Missouri province novitiate; also, the novitiate had built a costly new chapel.

[16] In an interview, Marshall Lochbiler, former rector at Colombiere, said that though he was on the original search committee that found the Colombiere property he advised against its selection. He preferred something nearer to the University of Michigan so that the young men, especially the juniors, might attend university classes. He also mentioned that Colombiere was the first structure built as a novitiate that provided all novices with individual rooms.

In 1969, Vincent O'Flaherty, the master of novices at Florissant, Missouri, wrote to the provincial to say, "Florissant has a long history and means much to many in the province. Nowadays the younger men like to return here for weekends and for retreats and tridua. I think the province would suffer a spiritual and psychological loss were it ever to completely close down or be sold."[17] But closed down it was the following year, after 148 years of continuous existence, the only Jesuit house in the U.S. with so long a record. (The closings of Florissant and of the one-hundred-year-old Woodstock were striking proofs of the end of an era.) In his last letter to the provincial of Missouri, the rector wrote, "We declined from a community of about 200 in 1961 to less than 20 in the summer of 1971. What happened?"

In 1970, Missouri sent its five first-year novices to join those of Chicago and Detroit at Colombiere, but they proved unable or unwilling to accept the situation at Colombiere. They found the amount of structure, diminished though it was, artificial and offensive. For example, they insisted on the naturalness of talking, quietly, at table during the thirty-day Spiritual Exercises. Tension between them and the novice director reached a point where it became necessary to return the Missouri novices to their own province. (Of the five, only two finally took vows, and both of these later left the order.) There, together with the second-year novices, they formed the first contingent of the new novitiate in Kansas City, Missouri. This novitiate was later (in 1975) moved to Denver, Colorado.

Shadowbrook, the New England novitiate at Lenox, Massachusetts, burned completely in 1956. It was rebuilt at considerable cost and was reopened in 1958, only to be abandoned in 1970. As in other places, the juniors had been siphoned off into the new collegiate program while the number of novices had diminished drastically. The novices were moved first to Weston (1970), which the theologians were leaving, then to Boston (1971). This latter

---

[17] At one point, in 1967, the Missouri province was discussing the desirability of moving both the novitiate and juniorate to St. Mary's, Kansas, which had been left empty that year when the theologians moved to St. Louis.

was a truly urban location—on a city street, with no grounds whatsoever. In an article written for the *SJNEws* (January 1973), Raymond Bertrand, novice director, listed three reasons for the move:

> It was hoped that a less remote place would allow the novices to develop a more apostolic dimension to their earliest Jesuit prayer, and that a smaller place might meet the needs of the fewer and older men who were applying. With dwindling numbers at Shadowbrook, the staff diminished; so it was also in view of finding more Jesuits willing to assist in teaching, directing, and living with novices that the move to Boston was made.

To the question "Has the move been a success?" Bertrand returned an affirmative answer, but he did add:

> I say this in spite of several drawbacks [that] life in the city poses for the novitiate. It takes longer for some men to tune in to the interior life or to curtail some of their customary recreations. The availability of very interesting apostolic and recreational activities disperses a lot of our energy for contemplation and leads to much wasted time and tension. It also has a negative effect on serious reading.

Much later, in 1988, the novitiate was moved again, this time to a former convent in the Boston neighborhood of Jamaica Plain. The location on Boston's Newbury Street had been judged to be too affluent; the Jamaica Plain location was in a poor neighborhood consisting largely of blacks and Hispanics.

The New York province relocated early (1969), closing St. Andrew-on-the-Hudson after sixty-six years of service and moving its thirty novices to Syracuse, New York, where they occupied the former residence of the Buffalo provincial, which was adjacent to Le Moyne College, a Jesuit school. This proximity was one of the chief reasons for locating in Syracuse, and for almost a decade the New York novices spent the first year of their novitiate attending the college on a full-time basis.

The last province to relocate its novitiate was Oregon. Though a decision to move had been made in 1961, the move did not actually occur until 1974. In a letter to the province dated November 1972, the provincial, Kenneth J. Galbraith, explained why a move had to be made:

> The problem is the novitiate's remoteness which frustrates the goals of early formation in at least two ways. First, although Father General has urged the team concept in novice formation, such a goal is scarcely realizable when the novitiate is located so distant from Jesuits who might assist in the program while they carry on other apostolates. Secondly, I can see the need to form men in a setting more in keeping with their future as Jesuits. Since that future would center on urban apostolates, it is fitting that early formation begin in an urban environment. For this reason it is my wish that the present novitiate program be moved from Sheridan [Oregon] and relocated in an urban setting at the earliest convenience (Galbraith 1972, 16).

An additional reason, of course, was the declining number of novices. Already in the fall of 1966, six years before the provincial's letter, the Sheridan community had shrunk from 107 to forty-seven. By 1972, Oregon had only twenty-four novices. The novitiate was finally relocated in January 1974, when it was moved from Sheridan to Portland, Oregon. The novices, who at the time of the move numbered thirty, were housed in a former convent, resembling in this respect the novices of the Chicago/Detroit novitiate.

New Selection Process

There seemed to be general agreement throughout the assistancy that the new breed, while probably more knowledgeable than its predecessors, was less mature emotionally. This description surfaces everywhere. For example, in the *Survey of American Jesuits* the question was asked, "What do you see as the most important reason for the departure from the Society of someone you know who has left?" The most frequent reply (31%) was "emotional immaturity".[18]

However, in a letter to the author, dated June 30, 1988, Andrew Brady of the New York province expressed some disagreement with this general impression: "In view of my experience with younger Jesuits, both at Plattsburgh and in other positions, I am inclined to think that the statement concerning the new breed being less mature emotionally than their predecessors may be much too general and perhaps hard to prove." Since Father Brady's experience with younger Jesuits was unusually broad—besides being master of novices at Plattsburgh (1955–61)—his judgment must be given weight.

Nevertheless, spiritual directors and superiors, whether on the East or the West Coast, in the Midwest or in the South, all include this characteristic in their descriptions of modern youth. The description appears frequently in the Santa Clara Conference (for example, in 2:1:227–28). Finally, it seems to have been accepted by G.C. 31: "To this end, sufficient human maturity is a requirement for candidates. Experience has shown, however, that in our own time affective maturity has become more difficult for adolescents" (Dec. 8.13). This perception had a number of effects on the novitiate. One was the decision—not universal and not absolute, but quite general—to accept only candidates who had been out of high school for a year or more. Thus, the typical novice became an older person, frequently a college graduate.[19]

Another effect was the development of explicit, detailed criteria for determining whether an applicant should be considered for admission to the novitiate. An assistancy-wide attempt in this area

---

[18] The next most frequent replies were "desire for independence" (16%) and "desire to get married" (13%) (S.C.C. 1967, 1:214).

[19] There is, however, a growing opinion that some high school graduates might well be accepted. The opinion is supported by two observations: (1) modern culture is so inimical to a religious vocation that a budding vocation needs the more favorable environment of the novitiate; and (2) the modern novitiate is so open to outside contacts that the young man will still be subjected to quite enough real-life testing.

was published in May 1981 by the Jesuit Conference Committee on Formation. Entitled "Criteria for Entrance into the Society of Jesus", this was a three-page document accompanied by a five-page questionnaire to guide examiners in the kind of information they should be looking for.

A third effect was the expanded use of psychological testing. Though some use of such tests had been made earlier, the practice was expanded greatly in the 1960s and subsequently.[20] Opinions and practice varied regarding these tests. There was general agreement that they could be useful in detecting the more extreme psychological aberrations. Beyond that, judgments differed considerably between provinces and over time. The Missouri province, for example, employed a much more elaborate psychological screening program before 1974 than it did later. The change came about as a result of an evaluation program that included consultation with a half dozen psychologists and psychiatrists, Jesuit and non-Jesuit. (A full account of the evaluation is in the files of the Missouri province.)

Some provinces used only Jesuit psychologists; but the majority of provinces used lay psychologists whom they instructed in the meaning of Jesuit life and in the kind of candidate they wished to attract. In at least two cases, the Jesuit administering the tests himself left the order. Most provinces seemed to put the main emphasis on interviews rather than on tests. A few used the psychologists only for interviewing, not for testing. There seemed to be general appreciation of the unavoidable subjectivity. For example, the Jesuit who accepted or rejected applicants might be inclined to favor those who tested much as he himself would have tested. Similarly, personal values might be operative in the instructions given to the psychologist as to the kind of novice the province wished to admit.

A 1967 doctoral dissertation found little correlation between

[20] William C. Bier, of the New York province, a psychologist, began such testing about 1950 and seems to have been the first to establish a formal province program. He has an excellent article explaining such a program in Lee and Putz 1965, 170–204.

the tests and later performance of the Jesuits who were admitted.[21] Several directors of novices reported that they did not look at the test results of those admitted until they had formed their own opinions of the novices. Though there has been a lowering of the earlier high expectations of the value of psychological testing, the practice has been found useful and is probably here to stay. G.C. 31 explicitly approved the use of psychologists: "Provision should be made in each stage of the training for personal maturity, especially of the emotions; the advice of trained psychologists should be used when it is necessary" (G.C. 31, Dec. 9.5).

A final effect traceable to the perception of delayed emotional maturation was the decision by many provinces to establish some kind of prenovitiate program.[22] In 1968, the Committee of Spiritual Review, consisting of representatives from the provinces of Maryland, New York, and New England, voted (27 to 2) to recommend to the provincials the establishment of a prenovitiate program. The expected result of such a program was "a heightened appreciation of the human values freely renounced by the religious vows, and also an experiential perspective enabling one to distinguish common human problems from those proper to religious life as such". The Committee of Spiritual Review had in view the typical applicant, who at that time was a high school graduate and might be in need of more maturing.

The Chicago province evidenced an early interest in the prenovitiate. Provincial Robert Harvanek saw the scheme in operation in India and was impressed by its potential as a vocation

[21] Entitled "Initial Psychological Prediction as Related to Subsequent Seminary Performance", this dissertation was the work of David W. Carroll, S.J., assistant to Father Bier at Fordham University. This study did not investigate the test results and the perseverance of those tested—probably for the reasons given in Lee and Putz 1965 (see p. 198).

[22] In a 1969 document, the Sacred Congregation for Religious recommended a series of stages in the formation of seminarians and religious. The first suggested stage was a kind of postulancy program to precede acceptance into the formal formation program.

developer. On his return to the United States, he introduced it into the Chicago province. Paul V. Robb, novice director in the Chicago province 1968–70 and a psychologist, was a strong proponent of the idea. He considered most modern young men to be incapable of making a perpetually binding commitment after only two years of preparation. A prenovitiate program would add a third year of preparation.

All the provinces took some steps in the direction of a prenovitiate. In the 1970s the Missouri Province had something called the Associates Program, whose members were listed by name in the province catalogue. While still living at home, these associates were in frequent contact with Jesuits and were given regular spiritual direction and sometimes financial assistance in pursuing their studies. Twice a year the associates were brought together for a three-day meeting that included "a short retreat, talks by active Jesuits in the apostolates, and visits to the various houses of the Missouri province".[23] After some years, this prenovitiate program became less formal, and the names of the associates were no longer carried in the province catalogue.

All provinces at some time or another established at least a candidacy program intended for those who were interested in the Society but were not yet ready to make a formal application and for those who had applied but were judged not yet ready to embark on a formal novitiate. These candidacy programs varied in details from province to province and within a province from time to time. Usually, in each of the larger cities a man would be assigned to care for these interested young men. The candidates in a given region would sometimes be invited to meet together for a weekend of prayer and socializing. Only very rarely was financial support supplied to the candidate. The New York province used a system, in connection with academic formation, that was a kind of prenovitiate program, insofar as it postponed by almost a year the time when the novices pronounced their vows (p. 232).

There was some continuing discussion whether the novice should

---

[23] Letter to the author from Joseph Damhorst, S.J., dated July 23, 1986.

be required at the end of two years to take perpetual vows. Among those who found the modern young man less mature than his predecessors, some drew the conclusion that two years was not enough time to choose between making a total irrevocable commitment and leaving the order. The suggestion was made that the Society, like some other religious orders, should make use of temporary vows, to be followed eventually by permanent vows. This suggestion received no official approval. On the contrary, Father General Arrupe was very forceful in declaring that the first vows must be perpetual.

On one occasion, while visiting the Maryland novitiate in 1973, I had a long conversation with three of the second-year novices about the perpetuity of the vows. None of them wanted the Society to change to temporary vows, and all of them were planning to take their vows at the end of the year and to mean them for life. However, when we got into more theoretical aspects of the issue, they manifested some ambiguity. One man, twenty-five years old, said that what one was permanently committed to was actualization, and that if life in the Society failed to provide actualization, it would not be a rejection of vows to leave. Another, twenty years old, seemed to accept this. The third, twenty-one years old, demurred. He was quite clear that he wanted to be bound irrevocably because he thought he needed this kind of help, the help provided by an outside pressure.

I put this question to them: Suppose that in taking your vows you were committing yourself in the same way that a Catholic man is when he is validly married; would you still take the vows?

All of them thought this an excellent way of getting to the heart of the matter. Each of them in his own way clearly indicated that he would take his vows under those conditions. There seemed to be no hesitation, as though this were a new view of the vows. Rather, they reacted as though they were saying, "Yes, this is a good way of describing how I look on the vows." (Note: as of 1990 all three were still members of the Society.)

VII

FORMATION IN THE NEW NOVITIATE

Once the candidate was admitted as a novice and established in the newly located novitiate, the central task of formation could begin. Changes in this task can be conveniently described under three headings: academic, apostolic, and lifestyle.

Academic Formation

In the new novitiate, studies became more formally academic and were allotted more time. They were given a more formal academic shape for several reasons. There was the immediately practical objective of gaining credits toward a college degree. Though this concern antedated the 1960s,[1] it grew markedly in the later period. There was, secondly, the desire to improve the quality of the novices' studies. In the traditional novitiate, especially in the earlier years, faculty was somewhat limited by the country situation, and studies could be interrupted for various reasons—for example, to pick fruit or stack hay on the farm.[2]

---

[1] During my own novice years (1926–28) at Florissant, Missouri, I earned—without my being aware of it—a number of credits, chiefly in Latin and English. Concern for credits seems to have begun somewhat earlier in the Midwest than in other parts of the country.

[2] In November 1966, the rector of Colombiere wrote to the province procurator asking for additional funds because expenses had increased: "The stepped-up academic program in the novitiate has reduced the manualia [manual

Finally, studies were intended to accustom the young man to balance the conflicting demands of prayer and work. As one novice director explained in a letter to the General, "I have insisted on maintaining a real academic challenge in these courses because I feel the novices need to learn how to integrate serious academic work with their spiritual and community life. . . . [Academic experience] will also ease the transition from the novitiate into studies, often a difficult and painful adjustment for many."

The new locations of the novitiates made it possible to have Jesuits living at the novitiate who had a principal job elsewhere but who could also provide, or at least guide, courses for the novices. This arrangement had the additional advantage of providing multiple role models for the novices. The novitiates also began to hire lay teachers. At Colombiere, for example, several had been added to the faculty at least by 1964, and perhaps earlier. In many cases, the new locations put colleges within reach of the novices. For example, some of the novices from Loyola House (Berkley, Michigan) attended the University of Detroit, while New England novices attended Boston College. The new novitiate of the New York province, in Syracuse, New York, went furthest in this direction: the first-year novices enrolled full time at the adjacent Le Moyne College. They did not make the thirty-day retreat until their second year, and they took vows in their third year, by which time they were in the collegiate program, outside the novitiate. This change was initiated by Novice Director Thomas F. Walsh on his own authority the year before the novices were moved to Syracuse. The General permitted this arrangement reluctantly, as an experiment, but after a decade ordered it to end.[3]

---

labor] hours of the novices and made it necessary for us to engage outside maintenance help. In the past three months we have hired three additional men, one for the dining room and kitchen and two for general maintenance."

[3] Beginning in January of their second year, the novices of Upper Canada took a full load of courses (five subjects) at the University of Guelph for two semesters in the regular B.A. program. At the meeting of the English-speaking masters of novices in Rome in 1970, the Canadian master reported that the

The courses taken by the novices varied a great deal, depending not only on the novitiate (whether, for example, it was connected closely with a college) but also on the individual novice. As novices grew to be fewer in number, older in age, and more educated, the course of studies could be and needed to be adapted to each individual. All the novitiates provided courses in theology, especially sacred Scripture, and in the Constitutions of the Society of Jesus. Nearly all, also, provided a course in the history of the Society. For a time, beginning in 1964, Fr. William Bangert moved from novitiate to novitiate teaching a course based on his book, *A History of the Society of Jesus.* Altogether, he taught in six provinces: New York, Maryland, New Orleans, Missouri, Wisconsin, and California. The Chicago and New England provinces provided similar courses taught by their own historians.

In 1967, a survey of the novitiate situation conducted by the Jesuit Educational Association (see Figure 5) found that the number of credits accumulated by novices in the various provinces varied from zero (New England and New York) to seventeen (New Orleans) for first-year novices and from six (New England) to thirty (Chicago) for second-year novices. Total credits earned in both years varied from six (New England) to forty-six (New Orleans). Thus, in some novitiates the young men accumulated a full year or more of college credit. Most of the credits were earned in theology and languages; but they were earned also in other fields, such as music and communications. At the time of the survey, the number of hours allotted to study in preparation for classes also varied considerably. In one novitiate, the ratio was a half hour of study for one hour of class; in another the ratio was one to one, while in several others the ratio was two to one.

During the period of the sixties, the relation of academic studies to the work of the novitiate was discussed widely with a variety of views expressed. At its third meeting (March 1965), the Committee on Spiritual Review reported, "This point was discussed

---

novices tended to overemphasize studies to the neglect of their spiritual life during the first semester and to pull out of this pattern in the second semester.

Figure 5

UNIVERSITY CREDITS EARNED BY NOVICES
IN SOCIETY OF JESUS, 1967

| | Credits Earned | | |
| | First | Second | |
Name and Location of Novitiate	Year	Year	Total
St. Charles College, Grand Coteau, LA	17	29	46
Milford Novitiate, Milford, OH	13	30	43
Novitiate of St. Isaac Jogues, Wernersville, PA	15	24	39
Bellarmine College, Plattsburgh, NY	11	23	34
Sacred Heart Novitiate, Los Gatos, CA	14	16	30
Jesuit College, St. Bonifacius, MN	15	15	30
College of the Queen of Peace, Santa Barbara, CA	12	15	27
St. Stanislaus Seminary, Florissant, MO	12	14	26
St. Andrew-on-Hudson, Poughkeepsie, NY	0	24	24
St. Francis Xavier Novitiate, Sheridan, OR	7	14	21
Shadowbrook, Lenox, MA	0	6	6
Colombiere College, Clarkston, MI	?	?	?

SOURCE: A Report on the Revision of the Program of Studies for Ours as It Is Developing in the American Assistancy, 1967. This report was presented to the 1967 annual meeting of the Jesuit Educational Association.

at some length, with no clear unanimity of view emerging" (C.S.R. 1964–68, 3:19).

At the Santa Clara Conference, Nicholas Predovich, novice director at Colombiere, urged that studies be given a high place in the novitiate:

> To many directors, the ascetical practices that were in the past considered a very important part of our training as religious— penances, fasting, refectory penances, bodily chastisements, etc. —though still considered valid forms of penance, are now considered more proper to the monastic forms of religious life. . . . Concretely, then, finding God in one's studies is as important as finding God in one's prayer (S.C.C. 1967, 2:1:115–16).

While approving of a more solid program of studies in the novitiate, General Arrupe voiced a warning:

> In the fervor of their desire for academic excellence, our young men must remember that such is not the prime goal of the novitiate. Often they need a reminder that time is needed to lay a firm foundation for the spiritual life. It is some of the more talented scholastics and young priests who are now having temptations against their faith.[4]

Apostolic Formation

In the allocation of the novices' time, the new emphasis on academics had to contend with a new emphasis on apostolic activity. While the allocation of time between these two varied continuously —between novitiates at any one time and within any novitiate over time—in general more time was probably spent by more novices on the nonacademic experiments. Altogether, experiments kept the novice outside the novitiate for about half of the total two-year period.

[4] From a letter to Robert Rimes, S.J., director of novices of the New Orleans province, dated May 26, 1966.

The experiments took a great variety of forms, such as the following: working in hospitals, old peoples' homes, and soup kitchens; going on a pilgrimage; or working on one of the multitudinous ministries of the Society, in a school, for example, or in a parish, or on one of the missions. A few of the assignments were somewhat unusual, such as traveling to India or Alaska or, in one case, participating in the Democratic National Convention.

G.C. 32 (1964–65) emphasized the apostolic element in the total formation process. Articles 137 through 149 assign unmistakable importance to this element and note especially two aspects of apostolic formation. One was contact with the poor: "An experience of living with the poor for at least a certain period of time will be necessary for all, so that they may be helped to overcome the limitations of their own social background" (G.C. 32, Dec. 6.10). The other was contact with functioning Jesuit ministries: "Contact, information and cooperation with other communities and works, especially those in the same province, should help young Jesuits to experience the whole province, indeed the whole Society, as an apostolic body united in one spirit" (G.C. 32, Dec. 6.16).

From the start, opinions differed regarding the relative emphasis to be accorded the inner and outer aspects of the novitiate life. For example, in the first issue of the New England *SJNEws* (February 1971) a front-page article described the new novitiate enthusiastically, largely in terms of the novices' many and imaginative apostolic activities. In the next issue (March 1971), one of the novices wrote to say that he found the article "embarrassing and misleading" because it had represented the novitiate as primarily "an organ for social activism".

All the novitiates inaugurated and maintained a high degree of social activism, though as time went on some directors began to share the thought expressed by Father Jean-Yves Calvez in regard to G.C. 32 (see p. 95) that the shift in emphasis from the internal to the external had been "perhaps too much". For example, after describing the enlarged work of his novices among the marginated, one novice director writing to the General in 1984 said:

I am happy for this improvement in our program. Nevertheless, I have been concerned that this emphasis on more social consciousness and engagement is not done at the expense of building the solid foundation of prayer and virtue so necessary and indispensable to perseverance and growth in religious life. . . . Some novices can use their engagement in social causes as a kind of compensatory mechanism to fill up personality deficiencies, to avoid growth issues, and to acquire a kind of derived identity based on their activities. My concern is that being a Jesuit becomes their primary identity, not being a social worker or a peace activist.

Lifestyle

Other changes in the novitiate may be grouped under the general heading of lifestyle. They range from essentials like prayer to incidentals like personal budgets. Of their very nature, such changes are less clear-cut than the changes, say, in location or in studies. Moreover, because lifestyles were in constant flux, the description of one novitiate will not necessarily fit another novitiate at the same time or the same novitiate at another time.

The practical solution is to emphasize general trends that were more or less common to all the novitiates, to concentrate on the earlier period when the changes were most clearly marked, even extreme, and to use as examples those novitiates which were most distinctive. The changes were governed largely by a perception "of the *de facto* pluralism in which Jesuits are living out their lives as Jesuits". This perception had resulted in "a movement from below within the Society to break through the straitjacket of the monolithic structure suggested in phrases such as '*the* course' or '*the* novitiate'." The quoted phrases are from a paper presented at the first meeting (January 22, 1970) of a new group called Eastern Inter-Province Committee on Formation. The paper, entitled "Plan for Novitiate", was prepared by Anthony Meyer with the support of Felix Cardegna and Joseph Whelan.

Silence

A change slight in itself but significant in its impact was the abandonment of the rule of silence. Traditionally, silence was the rule at all times outside of recreation.[5] The requirement that all necessary speaking be done in Latin acted as an additional brake on conversation. In the 1960s the rule of silence was criticized as being monastic and repressive of human growth. It was judged to interfere with the proper development of someone destined to work outside the walls of the religious house, and it was seen as inhibiting one of the most cherished values of the period, warm interpersonal relationships.

In 1970, the rector of one of the Midwest novitiates, writing to General Arrupe, reported:

> The living out of the ideal of silence and recollection, helpful to the spirit of prayer, is not as good as it was some ten years ago when I was here as a teacher. On the other hand, the lessening of strain and tension is noticeable too, and the more easy manner of dealing with each other in a friendly way may offset the loss of an atmosphere of recollection.

The change in silence began the way most changes of the period began—less by an official declaration than by an ever-expanding use of *epieikeia*. The reports of superiors everywhere—rectors, ministers, provincials—began to contain worried comments that the rule of silence was less faithfully observed and was difficult to enforce. There were also, however, some officially sanctioned early relaxations in the rule, for example at the Plattsburgh novitiate under Father Brady and at the Colombiere novitiate under Father Predovich. In the New Orleans province, the director of novices, Robert Rimes, informed his provincial (December 1965) that he was relaxing the requirements of silence

---

[5] When my parents visited me in the novitiate and juniorate at Florissant, it was this prevailing atmosphere of silence that most struck them. In their reports to the other relatives, it was silence they tended to emphasize as "different".

in certain specified situations, chiefly in the classroom areas and in the scullery (a room for cleaning and storing dishes and culinary utensils) during the work period.[6] In 1966, six novitiates (Buffalo, Detroit, Missouri, New Orleans, New York, and Wisconsin) did *not* have any rule of speaking Latin outside times of recreation; the other six novitiates (the two in California and those in Chicago, Maryland, New England, and Oregon) did have this rule. Of these latter, three wished to change (Chicago, Maryland, and New England). In this respect, as in most others, the novitiate of the Oregon province retained more of the traditional practice longer than did the others.

Daily Order

The new daily order bore little resemblance to the traditional one (pp. 162–64). In most novitiates, it became minimal. There was no set rising time or retiring time. Meals—cafeteria style—were available over an extended period of time and were not obligatory; there was, of course, no reading at meals. The time of the liturgy varied but was never early in the morning; usually it was just before lunch or just before dinner. Times for prayer, including meditation and the two examens (reviews of conscience), were entirely the responsibility of the individual. Such group prayers as the rosary and litanies simply disappeared. Some classes were common to all the novices, but others varied according to individual needs. Forms and periods of recreation were entirely an individual choice. When Father Arrupe met with the English-speaking directors of novices in Rome in 1970, he instructed them, according to the minutes of the meeting: "In the noviceship there ought to be an *ordo diei* [a daily order] which requires the novice to

---

[6] At the same time, he made a number of other changes in the daily order. For example, the reading of Rodriguez was reduced to selected treatises once a week.

submit himself for a period to a precise and monotonous life. And there should also be (at least in some periods of the noviceship) a due liberty in which he can organize himself." Subsequent developments saw the balance shift notably in the direction of the second goal.

Dress

In the traditional novitiate, the novice was given a Jesuit cassock (an ankle-length black garment with close-fitting sleeves, held together by a cincture) which he wore always and everywhere, except during manual labor and outdoor recreation.[7] The universal cassock, like the universal silence, tended to create an all-enveloping religious atmosphere.

The change in dress was made in all the novitiates, but at various times and in various stages. The first move seems to have been at Colombiere, where under Father Nicholas Predovich the novices were permitted to doff the cassock everywhere except in the chapel and dining room and substitute a black, coat-like garment. In most novitiates, the first step was a permission, not a command, to put off the cassock. For a time, the result was a split among the novices. I recall, for example, being present at Wernersville when the community held its annual party for the workers and friends of the house. The notice on the bulletin board specified merely "formal attire". At the party, the novices were divided into three groups of about equal number: those wearing secular clothes, those wearing clerics, and those wearing cassocks. In some novitiates, for a while, superiors supplied cassocks to those requesting them; later when the supply was exhausted and no more were ordered, novices who wanted a cassock had to ransack

---

[7] The cassock was washable but, even so, showed the marks of this severe wear. When the novice had his rare visitor, he could go to the brother in charge of the clothes room and borrow a new cassock to wear for the occasion.

attics and storerooms. Eventually, there were no more to be found. But even before that, in some novitiates, superiors explicitly forbade the use of the cassock.

Outside Contacts

In the new novitiate, the young man maintained much more contact with the outside world than formerly. He could write letters freely, without having to secure permission each time. Also, both the letters he received and the ones he wrote were unopened. Visits from his parents and former friends were encouraged; at some novitiates, the novice was allowed to go home for a couple of days after Christmas. Describing the situation at Colombiere in 1967, the father minister wrote to the provincial:

> The whole area of dealings with externs is undergoing considerable change. The young men have many more opportunities of meeting and working with lay people through their apostolic efforts, school and the like. There is more freedom with respect to visitors. Visitors now attend our liturgical services and eat in our dining room. The Juniors on occasion go out with their visitors and even go home at certain times. A woman is working in the kitchen, another in the dining room, another in the infirmary. This is necessary because the young men do not have time to do the housework as they used to, and laymen are not available.

The novice had full access to radio and television[8] and to magazines featuring news and entertainment. He was free to attend whatever films he wished and that his very limited allowance would cover. At one eastern novitiate, the majority of the novices attended a performance of the musical *Hair* with funds provided by the rector of the house. The novices considered

[8] The assistant director of one of the eastern novitiates remarked to me that on his shopping trip in town that day he had purchased two radios for the only two novices who had come without them.

Hair to be an important social statement of the new values, including a statement on nudity. These changes were introduced one after another, beginning in most novitiates with the late 1960s.

In the new novitiate, there were many more contacts with women than formerly. The novices met women regularly in their college classes and in the various experiments outside the novitiate. Such contacts were considered a desirable change for several reasons: they provided a realistic test of the novice's ability to keep the vow of chastity that he would pronounce at the end of the novitiate; they would prepare him to work with women in the ministry of the Church; and they would help develop in the novice the feminine values that are part of a balanced personality. A few of the novices inevitably fell in love as a result of these contacts and had to work their way through the difficulty.

Most novices also had more direct contact than formerly with the marginal sector of society. They worked in the wards of mental hospitals, in soup kitchens, and with the aged poor. In the pilgrimage experiment, the pilgrim novice experienced, at least partially and briefly, the powerlessness of the poor.

Novitiate Family

The ratio of staff to novices changed markedly. In my novitiate (1926–28), the master and his socius (assistant) were responsible for almost one hundred novices. Teachers from the juniorate would come over a couple of times a week to teach Latin or speech, but everything else was handled by the master and his socius. By contrast, in 1971 at Loyola House, the Detroit/Chicago novitiate, the ratio was seven staff members to sixteen novices. Most of the staff had other obligations outside the novitiate, but they were also available for work with the novices. The staff included an assistant director whose function was similar to that of the principal director; they would both, for example, direct some novices through the thirty-day retreat.[9] Some staff members were primarily teachers, but all were available for consultation. This team approach was approved by the General.

The new novitiate used the team approach for a variety of reasons. It provided the novices with multiple role models; it was thought that it provided a better academic formation; and it facilitated an individualized development, one that adapted the general values of the novitiate to the unique personality of each novice. In a notice dated April 22, 1975, Joseph Whelan, provincial assistant for formation in the Maryland province, explained the "current formation dynamic", which required that not more than twenty-five novices be in a single community. "This altered dynamic, which involves greatly increased time and attention from the novitiate staff, aims at taking each of your brothers precisely where *he* is and who *he* is, both at the time of his entrance and through each subsequent stage of his continuing growth in Jesus and in apostolic community life." When the novice directors of the United States met in 1971, they discussed the ideal size of a novitiate. The majority thought that a total of fifteen novices (in both years) was too many for a single novitiate. Only the two directors from the West Coast saw twenty to thirty novices as workable and even desirable.

The style of governance of the new novitiate was more open, flexible, democratic. The white paper of the Wernersville novices (1967) was only one of the more dramatic instances of participatory decision making. Well before that event, in March 1965, the Wernersville novices were invited by their master, Dominic Maruca, to express their views on five topics: the experiments, studies, location of the novitiate, a time order for the day (whether it should be uniform for all or adaptable by individuals), and the preferred relationship between master and novice. The great majority—nearly all—of the novices preferred the country rather

[9] In 1965, the Committee of Spiritual Review discussed the possible multiplication of directors. Some members expressed opposition to what they felt would be a duplication of responsibilities; they expected many difficulties to arise. Actually, the expected difficulties seem not to have been encountered.

than the city for the location of the novitiate. A slight majority thought a flexible time order would be better, but a substantial number thought it wiser to have a fairly fixed time order. There was no clear vote as to what the relationship of the master to the novices should be, but many more preferred "paternal" to "fraternal".

In 1967, the Florissant, Missouri, novices put together some novitiate guidelines. They explained that the guidelines were "largely the result of collaboration" and that "the various sections of our guidelines were substantially composed and formulated by different novices, while the project was overseen by our Assistant Director." The guidelines changed much but left more unchanged.

In all the houses the novices expected to be consulted on many matters, and were. Smoking was the subject of community discussion in a number of novitiates. In another instance, the question was debated whether to get a V.C.R. for the house television set. A majority of the novices voted to purchase a V.C.R., but the staff thought otherwise, and the staff prevailed. The novices accepted this decision without murmur. As early as 1963 at Florissant, the novices were having round table discussions. At one of these they discussed the differences between followers of the letter and followers of the spirit of the rule. A year later, the discussions were still continuing, with the master reporting to the provincial, "We have been having regular discussions of certain points of discipline, and I have been challenging them with more and more personal responsibility." At Loyola House, in 1972, the novitiate community held a discernment workshop on the question of fasting. They decided that the members of the community would fast up to six days a week, each according to his capacity, and with the approval of the superior. Many more examples, from all parts of the country, could be added to this list of novice participation in governance.

Another change in governance concerned permissions. Whereas in the traditional novitiate an extensive web of permissions exercised a constant influence on the novice, in the new regime permissions were needed only for the more unusual actions, and even these could be presumed in the case of genuine inconvenience. The one system sought to sink roots of humble dependence; the other, to produce fruits of creative responsibility. Responsibility was one of the most frequently mentioned virtues of the period. From G.C. 31 to provincials to novice directors and to novices themselves, responsibility (or a growth in it) was offered in explanation of most proposed changes.[10]

Relationships among novices became much more influential in the new novitiate. Many superiors remarked on the greatly increased influence of the peer group. At a meeting of the Committee of Spiritual Review in 1964, the New York master of novices reported, "The novice today feels extreme pressure arising from the demands of the group. He wants the recognition of the group and is despondent when he does not receive it." The minutes of the meeting record that the committee agreed that the novices tended to be independent of superiors but very dependent on the group; the problem for superiors was how to get them to stand on their own feet, to be inner-directed rather than other-directed.[11]

Closely connected with this development was the greatly increased need felt by the novices for dialogue—with superiors and, especially, with each other. As one master reported to his provincial in 1965, "The novices in the past five years seem to need more and more time for longer dialogue. They seem to have to do much more talking than before." In an appendix to their white paper, the Maryland novices objected to a strict time schedule because it did not leave enough time to develop "deep personal relationships" and thus enable each novice "to help his brother in getting to know himself". At Wernersville, the novices asked for, and got, doors on their rooms in place of curtains so that they could talk to each other in privacy. The novices were acquainted with and used the reasons provided by humanistic psychology for

[10] In the decrees of G.C. 31, for example, such usages occur in 9.6, 14.12, 17.11, and in many other places.

[11] The minister of one of the novitiates in 1965 remarked to the author that some of the juniors seemed immature. They would write notes to each other saying, literally, "I love you" or "May I see you? I need you." To the minister, the young men seemed to lack "manly courage to meet the problems of their lives".

"interpersonal sharing at the deepest levels". The ability and willingness to be "open with each other" became a critical norm by
which to judge desirable development during the novitiate.

In the New England novitiate, a heavy chain-smoker dropped
the habit completely under pressure from his fellow novices, who
were concerned about his health. As one superior reported to the
provincial, "The modern novices are very frank with each other
about such issues."

Penances

The traditional novitiate had a number of penitential practices
that were dropped in the 1960s. The discipline (a whip of small
cords to be used on the back) and the chain (a metal circlet with
dull points to be worn around the waist or thigh) were formerly
given to each novice during the thirty-day retreat. Thereafter, all
the novices used these instruments on prescribed days. After the
novitiate, the use of the instruments was to continue but at times
determined by the individual in consultation with his spiritual
director.[12]

The discipline and chain disappeared by gradual steps in most
novitiates. At first, each novice was given the instruments, but
there was no time prescribed for their use. Later, the instruments
were given only to the novice who requested them. Eventually,
their existence was not mentioned to the novices, nor were they
available to the rare novice who might hear of them and request
them.

The traditional novitiate provided also for various forms of
public penance, performed usually in the refectory and after
obtaining permission. The novice would confess a fault—"take a
culpa"—while kneeling in the aisle of the refectory at the begin-

[12] The new view of such penances was given typical expression by Novice
Director Nicholas Predovich during the Santa Clara Conference (S.C.C. 1967,
2:1:115).

ning of the meal. This public confession of fault might be accompanied by the practice of holding the arms extended or followed by kissing the feet of some of the community. On very rare occasions the superior might require such a penance. This was called a "pinned culpa", that is the superior might direct that someone's fault be read out from the pulpit in the refectory.

Gradually, all these practices fell into disuse—as the young men began to criticize or ignore them and as superiors ceased explaining, promoting, and providing them. Here, as in most of the developments of the period, the change proceeded by unpremeditated steps.

Budget

When the novitiates were out in the country, novices normally had no need for money. If in some unusual situation a novice needed money, he was given the exact amount required for the situation. An example would be a novice going to town to see a doctor; this was unusual because doctors and dentists normally came out to the novitiate. Most of the new novitiates, on the contrary, gave each novice an allowance which he could use at his discretion. The total allowance was the sum of budgeted items, but the novice was free to shift amounts between items. Normally, the novice made some accounting of his expenditures—in more or less detail, depending to some extent on the novitiate but to a greater extent on the novice himself. One would simply list "entertainment", whereas another would list "two movies, one magazine". The purpose of the new system was to develop responsibility both in the ordinary business sense and in the religious sense of preparing the novice to keep the vow of poverty he would pronounce at the end of the novitiate.

Spiritual Reading

For generations, spiritual reading had been identical for all Jesuit novices throughout the world. During a half hour each day, the novice read a work entitled *Practice of Perfection and Christian Virtues* by Alphonsus Rodriguez, a Spanish master of novices who composed the work in about 1600. When a novice completed the three volumes of "Rodriguez", he started over again. Translated into many languages, the work provided all members of the order with a common basic experience; even the stories, contained in sections entitled "The previous doctrine confirmed by sundry examples", were known to all and recognizable by a phrase or a single word.[13]

In the new novitiate, Rodriguez was perceived as out of date. Though there does not seem to be any written analysis of why Rodriguez was judged unusable, unofficial oral criticisms were directed to its old-fashioned style (even in the new English translation prepared in 1929 by Joseph Rickaby, S.J.), to its "monastic" values, to a psychology that did not reflect the new findings in that field, and to a theology which did not reflect modern scriptural exegesis or modern sexual morality.

Even while still officially prescribed, its use began to decline. In the Brady novitiate, after a novice had read the volumes once, he was free to choose other books for his spiritual reading (see p. 206). Some years after this system was already in operation, John Edwards, novice master at Grand Coteau, wrote to the General for permission to depart somewhat from the strict diet of Rodriguez. In a letter dated February 4, 1963, Vicar General John Swain replied, "After the three volumes of Rodriguez have been well assimilated, Your Reverence may assign other books to the novices." In the Predovich novitiate, the change was accomplished by the simple expedient of not mentioning Rodriguez. For a little while,

---

[13] Rodriguez was used also by many other religious orders, especially those which had modeled their constitutions on those of the Society.

some of the second-year novices continued to read it, along with a few of the first-year novices who had heard of it from the second-year men, but soon the work was seldom mentioned. In time, all the novitiates discontinued the practice of reading Rodriguez, and the typical modern novice has not so much as heard of the work. In its place, each novice director assembled what he considered to be a good spiritual library, and each novice, with direction, selected what seemed best suited to his particular needs and interests.

Psychology

The late 1950s saw the development of what came to be called humanistic or third-force psychology. "Third-force" psychology— so-called because it was neither psychoanalytical nor behavioristic— was a movement popular in the 1960s; its chief proponents were Carl Rogers, Abraham Maslow, Rollo May, and others. In this movement, attention shifted from the abnormal to the normal, from the pathological to the healthy. Humanistic psychology asked "What is a healthy psyche? How is one achieved?" This development brought psychology directly into relationship with ascetical theology, whose goal of human perfection includes a healthy psyche.[14]

Some of the goals and methods of the new novitiate show the influence of this development. In 1974, the Chicago Province Assembly requested Howard Gray, rector-director of Loyola House, the combined Chicago/Detroit novitiate, to describe the principles governing the recently established novitiate. In reply, Gray wrote: "The essential guideline for staff (our principle) and novices (their goal) is a developing maturity as persons sincerely

[14] As early as July 1961, a member of the community at Colombiere was writing to the provincial, "From various indications it would seem that direction and consultation with the juniors do not bear on ascetical matters but rather on social and psychological aspects of adjustment."

seeking to find God's will as Jesuits. It involves: self-knowledge and self-acceptance, the ability to inter-relate, and the growing desire to serve the Church and the family of man."

In contrast to this psychological language, the Jesuit Conference Committee on Formation, in a document approved on April 3, 1981, expressed itself as follows:

> In this document, we have tried to use religious and Ignatian language rather than to depend on any one psychological theory.... Thus, he [the novice] must be a man ... who has let Jesus die for him, a man who has come to know Jesus intimately, to love Him and to want to follow Him in serving the Father's cause with as much abandon as Jesus himself had. And the Jesuit follows Jesus in companionship with other Jesuits in a real union of minds and hearts.

The new novitiates recognized the importance of psychology in the daily formation of the novices. At their annual meeting in 1966, the novice masters of the United States and Canada made the following recommendation to the provincials: "The training of novice masters should include preparation in psychology, not only of a theoretical nature, but even more importantly of a practical (clinical) nature." Later that year (August 3) Father General Arrupe wrote in reply: "With the Masters I agree that spiritual directors should have a knowledge of practical psychology and psychiatry but they should take care not to substitute psychological for spiritual direction. At least for most of the Masters, *clinical* formation does not seem necessary."

The practice of utilizing the services of professional psychologists and psychiatrists in the formation of the young men increased significantly during this period. The extension of the practice to even novices and juniors led some community members to ask why the spiritual directors could not handle such cases or, if the cases were that severe, why the young men had been admitted before their difficulties had been resolved.

Increasingly, novice directors began attending psycho-religious institutes, sensitivity sessions, and similar activities of humanistic psychology. Also, the novice library began to include some of the popular works in the field. The Oregon novitiate, for example, though one of the more conservative in the assistancy, made significant use of such works. As described in the province's *General Exchange,* of November 1973:

> Regular instruction in asceticism ... [includes] contemporary non-fiction works such as Toffler's *Future Shock,* Roszak's *The Making of a Counter Culture,* Freire's *Pedagogy of the Oppressed,* Ochs' *God Is More Present Than You Think,* Skinner's *Walden Two,* Reich's *The Greening of America,* Harris' *I'm O.K.—You're O.K.,* Berne's *Games People Play,* Land's *An Overview,* Frankl's *Man's Search for Meaning,* and others.

Several of these were in the mainstream of popular third-force psychology. In one novitiate library in the East, I noticed on the shelves at least six copies of Thomas A. Harris' *I'm O.K.—You're O.K.,* a book that reflects one of the most characteristic features of the period, a declaration of self-worth.

The style of decoration used in chapels and private rooms seemed to reflect the optimistic, here-and-now mood of third-force psychology. In the chapel, there was a general tendency to replace statues by brilliant banners and abstract paintings.[15] In their private rooms, the modern novices exhibited all the popular banners, pictures, and buttons of the average college student. Religious pictures or statues were very rare. The room decorations favored a form of art that was optimistically psychological, cheery rather than strong, secular rather than sacral. They constituted one of the more obvious, even striking, differences between the new and the traditional novitiates.[16]

[15] In the early years, when the novices were part of a larger community which did not share the novices' tastes, the novices' insistence on making these changes led to some dissension within the community. Later, this source of friction disappeared.

[16] In my own novitiate, each novice had a desk, a straight-back chair, and a tiny kneeler—these in a large, open room called an ascetery occupied by about seventy-five novices. One's bed was in another large, open room divided by sliding curtains into cubicles about 8' × 6'. Each cubicle had a small cabinet,

The growing influence of psychology is probably reflected in the following two descriptions of the same novice master by successive provincials. One provincial, of the old school, writing to the General, reported in 1968 with obvious approval of the master's analysis of certain objective deficiencies in the novices:

> It has been found that it would be better to spend some additional time in grounding the novices in fundamental Catholic doctrine, about which they sometimes speak in very confused terms. Next year, the Master of Novices . . . plans to concentrate on aspects of Catholic doctrine to make sure that the novices have sound ideas about the Incarnation, the Mass, the Sacraments and so forth.

A few years later, in 1973, a new provincial, younger and of the new school, writing of the same man reported to the General: "He tends to objectify various problems which the novices have and remains distant from very personal problems which are of concern to the novices."[17] The master was changed the next year.

The objection to objectifying problems reflects a feature of the new psychology with its emphasis on nondirective counseling. This distinctive technique is designed less to measure the counselee against objective criteria than to increase the counselee's self-understanding. Instead of giving the novice the three volumes of Rodriguez with the instruction to mold himself on that ancient pattern, the master was rather to lead the novice, after an appropriate amount of instruction about goals, to a modern asceticism consistent with and congenial to his own unique personality.

---

about 3′ × 2′, in which the novice kept all his clothes. There was nothing else. The Jesuit Museum at Florissant, Missouri, re-creates the Jesuit novitiate exactly as it was at that time.

[17] The newer provincial also criticized the master for not emphasizing more the "reform of social structures".

Spiritual Exercises of Saint Ignatius

The principal novitiate experience has always been the Long Retreat, the thirty days spent in the Spiritual Exercises of Saint Ignatius. It was chiefly by this means that the novice was taught the essence of being a Jesuit. This feature of the novitiate did not change; the Exercises remained the centerpiece of the novitiate, the chief instrument of formation.

Certain changes did occur, however, in the timing and the method of presenting the Exercises. Whereas formerly the novices began the thirty-day retreat about a month after entering the novitiate, in the new novitiate this beginning was postponed for five or six months. (The General, a former novice master himself, was opposed to any delay longer than six months.) The postponement enabled the novice to become better acquainted with the religious life, especially with the art of prayer, before embarking on this major enterprise, this ascent of an ascetical Mount Everest.

The Missouri province was unique in having its novices make the Exercises twice, once in each of their two years of novitiate. Vincent J. O'Flaherty began the custom in 1966, his first year as master, continued it through 1970, but did not reinstate it after the turmoil of 1970 when the Missouri novices were first sent to Colombiere as part of the Chicago/Detroit/Missouri joint novitiate and were then withdrawn to start a novitiate of their own at Rockhurst College. In a letter dated March 22, 1988, Father O'Flaherty explained to the author:

> I felt that it was important for the novices to make the Exercises soon after their entry because I used to think (maybe I still would if I were on the job) that first-year novices didn't psychologically or spiritually begin their novitiate until they made the Exercises and also because I felt the Exercises were the best possible school of prayer for them. But I did not feel that they (most of them, at least) were in a position to make a definitive choice of a state of life in the Society until they'd had some experience of living in the Society both in the novitiate

residence and out on experiments. This was my reason for having them repeat the Exercises.

One important change was made in the method of giving the Exercises. In the novitiate of my time, when the single master might have forty or more first-year novices, the retreat was conducted by the method of group conferences. The master would develop "points" for meditation for the entire group; each retreatant would then make his own prayer on the subject matter just developed. Such points would be given to the group four or five times a day. The modern retreat, given to much smaller novice classes, was closer to Saint Ignatius' original form: it was personally directed, with the master seeing each novice individually once a day. Some use was made of group instruction, but much less than previously. The emphasis was rather on leading the novice to self-discovery and to conclusions reflecting his unique situation.

Whether similar changes occurred in the content of the Exercises is uncertain. A personally-directed retreat is of its nature personal and leaves no readily available traces of its content. Not much more can be said than that in a period of extraordinary overarching change reaching out in every direction, especially in the fields of theology and psychology, it would not be surprising to find that the content of the Exercises had been somewhat affected. While the text of the Exercises did not undergo any change, the actual use of the text may have been altered.

An illustration of the latter possibility is contained in Appendix 2, a description of Nicholas Predovich, the first of the "new" novice directors. The change he made in one of the key "Kingdom" meditations is described on p. 373. This incident also illustrates how difficult it is to ascertain the actual situation. In the interview, I had asked Father Predovich whether he felt a need to change anything in the Exercises, and he had said No. I then asked specifically whether he presented the Kingdom meditation as it was in the text of the Exercises, and he replied without qualification that he had. It was only when I had an opportunity to read the written text of his presentation that I learned the change he had actually made. In a subsequent interview, it became clear that the change was deliberate, though in answer to my question Why? he could give no more precise answer than that the omitted part "did not fit the American personality".

A decade after the Predovich incident, I attended a course on the Spiritual Exercises taught at a Notre Dame summer school by Howard Gray, then provincial of the Detroit province and formerly rector and director of Loyola House, the Chicago/Detroit novitiate. He presented the Kingdom meditation with the same alteration (omission of the oblation) as Father Predovich had made. Again the change was deliberate: Ignatius was being corrected, adapted to modernity.

Certainly there were many proposals to adapt the Exercises in one way or another. To take one of many examples, the scholastics at Alma College, in a 1965 paper entitled "A Re-evaluation of the Training of a Jesuit Priest", urged that "the 30-Day retreat should center on the plan of salvation scheme and its continuance in the liturgy rather than on an exclusively individualistic approach" and that "the neo-platonic words and expressions that were useful for St. Ignatius and used by him should be re-examined."

Another reason for thinking that the Exercises may have undergone some alteration in their actual use is the widespread influence of humanistic, especially Jungian, psychology among religious groups. Ascetical theology and psychology touch at many points. The Jesuit Renewal Center at Milford, Ohio, where future retreat directors are trained, provides an example of such influence. The directors-to-be are given the portraits of three types of retreatants, described in training manuals as *Person of "Whim", Person of "Law",* and a type described as "Principle and Foundation". Since the First Principle in the Ignatian Exercises describes the perfect principle that should govern every choice ("choosing only that which most leads to the end for which I was created"), the title of this group would seem to imply that the group described is the desirable type, the type the directors should try to form by leading retreatants through the Exercises.

This desirable type is described in eleven characteristics, the first

eight of which read as follows: "I am worthwhile. — Self acceptance. — Self-esteem. — Adult faith in God. — Healed of negative
self image. — Enjoys life, really spontaneous. — Creation is 'for
me.' — Experience of oneself as competent, able." This emphasis
on self-worth is one of the most characteristic features of the new
psychology in the therapeutic society. A description in these terms
of the person who exemplifies the Ignatian First Principle and
Foundation clearly reflects third-force psychology at work. The
extent of such influence is uncertain. It may be limited; it may be
considerable.

Prayer

Outside of retreat times, the novice was expected to spend about
two hours in prayer each day. It is impossible to know all the
changes that occurred in this part of novitiate life, the life of daily
prayer. The following may indicate general trends.

In the Maryland novitiate and probably in most of the others,
the novices were kept on a regular schedule for the first few weeks
but then were allowed to arrange their own personal order of the
day, including prayer time. I asked several novice directors how
this worked in practice. The answer, in the words of one director
was, "About the way it does with us", *us* meaning the formed
members of the Society. Some of the novices were very faithful to
the daily prayer; some of them were reasonably so; and some of
them allowed many things, especially work, to divert them from
prayer. Final judgment on the new system may have to wait for
long-term results.

The externals, including the technique of prayer, underwent
some changes. One novice director remarked that the modern
novice is sensitive about seeming to be put into a mold. Hence, his
first instructions to the novices were aimed to give them a sense of
the mystery and beauty that surrounds contact with the Divinity.
Only later, when they were devoted to the idea of prayer, did he
feel it safe to introduce instructions on the specific techniques of

prayer; even then he usually avoided traditional phrases such as "make a colloquy at the end".

Dress and posture at Mass tended to be less formal than previously. The cassock, of course, had disappeared; it was replaced by Levis, sweatshirts, and sneakers. The following description is from a note I made while living in the New England novitiate:

> The novices were in their usual casual attire. Most of them sat on the floor during the liturgy in various postures of relaxed ease. The only time this posture was disturbed was during the "Pax," when embraces were exchanged. Even during the consecration, the same casual postures (crossed legs, hands in pockets) were maintained. The young men tended to describe the formal attitudes as artificial, "phony," counter-productive.

More important than these externals, but also more difficult to ascertain, were the possible changes in the novices' interior prayer life. There were indications of some new developments. When Father Arrupe met with the English-speaking masters of novices in Rome in 1970, he said to them in his closing remarks on April 8, "As you know better than I, the young men of today pray in a manner different from our own. This requires of you an enormous amount of discernment and personal contact, a new type of direction." (See also pp. 259–60.)

At a meeting that same year of the novitiate advisory board of the California province, the vice-provincial in charge of formation reported that he sensed a lack of familiarity with Christ in the prayer life of some scholastics. They claimed they found it easier to pray while gazing at nature, and he worried that they might be edging toward a form of deism. At the same meeting, the California master of novices reported that, following the suggestion of the board, he had tried to interest the novices in Benediction of the Blessed Sacrament, but they did not respond. On a visit to the California novitiate in 1974, I made the following note: "After Mass, some of the novices remain for a while in the chapel talking and visiting. The Blessed Sacrament is there but gets no attention." In the fall of 1975, the Maryland novitiate reintroduced the morning and evening visits to the Blessed Sacrament: the morning visit (7:30) to make sure that everyone was up; the evening visit (9:30) to provide at least one religious exercise in the long period between dinner and late night, when most of them retired.

At the 1970 Roman meeting mentioned above, Father Arrupe reminded the novice directors that one of their essential tasks was to communicate "the knowledge of Christ, the present, personal, living Christ". He added, "Regarding the vertical dimension of one's relationship with Christ, there is no apostolic élan without a personal relationship to Christ . . . " At this same meeting, the General linked this goal with Christ's presence in the Blessed Sacrament:

> If he has the religious experience of this, he will willingly and frequently visit his friend and leader in the chapel. It is really very saddening today to visit the houses on my trips and find nobody in the chapel. How then can these men cultivate this vitally important intimacy with Christ, a real living friend, when they allow the personality of Christ to shrink and dissolve into an abstraction, a vague, misty concept? But he is a real person, the greatest man in the entire history of the world.

In a 1973 interview, I asked one of the more experienced novice directors about the modern novice and the Blessed Sacrament.[18] He told me that while the modern novice was not attracted to the Blessed Sacrament as previous generations had been, there had been some improvement (his term) in recent years—but that, in any case, he did not think it wise to urge the devotion on them. He mentioned that a few of the novices seemed to have some theological difficulty with the devotion. The difficulty seemed to be not so much a doubt about the real presence of Christ as it was a rejection of what they termed a "me and Jesus" mentality. For

---

[18] In the traditional Society, life revolved around the Blessed Sacrament. One made a morning visit to start the day and an evening visit to end the day. One made a visit after each meal. In times of special sorrow or joy, one sought out one's friend, to use Father Arrupe's term. Underlying the tradition was the theological perception of the sacramental presence as an extension of the Incarnation, with the same significance as Christ's first bodily presence in time and space: he was the one to go to, physically.

them, the living Christ was to be found in other people, especially though not exclusively the people who shared a common meal, which was the Eucharist.

There is probably some connection between this aspect of novitiate life and the findings of a questionnaire administered at Wernersville in 1966. One question was, "Who is Christ and where is He to be found?" A third of the novices gave the traditional answer of finding Christ in the Scriptures and in the Eucharist; another third answered that Christ was to be found primarily in others; another third did not answer this question at all.

An official at Weston, writing in September 1970, expressed some apprehension that the modern novitiate did not provide a congenial atmosphere for the experience of contemplation:

> Their whole tendency is to be out and doing things and the effort to be quiet, to read spiritual books reflectively and to pray in a calm atmosphere seems more than ordinarily difficult to put across. If they leave the novitiate with quite clear ideas about Catholic activism and quite unresolved ideas about their prayer life, their changes of survival are minimal. Several of the novices whom I would consider more mature and reflective by nature also possess this sense of uneasiness about an atmosphere that seems to stress the active more in practice than the contemplative. Perhaps it will take a few years to see what the new training is actually achieving, and it may well be much more effective than I can see at the moment. I think the next five years or so will give a much clearer picture.

The uncertainty expressed in this final evaluation was typical of much of the period. The same uncertainty was expressed by Nicholas Predovich, the change-oriented novice director of the Detroit province. Writing to the provincial in January 1967, Father Predovich said:

> A very basic, *erroneous* ascetical interpretation of an Ignatian principle is being propagated not only among the Juniors but among the younger Brothers as well, and seemingly nothing is

being done to stop it. It has to do with the principle of "finding God in all things." The erroneous interpretation is that . . . private prayer as well as liturgical prayer will always yield to present pressures of work.

I see so many of the Juniors fail to live what I consider a healthy spiritually oriented life with an active social consciousness that it makes me now question our whole novitiate training program. Yet, no one seems to be able to find anything wrong with this novitiate training program as set up since I have been here, and no one seems to want to make any further suggestions as to what must be changed, if anything need be changed.

Since he was writing of the men that he himself had formed (he had begun as novice director in 1963), his uncertainty was the more significant.

VIII

COLLEGIATE PROGRAMS: LOCATION AND ACADEMICS

Traditional Program

The traditional program of full-time college studies, consisting of a two-year juniorate and a three-year philosophate, was an amorphous stretch of formation lying between two relatively fixed sections, the novitiate and the theologate. These latter two derived their greater stability from their nature as professional schools— the first preparing novices for the profession which canon law terms *religious,* the other preparing seminarians for the profession of the priest. By contrast, the program that came to be called the "collegiate program" was much freer to take a variety of forms. Of its very nature, it comprised an indefinite large and varied area of human development within which particular choices had to be made, choices that had to omit at least as much as they included and that were always subject to change as the social environment in which they operated changed.

Traditionally, this vast area was accommodated to the particular needs of Jesuit formation in terms of the Jesuit's two professions, the religious and the sacerdotal. The demands of the religious profession chiefly affected lifestyle—for example, by affecting the allocation of the collegian's time; at least two and a half hours daily were to be allocated to formal prayer.[1] There was also a

---

[1] Meditation was to last one hour; Mass and thanksgiving, 45 minutes; two examens, 30 minutes; plus some spiritual reading. In addition to these

general concern in the order for keeping the collegiate life different and separate from secular life. This dictated some degree of religious silence, a religious mode of dress, a preference for life in the country rather than in the city. The religious profession had some influence on the academic life also insofar as it dictated an avoidance of works by authors who might impair the young man's morals or undermine his faith.

The demands of the other profession, the priesthood, not only enhanced the sacral character of the collegian's life but also directly affected its academic side. Collegiate studies were to prepare a scholastic to negotiate successfully four years of theology. This requirement operated chiefly through two emphases: on language and on philosophy. The scholastics were to arrive at the theologate prepared to read texts and listen to lectures in Latin. They were also supposed to be able to read theological sources in Latin and Greek. Most important of all, they were to come prepared to study divine revelation by applying the tools of Scholastic philosophy. As a result of this influence, stemming from the theologate, the juniorate emphasized the classical languages while the philosophate exercised the young levites in Scholastic philosophy to the point where they could actually use it as a tool.

Within each province the traditional collegiate program was marked by uniformity. Usually all the collegians studied the same subject at the same time. There were few, if any, electives and little adjustment of the course to individual differences of ability or interest. Everyone took "the course". Everyone was to be thoroughly trained in the fundamentals; after that, there might be an opportunity for individuals to pursue specialized knowledge or activities.

Within the United States in modern times the program was marked also by stability. The course followed by one generation closely resembled that followed by the generations before

---

daily spiritual exercises, there were the occasional exercises, all requiring time, such as house conferences, tridua, and the annual retreat.

and after it. The burden of proof was on the proponent of change, while the benefit of the doubt was awarded to tradition.

The traditional juniorate made up a single community with the novitiate. Though the juniors occupied a separate wing and lived a different life, the total community still carried a novitiate flavor. Silence and the ubiquitous cassock, the country location, the absence of movies, radios, newspapers, and secular magazines—all continued to characterize daily life for the juniors. The move from novitiate to juniorate was clearly governed by the principle of gradualism (pp. 197–98).

The practice of keeping the junior scholastics, those in the first two years of studies, separate from the other years of studies dates from the very early Society. The practice was given the force of law by the Sixth General Congregation in 1608 by unanimous vote. The purpose of the arrangement was clearly stated to be ascetical, namely, to protect the novitiate fervor from injury before it had become firmly rooted. It was for this reason that the masters of novices in the United States voted unanimously in 1964 against the idea of separating the juniorate from the novitiate and joining it with the philosophate. However, much of the debate in the 1960s over the separate existence of the juniorate tended to overlook this ascetical root of the institution.

Studies in the traditional juniorate concentrated almost entirely on the languages and literatures of the Latin, Greek, and English civilizations.[2] A junior would study a literary form—drama, epic, oration, lyric poetry, essay—simultaneously in all three languages. Without distractions of any kind, this life continued for two solid years. For those with literary interests, it was a remarkably rich cultural experience, probably not duplicated anywhere else in the country.

The three years of the philosophate represented a very different

[2] In my juniorate experience at Florissant, Missouri, in 1928 and 1929, I had no science or mathematics, a single, thin history course of one semester, and—during a part of one summer—a brief introduction to the French language.

experience for the young Jesuit. He moved to a new location and gave all his time now not to literature but to science and, chiefly, philosophy. The exact mix of sciences varied among the philoso-phates, but in all cases the total amount of science offered was minor.[3] There was also a small amount of time available for pursuing individual interests.[4] By far the greatest portion of the three years was spent on philosophy, and practically all of that philosophy consisted of Scholastic philosophy. Other philosophi-cal schools were treated as "adversaries", with a capsule descrip-tion of their positions. Such concentration had the advantage of developing that infrequently acquired skill by which philosophy can be used as a practical tool.[5] It had, of course, the disadvan-tage of leaving the student with a knowledge of only one philo-sophical system.

The lifestyle of the philosophate differed somewhat from that of the juniorate. The men were older; they were more in contact with the secular world through their studies and sometimes through their activities; and they had more responsibility for the allocation of their time. The rule of silence was still in effect, of course, but in the nature of things was less strictly observed. There were more frequent occasions for the doffing of the cassock and the donning of clerical suit and collar. Outside speakers made their appearance in the philosophate from time to time. On the whole, however, the life of the philosophate, like Jesuit life in general at that time, still had a distinctive religious look.

[3] In my own case, at St. Louis University, I had one course each in chemistry, physics, biology, and mathematics. They were special courses taught only to Jesuits and possibly thinner than the regular courses taught in the university.

[4] For example, I completed the courses required for an M.A. in Greek during my philosophy years at St. Louis University. For this it was convenient to be at the university but probably not necessary.

[5] During my years studying economics at Columbia University, I gained the impression that most of my fellow students and professors, though they had a grasp of the history of philosophy, did not know any one system well enough to use it as a tool. The fact that I did — and found it a very useful tool in economics — was noted and commented on by my professors.

In both the juniorate and the philosophate there was some small opportunity for apostolic work, chiefly the teaching of catechism to children. This work was highly praised by Ignatius among the experiments of the young Jesuits. It was, however, far removed from the kind of apostolic work chiefly admired in recent times, the "reform of sinful structures". Many of the scholastics, especially those less academically inclined, would have welcomed an increase in the proportion of their time spent on apostolic work.

Limitations

Any complex system will have disadvantages as well as advantages, and the traditional system had always had its critics. As time went on, the unchanged course suited its changing environment less and less, and the number of critics seemed to increase from a minority to a majority. The chief criticisms of the traditional course were four: the course was too long, too narrow, too rigid, and too monastic.

The traditional course occupied fifteen years after high school. Even in the days when the end of the course normally marked the end of formal study, fifteen years was criticized as being too long. The Jesuit priest was about thirty-three years old by the time he got out of school.[6] This criticism sharpened when modern conditions required some Jesuits to add three or four additional years in acquiring an advanced degree in some academic field. Time had to be made for working in these modern, specialized fields, such as the social and physical sciences. To make room, some traditional studies had to be dropped, or at least compressed. Since the two years of novitiate and the four years of theology were relatively

[6] In a 1965 letter to the New York provincial, John V. Curry wrote, "I am convinced . . . that the excessive number of years given to formal study in the Society has, in the long run, a deleterious effect on the spiritual and spiritual life of many of our men." Father Curry had taught in the juniorate for many years—at Plattsburgh, Shadowbrook, and St. Andrew's.

fixed by law, most of the shortening had to come out of the more flexible collegiate years.

By putting more class hours into the novitiate and by lessening the time spent on classical languages in the juniorate and on the more abstract questions in the philosophate, it would be possible, the critics argued, to obtain a bachelor's degree by the end of the fifth year after entrance and a master's degree—preferably in the specialty of the collegian's choice—by the end of the sixth year or during regency.[7] Some of the early critics proposed the amalgamation of the juniorate and philosophate. For example, a Commission on Philosophates of the Jesuit Educational Association, meeting in April 1961, discussed "a few recent studies on possible revision of the curriculum for the years now devoted to juniorate and philosophate". The studies envisioned an amalgamation of the two programs.

A second objection was that the course was too narrow, too concentrated. It was said to be training young Jesuits as though they were to enter the world of the Renaissance. During the Santa Clara Conference, Chairman Robert Henle flatly declared that the era of the classical education had ended and urged a "ruthless thoroughness" in eliminating a "Latin and Greek humanism". Since he himself was an outstanding product and former advocate of that education, his testimony was the more compelling (S.C.C. 1967, 2:1:264ff.). Some of the former emphasis on language, literature, and philosophy would have to be lessened, he said, so as to make more room for the modern social sciences, including history, as well as for mathematics and the modern physical sciences. Furthermore, the criticism ran, granted that much time should be

---

[7] Actually, this was possible even in the traditional system. In my own case, after entering from high school, I obtained a bachelor's degree at the end of five years and a master's degree in Greek language and literature at the end of my first year of regency (spent teaching the juniorate subjects of Latin, Greek, and English). In the theologate, I shifted to the field of economics and completed an economics major by the time of ordination. After teaching philosophy for a year, I went on to complete a doctorate in economics. By that time I was over forty years old.

spent on philosophy, it should not be spent so completely on Thomistic philosophy; space should be made for introducing the young Jesuit to other, more modern ways of approaching reality.

A third objection was that the traditional course was too rigid and uniform, making no allowance for individual differences in ability and interests. The literary man, the mathematician and the physical scientist, the social scientist, the abstract philosopher, and finally the pastor—all were run through exactly the same collegiate course. The Society should do, said the critics, what Harvard began to do in the 1920s: introduce more electives. The core courses should be constricted as much as possible and the opportunities for individual development widened correspondingly. This proposal fitted well with—and was greatly strengthened by—the characteristic individualism of the 1960s and the 1970s. The academic recommendations of the Santa Clara Conference in 1967 were guided primarily by the principle of flexibility: "Specifically we urge that the *Regional Order* [*of Studies*] incorporate that flexibility and willingness to experiment called for by the Conference" (S.C.C. 1967, 3:2:C20. See also pp. 72–73, "Scholastics' Statement".)

Whereas the other objections pertained to academics, a fourth objection was directed primarily at lifestyle. The traditional course, ran the charge, was too monastic in its whole mode of life. In the first place, it was isolated—out in the country, separated from the very life the Jesuit would eventually be expected to work in. Too much emphasis was laid on such monastic virtues as silence, religious dress, community prayer, abstinence from worldly entertainments. To some extent this objection also affected the academic life, insofar as it led to demands for travel to meetings and libraries and for greater opportunities to spend time in directly apostolic and pastoral work.

A second, closely related, objection to the traditional lifestyle was that it was institutional, monolithic. The critics urged that the traditional large collegiate community be broken up into a number of small communities. Daniel J. Shine, superior of the New England philosophers in 1968, explained in a letter to his province, "It is an age of personalism. The Scholastics are concerned with knowing one another, of knowing and being known by some Fathers, of being dealt with on a personal level."

In response to these objections, a number of changes were made in the traditional course, mainly changes in location, in academics, and in lifestyle. The history of the changes can best be told according to these three divisions, always understanding that the three are interlacing.

The history of the collegiate program is unusually complex for several reasons. First, the two separate programs comprising the Jesuit's "college" (juniorate and philosophate) changed, each at its own pace and in its own manner, even before they were amalgamated. Their amalgamation, furthermore, took different forms at different times in the various provinces. Finally, during the period of adaptation, the very persons to be formed changed, as the collegians grew fewer in number but more advanced and more varied in their education.

For most readers, a detailed history of these events would be tedious and not particularly useful. Instead the story will be related only in general outline, emphasizing those developments which were common to all the provinces and adding only those concrete details that may serve as illustrations of the general trend.

Changes in Location

Originally, all of the juniorates were in the country, each making up a single community with the corresponding novitiate. The location of the philosophates varied: two were on college campuses (at St. Louis University in Missouri and at Spring Hill College in Alabama); one was adjacent to a university (Mt. St. Michael's, neighbor to Gonzaga University in Spokane); the rest were in the country (Weston, Shrub Oak, West Baden). Six philosophates accommodated the ten provinces, with Maryland/New York, Chicago/Detroit, Missouri/Wisconsin, and Oregon/California sharing joint philosophates. Two (West Baden and Weston) comprised a single community with the theology students. Figure 6 shows the location of all the juniorates and philosophates as of the academic year 1964–65.

All the traditional collegiate programs experienced some change in location. In general, the reasons for the moves were much the same as in the cases of the theologates and novitiates. In particular, a change in location, especially to a college campus, was expected to work against several of the perceived limitations of the traditional collegiate system.[8] Such a move should enable more scholastics to make a more varied selection of modern courses; it should also work to remove any traces of monasticism; it should, finally, provide the opportunity to break up the large institutionalized community into small, personalized groups.

In the early 1960s the debate over the collegiate program still tended to distinguish between the juniorate and the philosophate, and in the case of the juniorate to stress the goal of "spiritual maturity". Thus, the Maryland province, in a long report on whether to keep the Wernersville juniorate or merge it with the philosophate listed the arguments for and against each option and in each case started with a religious consideration.[9]

For keeping Wernersville intact:
[Religious maturity] remains one of the primary reasons, if not *the* primary reason, for having a juniorate as opposed to some other program of studies—e.g., having the young religious go to a university. There are many theories as to how religious maturity is to be achieved and some doubt that the Juniorate is achieving it. Nevertheless the possibility exists and

[8] At its meeting in June 1968, the Three-Province Committee on Academic Formation asserted that "the basic problem is the isolated location of Shrub Oak rather than the length or content of the program of studies." The committee explained, "No matter what the program—its length or content—it could not be carried on successfully at Shrub Oak, given the difficulties of faculty manpower and declining student population."

[9] Joseph K. Drane, chairman of the committee producing the report, circulated the committee's conclusions to the province in a cover letter dated January 28, 1966. This report is one of the most penetrating and balanced analyses of the juniorate situation.

Figure 6

COLLEGIATE PROGRAM: LOCATION[a] CHANGES OF TRADITIONAL JUNIORATES & PHILOSOPHATES (1964–72)[b]

Province	1964–65	1965–66	1966–67	1967–68	1968–69	1969–70	1970–71	1971–72
California	J Los Gatos	↑	†L.A. (Loyola U.) 2 yrs.; then Spokane (Gonzaga U.)	↑	↑	↑	↑	↑
	P Spokane	↑						
Chicago	J Milford	↑	↑	↑	↑	†Detroit (U. of D.)	↑	↑
	P North Aurora	↑	↑	↑	↑			
Detroit	J Clarkston	↑	↑	↑	Detroit (U. of D.)	†Detroit (U. of D.)	↑	↑
	P North Aurora	↑	↑	↑	↑			
Maryland	J Wernersville	↑	†Shrub Oak	↑	↑	New York (Fordham U.)	↑	↑
	P Shrub Oak	↑						
Missouri	J Florissant	↑	↑	↑	↑	†St. Louis (St. Louis U.)	↑	↑
	P St. Louis	↑	↑	↑	↑			

Region		Location						
New England	J	Lenox	↑	↑	↑	†Weston	↑	↑
	P	Weston	↑	↑	↑	↑	Boston (Boston College)c	↑
New Orleans	J	Grand Coteau	↑	↑	↑	†Mobile (Spring Hill)	↑	↑
	P	Mobile	↑	↑	↑	↑	Mobile (Spring Hill) & New Orleans (Loyola U.)	↑
New York	J	Poughkeepsie	↑	↑	↑	†Shrub Oak	↑	↑
	P	Shrub Oak	↑	↑	↑	↑	New York (Fordham U.)	↑
Oregon	J	Sheridan	↑	↑	↑	†Spokane (Mt. St. Michael)	↑	↑
	P	Spokane	↑	↑	↑	↑	Spokane (Gonzaga U.)	↑
Wisconsin	J	St. Bonifacius	↑	↑	↑	↑	↑	↑
	P	St. Louis	↑	↑	↑	↑	†St. Louis (St. Louis U.)	↑

a All locations refer to living quarters. † Daggers indicate the formal beginning of collegiate programs, though juniors and philosophers may have been attending some college classes previous to this date. Arrows indicate continuation of previous location.
b Each date column shows academic year, fall to spring. After 1972, all locations remained unchanged for a number of years.
c Collegians began living in small communities around Boston College.

can be fulfilled if the Junior is given the proper combination of guidance and freedom . . .

Against retaining Wernersville:

The Juniors are at present keenly aware of their isolation and in some ways they do remain, because of this isolation, rather naive. They feel the thrust toward incorporation into society and a desire for continued awareness of society's needs and its modes. How much of this could and should be curbed is a problem too vexing for most observers; the fact remains, however, that no education is given *in vacuo* and the total responsiveness of the educand must be considered. A sense of incorporation into contemporary life can be a source of spiritual strength and intellectual impetus.

Proposals to move into the secular world came more easily with respect to the collegiate program than to the other stages of formation. After all, some critics observed, college was not a novitiate nor a seminary. Indeed, at the Santa Clara Conference in 1967 the proposal was made to transfer the collegiate program bodily to a secular campus and have the young Jesuit attend regular college classes just like other students (S.C.C. 1967, 2:1:229–30). This proposal did not meet with general support. In speaking against it, John P. Leary of the Oregon province remarked that the logic inherent in the proposal would close Catholic colleges by having all Catholic students go to secular universities.

A more acceptable proposal was to leave the juniorate in its protected environment but to transfer the philosophate to a Catholic college campus. This was not a new proposal. As early as 1952, when an expanding student body at Woodstock College necessitated moving the philosophers to another location—so that the theologians could have the entire plant—the Woodstock faculty proposed that the new philosophate be established on the campus of Fordham University. In its final meeting, the faculty voted favorably on this proposal 13 to 2. Fordham University offered space and was willing to meet all Jesuit requirements as to university relationships. The provincial, however, decided to retain the traditional structures; he purchased property and built Shrub

Oak, which opened in 1956, prepared to house at least 200 students.[10]

The major changes in the collegiate program may be followed in Figure 6. The actual process of change was not quite as neat, however, as the chart would seem to indicate. There were numerous partial adaptations before the final steps were taken. For example, the Jesuit scholastics at St. Louis and Spring Hill had for many years taken some courses with other students on the campus in addition to their regular philosophy courses. Somewhat later, other philosophates began to establish partial university contacts. For example, philosophers at Shrub Oak began attending some courses at Fordham University, while those living at Weston similarly attended Boston College.

Even some of the juniorates began to establish contacts with neighboring colleges. For example, in 1965 all the juniors at Milford were being bused into Cincinnati to attend classes at Xavier University. Likewise, in 1966 at Colombiere juniors were taking some of their classes at the neighboring Oakland Community College. At Shadowbrook one of the faculty wrote to the provincial that the impatience of the juniors to make outside contact was so strong that it seemed wise to allow them to take a few courses at a neighboring college, even though the level of education there was mediocre at best.

The process of amalgamating the juniorate with the philosophate into one college program began in 1966, when New York, Maryland, California, and Oregon closed their juniorates. In New York and Maryland the juniors joined the philosophers in a new four-year program at Shrub Oak. In Oregon the juniors joined the philosophers at Mt. St. Michael's. In California a new two-year program was begun at Loyola University in Los Angeles, during which the students covered subjects similar to those taken in the former juniorate, along with some studies relating to their

[10] While waiting for Shrub Oak to be constructed, the philosophers had been housed in a newly purchased hotel in Plattsburgh, New York. After the philosophers left, Plattsburgh was used for the novitiate and juniorate of the newly formed province of Buffalo.

fields of specialization. Upon completion of this program, they moved to Mt. St. Michael's for two years of philosophy. New Orleans began its collegiate program a year later, in 1967, and during the period covered by the chart made use of both Spring Hill College in Mobile and Loyola University in New Orleans. In later years, the province sent all its collegians to Loyola.

A joint, full collegiate program was established for the Chicago and Detroit provinces in 1969 at the University of Detroit. Also, in 1969, the Missouri province combined its juniors and philosophers in a unified program at St. Louis University. The Wisconsin province did not close its juniorate until 1970, after which it sent its collegians to St. Louis University. Even then, Wisconsin did not entirely abandon the juniorate. It kept one year alive at Creighton University doing work similar to the old juniorate. Other provinces made some occasional use of the Creighton arrangement and sent men there who needed the equivalent of a year in the juniorate.

All plans for the collegiate program were greatly affected by the steadily diminishing numbers of the collegians (New England, for example, had eighty-seven collegians in 1968 but only seven in 1974) and by the considerable increase in their average age. The latter change meant that the few who entered had already completed some years of college. Eventually, the New England province abandoned the attempt to maintain its own collegiate residences and adopted the policy of sending its collegians to one or more of the other centers.

As of 1988, there were five collegiate centers serving the ten provinces: New York (Fordham University), Chicago (Loyola University),[11] St. Louis (St. Louis University), New Orleans (Loyola University), and Spokane (Gonzaga University).

[11] In 1980, the Chicago/Detroit collegian program was transferred from the University of Detroit to Loyola University of Chicago.

Academic Changes[12]

General

An early question raised was whether there should be a collegiate program at all—whether there was a need for a separate, distinctively Jesuit program to supply whatever formation was required after the novitiate in preparation for theology. This question gave rise to frequent debate, as for example at the Santa Clara Conference on the "Total Development of the Jesuit Priest". (See S.C.C. 1967, 2:1, see Sessions 6 and 7.) Of those who gave a negative answer, some urged that no applicants be admitted who did not already have their college work completed. The system envisaged by this group would send men directly into theology from the novitiate. They argued further that even if men were admitted without college degrees, there was still no need for a Jesuit collegiate program. These Jesuits could get their college degrees in the ordinary way by going with other students to regular universities.

As time went on, the scholastics began entering at a later age, with more college studies already completed. This development bolstered the argument for doing away with a Jesuit collegiate program. The strength of this position was recognized by Walter L. Farrell, secretary for education in the Jesuit Conference, in an interview with the editor of the *National Jesuit News* (February 1973): "There is a trend toward accepting candidates only after their college education has been completed. If this continues, the whole need for a collegiate program will disappear."

The provinces have continued to judge that Jesuit formation is sufficiently different from regular collegiate formation as to require a separate and distinctive program. For example, applicants coming from engineering, or business, or medicine might need some

[12] In modern times, the formation of Jesuits in their studies is governed by two documents: *Normae Generales de Studiis* (1967) and *Regional Order of Studies* (1968, 1983).

strengthening in the humanities. This, in fact, is one of the functions performed for the assistancy by the one-year Jesuit collegiate program at Creighton University.

Even if applicants had sufficient backgrounds in general humanities, practically none would have enough philosophy to satisfy the requirements of the Society. In 1966, the Society required two full years of philosophy. This requirement, set by General Congregation 31, shortened by one third the previous requirement of three years (Dec. 9.22). Following the congregation, some Jesuit collegiate programs seem to have taken the reduction as an invitation to go even further in this direction. (At a meeting held in April of 1971 at the Jesuit School of Theology of Chicago, the statement was made that some Jesuit collegians at the University of Detroit were getting probably only half the previous requirement in philosophy.) G.C. 32, a decade after G.C. 31, found it necessary to state, "From different parts of the Society it has been reported that our philosophical studies in recent years have, for various reasons, suffered deterioration" (Dec. 6.24). This congregation repeated the two-year norm of G.C. 31 and added an admonition that seems to reflect some previous abuse: "But when these studies are combined with other subjects or with the study of theology, they must be pursued in such a way that the equivalent of two years is devoted to them" (Dec. 6.41).

In its *Regional Order of Studies,* published first in 1969 and revised in 1983, the Society in North America specified at least 36 hours of philosophy. Though less than the former requirement of three years, it was still far beyond what the ordinary college student took.

An important consideration in requiring this much philosophy was the relationship of the collegiate program to theology. Traditionally, theology acted as a lodestone for the whole of the formation program. The people in the theologate stated what skills and knowledge the young men would need when they came to the theologate, and this description guided the provincials in designing the earlier stages of formation. The former Jesuit theologates made much use of philosophy, especially Scholastic philosophy, in explaining the truths of revelation. Hence, the collegiate program spent much time on philosophy and emphasized a specific set of philosophical problems. Though philosophy was taught as a discipline in its own right, it was inevitably affected, in the seminary, by the theology which was to follow and for which it was to be a helpmate. This relationship was not stressed or, in my memory, even mentioned, but it was there and influential. Often in the course of four years of theology a student found himself saying, "So this is why we took this matter in philosophy!"

Two changes in the theology program had repercussions on the collegiate program. The time given to dogma, the branch of theology which made the most use of philosophy, was notably cut. Where dogma classes formerly occupied at least two thirds of the total theologate time, they now shrank to less than a half. Also, the entire approach of theology to revelation became less philosophic, more hermeneutic. Both changes worked to weaken the case for spending the traditional amount of time on Scholastic philosophy.

Apart from the influence of theology, there was an additional factor at work in the collegiate program. This was the change in philosophy itself, which had moved away from the traditional Thomism and toward some of the modern developments; it was more phenomenological, linguistic, existential. If Jesuits were to take their place in the modern world, they would need to be acquainted, the argument ran, with the way the modern world philosophized. In the interview quoted earlier, Walter Farrell listed as the second major problem a need to modernize Scholastic philosophy. The *Regional Order of Studies* (1969) specified that the study of philosophy was to include "both an intellectual respect for the perennially valid wisdom of our intellectual heritage and a well-informed understanding of contemporary philosophical issues and positions." (One might speculate whether a contrast was intended between "respect for" and "understanding of".)

Strongly abetting the move away from traditional Scholasticism was a fairly common attitude on the part of the scholastics.

They tended, many of them, to be bored by abstract philosophy. They could be interested only in a philosophy that had immediate relevance for daily life and action. There had always been scholastics uninterested in philosophy; however, in the 1960s, their numbers grew, and their dislike was directed especially toward Scholastic philosophy, perceived as irrelevant. They preferred courses with a heavy input of psychology or courses in ethics that dealt with concrete modern problems, especially problems of social sin. According to an account prepared by Arthur Madigan in 1968 while a scholastic at Shrub Oak, even such basic subjects as mathematics and history were rated lower by his fellow scholastics than such problem areas as poverty, peace, and power structures. The scholastics also favored the allocation of more time to training outside the classroom. G.C. 32 recognized a cognate problem when it spoke of the scholastics' difficulty of "remaining for a long time in the status of students" and "of their regret oftentimes at what appears an isolated existence" (Dec. 6.1).

In moving to a college campus, the scholastics did not simply mingle with the other students. In accord with the General's insistence, the Jesuits established a distinct school of philosophy which, while open to all students, was largely under Jesuit control and employed many Jesuit teachers. The reminder was offered more than once that although the Jesuits were college students, they were also seminarians and that the Dean of the Jesuit college must retain the power to decide what training was proper for men destined to become priests.[13]

In the new situation it became much more difficult to know what was happening within the Jesuit collegiate program. The program had become more individualized, not only because the men were entering later, with more of their own college work already completed, but also because values had become more

---

[13] This goal was not always reached in practice. At Loyola University (Chicago) in the 1980s, the scholastics took all their philosophy courses in company with the other university students. Two attempts were made to introduce at least one course specifically designed for Jesuits, but both attempts failed.

individualistic. Repeatedly the point was made that each man should be recognized as a unique individual and that his development should proceed accordingly (G.C. 31, Dec. 9.7). As a result, any general survey of the modern collegiate program would have to consist of an inspection of individual transcripts. Moreover, such a survey would have to be repeated at fairly short intervals. It is certain, however, that less philosophy was studied than formerly and that the philosophy studied was less traditionally Scholastic in tone.

With less time devoted to philosophy more time was available for other branches of study. From the beginning, this was one of the major objectives of the new collegiate program. The transition to the modern world was marked by the development of new fields of knowledge that the modern apostle should master. Even before the formal amalgamation of the juniorate and the philosophate, arrangements were made to permit scholastics to begin early specialization in such modern fields as the social and physical sciences. The move to a college campus accelerated this trend by putting a wide variety of courses within reach. (The new emphasis was in accord with the directions of G.C. 31; see for example, Dec. 9.2 and 9.4.)

The diminished demands of philosophy left more time available for direct pastoral work, and in the new collegiate program some of the young Jesuits made considerable use of this opportunity. The *National Jesuit News* for February 1973 describes two groups of collegians at Fusz Memorial (St. Louis) who lived separately from the main community in order to pursue apostolic work among the poor. One house was in a black ghetto, the other in a white ghetto. Other than the time spent in class at Fusz, the collegians lived in these houses, available to the neighborhood and engaged in organizing a Boy Scout group, tutoring grade-school and high-school pupils, counseling, and providing economic assistance. One of the enterprises, called Full Achievement, had a twenty-four member board of directors to help raise the needed funds. So much pastoral activity would have been out of the question in the traditional philosophate.

As time went on, differences developed among the various collegiate programs. For example, three of them (those at Fordham, St. Louis, and Gonzaga universities) were generally described as having a more strictly controlled system, with more required traditional courses.[14] This characteristic was not universally admired; complaints were sufficiently vocal at Fordham to engage the attention of an investigating commission. Most of the scholastics appearing before the commission defended the existing system, however, and asked that nothing be changed. The hearings produced some evidence of a generational gap. When a man of the 1960s (ordained in 1966) attacked such courses as the classics and philosophy on the grounds that they set up a frame of mind inimical to a social consciousness, the scholastic members of the commission repudiated this line of reasoning, saying that it certainly did not apply to them.

There are two reasons why the present fluid situation may continue to characterize the collegiate program. In the first place, as mentioned in the opening paragraph of this chapter, the collegiate program is of its very nature peculiarly subject to change, continual change. In the second place, Jesuit professional philosophers are quite unable to agree on what would be the best philosophical training for the scholastics.

Particular Examples

Some historical details may complement this streamlined account of academic changes. While the added details relate to specific provinces, they are sufficiently typical to have general relevance.

— Some discussion of structural change was always going on but became more pointed in the 1950s. At West Baden, for example, a committee was established in 1956 to look into the growing apathy of the scholastics toward the study of philosophy. Out of

[14] In the 1980s, however, St. Louis dropped metaphysics from its required courses.

this committee, chaired by Robert Harvanek, eventually came the Bellarmine Plan, an attempt to integrate philosophy with theology and the spiritual life—starting in the novitiate and continuing throughout the entire course of formation. (This goal was in accord with G.C. 31, Dec. 9.2.) The Chicago province put the plan into operation for a few years but had to abandon the experiment under the flood of other changes that were occurring— including the move of the philosophate to Detroit (1969) and away from direct contact with the theologate.

— As early as 1960, one of the eastern philosophate deans was writing to his provincial that many of the scholastics were completely uninterested in Scholastic philosophy, partly "because they are filled with an exaggerated consciousness of what they think to be the modern predicament". The modern student, he wrote, was very little interested in what he considered to be the abstractions of Scholastic thought "far removed from the real world". The dean also wrote: "He finds the thesis method dull and boring; and it is my sincere conviction that the amount of weariness of which so many of our scholastics complain is due not to labor, but to boredom." His recommendation: "More emphasis must be given to the subjective side of philosophy, while we must not abandon the objective emphasis which has been the tradition." In the period 1967–69, scholastics at Shrub Oak would sometimes preface their oral examination with a protest against having to spend so much time on philosophy, time that could more profitably be spent on their specialties. Somewhat related to this student attitude was the statement made by a tertian that "our generation finds philosophical proofs unconvincing."

— At their meeting in April 1961, a Commission on Philosophates of the Jesuit Educational Association discussed "a few recent studies on possible revision of the curriculum for the years now devoted to juniorate and philosophate studies". These studies sought for ways to integrate the juniorate and the philosophate. In early 1961, the program at Shrub Oak was reorganized to enable the scholastics to get credit at Fordham University, and later that year the scholastics were allowed to travel to Fordham for classes on Wednesday afternoon. Regarding the move, the rector reported to the provincial, "Strange as it may seem, I am coming around to the point of favoring it." At about the same time, the New England philosophers, at Weston, began to commute regularly to Boston College.

— Somewhat later, the Weston philosophy faculty embarked on one of the most intensive planning sessions of that period. The provincial of New England, J. V. O'Connor, had suggested to the rector of Weston "the possibility of having officials and faculty at Weston College initiate a self-evaluation program as a step toward continuing academic improvement at Weston." The decision to make such a study was announced on September 13, 1963, and Paul T. Lucey, dean of the philosophate, appointed William J. Connolly as chairman of the Weston College Self-Study Committee.

The study occupied the entire period of May 1964 to June 1965. Over the course of these fourteen months all philosophy faculty members met in committee sessions two or three times every week for an average of three hours each session. Faculty members also traveled about the province in pairs, informing the communities of what was being done and asking their judgments on the past and future education of the scholastics. They asked the members of each community: "Do you wish your philosophy years had been different? What changes would you like to see made?" As the work proceeded, Chairman Connolly kept the scholastics informed, meeting with them every two weeks to report on problems and proposed solutions. Among other effects, this kept the scholastics in a position to exert effective pressure.

At an early stage the committee reached a basic and radical conclusion: "Our first fundamental decision unanimously concurred in by the Committee is the recommendation that the Juniorate and Philosophate as we have known them cease to exist as such, and that the juniorate and philosophate studies be integrated into one unified program."[15] To guide the construction of the philosophy sector in the proposed new collegiate program, the report offered the following observation:

> The dissatisfaction of many philosophers with much of the course content and with some of the methods presently employed in the teaching of philosophy, and the inability of a large number of students to understand what relationship philosophy as it is presented to them—"tract philosophy"—should have to their personal and professional development, all indicate the need for an energetic and searching study of the professor-student encounter in the philosophy courses themselves, and of a study of course content that might "prove the worth of each course and of each thesis" before a decision is made to continue them (Weston Self-Study Committee, 1965, 8).

Traditionally, the scholastics at Weston took at least sixteen courses in philosophy; the committee recommended ten. There was much objection to even this. A minority report signed by Fathers John R. McCall, John R. Vigneau, and Walter J. Feeney would have limited the required philosophy courses to six. The majority of the members accepted the proposition that philosophy was to be studied by the scholastics not only for itself but as a tool for the study of theology. The committee also recommended that, in the purchase of new books for the library, emphasis be placed upon modern, non-Scholastic thinkers.

The final report of the committee appeared in 1965, shortly after G.C. 31 began. A year later, in a letter to the General dated June 6, 1966 the provincial wrote, "It was heartening to all the province to witness the remarkable resemblance of the Self-Study recommendations to the General Congregation's decree 'On the Training of Scholastics, Especially in Studies.'" The report, like the congregation, sought ways to shorten the general curriculum, distinguished between graduate and undergraduate studies,

---

[15] The full report, from which this excerpt is taken, has been lost or misplaced.

recommended that scholastics be permitted to pursue graduate degrees outside the house of studies, provided for more individualized formation, and included in its goals personal maturity and responsibility.[16]

In his letter, the provincial urged on the General the wisdom of accepting the report's recommendations. He also remarked that the scholastics knew the contents of the report, including the recommendation to move the scholastics from Weston to Boston College, and were under the strong impression that other provinces were moving more rapidly and progressively than was New England. (In fact, the scholastics of the various provinces were in constant touch with one another, by letter, by phone, and by ham radio.) The provincial's long letter ended with a plea to begin the program with the new academic year and concluded with the usual justification that it could be done "by way of an experiment".

— John A. McGrail was dean of the juniorate at Milford (1944–54), rector of the combined philosophate and theologate at West Baden (1954–58), and provincial of the Detroit province (1958–65). This long experience, he said in an interview, left him ready to approve adaptations in the course of studies. For example, he had been acutely aware that some of the scholastics had little interest in or aptitude for the classics or for philosophy. When he returned from G.C. 31, he was prepared to depart from traditional patterns in both fields. Practices that he had chafed under before but had not felt free to change he now proceeded to modify or abandon without first getting permission from Rome.

— At Colombiere, one of the faculty, writing in January 1965, reported, "The several laymen who have been hired to supplement the Jesuit faculty are fortunately men well trained in their fields." He went on to offer the judgment that either more faculty would have to be hired or else the juniorate would have to be moved to a college campus. Later in 1965, the juniors did begin to attend classes at Oakland Community College and at the University of Detroit.

[16] Similar reviews of the collegiate program were made in other provinces at about this time but none, as far as I know, so intensive as this one.

— The New England collegiate program may be said to have started in May 1966, when the second-year novices at Shadowbrook were permitted by Rome to follow a combination of Latin and theology classes for three hours a day, five days a week. By means of summer work and one year of juniorate, they completed two years of college and were ready to move to Weston for the two years of philosophy needed for their college degree. Thus, there was a collapse of the previous seven years into a five-year program; a year had been cut from both the juniorate and the philosophate.

— In the school year of 1963–64 at West Baden, Latin was the prescribed language (in systematics courses) during the three years of philosophy. During the next year, 1964–65, the school had been moved to North Aurora, Illinois, philosophy had been reduced to two years, and the language of instruction had become English.

— At Weston College, Rector Paul T. Lucey decided in March 1964 that the oral examinations would be held in English instead of the customary Latin. He made this decision without previously clearing it with anyone—not with the provincial, or his consultors, or the faculty.

— In November 1964, the deans of the houses of formation in the assistancy met at North Aurora. It became clear that nearly all of their philosophates had shifted from Latin to English. The changes had spread gradually among them, with New York being one of the earliest. At this time the St. Louis philosophate had not yet made the shift, but when the dean returned to the city, he immediately contacted the provincial and obtained a dispensation from the rule of using Latin in the classes, in the disputations, and in the examinations.

— When the Oregon Committee on Juniorate-Philosophate Integration held its first meeting (October 16, 1965), a question was raised as to how free the committee should feel of existing legislation. According to the minutes of the meeting,

it was pointed out that we must attend primarily to the letter and spirit of the latest decree on studies from the present General Congregation; that the outmoded or dead letter of the past should not be normative for us; that many previously unheard of experiments are already existing and approved in other Assistancies—including the Roman province, where the novices begin philosophy studies outside the novitiate.

— In its 1966 revision of the traditional program, the Oregon province provided for thirty-six hours of philosophy and twelve hours of theology. Of the philosophy hours sixteen were to be historical and twenty systematic. Of the twelve hours in theology, six were to be taken in the novitiate. The other six would be taken in the remaining four years of the collegiate program. The philosophy was to be mainly that of Saint Thomas, combined with an introduction to modern and contemporary philosophy.

— At West Baden, at least as early as 1960, the scholastics were beginning to get a taste of a different philosophy, one touched by existentialism and by philosopher Bernard J. F. Lonergan's experiential approach.

— According to Frederic M. O'Connor, spiritual director at Shrub Oak, the scholastics exerted continuous pressure to lessen the importance of philosophy and substitute other areas of study such as psychology and sociology. There was a marked tendency to find psychological and sociological solutions to problems and thus to relativize what was taken formerly as absolute.

— As the scholastics at Shrub Oak increased the amount of time they chose to spend on nonphilosophical subjects, the faculty responded by increasing the pressure to study the assigned matter. The result was serious tension. Similar tension was generated at several of the other philosophates also but not, apparently, to the extent that marked Shrub Oak.

— According to its minutes for April 19, 1970, the Eastern Inter-Province Committee on Formation, composed of representatives of New England, New York, and Maryland, debated the proposition that philosophy was not necessary as a preparation for theology but that any humanistic subject area would do as well. The proposition was defeated by one vote.

— At most of the philosophates, the students expressed opposition to the Latin oral examination called the *"De Universa"* (more fully, *De Universa Philosophia* — on all of philosophy), which covered all the matters studied in the previous three years and which determined whether a scholastic would be assigned to the long or honors course or to the "short" course in theology.[17] One root of the opposition was basic: the scholastics objected to being required to learn an established set of theses in Scholastic philosophy; they wanted philosophy to be a free-ranging, subjective investigation of open problems. The established theses were dictated partly, of course, by the requirements of the theology to come. Another root of the opposition was the desire of the scholastics to spend more time on other subjects; preparation for the *De Universa* traditionally occupied many weeks. The opposition was most vehement at Shrub Oak, where the scholastics threatened to strike against the requirement (pp. 302–3).

Drift from Thomism

There were indications that a new philosophy was becoming part of the traditional course and was causing some alarm. For example, as early as January 1962, the dean of one of the eastern philosophates was writing to his provincial as follows:

> It cannot be stressed too strongly that our scholastics are not immune from the mental uneasiness which is observable in every Catholic campus at the moment. The attraction of relativism, process, rupture with the past is most strong. As a consequence our young men, talented and untalented alike, have a deep suspicion of the *philosophia perennis* and a deep distrust of its conclusions. This is a matter of most grave concern, since we no

[17] In 1966 at Weston, fourteen out of fifty-two scholastics failed in the *De Universa* examination. In writing to the provincial about the failures, their superior, Daniel Shine, suggested two reasons: "Scholastic philosophy as presented does not seem meaningful to them in their own lives. Another reason might be lack of study due perhaps to overcommitment to extracurricular concerns at Boston College."

longer are confronted merely with the attitude of students bored with a dull course. Neither are we confronted merely with the indifference of students to scholastic quarrels over medieval niceties. There is a genuine danger of these young men throwing over basic philosophical principles which are necessary for the maintenance of Catholic theology.

W. Norris Clarke taught in the philosophate at Woodstock until 1952 and at Plattsburgh thereafter. To acquaint his students with modern trends, he incorporated elements of existentialist and personalist philosophies. His students were writing to the scholastics in other philosophates and announcing that a personalist revolution was in the making. Some members of the faculty, however, were uneasy over this development. Gustave Weigel, a noted theologian and a friend of Father Clarke, warned him that he might be "releasing the irrational id on the young men in the province". Also, a psychiatrist working with several of the scholastics expressed the opinion that such philosophy had best be postponed until the years of theology, when the young men would be older and more balanced.

The provincial, Thomas E. Henneberry, grew apprehensive and in 1955 removed Clarke from the scholasticate, assigning him to the philosophy department of Fordham University. In later years, at Fordham, he found the students already immersed in existentialism and personalist modes. They were coming to class influenced by all the media of modern life. To achieve balance, he emphasized traditional Thomism. By thus putting existentialism and personalism in their metaphysical framework, Clarke sought to prevent excessive personal independence.

There were other instances of professors being moved out of a philosophate because they were teaching a new philosophy which superiors judged to be unsafe. At Shrub Oak, for example, at least three professors (Giles Milhaven, Robert Johann, and William Richardson) were transferred for this reason. Frederic O'Connor, spiritual father at Shrub Oak for many years, thought that these men had aided the philosophers by helping them articulate their restlessness.

At West Baden, the new philosophy appeared in various courses, but especially in the course Philosophy of Man taught by Michael J. Montague. A course in psychology taught by Walter L. Farrell for many years was congenial to the new approach. Montague's reading assignments included references to Robert Johann and Bernard Cooke but did not include, for example, the opposing writings of Robert Harvanek.

In his course, Montague taught an individualist—often termed personalist—type of philosophy with emphasis on self-fulfillment. This was taken up by the young men so enthusiastically that when they went out to regency some proved hard to handle. "Montague's men" were openly criticized in houses throughout the province. The criticism was so acute, Father Montague reported when interviewed, that he was reluctant to visit some houses. In time, with experience, the approach was moderated so as to include a balancing emphasis on self-transcendence as the most effective way of achieving self-fulfillment.

Joseph D. Devlin, of the New England province, recalled from his days in the Weston philosophate that Reginald F. O'Neill taught a seminar in existential philosophy in 1958. In the seminar, the students made the acquaintance of Martin Buber, Gabriel Marcel, Emmanuel Mounier, Jean-Paul Sartre, and others.[18]

In the traditional philosophate, a major event was the disputation, in which one of the students defended the house doctrine against all objectors, who included several preselected scholastics and any of the faculty who cared to enter the lists. At West Baden, in the spring of 1964, the disputation tackled the problem of "knowledge, objectivity and the real" and also the problem of "a transcendental method in metaphysics". Significantly, in this disputation it was the *objectors* who had the task of presenting traditional Thomism.

In Oregon, in 1962, the provincial reported to Rome:

---

[18] According to Devlin, the road had been prepared in the juniorate where in their English classes the scholastics came across what was then called personalist literature in the writings of such authors as Ernest Hemingway and F. Scott Fitzgerald, from whom they learned an emphasis on courage, openness, individualism.

During the past several years, a number of the scholastics have become strongly partisan for the philosophical position of Father Lonergan in a way that makes some of them hostile to the content and method of certain more traditional teachers at the Mount. There was some rather sharp criticism about "ghetto Thomism" and "naive realists" that went beyond the limits of the proper respect owed by our scholastics to their professors.

Also in Oregon, two years later, a province committee on philosophy completed its work. Among its conclusions was the following: "The historical, developmental, evolutionary viewpoint seems to call for something from metaphysics. Metaphysics should not be dumbfounded before this surge. It cannot, of course, detail a philosophy of history or evolution, but it can manifest the profound, dynamic framework within which history can be interpreted." The call for some change in the *philosophia perennis* is clear here.[19]

In April of this same year, 1964, the Jesuit professors of epistemology met in Rome. The dean of the Missouri philosophate, George P. Klubertanz, attended the meeting and reported to his provincial that the vicar general of the Society, John L. Swain, "expressed concern about the state of doctrine in the teaching of philosophy, especially in the field of epistemology." With respect to the Jesuits at the meeting, Father Klubertanz was optimistic. He reported, "As regards conclusions, the group was pretty solid on realism, on the plurality of possible methods, and on the solid content of most of the traditional stuff." This was, however, early in the period of change; as time went on the shift away from traditional Thomism became more pronounced.

Thus, the philosophical formation of Jesuits has been influenced

[19] Thomas Merton, one of the more popular guides of the 1960s, challenged "the American Church to move ahead in the spirit of the Second Vatican Council, to seek truly to make the Church indigenous to America, and to examine honestly the need for a new philosophical base for our theological teaching and the potential of Christian existentialism to serve as that base" (Pennington 1987, 167).

by three developments. First, they are spending less time on philosophy—two years instead of three years. Second, in this shorter time they are addressing themselves to diverse philosophical systems. Third, philosophy is used less in theology, where traditionally the scholastic learned philosophy by applying it daily for four years.

IX

COLLEGIATE PROGRAMS: LIFESTYLE

Introduction

In a religious order, changes in lifestyle are more important than changes in location or academics, for the religious life *is* a lifestyle. As Frederick McLeod, superior of the Weston collegians, put it: "The selection of a life style powerfully shapes an individual for the future. For a life style goes deeper than external behavior, not only manifesting but engendering attitudes and values" (McLeod 1973, 12).

Lifestyle changes in the collegiate program were generally the same as in the theologates and novitiates. The causes of the changes were also basically the same. Though the timing of the changes varied somewhat among the provinces, the variations were not large enough to be significant. If will suffice, therefore, to describe these changes in broad outline, confirming familiar patterns with new illustrations.

The following description of the new scholastic may serve as an introduction to this section—and as a partial explanation of many of the lifestyle changes recounted. The description emerged from an interview with John V. Curry, who taught in three different juniorates in the early sixties to mid-sixties and had witnessed the evolving situation at first hand. According to Father Curry, the new scholastic was marked by four characteristics:

1. An antipathy to status and defined roles and especially to control by tradition.

2. As a fruit of No. 1, an insistence on deciding matters (both practice and principle) for himself.
3. A personalist interest which caused him to be greatly concerned with friendship.
4. A marked dependence on the support of his peers, a combined fruit of No. 1 and No. 3.

While external changes among the collegians did not appear, generally speaking, until the later 1960s, internal changes seem to have appeared earlier. In a series of long letters to this writer, Bruce F. Biever, then provincial of the Wisconsin province, recalled his experience as a scholastic at Fusz, the philosophate of the Missouri province, during the period 1956–59. Even at that early date, some of the characteristics of the new breed were already evident. As Biever described the situation (letter of July 1, 1974), traditional restrictions were beginning to generate resentment and restlessness:

There was silence through the day, conversations were to be in Latin, there was no allowable interaction between the scholastics and students at St. Louis [University], socialization was forbidden, all forms of secular entertainment were rigorously curtailed, etc. . . . There was a lot of resentment at Fusz during the three years I was there, and I don't think that it is an exaggeration to say that it was quite a "sick" community. . . . Things were beginning to crest, attitudes were changing, demands were being made which were not in consonance with the accepted policies and life style of the philosophate, and while none of us could predict the crest of the 60s, when all of this broke forth in a systematic pattern, nevertheless I do think it is fair to say that there were many indications that the crest would come. I suppose what I am saying in summary is that the Vatican Council [1962–65] was a watershed of values that those of us who were scholastics were feeling deeply as early as the 50s.

It is noteworthy that the changed values in the scholasticate antedated Vatican II and thus did not directly depend on the council. Rather, both developments seem to have had the same roots.

G.C. 31 marked the formal beginning of Jesuit change, but there were many examples of a changed spirit antedating the congregation. To take just one such example, the traditional law of the Jesuit order forbade trips home for the scholastics except on the occasion of the death or serious illness of a parent (Curia 1931, #247). Yet by 1964, the rector of Shrub Oak, Thomas E. Henneberry, was writing to the provincial to say that this provision was no longer enforceable, adding "nor do the scholastics accept the reasons (ascetical, economic, use of time) on which the norms were based."

While the earliest stirrings of unrest seem to have been felt by only a minority, they gradually spread to a wider circle. They also became externalized in confrontational action. In this form they posed serious disciplinary problems. Local superiors had to choose between trying to hold the line with little community support — and sometimes indecisive support from higher superiors — or beginning to make concessions — either in the form of ignoring violations or formally changing the rules. When they chose the latter roads, usually tentatively and doubtfully, sometimes they were then charged by the rest of the province with a "failure of nerve".

The most general lifestyle change was a revolt against rules: against rules requiring attendance at class or at daily Mass or at a particular Mass; against rules requiring prayer at a particular time or place or of a particular form; against rules forbidding talking in certain places or at certain times, or going to movies and plays, or being out of the house at night, or wearing certain clothes. The revolt was motivated by two values, not always clearly differentiated: the conviction that a real *person* should be responsible for making such decisions for himself, and the conviction that some of the things forbidden were desirable and some of the things commanded were not desirable.

The following correspondence, dated early 1966, between the rector of one of the philosophates and his provincial and referring to developments during 1964 and 1965, illustrates the general situation. The rector had been trying to enforce all existing rules and had been experiencing less and less success. In reporting to the provincial, he described the attitude of the scholastics as doing "what he [the rector] wants if he is reasonable, but of course if he isn't we do it anyway." He asked the provincial for instructions. In reply, the provincial wrote:

> It is pretty clear that in this year of Our Lord discipline cannot be managed and ordered with a precision that might have been possible a few years ago. In this generation of "war-babies" the built-in opposition to control and direction by authorities of whatever status is so deep and the sense of personal liberty is so delicate that merely for prudential reasons Superiors have to be not merely receptive and open to whatever the young men may want to say but much less ready than before to correct and impose regulations. It is certainly no simple task today to be a Superior.

The rector expressed relief at having "a directive as to what attitude I should take toward the younger men".

In the article quoted at the beginning of this chapter, Frederick McLeod attempted a description of the changed world that was forcing a changed lifestyle. It is a penetrating description based on his years as superior of collegians and reflecting a keenly analytical mind. He sums up the goal of modern formation by saying that it is

> to enable a man to deal with change in his life, to cope with a pervasive and often subtle spirit of relativism, and to live with a balanced outlook in an age that emphasizes personalism, experience and freedom. No matter what one may think of it, we have to come to terms with a cultural shift of vast proportions. Emphasis has moved away from objectivity according to juridical norms to subjectivity of personal experience, from uniformity of observance to multiformity of ways of living, from closeness and conformity to openness and a critical attitude (McLeod 1973, 12, 13).

The present chapter provides concrete examples of this general process of change in collegiate lifestyle. The particular illustrations, taken from the experiences of the various scholasticates, are arranged according to province and, roughly, period.

New York/Maryland

The philosophate of the New York and Maryland provinces was established in 1956 on a beautiful and extensive estate near the Hudson River in an area called Shrub Oak. From the beginning it was a disturbed house. A significant proportion of the scholastics resented its country location, all the more because they knew that the New York provincial had rejected the offer of Fordham University in New York City to host the philosophate. Though located in beautiful surroundings, the new building was criticized bitterly as being too institutional. From the opening of Shrub Oak until its closing in 1969, the drum beat of criticism and a certain restless stirring never ceased. Frederic M. O'Connor, a long-time spiritual director at Shrub Oak, recalled the history of the house as falling roughly into three periods: a gradual escalation of unrest, 1955–60; a sharp increase in restlessness, taking the form of overt agitation, 1960–65; and a slowed state of disturbance, 1965–69.

It was primarily because of the unrest at Shrub Oak that the Committee of Spiritual Review (C.S.R.) was set up in 1964 at the request of Father Arrupe. Hence, most of the discussion of that committee (see Chapter I, Section 4 above) may be understood as reflecting to some extent the situation at Shrub Oak. At the first meeting of the C.S.R. (July 1964), one member declared:

> Something must be done to counteract the "retreat to the group" for support and guidance. In an attempt to break down this gap between the body-scholastic and authority, Shrub Oak plans to introduce a new program whereby each Saturday evening a conference will be given revolving around a specific theme for each month. The talks will be given by the Rector, the two Spiritual Fathers and a faculty member (p. 1:7).

At the same meeting, a member reported that a tendency to form cliques was prevalent and opposed to the universalist tendency of former generations of Jesuits. Another member observed, "This need to experience a real love for other scholastics is a dominant goal for them" (C.S.R. 1964–68, 1:9).

At Shrub Oak, the incoming class of 1963 was different (see the similar experience at Spring Hill pp. 317–18). They seemed to have been different even in high school. Donald Hinfey, who graduated from Regis High School in New York in 1950, returned as a Jesuit regent in 1957. He found the students at his alma mater, especially the lower classmen, very different from when he had been there: they were more questioning, less docile, less grateful for their free education (Regis was an honors-scholarship school), more self-centered. These would have become the collegians of the early 1960s.

Writing to the New York provincial in November 1963, one of the faculty offered the following analysis (surprisingly prescient considering its early date):

What is truly alarming about the present decline in religious discipline, however, is not simply that it manifests a poor state of external observance. That has existed in the past. The Woodstock of my own philosophy days was a glaring example of it. It is rather that we are now confronted with a new and qualitatively different phenomenon: the absence in a sizeable and growing body of our scholastics of an interior understanding and appreciation of Jesuit community life as such. . . . [They] are engaged, more than half-consciously, in an endeavor to remould the Society to their own image, to their own concept of religious life, apostolic activity and the life of supernatural perfection.

One of the members of the C.S.R. advanced the following explanation of the situation at Shrub Oak.[1] The explanation is the

[1] This quotation is from the minutes of the Committee of Spiritual Review, probably in 1964. A more exact designation cannot be given because the minutes from which this quotation was drawn have been lost in or from the Center library.

more significant because it probably applies to the other scholasticates as well.

> I think the young man of today finds it extremely difficult to conform himself to a set time order where everyone does the same thing at the same time. I cannot begin to analyze all the reasons for this, but it is a fact. Perhaps it is because this runs counter to the young man of today's preoccupation with personalism and action. He feels less a person because he is pushed into the anonymity of a uniform order.
>
> Perhaps this partially explains the explosions which have occurred at Shrub Oak in recent years. After four years within a structure which he never wholeheartedly accepted, in which he felt no real growth but where he never articulated his objections, he came to Shrub Oak where the "official" structure was still fairly rigid but where in philosophy class he was bombarded intellectually with the demands of personalism, self-realization, and "authenticity." The result was that he began to operate outside the structure in his quest for individuality, often in a bizarre way.

The following are a few particular instances that mirror the general situation. In all cases, the reference is not to the entire scholasticate, but to an active minority. When Thomas E. Henneberry, rector of Shrub Oak, spoke to the fifth session of the C.S.R., the minutes reported as follows:

> At the outset, Father Henneberry emphasized that the problems that he would discuss were not problems which could be said to be universal at Loyola [the official name of Shrub Oak scholasticate]. Many of the scholastics were not involved in the matters which he would treat, but there was a relatively large *minority* of the scholastics who were. It is about this minority group that he would speak (p. 5:17).

In 1964, one of the spiritual fathers reported to the provincial that the scholastics were beginning to violate rules to an extent unheard of before. He instanced the following: playing cards until 2:00 A.M., coming to Mass late on Sunday (fifteen or twenty would come in as late as the offertory), being away from the house all day Sunday until midnight without permission, laughing and joking about the Profession of Faith by the third-year men in connection with their taking minor orders.

In that same year, the provincial reported to the General that five members of the Shrub Oak community were being treated by psychiatrists. He also spoke of being "surprised at the number of scholastics who mentioned the tranquilizers they were taking."

By 1966, the reports reflected increased concern. One community member reported to the provincial:

> There can be no question that a serious decline in religious life has taken place at Shrub Oak. At the community exhortation yesterday, I counted eighty scholastics present. This means that the majority of our scholastics were not in attendance at the one required spiritual instruction of the month.... To put it very bluntly, it is becoming more and more difficult to determine in what way we are a religious house and not simply a college. In all honesty and without emotion, I have to say that we have reached the stage where interior confusion, lack of exterior order in their lives, and extreme emotionalism have brought our scholastics to a state where they are incapable of hearing and absorbing rational instruction.

He did recognize that the scholastics seemed to be currently more content. He added, however, "We can well ask if some of the 'contentment' of our scholastics is not due to the relaxation of many of the requirements of rule and non-enforcement of others. Indeed, much 'contentment' is a very surface thing, for underneath it our good scholastics are confused and dissatisfied with a life that does not really challenge them."

One of the faculty writing at this same time (February 1966) reported that a "serious situation" existed because of lack of control over the scholastics. He wrote, "After dinner at night there are frequently as many as thirty or forty scholastics absent without anyone knowing even where they are, and as for general house discipline there is no longer even a pretense at keeping it up."

According to John A. Dineen, rector at Shrub Oak, who succeeded to the post after the brief incumbency of Robert A. Mitchell, the pressure for most of the changes definitely came from the scholastics. Sometimes the changes would be requested; sometimes they would simply begin and would continue when no official notice was taken of the change.[2] He said that he was faced with a serious division of opinion among his consultors during the most turbulent years. He also said that in his meetings with the scholastics he found many of them reporting that they themselves were happy but wondered if they should be because of the chorus of criticism they heard all around them.

An unusual number of departures from the Society during this period both contributed to the seriousness of the situation and influenced the superiors' actions in dealing with it. In 1964, Shrub Oak held a "Conference on Religious Life". Of the four speakers chosen to instruct and inspire the community on this topic, two (Edward J. Sponga and Robert O. Johann) left the religious life not long afterward.

Perhaps the most significant change during the sixties was the altered concept of law and authority. While this change was universal throughout Western society, it had special import for religious orders, with their vow of obedience. The following items chosen from the Shrub Oak experience illustrate how far the altered attitude toward law had progressed. The point in each case is not that a rule was broken but rather that there was an implied, and sometimes an explicit, judgment that the rule was illegitimate and carried no moral force.

It was customary for the beadle of the class to take attendance and report to the dean. The beadle would report perfect attendance. A month later the dean would hear from a professor that less than half of the class was in attendance. When the beadle was confronted with this discrepancy, he would say, "I was sitting up front and I took for granted that everybody was there behind me."

---

[2] Some of the scholastics were in touch with canonists in Rome; the scholastics were seeking to establish what rights they had against superiors.

In an interview, the rector of Shrub Oak, Father Dineen, recounted the following incident. During a holiday at Shrub Oak, eight men absented themselves from the house and did not return for two days. They had obtained the necessary funds from their parents, who had been instructed to pick them up at a prearranged spot. When the scholastics were called to order on the matter, they were not contrite. While accepting the punishment that might be involved, they did not consider their action to have had moral significance. Their attitude seemed to be, "O.K.—if this is the way the game has to be played, we'll go along." When asked why they had done it, they replied simply, "We felt we needed the change."

In 1965, Father Henneberry, the superior at Shrub Oak described for the provincial the problems the current situation was posing for some of the more religiously observant men. A scholastic had come to the superior's office to say that there were many men like himself—they loved the Society, wanted to pray, wanted to study, wanted to obey but were having great trouble at Shrub Oak. "He said that either what is tolerated by the superior at Shrub Oak is Jesuit life—and he cannot make this meet the ideals he has—or it is not, and something should be done about it." Among examples adduced by the young man was the way the superiors tolerated a hard core of half a dozen scholastics who refused to go to daily Mass and publicly announced the fact. Another example was the way superiors tolerated group defiance. As Saint Patrick's Day approached, the word went out: "If the Rector doesn't give us *Deo Gratias* [permission to talk] at breakfast, we just start to talk." No permission was given, and the scholastics just started to talk. No action was taken by superiors either on the spot or later.

Shrub Oak scholastics were in communication with the other philosophates, especially West Baden and Weston, through short-wave radio. They also used long-distance telephone, making many calls without permission.

At about the same time, the vice-rector of Shrub Oak, while recognizing the problems, took a more optimistic view:

There seems no doubt that today's generation of young Jesuits reflect the emotional immaturity and insecurity of their American generation. Since we admit them as such, we have to work with them as such, with patience and kindness as well as with firmness, in the knowledge that it may take longer to form them as Jesuits, but also with the hope that they will become fine Jesuits.

In July 1966, Shrub Oak became a collegiate institution with a new order of the day. Rising was between 5:30 and 7:00, at the individual's discretion. All were to be present at breakfast at 7:30. Luncheon was buffet, but dinner was still a served meal. Eleven o'clock was the beginning of evening silence, at which time everyone was to be in his room. There was no set retiring time. There was no regulation of television, except that it was not to be used after 11:00 P.M. It was necessary to obtain the rector's permission to smoke or to possess a radio. Each scholastic was permitted to have $5.00 in his possession; when the $5.00 needed to be replenished, he was to give a note to the subminister indicating how the previous $5.00 had been spent. There was a list of activities open to scholastics at Shrub Oak; the list included the Democratic party and the Republican party.

In 1968, two years later, the problems at Shrub Oak came to something of a climax when the scholastics threatened to strike against the traditional oral examination, the De Universa. They held two meetings (May 22 and 23, 1968) to decide whether or not they should go through with their threat. About one third was strongly in favor of the proposal, another third saw some possibility in it or was doubtful, while the remainder was opposed to it as being un-Jesuit. They did agree to issue a paper directed to superiors but were divided on whether to make it a petition that the examination be canceled that year or a flat declaration of a boycott of the examination. In the voting, thirty-three favored a boycott while forty-four opposed this action in favor of a petition.

The commotion was loud enough to reach Rome and to involve Vincent T. O'Keefe, one of the consultors to the General. In the event, the examinations were postponed for a day but, nevertheless, had to be taken. Some took it only under protest, each making a speech to that effect before his examination started. A few scholastics were so tense over the whole affair that they were in no condition to take the examination at that time and were allowed, instead, to take it the next fall.

As regards prayer, the scholastics tended to find traditional forms unappealing and either to abandon formal prayer or to develop other forms for themselves. Most congenial was the kind of prayer practiced by a group of ten philosophers from Shrub Oak, who in June 1964 spent a couple of weeks working in Harlem with Father Frank Winters as their chaplain. Their prayer was described by John L'Heureux:

> They stand in a semicircle around the altar, sing hymns not out of obligation but as an expression of devotion (one chap leads them on a guitar), place their hosts individually on the altar during an Offertory procession, receive Communion standing, and sing "We Shall Overcome" as a recessional. More remarkable, one of them gives a homily each day.... They are devastatingly open young men. Witnessing their liturgy, you have no choice: you must laugh at them or you must admit that this comes close to what Christianity should be—lives lived in Christ forming a continuity of revelation (L'Heureux 1967, 184).

New England

Until 1968, the New England collegians lived in separate locations, the juniors at Shadowbrook and the philosophers at Weston. The burned-down Shadowbrook was replaced in 1958 by a larger building in anticipation of continued growth, but this soon was extra space. For a time the additional space was used for lay retreats. John Swain, the vicar general in Rome, was concerned lest this development impinge on the desired isolation of the novices and juniors. He explicitly ordered that the retreatants were not to take their meals with the Jesuits in the community refectory, as they had been doing. In a 1960 letter he wrote, "We must beware of little changes which gradually (*sensim sine sensu*) change our customs in such a way that they are difficult to eradicate later on."

This incident reflects much of the previous lifestyle: a scale of building based on the confident expectation that the previous rate of growth would continue; the reporting to Rome of local details; the relative weight assigned to religious lifestyle and apostolic ministry; the belief that principles can be undermined by "little changes". Within half a dozen years, such a view of Jesuit life disappeared.

One of the early signs of a new era was the inability of superiors to agree on a house custom book—a manual of lived practice and procedures. When the new Shadowbrook went into operation in 1958, it seemed like an appropriate occasion to revise the previous book. Shadowbrook obtained copies of the custom books of all similar houses in the assistancy and set to work to revise its own book. By 1962, the task had not yet been completed, though still in process. By 1965, the task was abandoned; a custom book was no longer desirable or possible.

In 1966 a retreat for lay students was being conducted at Shadowbrook. The retreat was proceeding in silence according to tradition when a junior took a couple of the retreatants aside and explained that silence was an outmoded, monastic custom. He went on to urge the young retreatants to make their own decisions: "Why do you let them impose silence on you?" The faculty member who reported this incident to the provincial thought that the most significant aspect of the affair was that nothing was said or done to correct the junior and his action.

In 1967, there were numerous mentions made in the Shadowbrook house diary of juniors going to various towns in the area to partake of cultural events, including plays. The diary also mentioned that "five Smith College girls arrived for dinner in the parlor and discussion on James Joyce." At this same time, the rector and minister of Shadowbrook differed considerably in their attitudes toward house discipline, with the rector being much less inclined to enforce existing regulations.

The beadle's diary consisted of daily entries by the beadle, a scholastic designated as the intermediary between the rest of the scholastics and the superiors. His keeping a diary was an old Jesuit tradition which was regularly used to settle questions as to whether something should or should not be done and, if it should be done, how it should be done. The following are a few selections to illustrate the gradual change of lifestyle.

In 1962, the beadle's diary noted that the *missa recitata* had begun; that movies were being made available to the scholastics; that the young men had to be reminded that they should be at Mass every day. In 1963, the diary recorded the following: sports shirts were now acceptable wear in the refectory in the hot weather of summer; the weekly house holiday was changed from Thursday to Saturday, to be in harmony with the secular world; Hans Küng lectured to the scholastics at Weston on "The Church and Freedom"; the house retreat, conducted by Father William C. McInnes, incorporated discussion. In 1964: the scholastics heard a lecture on Teilhard de Chardin; some of them attended summer school at Boston College; three telephones were made available to them. The diary's final entry, March 5, 1965, read, "Father Rector gave me permission to discontinue this diary." Thus simply, another long tradition ended.

As mentioned earlier, the custom of town hall meetings for the Weston collegians (philosophers) began about 1965 under their superior, Daniel J. Shine, who would chair the meetings. At least one meeting dealt with the principle of the Third Way and its applicability to celibate religious. There were some problems with practice as well as with principle when the collegians began to go to Boston College for their classes and mingled with the female students. On the basis of this experience, several of the men were induced to withdraw from the Society.

At about this time, also, the scholastics were quite active in various "social actions". For example, at one time, they were getting up at 4:00 A.M. to go to the farmers' market with placards to protest the selling of grapes. Whenever the young men engaged in one of these actions, they wore clerics, though they were not wearing clerics at school.

When the New England provincial made his visitation at Weston in 1968, he reported that the scholastics were "hungry for more leadership". He went on to explain that this was "not so much a need for spiritual direction as it was a need for psychological support". The young men were unwilling to be fitted into the old structure but were understandably unable to create a new way of religious life. They were, after all, beginners in that life. The frequent complaint of lack of leadership seemed to the superiors really to be a confession of their inability to see their own way, along with an unwillingness to accept the old way. A part of the problem, as described by the provincial, was that after the changes "they feel that they differ little from any other student on the Boston College campus."

In this same visitation, the provincial reported, "There is no common rising or retiring time. People are allowed to follow individual time orders. The majority of the members of the community do not abuse this mark of trust and opportunity for a display of personal responsibility." It was at this same time, 1968, that the provincial approved of an experiment with secular clothes. The scholastics were to be allowed to wear such clothes during the spring semester, and then the experiment was to be evaluated. If such a formal evaluation ever took place, it must have been favorable, because the custom continued.

With the permission to wear secular clothes on the Boston College campus came a directive from the General that the Jesuits were to wear a small crucifix pin. The crucifixes were distributed to the collegians, but few of them chose to wear the identifying sign. According to the father minister, while the collegians were still living at Weston but taking their classes at Boston College, they went out at night more than did the theologians and also had more girls coming to see them from their Boston College contacts. (This same difference between collegians and theologians seems to have marked experience at St. Louis and North Aurora; the collegians were, of course, younger and probably less mature.) To provide adequate spiritual direction for the collegians in this new situation, their superior brought in young Jesuit priests from the high schools and colleges. There was one priest-director for every ten collegians. In the case of one director, a very modern young man, all ten of his group left the Society.

The academic changes made in collegiate life were the root of many lifestyle changes. The Weston Self-Study Committee (1964–65) had recognized that if their recommendations on academic matters were carried out, especially if the scholastics began to take courses on the Boston College campus, many changes in lifestyle would have to be made at Weston. The prediction was accurate. Changes followed, for example, in the community meals and the community Mass and the garb of the scholastics. Describing the situation of the collegians in 1966, Daniel Shine, superior of the collegians, stated in a report to the provincial that going to class at Boston College had much significance, also, for the spiritual life of the young men:

> They are no longer in isolation from the academic community, and they have the opportunity for growth and personal responsibility. Not a few of them have expressed themselves to me as finding the whole situation such that they "re-choose" their vocation. Briefly, the situation seems to encourage personal growth, responsibility, and a mature exercise of freedom.

When in 1969 the collegians left Weston entirely, they moved into eight small communities in the vicinity of Boston College. (As in Chicago, the incoming collegians were asked which community they preferred, though the superior made the final decision.) In connection with this move, New England analyzed the potentialities and problems of the "small community". For example, in the spring of 1970, James F. Powers examined the experience of twenty-five communities (theologians as well as collegians) and chronicled both the accomplishments and the difficulties of small communities.

In the fall of that same year the superior of the collegian communities, Frederick G. McLeod, addressed a thirteen-page letter to the members of those communities in which he described the goals of the New England program. He wrote:

> The major goals of our experiment are threefold: first and foremost, to develop a supportive community, not merely on the affective level, but also on the level of shared religious commitment; secondly, to develop an atmosphere in which a collegian can grow in a religious sense of personal and corporate responsibility; and lastly, to provide an intellectual and apostolic milieu in which one can become aware of his talents, develop them and use them fruitfully, not only for his own self-development, but also for the service of the Society and the Church (McLeod 1970, 2).

Father McLeod proceeded to point out that "the move was implemented in a period of profound historical and cultural adaptation when the cry for relevance, personal freedom, and, above all, change became dominant and widespread." He went on to describe to the collegians the significance of this move from Weston to Boston:

> Undertaken in this situation, the move to Boston College— however you may want to view it—directly or indirectly caused or contributed to several results, such as the end of the Juniorate, the erosion and disappearance of former Weston structures, a real and deep separation between the academic and community aspects of a collegian's life, a change-over from traditional religious garb to lay clothing, an assumption of attitudes and study habits prevalent among other students at B.C. [Boston College], etc. Although you may not frame your thinking consciously in terms of existentialist philosophy, you are nevertheless deeply influenced and concerned over what is authentic existence in the kind of world in which you now live—about the immediate present, about man himself, about your personal relationships with others, and about your personal experience as being the basis of real knowledge (McLeod 1970, 3).

McLeod remarked at the end of that description, "No wonder then that a storm of centrifugal forces was unleashed at Weston" (ibid.).

In another report (January 11, 1970) which surveyed the first year's experience, McLeod found many failures to achieve the goals of the small communities. In that same month, a member of the community reported to the provincial that the younger men were suffering "from a general state of ennui of not being either a layman or a religious". Some sought reorientation by visiting the novitiate at Shadowbrook, but this practice was discouraged by Father McLeod. Meanwhile, the number of collegians continued to drop. The eighty-seven in 1968 had become seven in 1974. The number of small collegian communities also, of course, shrank each year. In 1973, there remained only two collegian communities, which differed greatly. One was very open, with much "sharing". Its members were activists, involved in the apostolate. The other house was quieter, its members primarily concerned with studies.

Changes in the prayer life of the Weston collegians were similar to those in the other scholasticates. For example, in 1970 the superior of the collegians noted that "many do not see or sense a value in a daily liturgy." Of the eight extant communities, he mentioned two that seemed to be particularly unimpressed with the need for spiritual direction and daily prayer.[3]

In 1971, one of the collegians who was a house consultor wrote an analytic letter touching on a topic that was discussed frequently in those days, the topic of Jesuit identity. He wrote:

> Within the collegian community right now there is little understanding of *Jesuit* spirit and spirituality. One collegian whom I respect highly told me recently that as long as we have Jesus Christ as the center of our personal spirituality, we are in fine shape. I rebel against this simple but false pronouncement. The spirituality of the Society, which is the source of our identity as Jesuits, is a definite regime for holiness. We cannot live without

---

[3] These two communities totaled twelve scholastics. As of 1989, only two of the twelve were still Jesuits.

the strength, the accumulated wisdom, the way of holiness of
our predecessors. The collegians tend to assess their identity in
an absurd vacuum. At the present time, I feel that the community has little or no sense of our tradition, our heritage, our
history of holiness. A small number are tempted to enter monastic communities, while others leave.

The last observation caused him to add, "I cry out that we can no
longer let people 'grow out of their vocation'."

Chicago/Detroit

For a time at Milford (of the Chicago province), in the late 1950s
and early 1960s, the number of scholastics needing psychiatric care
brought a remonstrance from Rome that the province might be
more careful in testing applicants before accepting them. There
was no recognition at that time that the problem might be one of
putting new wine into old wineskins. The young entrants had a
set of values that did not easily fit within the traditional structures.
    At least as early as 1962, small changes were occurring at
Colombiere that bore a marked similarity to the later revolution.
For example, in a letter dated January 1961, an official reported a
change among the juniors with regard to customary penitential
practices. "The Juniors rarely take Little Table, which as a result is
filled by the Fathers and Brothers. It is also very rare that a Junior
takes a culpa; maybe a generous number would be two a month."
At Colombiere in 1967, the juniors developed a liturgy in which
the entire congregation sang the canon of the Mass, including the
consecration, in four parts. At Milford at this time the daily
community Mass became a concelebrated Mass with many variations and with many disagreements over what form the liturgy
should best take. In 1968, obligatory attendance at the community
Mass was limited to Sunday and Wednesday. Also, the congregation no longer attended Mass divided according to their status

(fathers, novices, junior scholastics, brothers) but all mingled. (They also began to mingle, at about this time, in the dining room.)

At Milford, a community council was formed in 1968. It consisted of priests, brothers, juniors, and novices, and the council met with the rector and his consultors. Beginning in this same year, the juniors, now called collegians, were allowed to visit their family homes, even outside the Cincinnati area.

One of the professors at Colombiere wrote to the provincial in 1966:

> The Juniors, by and large, have a tendency to use "self-improvement" as a norm for accepting work and setting goals. "Peace of mind" and "intra-personal development" are the watchwords. While the scholastics should be conscious that they are developing, an egocentric emphasis seems to be harmful. I must spend a good deal of time trying to convince them that this self-development is a by-product of self-giving.

At West Baden College, a joint house of Chicago and Detroit provinces, few external changes were made before the move to North Aurora in 1964. The cassock was still worn, there was reading at meals, mail was censored, and so forth. This traditional lifestyle prevailed for a while at North Aurora also, but the changes soon began.

Changes in values, however, were being reported well before external changes occurred. Some observers saw a connection between the new values and the personalist philosophy being taught by Michael J. Montague and Walter L. Farrell. Other value changes were connected with the new interpretations of Scripture. The philosophers were in the same house as the theologians, and developments in the theologate—at least the more exciting ones, like questions regarding the historicity of the Gospels—tended to percolate to the philosophers and to have the greater impact because the latter lacked the theological background necessary for a balanced interpretation (see p. 288).

W. Henry Kenney was superior of the philosophers at North

Aurora beginning in 1967. In an interview, he reported that he found the young Jesuits harder to deal with than the college boys he had been teaching at Xavier University. The scholastics were more restless and questioning and also more aggressive. About a half dozen were the leaders in causing the unrest. All of them later left the order; but while they were there, they were the storm center of disturbance.

A traditional community prayer had been the recitation of litanies, usually just before dinner or before retiring at night. In the 1960s, this devotion came in for widespread criticism, and the scholastics began to ignore the rule requiring their attendance. After some attempts to enforce the regulation and the usual failures, attempts were made to replace the litanies with another form of community prayer. At North Aurora, for example, in 1967 a community prayer service was substituted. The new prayer service, however, was no more acceptable than the displaced litanies and eventually was abandoned. As in other houses, litanies then ceased, and nothing took their place. The young men declared that any form of community prayer, especially obligatory community prayer, was monastic.

Missouri/Wisconsin

The philosophate of the Missouri province, which had always been on the campus of St. Louis University, was the only one not to change its location during the upheaval of the 1960s. It did move to a new building called the Fusz Memorial, but this was also on the university campus. Built in the traditional manner, Fusz could house almost two hundred scholastics, along with faculty, classrooms, dining and recreational facilities, and a chapel; it was a very large, self-contained unit in which everyone operated on the same schedule in a uniform lifestyle. By 1973, Fusz housed five distinct communities of collegians with different lifestyles. (For a detailed description of the new Fusz, see *National Jesuit News* February 1973: 6.)

The following description of lifestyle changes at Fusz during the 1960s is based chiefly on an interview with Robert A. Doyle, who held the positions of minister of scholastics (1964–66) and of rector (1966–73). When he came to Fusz in 1964, the prescribed order of the house was the same as when he himself had been a philosopher there seven years earlier. The spirit of the house, however, had changed, and this was Doyle's first experience with the new Society. In his own course of studies, he had been moving just ahead of the wave of change, and he was coming to Fusz from tertianship. The two preceding ministers of scholastics had, for the most part, simply avoided confrontation with the young men. Doyle's immediate forerunner had been ill much of the time.

Since approximately 1962–63, a certain independent spirit had begun to manifest itself, and some existing rules were not being observed. For example, as much as one third of a class—not always the same third—would be absent and nothing would be said. Also, there was widespread violation of the rules regarding silence, attendance at Mass, and the first morning visit to the Blessed Sacrament. In addition, there were failures to obtain necessary permission—for example, permission to be out of the house in the evening.

The rector was disturbed over the situation and urged the new minister to restore order. Doyle began by insisting on the observance of all the rules. He worked on the principle that if you allowed one man to violate a rule, there would be two violations the next day, then four, and soon all discipline would be lost. So all violators were to be called to account immediately.

For several months he attempted to operate on this principle but ran into formidable obstacles. For example, according to the traditional rule, a visitor was to check on the scholastics during times of prayer. Because the scholastics appointed to this task enjoyed so little community support, they were performing the task ineffectively, if at all. In an attempt to establish the principle of the rule inescapably, the minister himself sometimes took on the task. He encountered, however, such a massive resistance that eventually he abandoned the effort.

There was constant confrontation. For example, two of the scholastics had returned to the house after 10:00 P.M. and were standing by the bulletin board talking. After they had been talking for five or ten minutes, the minister challenged them on the score that this was the time for prayer in their rooms. The next morning one of the scholastics was in the minister's office lecturing him on his "fascist" way of running the house. For another example, the minister on his rounds would find a scholastic sleeping after the rising bell. The minister would get the man up and reprimand him; but the next day the man would be following exactly the same course of action. Short of dismissal from the Society, there was little that could be done. There were no adequate middle penalties that could be applied. The minister might send the man into the chapel to pray for an hour as a penance; but as soon as the minister went away, the man was likely to leave the chapel.

The disciplinary problem had a psychological-ascetical component that made its solution extraordinarily difficult. The minister would call a man into his room and lecture him on a strict spiritual basis, explaining that it was necessary for him to obey the house regulations if he wanted to keep his vocation. Then the man would argue that he could not in conscience allow himself to be so regimented; he could not allow himself to be treated as a "non-person"; he ought to be "inner directed" and not "other directed". The confrontation would be so intense at times that the young man would burst into tears. But at the end he could not in conscience bring himself to say that he would follow regulations. There was a great deal of strain in the house. Many of the scholastics were on medication, and there were at least thirteen getting professional psychological treatment.

Not all of the scholastics followed this course of individual determination. Out of a total community of 180 scholastics, one third might be of this sort. But the third included many natural leaders, and the entire scholasticate tended, in a confrontation, to support the dissenting individual. When a Wisconsin scholastic was sent home to his province because of a steady, formal resistance to authority, the other Wisconsin scholastics, when they returned to the province that summer, went as a group to the Wisconsin provincial, to criticize the Fusz minister.[4]

After a time, the minister came to the conclusion that he would have to follow some different procedure. He began to distinguish between positions that must be held at all costs and those that could be relinquished. For example, beer was served daily instead of only a couple of times per week; attendance at litanies was not checked upon; and the scholastics could be out until 10:00 P.M. without the minister's calling them to task. On other matters, however, he drew a strict line and enforced compliance. For example, the scholastics had to attend daily Mass; they could not be out after 10:00 P.M. without permission; they had to wear the cassock at Mass and in the refectory and to wear clerics outside the house.

The rector did not like this compromise, which he considered to be a retreat from principle. He wanted the minister to enforce all the regulations that were still on the books. The provincial, however, agreed with the minister that the compromise was probably the best that could be achieved. During the following two years, 1965 and 1966, morale improved and so did the health of the scholastics.

The next two years, 1967 and 1968, were again difficult. For one reason, the climate of experimentation and permissiveness was picking up strength throughout the assistancy, and changes made in one house were acting as a pressure on all other houses. For another reason, the theologians had moved in from St. Mary's to St. Louis University (1967), and there was much contact between them and the philosophers. The philosophers were being introduced to the new convictions of the theologians—for example,

---

[4] The dismissed scholastic was engaged in some political activity with a black group and was often kept out until 3:00 in the morning. Repeated commands brought no change of behavior.

that regular, frequent confession was likely to be unhealthy and that Benediction, which was still on the regular order of the philosophers, was little short of idolatry. During this period, superiors were under constant pressure again to make more changes.

St. Louis, along with California, seems to have been a center of scholastic interest and experimentation in the theory of the Third Way (see Chapter II, footnote II). There was much discussion of the necessity of warm intimate relationships with each other and with women. Superiors were concerned for a time with possible homosexual developments, but mostly the scholastics developed new relationships with women. After Mass on Sundays, at the college church, the young scholastics would spend an hour in front of the church chatting with the young novice sisters from the neighboring novitiate down the street. Or on a summer evening, a half dozen pairs, each consisting of a scholastic and a novice sister, would be strolling up and down Lindell Boulevard talking. There was also some experimentation with dating.

The General's letter on the Third Way was well received by most of the collegians. The scholastics who came along later, after about 1970, exhibited little interest in the Third Way but tended rather to judge it as immature on the part of their predecessors.

In the years 1969 and 1970, superiors continued to make concessions to the scholastics' demand for adaptation to modernity, and the morale at Fusz again improved. These years were peaceful and pleasant ones. The scholastics were prayerful, hard working, and happy. Father Doyle recalled it as a time when he felt he had them in the palm of his hand—a very different situation from that which existed in the period 1964–66. There remained three problem areas: late night hours, travel, and dress. The question was debated among the house authorities whether Father Doyle should move on these three areas or let them be. Advice was divided. In the end, he decided not to move lest he spoil a good situation. A prayerful, hard-working, happy community seemed too good a thing to imperil.

Fusz saw the development of considerable T-group activity. At the peak, about two thirds of the house was engaged in such groups. Those who belonged to T-groups met weekly and accorded this meeting the highest priority in the week. (See also p. 90.)

During this period, the rate of scholastics leaving the Society was unusually high. This, and the numerous changes made at Fusz, led to considerable criticism throughout the province. Father Doyle made a tour of the province and explained why changes had been made. His impression of the results of the tour were that it altered the minds of only a few.

New Orleans

The juniorate at Grand Coteau had been quite traditional, as may be seen in the following items taken from the custom book regulating the life of the juniors before the sixties:

> All must be in bed and the lights must be out by 9:30 P.M.
>
> The customary appellation for a Junior is "Mister" in English and "Frater" in Latin.
>
> No Junior is allowed to enter the cubicle of another Junior. If he wishes to speak to another, he must obtain permission from the Beadle and speak at the entrance of the cubicle. If he wishes to speak for some length of time (more than three minutes), he must obtain permission from Father Minister.
>
> The biretta is to be worn whenever a Junior leaves the third floor. When the server approaches Father Rector's table for the first time only, he should raise his biretta.
>
> Letters and clips should not be shown to others without permission of Reverend Father Rector.
>
> Card playing is not allowed at any time. Sunbathing is never allowed.

While these external provisions were still in operation, the spirit of the juniorate was gradually changing. The 1963 class, for example, was clearly much more independent than its predecessors. Repeatedly, officials' letters mention this class as having "a different spirit". One letter predicted that the class would continue to be a disturbing influence when it moved into the philosophate.[5]

By 1966, house officials were with one voice telling the provincial and the General that a new spirit had overtaken the juniorate: "A spirit of restlessness exists among some of them most definitely. ... They are eager to seek direction outside normal channels and especially outside the Society. A chance remark of a philosopher in a letter carries more weight than a directive from the Holy See or from the Provincial."

It was a common observation that silence was disappearing: "The young men find it frustrating not to be free in communicating when the spirit moves them." Even silence at table was disappearing: "The talk is both loud and prolonged at times. The Rector and the Minister are among those provoked, but they seem to do little to remedy the situation."

The restless juniors of 1963 became the restless philosophers at Spring Hill, Alabama, in 1965. In that year, the philosophers asked the provincial to come out to the scholasticate for an open discussion for which they would set the agenda. They may have had in mind something similar to the Alma confrontation (see p. 186). The vice provincial, acting in place of the provincial, who was out of the country, declined the invitation, following the advice of those he consulted.

Perhaps as a substitute for the meeting with the provincial, the scholastics arranged a meeting of their own.[6] The rector and the minister were invited to attend and sat in the rear of the room. The meeting went on from 8:00 in the evening until 9:30. People got up all over the room and voiced their unhappiness with various aspects of the life. Some of them even wept. After an hour and a half, there was nothing more to say, and the meeting broke up. There was a general feeling of frustration because nothing had

[5] This class also left the Society in large numbers. The 1963 juniorate had fifteen members in first year and thirteen in second year. As of 1975, ten of the first-year men (67%) and eight of the second-year men (63%) had left.

[6] This account is from an interview with one of the scholastics who was present at the meeting.

been settled. About 10 o'clock word went down the corridors that the meeting was being reconvened—by the rector.[7] The rector was in the front of the room. He told the scholastics that he had been unable to sleep and wanted to address the group that night. In effect, he said two things. He said that he had been unaware of how deeply disturbed the community was and how unhappy.[8] Second, he promised that he would take immediate steps to improve or remove many of the conditions that they had spoken about earlier that evening. He spoke only about fifteen minutes and then sent everybody back to bed.

Later that year one of the faculty commented on this meeting. The writer was a relatively young man who in his previous letters had tended to take the side of change and progress. After mentioning the confrontation between the rector and the scholastics, he said: "Prior to that discussion, I had believed that the major problem in the scholasticate was academic. The one thing that became clearly evident during this discussion was that the major problem seems to be spiritual. Many of the men seem to have a very deficient conception of the religious life." He then listed concretely some of the attitudes that seemed to him to be defective.

1. The scholastics were taking the Society on trial and were seriously questioning whether or not the Society had lived up to their expectations.
2. They had a distorted understanding of the precedence that private conscience takes over law.
3. They condemned almost without exception the apostolate of the Society. (The writer did not explain this ambiguous statement.)
4. They had an excessive concern to build up friendships in

[7] The rector, James C. Babb, had entered the order in 1933 and had been rector since 1962.

[8] There were a half dozen instances of this, where the superior told the scholastics that he had not known how unhappy they were. Usually this discovery came about through the manifestations of conscience, which grew much longer during this period.

the Society, which then became cliques "within which others in the community are criticized and mocked privately while avoided publicly".

5. "The fundamental notion of self-abnegation and generosity in the service of Christ seems to be given second place to the ideal of self-development in a purely secular way."

6. There was a tendency to think of obedience in the Society "in terms of political maneuvering in a way disastrous for religious spirit".

At about the same time, the minister of the house wrote to the provincial, "They ask me why they cannot associate with the college girls, why they can't mix with externs in general, why they can't go places and be treated and trusted like men. The fact is that they are treated like men, religious men." In the same letter, he mentioned that four of the scholastics had gone to a drive-in movie and then to a bowling alley, returning home at about 4:00 A.M. They insisted that there was nothing reprehensible in their actions even though they were contrary to house regulations. They had reached a responsible decision that they needed this recreation in order to do their work.

In 1969, the dean of the philosophate wrote to the General about an almost universal problem of the period: "I find that a good number of the young men have what is referred to popularly here as 'authority hangups'. They resent having to do something because it is in a schedule or laid down by someone else." He ended, however, on an optimistic note: "Most are able to talk intelligently about this problem and to work it out gradually." He added that the process required an exhausting amount of dialogue.

In a letter written at about this same time, a community member voiced a common complaint of the period: "I have been somewhat distressed by an attitude of seeming permissiveness on the part of Superiors. This is true from the Provincial down. There is an apparent hesitation to give positive, definitive directives in areas that are being challenged." He added that in his own dealings with the scholastics, he put great stress on the documents

COLLEGIATE PROGRAMS: LIFESTYLE

of the Thirty-first General Congregation. This led some of the scholastics to warn him not to be "a man of the book".

Oregon/California

In general, changes came somewhat later to the Oregon province than to the scholasticates on the East Coast. For example, a completely new daily order was established at Shrub Oak in 1966, at Colombiere in 1967, and at Mt. St. Michael's in 1968. A frequently heard argument on the part of the scholastics at the Mount was, "Why can't we do the same as they are doing at other places?" Nevertheless, changes came.

The juniors of the Oregon province (at Sheridan, Oregon) presented a petition to use their Christian names rather than the title "Brother". The petition contained two pages of reasons and was signed by most of the juniors. In the fall of 1965, the provincial, John J. Kelley, granted the petition, but only for use within the family. "In all introductions to any externs, the formal title should be used."[9]

One of the characteristic developments of the new era, and one of its shaping forces, was the ascetical institute. The Mount had three of these—one on "Jesuit Community" (1964), another on "Authority in the Church" (1968), and a third on the "Psychosexual Maturity of the Jesuit" (1969). All three of these topics involved characteristic issues of the 1960s.

At the Oregon philosophate, Mt. St. Michael's, Timothy Fallon, who taught the history of philosophy, publicly held in 1963 that every scholastic should have a psychiatrist. A disagreeing member of the community remarked, "If I had a son who said he was going to join an order where every young man had a psychiatrist, I would forbid him to join it."

---

[9] For a contrast in the date of the change and in the method of making it, see

In March 1963, Hans Küng had spoken at Jesuit-directed Gonzaga University, with the result that the progressives in the community felt strengthened. In May 1966, Father Pedro Arrupe visited the university and spoke on the need to update the Jesuit outlook and in general to be open to change. In April 1967, there was a meeting of the province on the spiritual formation of Jesuits; delegates to the meeting included scholastic representatives and even two novices.

The superiors' view of the future was not very clear. In October 1967, they built at the Mount a costly complex consisting of a new gym and a swimming pool—just two and a half years before they moved the scholastics out of this scholasticate entirely. In February 1969, the provincial's advisory committee advised him not to issue *any* directives on attire or on liturgical rubrics; the entire situation was too foggy.

In May 1970, the scholastics were put on a personal budget, each scholastic receiving $30.00 per month.[10] In September 1970, the scholastics of Mt. St. Michael's moved to Gonzaga University and began quite a different lifestyle. Some changes came more slowly than others. It was not until 1975, for example, that the Gonzaga yearbook showed a few Jesuit collegians wearing secular clothes; even then the majority were still wearing clerics.

Various experiments were tried in replacing traditional prayer forms with something different. One experiment made use of psychological techniques such as T-groups and sensitivity sessions. In 1969, for example, nine members of the community chose to make the house triduum in group-encounter style.

Albert A. Lemieux was the rector of Mt. St. Michael's during the time when the changes began. In an interview, he said that two factors chiefly inclined him to look with favor on the forces making for change. One was his growing knowledge of the scholastics. This knowledge was gained mainly through the mani-

---

[10] At this time at Weston the scholastics were receiving $60 per month. In all probability there were some differences in what the respective communities supplied to their scholastics in the way of goods and services.

festations of conscience, which were averaging over an hour each. He was one of a number of superiors who found this experience a revelation of a new type of young Jesuit. The other factor was his experience at G.C. 31. The congregation had repeatedly recognized a need for adaptation to a new era.

As rector, he dealt with the scholastics who were leaving the order. In his experience, the two chief causes of the departures at that time were problems with faith and problems with celibacy. He mentioned also that these were young men who had come into the collegiate program directly from the novitiate without the protective period of the juniorate. He could see the possibility that some needed a longer period of protection during which the new patterns of life developed in the novitiate would have a chance to deepen and become firm.

California, as a matter of fact, kept its men for two years after the novitiate in a kind of juniorate at Loyola University of Los Angeles.[11] It sent its scholastics to the Mount for only the last two years of the collegiate program.

---

[11] During this transitional period, however, the young men were to be introduced gradually into new aspects of the religious life. The superior was urged, by the provincial, to develop in them a strong sense of individual responsibility, and to that end it was suggested to him that he might absent himself from the house for half the time.

X

CHANGES IN REGENCY

After two years in the novitiate, two in the juniorate, and three in philosophy, the young Jesuit traditionally entered on a very different stage of formation. It usually lasted for three years, usually took the form of teaching in a Jesuit high school; it was called "regency".[1]

Purpose

The primary purpose of the regency period was to form the scholastic—in three ways especially. One was to exercise the young Jesuit in self-giving. After nineteen years or more of attending school, where he was the center of the enterprise and was constantly urged to develop himself, he needed the experience of expending himself for others, to give rather than to receive. Second, regency was to exercise the young man in practical skills. He would have many responsibilities and have to make many decisions, both in teaching his classes and in managing extracurricular activities. Third, regency would also restore the scholastic's relationship to the outside world. After seven years of isolation, he would again be mingling on a daily workaday basis with others than Jesuits.

For practically all the scholastics, regency was a welcome change. They were weary of the life of the student. It is true that they

---

[1] The use of the term in this sense seems to be limited to the Jesuit order.

were still in the classroom, but with an altogether different function to perform. Instead of being taught, they were teaching. For the scholastic who was not primarily academic in inclination and who had occasionally wondered if he really had a vocation to be a Jesuit, regency supplied a welcome reminder that there was more to life than was contained between the covers of books. Some of the less academically inclined philosophers often proved to be among the most successful regents.

A secondary, but significant, purpose of the regency program was to supply the Jesuit high schools with needed personnel. The scholastic teachers were an important part of the traditional high school. Though some of them moved on each year, they were replaced by others, so that the school could count on a steady supply of perhaps a dozen well-educated, highly motivated teachers— who worked without salary. While in some ways inferior to the priest teachers in the school, the scholastics had their own advantages. Closer to the students in age (the average scholastic was about twenty-five years old), they bonded easily with the boys. They played sports with the students and managed many of their extracurricular activities, such as the school newspaper and yearbook or the debating club. Since the scholastics had no families but lived at the school, they and the boys felt they belonged to each other in a unique way.[2]

In earlier times, the scholastics were so needed that their regency period often lasted five years. The General would write to a provincial complaining of this prolongation, and the provincial would answer that it was a temporary expedient adopted to meet the floodtide of the immigrant church and that "next year" he hoped to be able to reduce the teaching period.

This dependence on scholastics did not last. Under the impact of two simultaneous developments—the growing size of the schools and the diminishing number of scholastics—many more lay teachers were hired and the reliance of a school on Jesuit scholastics grew

[2] Though my own regency days are fifty years in the past, some of the boys I taught then (retired grandparents now) still correspond with me.

less and less. Eventually the whole institution of regency was of minimal importance to the schools.

In the late 1960s, two questionnaires were administered to the theologians, asking them about their experiences during regency. One questionnaire was constructed by and administered to the theologians at Alma (California) in 1966; the other was constructed by the theologians at St. Mary's (Kansas) and administered to the theologians at St. Mary's, North Aurora, Weston, and Woodstock.[3] The very existence of the questionnaire is significant: in previous times, the scholastics in theology did not occupy themselves with analyzing the process of formation and making recommendations for its modification. They might have vented their personal complaints in "bull sessions", but they would never have launched a formal investigation aimed at changing the traditional system.

In the St. Mary's questionnaire, many reported limited success in performing the required spiritual exercises.[4] For example, 40% reported that they meditated less than fifteen minutes daily. Most identified their workload as the chief cause of their failure to pray. Some criticized their novitiate formation for teaching them

[3] The returns from North Aurora and Weston were too small to be significant, while those from Woodstock arrived too late to be usable. The returns are summarized in Santa Clara 1967, 2:1:153–201.

[4] Father Joseph F. Small, who was a regent at St. Xavier High School in Cincinnati in the early 1940s, recalls that the scholastic started the day as follows:

5:00	—	rising time
5:15	—	check to see that the man was up
5:30	—	a visit to the chapel (the Father Minister was kneeling at the back to check)
5:30–6:30	—	meditation in one's room (checked once during the hour)
6:30	—	serve a Mass
7:00	—	examination of meditation made in the chapel (Father Minister kneeling in back)
7:15	—	breakfast

While the order in some houses may have been somewhat less strictly administered, this was basically the order regents were expected to follow in the years preceding the sixties.

a monastic spirituality rather than one that would enable them to see their work as prayer and thus to be at peace when they substituted work for formal prayer. One reported: "I was inadequately prepared for the problems and situations I met. Training for a monk-oriented life gave me no comprehension of the stress and strain of the active life. Seven years of secluded study did not prepare me for dealing with students, parents, or the community as a working apostolic unit." Another said:

> A man faces head-on for the first time the reality that what he was told in the novitiate is misleading and just plain incorrect. The time-clock exercises of his spiritual life are not the practical way of living and growing in the religious life. Readjustment must come during regency, or the man is heading for a nervous breakdown attempting to live a life that is impossible to live (S.C.C. 1967, 2:2:170–71).

Regent Harry Fleddermann agreed with John Vigneau's proposal at the Santa Clara Conference that the novitiate training be restructured to provide "an apostolic spirituality of contemplation in action". With such a spirituality, the regent could more easily recognize work as prayer (p. 3:1:192). Both men later left the order.

A majority (71%) agreed with the proposition that the primary purpose of regency was the personal development of the scholastic. From this they drew the conclusion that the needs of the individual rather than the needs of the school should dictate the nature and duration of the work assigned. An eloquent minority, however, observed that true self-development involved a self-transcendence, that is, involved working for the good of the school, which was the good of the students. As one of them wrote: "I don't understand this. A Scholastic should be expected to shoulder the responsibilities of someone teaching in a modern educational enterprise. The institution should *not* have to adapt itself to the needs of the Scholastics!" (S.C.C. 1967, 2:2:166).

The following are some of the findings of the 1966 Alma questionnaire. Asked if they had a sense of satisfaction about their regency experience, 91% replied in the affirmative. Asked if they had had enough freedom to develop as a person during regency, 68% said they did.

Regarding time devoted to daily meditation, one third reported spending the full required fifty minutes, while another third reported a daily average of thirty minutes; 9% spent no time in meditation. Asked if they thought the requirement of fifty minutes daily was practical for regents, 95% replied No. A substantial part (59%) felt that their daily experiences with the students were more effective in developing their spiritual life than the time spent on formal spiritual exercises.

There was general agreement that a single standard should obtain for scholastics and priests in the use of cars, money, television, and all other things. Most (61%) thought that apostolates other than teaching should be open to scholastics; as examples of "other", they mentioned census taking, race relations, and poverty programs.

The editors of the questionnaire summed up the responses dealing with superiors by saying that the scholastics wanted the rector to be a "pal" and someone who was "at ease in non-structured situations". One editor offered a personal summary of the dominant theme struck by the answers: "To me the question-naire seemed to be shouting 'too much formation; too much idealism; too much effort to mould us into some ideal Jesuit; too much rule, law, objectivity, obligation.'"

Lifestyle

The regents' experience with changed lifestyles varied consider-ably according to both time and place yet had some common characteristics. In general, the high schools and colleges changed less and later than did the houses of formation. There was thus a degree of built-in tension between the regents and the communi-ties that they were joining, especially after about 1966. From coast to coast the complaint was heard from the older faculty members, "What are they *doing* in the houses of formation?" Some of these houses tried to explain themselves to the rest of the province by sending an emissary on a tour of the major local communities. (See, for example, pp. 179, 317, and 365.)

In one New England high school, in 1968, a house official commented on the slowness of the community's adjustment to modernity. Having noted that the high school consultors had voted to allow members of the community to come to lunch (not breakfast or dinner) on Saturdays and Sundays (not every day) in informal dress, he said, "St. Ignatius would be very disappointed in such 'pioneers' who are afraid to do what is done even in houses of probation." In another New England high school, a scholastic was the first to teach without the cassock. He made this break with tradition entirely on his own authority, and for some time this regent stood entirely alone in the school. Eventually everybody adopted his pioneering practice.

The St. Mary's questionnaire (1967) had some questions relating to community life, but the responses do not add up to a unified picture. For one thing, the responses reflect a period of experience covering six years (1960–66). In the early part of this period, changes were few and small, even in the houses of formation, whereas toward the end of the period, they were greater and more numerous. Thus, the responses, which were not identified by period of regency, could reflect very different individual experiences. Also, the houses among which the regents were dispersed varied in the size and timing of their lifestyle changes; the pattern often depended on a particular rector. Thus, the experience of the regents, scattered among the various houses, was more diversified than that of the other periods of formation.

In all of the communities, the degree of any friction between regents and other members of the community was moderated by two factors. First, regents were a small part of the total community. Whereas in the houses of formation, they were gathered together in one group, here they were dispersed in small units. Inevitably they tended to conform more to the existing community than to attempt to reform it.

The regents also had somewhat less motive to agitate for change than did the scholastics in other stages of formation. Life in the schools had always been much freer than life in the houses of formation. The regents already had many of the freedoms that the other scholastics were demanding. They were in daily contact with the outside world; they had access to newspapers, television, and movies; they had much more control over their own time; they had some access to cars; and so forth. Though they wanted more of all these things, they already had more than had been granted them in the earlier stages of formation, especially during the years before about 1968.

Eventually regency ceased to have a fixed form. As the regents grew fewer and older, regency was fitted to their needs on an individual basis. If it took the form of teaching, it might be in a college as easily as in a high school. But it might not take the form of teaching at all. It could be some kind of pastoral or social work. Or it could be special studies. And in all cases its duration was adjustable. At the end of regency, all returned to a life of study and to the lifestyle of a house of formation.

XI

CHANGES IN TERTIANSHIP

Traditional Structure

Tertianship, the last and shortest stage in the formation of a Jesuit, follows the completion of theology. In its traditional form it lasted eight to ten months. It was called "tertianship" because it was thought of as a "third" probation. Traditionally, there was a first, very short, probationary period before the applicant was admitted as a novice. This was followed by the novitiate, a second period of probation. At the end of the entire process, there was this third, and final, probation. It is probably more helpful to think of this "third" year as extending the work of the two years of novitiate; for the tertianship is a return in some ways to novitiate values and lifestyle—modified appropriately to suit older and more mature men.[1]

The tertianship seems to have been original with Saint Ignatius and to have stemmed in part from his personal experience. During his studies at the University of Paris, he experienced less felt fervor in his prayer life. Upon the completion of his studies, when he could spend more time in prayer and in direct spiritual works for the neighbor, "he found his affections again warmed, and he experienced anew his former consolations and even mystic visitations" (Ganss 1970, 234). Because scholastics would be in studies

---

[1] The 1931 edition of the *Epitome* prescribed that the kinds of experiments and the amount of prayer were to be similar for novices and for tertians (Curia 1931, no. 434, no. 436). (The *Epitome* was a collection of precepts taken from various authoritative sources.) The two prescriptions are omitted in the *Practicum,* which replaced the *Epitome* in 1977.

for many years, Ignatius legislated a final year of formation very different from studies and calculated to restore any fervor they might have lost.

Ignatius termed the tertianship the "school of the heart"—in contrast to the "school of letters". He described it in the Constitutions as follows:

> After those who were sent to studies have achieved the diligent and careful formation of the intellect by learning, they will find it helpful during the period of the last probation to apply themselves in the school of the heart, by exercising themselves in its spiritual and corporal pursuits which can engender in them greater humility, abnegation of all sensual love and will and judgment of their own, and also greater knowledge and love of God our Lord (ibid.).

This description of the tertianship—its goal and its means—has come down unchanged from the time of Ignatius. General Pedro Arrupe, for example, repeated it verbatim when he distributed his questionnaire to all tertian instructors in 1967 (Curia 1969, 15:53). G.C. 31, it is true, reworded the description somewhat, with less emphasis on the value of self-abnegation (Dec. 8.43).

In the earliest years of the Society, while it was still small, the tertians, like the novices, were scattered among already existing houses; but as their numbers grew, they were gathered together into one house, where they lived under the direction of a full-time tertian master. By the time of the Fourth General Congregation, which elected Claudio Aquaviva as General in 1581, the tertianship had taken on its characteristic form: "It entailed a group of "tertian fathers" under the guidance of an instructor, the Spiritual Exercises made during an entire month, a life of retirement, prayer, and penance, of formation both interior and pastoral but to the exclusion of all study properly so called and of all ministries which are conspicuous or absorbing" (de Guibert 1964, 236).

This form was approved by congregations, generals, and tertian masters for over three centuries. The tertianship of St. Stanislaus, in Cleveland, Ohio, for example, fitted this general description closely. It was under the direction of Francis X. McMenamy, who held the position for twenty years and had the complete confidence of the General.[2] He conducted a tertianship probably somewhat stricter than the average. During his first ten years as master, Father McMenamy did not allow the tertians to work even on the retreat they would give some day, lest it prove too distracting. In later years, however, he did permit this work. Each tertian had half a week of hospital ministry and only rarely, very rarely, went out to live at a parish over a weekend. During the Lenten experiment, however, all the tertians lived out of the house.

Though speaking in another context, Henri de Lubac succinctly described in modern terms the function of the Jesuit tertianship:

> A continuity is indispensable between theological work, apostolic action, and the currents of spiritual life. This continuity does not run only one way: there must be action and reaction, exchange. Theology, apostolic action, spirituality: each of these three functions is essential and none of them can be exercised authentically without the contribution and help of the other two. A theologian who, even in his work of theologian, would be cut off from the apostle and the spiritual man within himself could not properly accomplish this work (de Lubac 1987, 56).

The tertianship was to assure, after four years of theological study, the presence of "the other two".

The tertianship is a kind of finishing school designed to impart a final and definitive shaping. Because that shape includes two equally essential but quite different elements, there has always been and probably will always be some debate over the proper mixture of the two in this final formative action. The Jesuit is to be a "contemplative in action". In the tertianship, how much should contemplation be emphasized and how much action? As we have seen, this issue surfaced at every stage of formation during the changing sixties; but it was especially sharp at the stage

---

[2] Pedro Arrupe, who was to become General, made his own tertianship under Father McMenamy. Arrupe's successor, Peter-Hans Kolvenbach, also made an American tertianship.

of the tertianship. More than any of the other stages except the novitiate, the tertianship emphasizes the contemplative, prayerful side of the Jesuit vocation, whereas the trend of modern times has been toward finding God less in formal prayer and more in action, action that directly touches one's neighbor.

The balance between these two values has been at issue in nearly all the debates over the best structure for the tertianship. As early as the 1600s, for example, when Louis Lallemant was tertian master at Rouen, Father General Muzio Vitelleschi was called upon to judge whether the master held and was imparting a correct view of the relationship between contemplation and action. Lallemant's critics said that he was overemphasizing contemplation.[3] Given modern trends, it was only to be expected that today's tertianship would reflect this tension to an increased degree and would begin to experience special difficulties.

Signs of brewing trouble appeared early. In one tertianship in 1963, for example, a very perceptive young man said to the tertian instructor, "Ours is probably the last class you will be able to take through the traditional tertianship." A few years later, in the same tertianship, a tertian said publicly in class, "If you insist on this outmoded, traditional stuff, you will drive half of us out of the Society."[4] In 1968, this instructor wrote to the General, "My own effectiveness with the Fathers has seemed to be less each year."

Difficulties

This traditional tertianship was subjected to widespread criticism in the 1960s. Sufficient opposition surfaced to capture the attention of G.C. 31, which dealt with the tertianship in its tenth

---

[3] After investigation, the General approved the tertianship as conducted by Lallemant (de Guibert 1964, 357).

[4] The speaker did leave the order three years later.

decree.[5] After expressing its high regard for the institution of the tertianship and clearly rejecting any proposal to discontinue it, the congregation nevertheless recognized that "many modern difficulties" had arisen and that changes might have to be made. It decreed, therefore, that "for the present new experiments are to be attempted . . . before anything is definitively decided for the whole Society." The experiments were to continue over three years, after which the General was to make whatever changes seemed to be indicated.

The difficulties of the tertianship in the United States were discussed at the Santa Clara Conference. Two long-time tertian directors presented papers, which were then discussed at length by the conference. The fullest exposition was that of Henry F. Birkenhauer, who had attended G.C. 31 and had served on the congregation's tertianship commission. He based his analysis on his own five years of experience (1963–67) and on the experience of the other directors with whom he had worked during the congregation.

All agreed that the core of the tertianship and the chief determinant of its success was the month-long Spiritual Exercises of Saint Ignatius. According to Father Birkenhauer, some of the tertians "believe that the Spiritual Exercises have lost meaning" (S.C.C. 1967, 2:2:257). At about this same time, the Committee of Spiritual Review was reporting that the tertians did not "buy" the Spiritual Exercises any more; they asserted that one needed "a Renaissance mentality" to profit from them (C.S.R. 1964–68, 11:7).

Closely connected with this difficulty was an attitude toward prayer in general. "Some wish their prayer to consist exclusively" in finding Christ in their neighbor; they "see no value in private, personal prayer" (S.C.C. 1967, 2:2:258). In the discussion of the Birkenhauer paper, Harry T. Fleddemann, a scholastic, said with apparent approval, "There is a group of Jesuits who do not see

[5] The following quotations are from Decree 10.3, 10.4, 10.5. For an account of the congregation's work on the tertianship, see James P. Jurich, S.J. in volumes 95, 96, and 98 of the *Woodstock Letters* (Jurich 1966a, 1966b, 1967a, 1967b, and 1969).

value in formal prayer. Their dialogue with God goes on in the background of their dialogue with man and with the world" (P. 3:2:37). (Changes in the theory and practice of prayer will be treated more at length in Volume II.)

Another difficulty was that some of the young men had "no genuine desire for tertianship"; they lacked the desire "for greater intimacy with Christ, for prayer and self denial" (S.C.C. 1967, 2:2:258).

Difficulties were raised also regarding the location of the tertianship, on the ground that it was too secluded (p. 2:2:260, 263). Another difficulty was that the tertianship was too long, and for this objection there seemed to be considerable support. Given the new structure of formation in which the young men had abundant experience with pastoral work before reaching tertianship, given also the fact that a seminar during theology years could cover the study of the Constitutions (some men did have this experience), the tertianship (said the critics) could be shortened to not much more than the thirty-day retreat (p. 2:2:261–62). Some would have gone so far as to eliminate the tertianship entirely (p. 2:2:266).

A full session was devoted to a discussion of the Birkenhauer paper (S.C.C. 1967, 3:2:34–51). At the very beginning of the discussion, however, someone raised a point regarding prayer, and the discussion never left that topic. At the end, Father Birkenhauer said, "I think that the Holy Spirit has definitely been with us this morning. As all of you are aware, this was supposed to be a session on the problem of Tertianship, but really the essential problem is the problem of prayer" (p. 3:2:50).

The general direction of change was the familiar movement away from anything having a monastic coloration. The leaders of the changes objected to legislated silence. They also opposed a fixed, common daily order; in its place they wanted freedom for the individual to create his own pattern. They also wanted more contact with the world they would eventually be working in. This included contact, as the individual saw the need, with secular magazines and books and with television, films, and plays. They wanted the tertianship to consist of smaller groups, so that each tertian could have the benefit of personal direction and so that the group could enjoy warmer interpersonal relationships. They wanted much more time devoted to the experiments, which took them out of the tertianship house. They wanted to be consulted in the selection of these experiments, and they expected their preferences to be followed if at all possible. Tertian directors reported that some tertians arrived with a detailed experiment that would effectively take them out of the house for almost the whole period following the retreat.

One tertian instructor, writing to the General in 1969, essayed this description of attitudes prevalent among his tertians:

> an eagerness to structure their own tertianship and "to do their own thing" by arranging programs and projects for themselves far in advance, even for the whole time of tertianship; a greater self-reliance in judging what they consider useful for themselves in matters of prayer and the like (including a rather free excusing of themselves from saying the Divine Office); a disinclination for anything in Latin, especially something like the *Epitome;* a lack of interest in documents pertaining to the past history and legislation of the Society as being somehow less relevant.

Proposals were heard to abandon the tertianship entirely on the ground that its essential goals were already achieved by the end of the regular course, or if they were not, that they should be and could be. The experiments of the tertianship were no longer needed because the modern novice and scholastic had been exposed to many experiments during the regular course.[6] The men had been making the Spiritual Exercises for eight days each year of their Jesuit lives; if they were not imbued with the Ignatian spirit by the time they were ordained, they would never be. As for the study of the Constitutions, that could be handled by a seminar during the theologate years. If, nevertheless, there had to be a

---

[6] For a detailed description of collegians embarking on a ten-day experiment in Harlem, working intimately with the poor there, see "Harlem Diary" by Joseph F. Roccasalvo, S.J. (*Woodstock Letters,* 1965, 94:427–44).

tertianship, at the very least it should be shortened. This proposal was linked with the general demand heard in many places, that the entire course should be shortened.

As noted earlier, G.C. 31 legislated a three-year period for experimentation with the new forms of tertianship, after which Father General Arrupe was to make what changes seemed to be indicated. To begin this period of study, the General distributed a questionnaire (April 1967) to the rectors and instructors in all tertianships.

In a later document (September 8, 1967), he summarized the replies to the questionnaire and provided guidelines for the three years of experimentation. He reported that the responses had been full, often very long, and had provided clear evidence that the institution of the tertianship was in a crisis (Curia 1969, 15:52).[7] Nevertheless, he rejected any judgment that the institution of the tertianship had outlived its usefulness. After quoting the Pope and G.C. 31 in support of his position, he said, "Who will dare to say that modern Jesuits no longer need a third year of probation? Who except perhaps the one who does not sufficiently value the goal of the tertianship?" (p. 15:53). He then proceeded to outline permissible lines of experimentation, with an indication that he intended to maintain control of the process.[8]

After the three-year period of experimentation had elapsed, Father Arrupe brought all the tertian instructors to Rome. In an opening allocution delivered March 1, 1970, he touched on a number of topics that might guide their work in the following week. The utility of the tertianship had been questioned before, he said, as in the time of General Ledochowski (1915–42), but the Society had always reaffirmed the institution. Arrupe did the same, very strongly (Curia 1969, 15:548–49). The vehemence of his defense is probably a measure of the seriousness of the 1960s' attack.

[7] The English quotations of this work are the author's translation.
[8] He remarked it happened *non raro* that changes were made which had never been submitted to his approval; if this continued, he warned, the global situation would become "chaotic" (Curia 1969, 15:34).

One difficulty that always limited the success of the tertianship was a lack of "that generosity of soul" which Saint Ignatius described and supposed in the Constitutions (549). Father Arrupe outlined also a number of "new difficulties". The first of these is worth quoting in full: "There are theological problems today which affect religious life and upset our men— not only those who are in the various stages of formation, but even those in charge of the institutions, who frequently do not know which road to choose or what concrete position to take in the midst of this changing flood of ideas" (p. 549).

He describes some of the other difficulties that were affecting all parts of the Society and asks, in effect, "Should we expect the tertianship to be free of these same difficulties?" He notes how these difficulties were upsetting some tertians and inviting others to abuse the situation. He notes how important it is, therefore, to make sure that only those who are fitted for it are admitted to tertianship (p. 550).

Father Arrupe notes how the task of the tertian instructor is affected by the turbulent times and, after listing eight qualities needed in the modern instructor, concludes that normally no one man will have all the needed qualities. He therefore approves the team approach—with the instructor, however, definitely in charge of the team (pp. 551, 545).

A final difficulty is the current uncertainty regarding the most desirable structure for the modern tertianship. Arrupe reminds the instructors that they are in Rome precisely to solve this difficulty. To help them perform this task successfully, he reminds them of what the tertianship is all about, what is its "primary goal":

> a total consecration of oneself to the love of Christ, of that Christ who is intimately grasped in his historical reality and in the certainty of ecclesiastical faith; not the Christ who seems to be dissolved in a kind of tireless concern for the secular advancement of mankind—although no one would deny that such concern is also necessary and meritorious (p. 552).

Solutions

At the conclusion of the General's address, the assembled tertian instructors began their eight-day task of responding. Their final answers may be summed up as follows.

After affirming in the strongest terms that the tertianship should continue to be the climactic stage of a Jesuit's full formation, they restated the goal of the tertianship. It is, indeed, the "school of the heart", which is to be understood as an intensification of union with God, both in action and in personal prayer. They were in general agreement that the notion of probation in the judicial sense should not be made the chief goal of the tertianship; the main goal should be formation. They were divided on whether or not the thirty-day retreat would best precede ordination.

Nearly all the instructors were in agreement that the tertian instructor should be aided by a team. They approved the idea of the instructor engaging in some outside ministry. Their main reason seemed to be that he would thus be kept abreast of modern life. (This reason seems to imply the double conviction that modern life is a rapidly changing reality and that the tertianship should be marked not by seclusion but by involvement in ministry.)

With regard to the tertians themselves, the instructors were unanimous in stating that only those should be admitted to the tertianship who have, at the minimum, an elemental trust in the fruitfulness of the tertianship. Nearly all were in agreement, also, that the tertianship would be more productive if the men came to it after two or three years of apostolic experience. They commented on the growing problem of those who seek to escape the third probation; if the young man cannot be brought to see the value of the tertianship and desire it, this should probably be understood as indicating a lack of a true Jesuit vocation.

They had a number of comments on the structure of the tertianship. They agreed unanimously that the tertianship should be pluralistic in the sense that there should be a number of methods of doing it, and they explicitly approved five methods.

One was the traditional form, lasting seven to nine months. Another was a three-stage format described by the General.[9] The third form consisted of two intense summers, with close contact with the instructor during the intervening period. A fourth format also had three stages: a preparatory period of at least a year; then a dwelling in the tertian house for two or three months; then a period of confirmation, which was to extend for at least a year. In the fifth form, the tertian would be engaged in apostolic action for three years under the close tutelage of the instructor and with time for the cultivation of a more intense spiritual life.

The instructors agreed that the Spiritual Exercises constituted the center of the tertianship and that the Exercises should be given "individually" rather than made as a group. They recognized that there was some prejudice against the Exercises, but they thought it could be overcome.

In what kind of ministries should the tertians be exercised—in hard, lowly work, such as Ignatius praised, or in work similar to that which they would be doing after the tertianship? All of the directors saw the usefulness of the latter choice, and some judged it to be the better choice; but they also praised the first choice. In his earlier letter of September 8, 1967, the General had commented on the kind of ministerial work proper to the tertianship: "I do not forbid that these experiments resemble somewhat the future work for which the Fathers are destined" (Curia 1969, 15:55). This unenthusiastic phrasing may reflect an apprehension lest the tertianship be reduced to two summers with life-as-usual intervening. He also said that the instructor was to protect the tertians "against overwork and other abuses" incompatible with the goals of the tertian year. (The warning against "overwork" probably reflects a concern that the tertian have adequate time for personal prayer.)

[9] In this format, the first four months are spent at the tertianship, the next five months are spent in experiments outside the house, and the final three weeks are spent back in the tertianship. See Curia 1969, 15:55.

The instructors saw great importance in the study of the Institute. Such study was necessary, they said, because they were encountering widespread ignorance in young Jesuits of the Jesuit vocation. Such study was to include not only the Constitutions and the decrees of general congregations but also the Spiritual Exercises and other sources of the Ignatian charism.

A week after the instructors had submitted their report, the General replied by way of a letter (April 15, 1970) to all provincials expressing his agreement with the report and making some decisions. He quoted, with approval, the instructors' description of the tertianship goal ("a more intense union with God in action and personal prayer") and expanded on this at some length. He agreed that a team was needed for the modern tertianship but insisted that it be under the control of the tertian instructor. He approved, as possible options, all five of the structures described by the instructors but required that the choice of some of them be cleared with himself in each case. In approving this pluralistic tertianship, he remarked that Saint Ignatius had determined "little or nothing" with regard to the method of tertianship. He agreed with the tertian instructors that too many of the young men were postponing tertianship too long. He judged that generally the tertianship should not be postponed more than three years.

Meeting four years after the events just described, G.C. 32 confirmed what the tertian instructors had recommended and the General had approved. It decreed that the individual provinces were free to adopt, with the General's approval, either of two tertianship plans. In Plan A, the candidate begins his tertianship immediately upon completion of theology and before ordination. He first makes the month-long Spiritual Exercises, after which he is ordained to the priesthood. A notable part of the tertianship is then to be devoted to ministries, primarily pastoral, under competent supervision. At the end of this year, the priest can be promoted to final vows. In Plan B, the traditional order is followed; that is, the Jesuit completes theology and is ordained before beginning tertianship, which is to occur not later than three years after ordination. This tertianship may take any of the five forms approved by Father General.[10]

The New Tertianship

All five of the traditional tertian houses had closed by 1971 (see Figure 7). Three had closed by the spring of 1968, another by the following spring, while the fifth, at Auriesville, held on until 1970–71. Two followed a pattern not uncommon in the swirl of change that was the 1960s. Each undertook the trouble and cost of moving to another location and then, after only one year, closed. The Port Townsend tertianship moved to Seattle, where it became a part of the university community; the Cleveland tertianship moved to the former novitiate, Colombiere. In the year following the moves, each was discontinued.

Several reasons explain the changes in location. In the first place, the number of tertians had declined greatly, chiefly because the number of Jesuit priests had declined, but also because the proportion of priests who were postponing tertianship had increased. Where in 1964–65 there had been 171 men in tertianship in the U.S. provinces, there were only forty-eight in 1968–69 and only eighteen in 1970–71. The numbers coming from a particular province were, of course, even smaller. For example, in the last year of Port Townsend, only two tertians were from the West Coast; likewise, in the last year of Auriesville, only one was from the East Coast. These small numbers of native tertians would cause a province to ask itself whether it wanted to continue to conduct its own tertianship.

The rejection of anything monastic was also at work, of course, in explaining the disappearance of separate tertian houses. An additional reason was the availability of new methods of going

[10] For the advantages of each plan, see Cecil McGarry in Ganss 1976, 117–19.

Figure 7

TERTIANSHIPS, NUMBER OF TERTIANS,[a] AND TERTIAN INSTRUCTORS, BY YEAR[b] (1964–71)

	1964–65	1965–66	1966–67	1967–68	1968–69	1969–70	1970–71
AURIESVILLE (NY)							
Total number	46	43	32	36	22	12	18
Maryland tertians	13	13	12	9	3	0	0
New York tertians	16	8	11	12	8	2	1
Tertian Instructor	McMahon	McMahon	McMahon	McMahon	McMahon	McMahon	McMahon [CLOSED]
POMFRET CTR. (CT)							
Total number	29	24	34	26			
New England tertians	9	10	20	12			
Tertian Instructor	W. Murphy	W. Murphy	Coleran	Coleran [CLOSED]			
DECATUR (IL)							
Total number	33	22	25	24			
Missouri tertians	4	6	11	8			
Wisconsin tertians	13	7	6	9			
Tertian Instructor	Coleran	Coleran	Hunter	Hunter [CLOSED]			

CLEVELAND (OH)[c]				
Total number		30	34	30	14
Detroit tertians		3	4	1	1
Chicago tertians		5	5	8	6
Tertian Instructor	Birkenhauer	Birkenhauer	Birkenhauer	Birkenhauer [CLOSED]
PORT TOWNSEND (WA)[d]				
Total number	33	33	22	22	26
Oregon tertians	6	9	5	11	1
California tertians	13	12	4	1	1
Tertian Instructor	Frajole	McDonald	McDonald	McDonald	McDonald [CLOSED]

SOURCE: Province catalogs

[a] In all the tertianships, there were some men from other provinces. In some years the outsiders outnumbered the natives.
[b] The fall of one year to the spring of the next.
[c] The tertianship moved in the fall of 1968 to Colombiere. At the end of this year it was discontinued.
[d] The tertianship moved in the fall of 1969 to Seattle. At the end of this year it was discontinued.

through tertianship. Most of the new methods did not require a large, stable house; the tertians could be accommodated in existing institutions. If the host institution was in a city or on a university campus, there followed the advantage of easy access to experts and to a greater variety of experiments.

As mentioned, the dwindling number of tertians was related to a growing pattern of delayed tertianships. Instead of beginning tertianship almost automatically at the end of the theology years, a man now had a choice as to when to make his tertianship. For a number of reasons, men began to postpone their tertianships. The very indefiniteness of the starting date contributed to the phenomenon; if tertianship could be made any year, there was no necessity that it begin this year. Also, when the tertianship had been postponed for a few years, the man was more likely to have become an important part of some enterprise, which could not easily release him—at least not this year. Further, the sixties were critical of "creeping monasticism"; to some the tertianship seemed too monastic to be worthwhile.[11] This lack of desire for the tertianship was frequent enough to elicit strong comment from the tertian instructors gathered in Rome and also from the General.

The new tertianship world was variegated and fluid. Though none used Plan A, the provinces did use the varieties available under Plan B. Of the various methods available, the most popular became that of two summers separated by a year of regular work during which the tertian kept in close touch with the tertian instructor. The experience of the Chicago province supplies one example of this method. After three years without a tertianship program (1968–71), the province began a new one in the summer of 1971.[12] The tertian instructor first interviewed all applicants

[11] Even in the author's day, tertians were known to say, "The only people who like tertianship are the very lazy and the very holy." The speakers were likely to be men anxious to get on with their work.

[12] An attempt had been made earlier to begin a tertianship, but the man selected as tertian instructor left the order. This is one of the many examples of obvious inadequate knowledge of individuals on the part of

and asked six questions of each applicant: (1) Does God exist (for you)? Is Jesus Christ God? (2) Are you presently in love with somebody? (3) Are you presently under therapy? (4) Are you angry at the Society of Jesus? (5) Are you angry at your own blood family? (6) Do you have a drinking problem? These questions came out of the experiences of the tertian directors, who were meeting annually at this time. In their view, the tertianship was intended not to solve basic problems but to improve an otherwise sound spiritual life. These screening interviews actually functioned to exclude some applicants.

During the year between the two summers, the Chicago province instructor saw each man on a monthly basis. He drove around the province visiting each man for a day—a tertianship on wheels. The object of this monthly visit was to assist the man to live his regular Jesuit life according to the mode he had determined upon in the thirty-day retreat. He also gathered the tertians together for a triduum (three-day retreat) at Christmastime and again at Eastertime. Both tertians and instructor were busy at other times with their regular work. (The instructor was a university professor.) The second summer was devoted partly to various experiments for the individual tertians and partly to study the Jesuit Constitutions, the congregations, and the spiritual life in general.

Wisconsin and New England together also embarked on a summer/nine months/summer program, under the direction of a Wisconsin instructor. In this program, the first summer was taken up entirely with the Spiritual Exercises: a ten-day preparation, the retreat itself, and a ten-day period for processing the retreat. The second summer was devoted to a study of the Constitutions and Jesuit history, along with an analysis of the Ignatian retreat. The intervening nine months of regular work was considered a tertian

---

superiors. Another example is mentioned by Cecil McGarry: "In recent years a large proportion (40%) of priests who have left the Society have done so after ordination and before final vows" (Ganss 1976, 117–18). The manifestation of conscience, upon which the Jesuit system of administration is based, was not working efficiently.

experiment, during which each tertian had genuine spiritual direction as far as the instructor could arrange it, though he himself did
not supply it.

New York adopted the summer/nine months/summer program
for a few years but then returned to something like the traditional
program. In 1978, under Joseph T. Browne, a tertian house was
established on the campus of Fordham University.[13] The tertianship year took up seven months, September to April, and thus
precluded teaching or studying for a full academic year. After the
thirty-day retreat, the tertians first engaged in various projects
dealing with the poor; then they engaged in such spiritual ministries as retreats, days of recollection, and missions.

The New Orleans province also established a stable tertian
house, at Austin, Texas. This program operated for one semester
each year. Thus, men connected with educational work needed to
absent themselves for only half of the academic year.

In 1990, the Detroit province began a ten-month program with
three parts: (1) three months for introduction, Constitutions, and
thirty-day retreat; (2) five or six months in ministry in a third-
world setting; (3) a final month or six weeks back in the United
States to reflect on the entire tertian experience.

There were other variations between provinces and over time.
A survey of the assistancy made in one year would not likely be
accurate a few years later.[14] Individuals sometimes arranged for
special programs. A number obtained permission to make their
tertianships in Australia, where there was a traditional program
similar to those in the New Orleans and New York provinces.
Others devised a long experiment in the third world, for example
in India. Some made their tertianships in Europe.

The team approach was adopted in all the tertianships. The individually directed retreat meant that one director could not handle

[13] Previously, since 1975, Browne had been assistant to the former instructor,
John McMahon. As of 1990, therefore, Browne had been forming tertians for
fifteen years.

[14] A continuous record of changes in formation is maintained by the Jesuit
Conference (Washington, D.C.).

more than four or five retreatants—six at the most. An assistant could also aid the instructor in the study of the Constitutions.

The variety of programs seems likely to continue, for each type of program has its own advantages. By having many different programs available in the assistancy, the differing needs of individuals and of provinces can be accommodated. In the late 1980s, a survey of all the young Jesuits eligible to make tertianship found that a substantial majority preferred the traditional type of tertianship over the two-summer type. Their reason: the longer, more concentrated tertianship promised to achieve the goal of the tertianship more adequately.

XII

POSTLUDE

Arriving at the end of our long trip through six stages of formation, with a hilltop view of the many twists and turns of the road, we face insistent questions: What is the meaning of it all? How did it all come about? The explanation must be, of course, in terms of causes. What were the causes of it all? The list of causes had best proceed from the more immediate and particular to the more remote and general.

The new breed was certainly one of the causes. The first and most continuous force making for change was the changed character of the scholastics. When General Pedro Arrupe remarked, "The young men coming to us these days are different", he was repeating a judgment being voiced by superiors all over the United States.

Who were the new breed? At the Santa Clara Conference, Gordon Moreland, who had been in touch with the young Jesuits of the Oregon province for many years, identified a group of scholastics as constituting the core of the new breed. Speaking in 1967, Moreland identified this group as occupying the four years of theology and the last two years of regency. Figure 8 shows this group as it made its way through the course of formation.

The edges of the group are not, of course, as sharp as the figure would indicate; moreover, the exact outlines of the group would vary somewhat from region to region; but, in general, this seems to be an identifiable group. The earliest members of this core group would have entered the order in the mid-fifties, a pattern that fits the memory of some masters of novices who recalled that

Figure 8

CORE OF THE NEW BREED[a]

Novitiate	Juniorate	Philosophate	Regency	Theologate
1954, 55	56, 57	58, 59, 60	61, 62, 63	64, 65, 66, [67]
1955, 56	57, 58	59, 60, 61	62, 63, 64	65, 66, [67,] 68
1956, 57	58, 59	60, 61, 62	63, 64, 65	66, [67,] 68, 69
1957, 58	59, 60	61, 62, 63	64, 65, 66	[67,] 68, 69, 70
1958, 59	60, 61	62, 63, 64	65, 66, [67]	68, 69, 70, 71
1959, 60	61, 62	63, 64, 65	66, [67,] 68	69, 70, 71, 72

[a]All dates are as of the fall of the year. Boxed years show location of the "new breed" in 1967.

the young men coming to the novitiate began to be "different" about 1955. They were different as having a new spirit of independence, as being uncomfortable with traditional answers, and as wanting evidence that grew out of their own experience. Everything, without exception, was to be open to questioning and testing.

As the years went on, this questioning attitude grew more explicit and insistent. The earliest members of this group would have had, from the beginning, the seeds of change in them, needing only a favorable environment to sprout. This favorable environment would have come with Vatican II or even with the earlier forces that produced Vatican II.

All the entering classes coming after the core group would have participated in this new attitude, but with a difference. Moreland made the additional observation that the scholastics coming behind the core group were less restless with authority, more comfortable with the externals of religious life, and in some ways felt more affinity with the pre-Vatican II Jesuits (their grandparents) than with the cohort immediately preceding them, the generation of the sixties. This development of a third group has been noted by a number of persons in various situations and seems open to two explanations. First, since most of the battles had already been won by the sixties generation, there was no occasion for the following group to be equally pugnacious. Secondly, the post-sixties group may have been motivated by a different set of values. Very likely, both explanations apply.

Another significant source of change was the faculty, especially the younger members trained in Europe, where new developments, especially in theology, had begun somewhat earlier. Faculty members sometimes lent support to the scholastics in their pressure for change. More importantly, they sometimes taught the young men the values that fueled the revolution.

Superiors also played a part in guiding the movement of change. The pattern of participation varied not only with persons but also with the kind of change involved. Superiors were more active, for example, in initiating and designing changes in academics than in lifestyle. In the latter area, they operated chiefly by yielding—selectively and gradually—to the requests, demands, and sometimes actions of the scholastics. Intermediate and local superiors especially had to make difficult choices between insisting on the observance of rules still formally in place and allowing, sometimes simply by ignoring, actions contrary to existing regulations. As the avalanche of change gained momentum, local and intermediate superiors made less effort to oppose or control it. In this negative sense, they could be said to constitute one of the significant causes of change. It is worth noting, however, that as superiors grew in knowledge of the new breed—usually through the long individual manifestations of conscience that marked this period or through group meetings like the one described on pages 318–19—they became more supportive and to this extent, usually a minor extent, became a positive cause of change.

G.C. 31 was undoubtedly a major cause of change with its emphasis on the need to modernize and with its explicit invitation to embark on experiments, even such as ran counter to existing legislation. The congregation approved of the establishment of agencies in every assistancy, indeed in every province, whose function was—in the congregation's terminology—to renew all Jesuit activities.

The general congregation was only responding to the invitation, even to the command, of the Second Vatican Council to seek *aggiornamento.* Vatican Council II must be accorded the principal place among all the immediate causes of change in the Catholic Church. The council directed every religious order to hold a general chapter precisely to ascertain if changes were needed. This was a force of earthquake proportions, a seismic shock that left no order untouched.

This has been a review of a concentration of efficient causes, one following another. At the end, we are still left with a question: *Why* did these efficient causes work the way they did? This is a question of final causes, and the answer or answers are buried deep in the explanation of human values. An attempt to identify the roots of this shift in Western values will be made in Volume II.

Here it must suffice to sketch such a shift in a very general, panoramic way.

It was a shift along four axes of vital tension in the Western world. Because these tensions reflect basic understandings of reality, any change in them inevitably produces at least temporary dislocations in society. As shifts in the earth's crust have produced earthquakes, so shifts in these basic tensions have produced shocks felt by all the major social structures of Western society—by the family, the school, the military establishment, the labor union—but especially by the Church and her religious orders.

The four tensions are shown schematically below.[1] The four are not adequately distinct but are rather like the intertwining strands of a single cable. The arrows signify mutual interaction and (almost) constant movement. The double arrow indicates the direction in which the center of balanced tension has moved in modern times.

$$\text{SUBJECTIVE} \longleftrightarrow \text{OBJECTIVE}$$
$$\text{RELATIVE} \longleftrightarrow \text{ABSOLUTE}$$
$$\text{SECULAR} \longleftrightarrow \text{SACRAL}$$
$$\text{INDIVIDUAL} \longleftrightarrow \text{INSTITUTION}$$

The shift along the subjective-objective axis is put first because it seems to be the key movement, the one which, understood, leads most naturally to an understanding of the others. The move along the relative-absolute axis is very closely related to the increased emphasis on subjectivity. Together, these two shifts produced a giant, Heraclitean tremor that literally shook to its foundation the post-Tridentine Catholic world. The Jesuit order had its origin in that world and was especially shaken because its intellectual apostolate and flexible constitution made it especially sensitive to new developments.

The shift from the sacral toward the secular was of its nature, of course, disturbing to sacral institutions. This shift was the direct result of independent developments in Western culture, especially

[1] The following analysis is adapted from an early monograph of mine appearing in *Studies in the Spirituality of Jesuits* (Becker 1977).

in the field of science. It was further fostered, however, by the other three shifts, which together could produce a Sartre-like type of individual, one who is the sole norm of reality. Such an individual does not dwell at ease in the realm of the sacral, which postulates an absolute reality on which all individuals are dependent and from which they derive their meaning.

The shift toward individualism was felt by all institutions—the family, the school, the state, the church, the armed forces—but was especially felt by the religious orders, for the traditional religious order was the epitome of institutional life. In the traditional order, the individual did not determine his own dress or work or order of the day. He gave up individual property and the hope of a family of his own. Above all, by his vow of obedience, he gave up his own will. If any one change could be said to mark the 1960s, it was the altered understanding of authority, both of law and of tradition. The impact on institutions was enormous.

The trail of the "whys" never ends. It can be asked: Why did the four shifts occur? An attempt to deal with this deeper "why" will be made in Volume II.

APPENDIX 1

THE EXPERIMENTAL EIGHT

At Woodstock College, Maryland, in the spring of 1969, a first-year theologian named Anthony Meyer proposed that on the occasion of the college's move to New York a different method of studying theology be tried. He had been dissatisfied with his first year of theology, which he described as learning predetermined answers to questions that were of little pertinence in the modern world. He envisioned a small group living together in an apartment, with each man free to follow his individual interests—under the direction of a faculty advisor—but with the group sharing intimately the common experience of "theologizing". Meyer's proposal was favorably received by Peter Neary, another first-year student, and the two of them enlisted six additional students, constituting the Experimental Eight. Father J. Giles Milhaven, who had encouraged them from the start, agreed to live with them and act as faculty director. The nine members of the group, their respective provinces, and their later history were as follows:

Name	Province	Left S.J.
J. Giles Milhaven (Mentor)	New York	1970
Michael R. Fargione	Wisconsin	1970
Richard D. Hunt	New York	
Joseph W. Lux	New York	

John W. McDaniel	Maryland	
Anthony J. Meyer	New York	1977
Peter J. Neary	New York	1984
Thomas F. Ritz	New York	1971
William J. Sneck	Maryland	

Though the faculty was divided on the desirability of the experiment, Dean Robert E. O'Brien supported the idea, and the provincials gave their approval for a semester trial. The group, composed of second-year theologians, began to function in the fall semester of 1969 and continued for two years, until ordination.[1] They lived together in three apartments in a large building on 98th Street in Manhattan. Walls were pierced with doors, so that all the rooms could be reached without going into the corridor. This arrangement provided a private room for each man, a common room where the group could recreate and hold meetings, and a kitchen where they could prepare their own breakfasts and lunches. For dinner, they usually joined the large community on the eighth floor. Their mentor, Giles Milhaven, lived on another floor but in the same building. (A convenient summary of Milhaven's views on how scholastics should be formed during their theology years is provided in a piece he wrote for the Santa Clara Conference [1967, 2:1:145–53].)

Each man obtained his own funds from the father minister as need arose. From these personal funds, each contributed to common expenses such as food and the entertainment of guests. At this time there were no budgets, either for individuals or for the group.

The group did not usually celebrate the Eucharist together. While there was some discussion of meeting for common prayer, this goal was not often achieved. An academic meeting was held each week, with Milhaven present, and occasionally (once or twice a month) a kind of encounter meeting.

[1] The places of those who left the Society or went elsewhere for third-year theology were taken by other scholastics of the Woodstock community.

They were freed of the obligation of attending classes but had to take the same comprehensive examinations as the other students, and they had no guarantee that the college would grant them a degree at the end of the experiment.

Each of the members of the group made a detailed report at the end of the first semester and described his activities. The reports indicate that each student followed his own path, with no two alike. They all exhibited, however, two general characteristics, which may be termed the psychological and sociological dimensions of the experiment.

The approach of each was marked by a strong subjective, psychological quality. "To be in touch with myself" was a phrase frequently employed to describe an essential goal of the experiment. The truth of theology was to be found in its meaning to the self. There was much stress on the necessity to be free. The freedom they spoke of was not that of the Ignatian Spiritual Exercises ("freedom from inordinate affection") but rather freedom from outside pressures—especially that exerted by past custom and prescription as codified in institutions.

In his report, Peter Neary included a three-page description of five "principles for learning" and eight "conditions which facilitate learning". Neary stated, and other reports agreed, that this description fitted the group's approach to the task of learning theology. The five principles were highly subjective, with two implications for the learning process: (a) the final norm of what is desirable (true) is myself, rather than anything outside myself; and (b) the content of learning is evolutionary, hence changeable. The eight conditions of learning all declare the need to be free of external constraints. For example, in good learning conditions there are no rewards or punishments for being right or wrong; there is encouragement to confront and judge tradition; and there is acceptance of ambiguity, even at the end of the search.

Though the members of the group had had only one year of formal theology, they felt themselves capable of deciding on the proper goals of theology and the most efficient methodology.

The adoption of the norm of self-realization was essential to the rationale of this position. There was no discussion of the distinction between the goals and methods of a seminary and of a secular college, or between revelation and reason as sources of learning. One of the reports, Neary's, recommended that Woodstock College cease to grant degrees because degrees led to control by accrediting agencies, which in turn prevented the free development of innovative approaches to learning and the unhampered growth of the unique individual.

The group's emphasis on the psychological dimension of their experiment was reflected also in their emphasis on community. The truth was to be found in and through other human beings— rather than in abstract ideas or in verbal formulations, especially traditional formulations. To launch their experiment, the group arranged for a week-end sensitivity session, for which they brought in psychologist Father John Burton as director. Thereafter every other week the group engaged in an encounter experience. All their reports emphasized the value of their daily encounters with one another. Typical statements: "I have gained a theological perspective due primarily to the community aspect of our experiment." "The greatest benefit to me has been in the community dimension of our experiment."

The work of the group was marked also by what might be called a sociological dimension. Theology was best learned by studying its significance for modern secular problems such as war, poverty, racism, family relations. One of the essential fruits of the study of theology is the courage to oppose and change what the individual judges to be un-Christian. Even purely theological topics, such as the priesthood, were studied with an emphasis on some sociological problem, for example, its relationship to celibacy.

The report of Anthony Meyer reflects this emphasis the most clearly. He seems to have taken no formal courses in the first semester, but to have occupied himself with readings, meetings, and "actions". Of the twelve pages of his report, the first nine are devoted to ethics (not moral theology) and to "the theology of the radical stance". He adopts Louis Monden's definition of ethics ("an ordering of man towards his self-perfection and his self-realization") and concludes that this "makes a traditional natural law ethics effectively useless". He adopts Giles Milhaven's model of "ethical consequences" and concludes that this is essentially the same as situation ethics. He lists the films he had seen, all "questioning our whole American way of life" and records his many "actions" taken against war and consumerism. He mentions that he had been gassed four times in Washington and feels "the need to go to jail in the face of this war".

He devotes two pages of his report to his work in "the theology of spirituality". Since all his past reading in this field had been in the Western tradition, he turned to Zen and discovered an essential similarity between the Buddha-nature and the Christ-nature. He devotes the last half page of his report to his study of ecclesiology. He reports that he directed his attention primarily to Church structure in order to find an answer to the question, "How does one make her change?" His goal was to find the means "to move her forward with creative alternatives".

All the members of the group report much use of Union Theological Seminary and other non-Catholic sources; indeed, some report no work at all taken with the Woodstock faculty during this first semester. The reports mention the cultural opportunities offered by New York as contrasted with Woodstock in Maryland. They list attendance at the ballet, the opera, concerts, plays, including the play, *Hair*. While recognizing that these activities were primarily entertainment, the reports see in them a theological dimension.

The group invited many guests, usually for a dinner followed by an evening of discussion. All the reports highlight this aspect of the group's operation, which evidently succeeded in attracting prominent guests, especially from the other faculties of the consortium. Because Jesuits on Morningside Heights were a novelty, there was considerable curiosity about what they planned to do. The faculty report warned against inviting guests who primarily asked questions rather than made positive contributions. One visitor, a prominent Protestant theologian, reported to a friend on the Woodstock faculty that he had found the evening "fascinating" because it was the closest he had ever come to "genuine Anabaptists". He was referring to the group's enthusiastic attack on tradition, authority, and institution. The number of guests declined notably after the first semester.

One of the more active members of the group was William J. Sneck, who functioned as secretary and composed the group's general report for the first semester. He also kept a full account of his own activities from the beginning to the end of the experiment. (He seems to have been the only one who did this.) Looking back on his first year of theology, in Maryland, he rated it very satisfactory and judged that for a freshman the regular classroom methodology had probably been the proper approach. With that behind him, however, he felt eager and able to take a more active part in structuring his own education. But he explicitly states, "My reasons for joining the experimental group were not a repudiation of the 'system.'" In this he differed from Meyer and several of the others.

His report on the first semester shows that he continued to follow some of the regular Woodstock courses at the same time that he was branching out in individual ways. He was attempting to structure his theological studies so as to integrate them with studies in his own field of psychology. He joined Anthony Meyer in preparing a paper on how the modern novitiate should be conducted and spent three days with Meyer at Wernersville explaining their ideas. He did work at both Columbia University and Union Theological Seminary. At the end of the two-year experiment, he rated it the most satisfying intellectual experience of his life.

In preparation for his comprehensive examination, Sneck supplied his examiners with a set of "brief statements to get things going" which he entitled "Conversational Hooks for Comprehensives". These pages provide an excellent view of how differently theology was being approached at this time even by the member of the group who seemed to be closest to traditional values.

The group's two originators stayed with the group only one year. Peter Neary accepted the invitation of a Protestant professor, Dietrich Ritschl, to return with him to Germany and function as his assistant for a year or more. The Woodstock faculty agreed to accept this as fulfilling the requirement of third-year theology. For his third-year theology, Anthony Meyer enrolled as a full-time student in communications at Stanford University. This work was structured with a strong link to the task of preaching the Good News. After coming to New York to be ordained and to beard the cardinal,[2] Meyer returned to Stanford to complete his work in communications, which counted as his fourth-year theology, and shortly thereafter left the priesthood.

The group's mentor, Giles Milhaven, announced in February of 1970 that he intended to marry but requested to stay on, as a Jesuit or Jesuit associate, in his position as a Woodstock professor. Anthony Meyer had a sign posted inviting signatures to a petition supporting Milhaven's request. The petition was signed by about half the students, including all of the Experimental Eight. One second-year theologian wrote to the Woodstock president to argue, "We say almost as a commonplace that we attach no stigma to the religious priest who decides to follow out his vocation in the Church by leaving the religious life to marry; Woodstock's decision to have Giles remain on its faculty would make clear that we believe what we say, and are willing to put it into practice."[3] After the trustees of Woodstock College had rejected his request by a vote of 11 to 2, Milhaven submitted his resignation and married in the summer of 1970.

In summary, while the experiment produced excellent effects for two of the participants, on the whole it failed to meet its early expectations as a better method of forming Jesuit priests. Of the

[2] During the ordination ceremony, Meyer and Joseph O'Rourke used the occasion (contrary to an assurance given to the New York provincial) to seize the microphone and denounce the ordaining prelate (Cardinal Terrence Cooke) for functioning as military chaplain.

[3] The writer of this letter also left the Society the following year.

nine Jesuits originally involved in the experiment, only four persevered in their vocations. Of these four, only two passed their comprehensives.

APPENDIX 2

NICHOLAS A. PREDOVICH:
PIONEER OF CHANGE

The following account of the changes inaugurated by Nicholas A. Predovich at Colombiere, the novitiate of the Detroit province, is based on a long session I had with Father Predovich in 1974, a year before his death. The views expressed are entirely his, and I have not attempted any evaluation.

The quality of the Predovich approach to change is caught in an early incident that faithfully reflects several characteristic features of the 1960s. The community of the new Colombiere College automatically followed the province custom of burying the priests apart from the others. When the first Jesuit brother died and was buried at a little distance from the priests, the recently appointed novice master protested, first to the rector and then to the provincial. The basis of the protest was typical of the 1960s, a rejection of status in favor of equality of all individuals.

When action did not follow upon his protest, Predovich resorted to the typical technique of the 1960s—confrontation. He told the rector that if the grave were not immediately moved, he and his novices would go out and move it themselves. He also contacted the relatives of the deceased brother and informed them of his efforts. This going public with its consequent pressure on authorities also characterized the 1960s. Two other characteristics of that period are reflected in this incident: the confrontation resulted in victory (the grave was moved), and the principle underlying the confrontation eventually won widespread acceptance and approval.

Nicholas Predovich was probably the chief center of controversy in the Detroit province during the 1960s. Even up until his death, he was looked upon by some in the province as the man who had, with all the good will in the world, destroyed the province. Shortly after General Congregation 31, the provincial had asked Father Predovich to tour the province and explain the changes in the novitiate. It was hoped that in this way some of the uneasiness and bitterness in the province would be mitigated. According to Predovich, the largest community in the province refused to extend him an invitation. When I interviewed him in 1974, he reported that he felt uncomfortable in some houses because more than a few of the brethren obviously went out of their way to avoid him.

Born in 1921, Nicholas Predovich entered the Milford novitiate in 1942. Coming as he did from a large affectionate family whose members freely displayed their affection, he found the Society's lifestyle cold. He made the usual studies and was ordained at West Baden in 1954. "Since your entire formation was thus in the old school," I said to him, "why are you different? What caused you to change? And when?" He thought long over this question, and in the course of two days produced a number of answers but seemed to settle on two experiences as the critical ones.

The first was his teaching experience after ordination. He taught theology at John Carroll University for four years (1957–61) and during most of this period was chairman of the department. He found his students complaining—mildly at first, later more strongly—about the irrelevancy of what he was offering them, what his own studies had prepared him to offer them. He grew more and more sympathetic to this student reaction. He recalled how, while going through the course at West Baden, he himself had found the matter generally dull and would often ask himself, "How can I possibly use this in teaching students or in preaching to the people?" Thus, his teaching experience brought to life with greater vigor an inclination that was already present.

In counseling students, he found himself less and less comfortable with the traditional moral and ascetical theology. An explicit judgment began to form, which in retrospect he believed had been implicit for a long time, that the traditional methods of spiritual formation were inapplicable to modern conditions. In his actual dealings with students, he found more guidance in the new humanistic psychology than he did in the traditional methods by which he had been formed. For all practical purposes, Carl Rogers became his moral-ascetical text. He had become acquainted with the humanistic or third-force psychologists while he was a theologian at West Baden, largely through the instrumentality of his study partner in theology, who was specializing in psychology. At first, primarily interested in humanistic psychology as a counseling technique, he was gradually influenced—he saw this more clearly in retrospect than at the time—in his fundamental views of human nature and human perfection. Where he perceived conflicts between traditional ascetical formation and modern psychology, he generally preferred the latter.

At the university he had inherited a course entitled "Modern Heresies". Whereas his Jesuit predecessor (James McQuade) had taught the assigned authors in order to refute them, Predovich found himself explaining them with considerable sympathy. He found them saying things with which both he and his students resonated favorably. He recalled, somewhat vaguely, that the course included some existentialist authors, such as Jean-Paul Sartre, some writings of Maurice Blondel, and some church-state writings which he later came to associate with the approach of John Courtney Murray.

He became aware of two issues that seemed to run through all of the course readings like a golden thread. One issue was the freedom of the individual person. Predovich began to see, or feel, in a new way that institutions and rules were subordinate to the individual. The other issue was the sacredness of the secular, or the naturalness of the supernatural. The traditional distinctions between the secular and the sacred or between the natural and the supernatural began to lose their authenticity and appeal.

The second formative experience was his graduate study. While teaching theology at John Carroll, Predovich began to feel more and more inadequate. Though only four years out of the course, he felt the need for a wider—and a different—theological education. Superiors approved his request to go on for a doctorate in theology and asked him where he would like to go. He examined and rejected the Gregorian University in Rome because it was clearly traditional, "just more of West Baden". For the same reason he decided against the theologate in Canada. It is significant that already at this early point (1960) Predovich was explicitly rejecting the traditional.

His final choice was Woodstock College in Maryland. He was moved by a variety of considerations but chiefly by the presence of John Courtney Murray on the faculty. He studied at Woodstock during 1961-63 and wrote his dissertation under Murray. While at Woodstock, he was also influenced by Joseph Fitzmyer (Scripture), by Gustave Weigel (liturgy and ecumenism), and by Avery Dulles (revelation and ecclesiology). He recalled gratefully that he had been introduced to Karl Rahner by Thomas Clarke. He thought of Murray, Weigel, and Dulles as "pre-Vatican II" in the sense that the emphases which characterized the council had been pioneered by these men earlier at Woodstock.

He completed his doctoral work in time to be assigned to West Baden for the winter session of 1963. To Predovich, his return to Baden was a heavy burden. "It was like regressing to a period of history twenty years earlier. I could not find anyone with whom to talk about my experience at Woodstock."

By this time his rejection of the traditional approach was complete. In retrospect, he saw the change as taking place in him, first in terms of the new psychology, then in terms of the new theology, especially in Scripture and ecclesiology.

In the one semester that Predovich taught at West Baden, he did not fit smoothly into the house patterns and was the source of some friction. For example, he urged his students to read Teilhard de Chardin. According to the directions of the General, all writings by Teilhard were kept in the dean's library under the dean's personal control. Father Predovich circumvented this difficulty by simply borrowing the books from the dean's library and circulating them among the students. He mimeographed and circulated, also, controversial articles of Karl Rahner. Some members of the faculty were critical of such procedures on the ground that students were "reading marginal authors without direction".

Master of Novices (1963–69)

During his visitation at West Baden in 1963, the Detroit provincial, John A. McGrail, told Father Predovich that he might be appointed master of novices at the Colombiere novitiate. The current master, who had been in the post for many years, was being seriously challenged by the currents of change. Novices, particularly those with college degrees, were openly expressing dissatisfaction, for example, with traditional Scripture and ascetical theology. Also, in the previous year of 1962, twenty-one novices, sixty percent of the entire novitiate, had left or had been dismissed.[1]

Father Predovich's first reply to the proposed appointment was one which most prospective masters probably have had to make, that he had no previous training for the task. But Father Predovich went on to say what probably very few have said before, that if appointed he would make significant changes in the whole program of formation. He warned the provincial that he had learned to disapprove of many features of the customary program and that he could not in conscience conduct the novitiate in the traditional manner. The provincial, as Predovich remembered it, simply said, "Do what you have to do."

[1] In Predovich's last year as director of novices, the record was not significantly better; out of fourteen novices (first- and second-year combined), only seven persevered to take vows. Of course, by that time the whole situation had changed, and Jesuits were leaving in extraordinary numbers from every level of the Society.

The provincial offered Father Predovich the opportunity to go anywhere in the United States to see what was being done in the other novitiates. Predovich replied emphatically that this was precisely what he did not want to do. He did not want help in perpetuating the old pattern. He did spend two days at Colombiere with the then master of novices for purposes of general orientation. As Predovich recalled the experience, he gave the orientation only half his attention, if that much. The whole structure seemed to him an endless amount of complex legislation about things of little importance.

When he came to Colombiere as master of novices in the fall of 1963, he had prepared the first ten days of the thirty-day retreat and little else. During the retreat he prepared a total of 180 talks and assembled many visual aids. He never used the material again; indeed, he never opened the boxes again. In subsequent retreats, he moved further and further in the direction of individually directed retreats. He never attained this goal because the number of novices was too great, but each year he moved closer to it.

After the first thirty-day retreat, many changes began to occur in the novitiate. Some of the changes were initiated by the master and some by the novices with the encouragement of the master. Some changes were formally announced, while others "just happened". An existing regulation while remaining on the books would no longer be enforced, or a new mode of acting by a few individuals would go unchecked and be adopted by many. There was never a blueprint. Father Predovich handled problems as they arose, and his usual norm was "common sense".

A typical example is the way in which the change was made in the traditional requirement that all the novices read the three volumes of Rodriguez (see p. 245). In class one day, a novice raised his hand and asked whether any other reading could be substituted for Rodriguez. The new master replied that as far as he was concerned no one need read Rodriguez. Reading schedules could be worked out according to the needs of each individual. As Father Predovich recalled, a few of the second-year novices—

possibly loyal to their first master and trusting in tradition—continued to read the work, but the first-year novices largely abandoned it.

At the annual meeting of the novice masters, he described some of the changes he was introducing into the novitiate program, such as the elimination of the requirement to read Rodriguez. When asked by what authority he had made this change, he replied, "It was simply common sense." This method of direct action, of voting with one's feet, was characteristic of the revolution of the 1960s. Characteristic also was the final result. Since then, all the novitiates have abandoned the required reading of Rodriguez.

Almost from the start, the new master of novices dropped the practice of explaining the Rules of the Summary and the Common Rules. Instead he provided the novices with mimeographed copies of those parts of the Constitutions that were available in English. This practice was adopted eventually in all the novitiates, especially after the George Ganss translation appeared in book form.

The cassock never entirely disappeared during Father Predovich's time. The provincial wanted it retained at least for the liturgy and in the dining room. But Father Predovich invented the "mini-cassock" (a light-weight black jacket), which he allowed to be used in place of the cassock in most situations. He also allowed a wider use of the Roman collar and suit. The net result was a steadily diminishing use of the cassock.

He dropped the use of the public culpa because a psychologist friend told him that damage might be done by such a procedure. For the same reason he replaced the "exercise of modesty" (mutual public correction) by a form of encounter-group action. He discontinued the regular use of the chain and discipline. If any of the novices used them at all, they did so privately and at their own discretion. The traditional use of titles was discontinued—whether by a formal change in the regulation or by simply ignoring it, I do not know—and the novices began to use first names instead.

The new master discontinued the practice of the official visitor during spiritual exercises. He did so by the simple expedient of not appointing anyone to the function. He also discontinued the censorship of mail—again not by a formal change of rules but simply by delivering the mail to the novices unopened and providing a box into which they could put outgoing mail sealed. Likewise, the previous ban on smoking was allowed to lapse by simply not mentioning it. The former strict daily order of the novitiate became ever more open and included flexible individual times for rising and retiring.

In his semi-annual letters to Rome, Father Predovich reported such changes in guarded, general terms "so as to avoid making issues of them". However, he did have at least the tacit approval of his provincial, who knew all that was going on. Some friction in the house did arise because the novices were permitted more freedom than was allowed the juniors. This involved nearly everything—the daily order, clothes, silence, smoking, even beer. The juniors became restless and protested against being held to the traditional restrictions. There could, of course, be only one outcome to this situation of tension. If the provincial did not require Father Predovich to change, the juniorate would have to change. And it gradually did. Though the rector, minister, and many of the teaching faculty in the juniorate resented this unilaterally enforced alteration of house customs, others on the faculty welcomed and promoted the changes in the juniorate.

Some Predovich Positions

Father Predovich had a general aversion to legislation as a means to regulate ascetical practices, such as the ban on smoking. He warmly defended the position, which he attributed to Karl Rahner, that religious obedience does not properly extend to many matters covered by rules in the past. The public reading of Saint Ignatius' Letter on Obedience was dropped shortly after Father

Predovich's arrival at Colombiere. He recommended to his novices that they should not read the letter until it could be taken up in class and explained in its context.

I remarked to Father Predovich that a particular concept of law seemed to underlie his methods of achieving change. He nodded, grinned, and said, *"Epieikeia."* I am not sure that Father Predovich was acquainted with the distinction between the Suarezian and Thomistic version of *epieikeia,* but it was clear that he worked with the latter form. His concern was not whether a superior knowing all the circumstances would approve of his (Predovich's) going against an existing rule; his concern was whether the rule made sense in the circumstances as he, Predovich, saw them. If a rule was not reasonable, according to his discernment, he simply ignored it. He was intensely convinced of the correctness of his discernment—in this respect, also, faithfully reflecting a characteristic quality of the 1960s.

His individualistic approach was applied to many regulations which other superiors at that time took very seriously. He offered as one example the requirement in canon law that the "canonical year" must have a certain number of days to assure the validity of vows. Because such complex regulations got in the way of more important objectives, he explained, he gave them only passing attention.

Father Predovich rejected the traditional position that the life of the counsels was in some prior, objective sense superior to its alternative. Each way of life had its advantages and disadvantages; it was the task of the individual to discern to which way of life he was being called. He remarked that his own concept of a religious vocation had changed as much as had his concept of the "Church".

He said that he taught his novices the relativity of the Spiritual Exercises. He reminded them that Ignatius was working out of his own environment of the later Renaissance and must now be reinterpreted in terms of the twentieth century. "The Spiritual Exercises, like the Bible, must be demythologized."

Father Predovich was closely connected with the famous discussion of the Third Way at the Santa Clara Conference in 1967. He was the sole survivor of a small committee of four who drew up the final statement on the Third Way. The other members were Richard Braun, Giles Milhaven, and Felix Cardegna, all of whom later left the Society and married.

In the short time I had to examine the notes he had prepared for the first thirty-day retreat at Colombiere, I concentrated on the Kingdom meditation and its oblation.[2] I had observed that the way the oblation of the Kingdom was treated in a retreat was a usually reliable indication of the retreat master's general psychological-ascetical approach. Father Predovich gave four talks on the Kingdom meditation. On the whole, the notes looked very interesting and attractive. They made considerable use of his background in psychology. But none of the four talks touched on the oblation at all. When I asked him about its omission, he replied that it was a rare novice who could distinguish such fine points in the Spiritual Exercises. Here, as well as in the meditation on the three degrees of humility, he contented himself with presenting the general thrust of the meditation. As a student of Carl Rogers, he might have found distasteful the negative emphasis in these meditations.

Halfway through Father Predovich's term in office an event occurred which he considered to provide the strongest kind of support for the general direction in which he had turned the novitiate. This was General Congregation 31 (May 1965 to November 1966), which was unmistakably affected by the prevalent spirit of change. More postulates for alterations in the Society's life were received by this congregation than had been received by all previous congregations combined. The decrees of the congregation itself (see those quoted earlier on pp. 40–41) clearly reflected the spirit of change. He especially liked the decree which said, "New experiments . . . ought to be prudently and boldly pursued" (Dec. 8.14).

---

[2] In making the "oblation", the retreatant asks to be "chosen" (Ignatius' term) for a life of humiliations and poverty. This is explicitly described as something greater than merely "offering one's whole self for labor".

A Final Glance

Father Predovich was replaced as master in 1969, after six years in office. I do not know all the circumstances of the change. He himself had always contended that no master of novices should remain in the post longer than six years. Also, the Chicago and Detroit novitiates were about to amalgamate and he had expressed disapproval of the move.[3] At any rate, a new director (no longer "master") was chosen to launch the new combined novitiate.

The career of Nicholas Predovich is a window onto the larger Jesuit revolution of the 1960s in a number of ways. This microcosm resembles that larger world in its objectives, its methods, and its results. As master of novices, he sought to redress the balance between the individual and the institution, between liberty and law, between the relative and the absolute, between the secular and the sacred—and always in favor of the first of each pair. He used the methods of direct action, confrontation, openness, and publicity, and he relied heavily on personal discernment and the Thomistic *epieikeia*. He gained most of his immediate objectives, and he lived to see the patterns he favored become common in all the novitiates. At the end, he expressed some doubt of the final fruits (p. 260).

[3] Further, his record in keeping novices had become not very different from the record of the man he replaced. In the academic year of 1968–69, of the eight novices who entered the Detroit novitiate, only two were left to begin the second year of novitiate. Finally, doubts were beginning to surface regarding the efficacy of his methods. At a meeting of the Chicago Province Novitiate Committee (May 3–4, 1968), the conclusion was reached that "the training under Father Predovich is deficient in spiritual depth".

APPENDIX 3

GRAND COTEAU: CALENDAR OF CHANGE

Changes in the New Orleans novitiate can be followed in a series of "Novitiate Directives" announcements made each year and put on the novitiate bulletin board. The alterations in this document provide a convenient example of the gradual diffusion of change. In general, Grand Coteau changed later and more slowly than the other novitiates.

1956

In 1956, before the changes had begun, the novitiate directives included such detailed instructions as the following:

> On rising in the morning, beds are not to be made but the covers thrown back for airing. After breakfast the beds should be neatly arranged. On Wednesday and Saturday they should be completely stripped, and mattresses turned, before being made up. During the Ember Days, mattresses and pillows are taken outside for sunning. The Beadle posts a reminder to this effect at the appointed times.

> While waiting for the beginning of conference or class, the novices stand behind their chairs. As soon as the one conducting the exercise enters, all books should be closed. In general, when

one is spoken to, or speaks, he should rise and stand behind his chair.

The use of first names is not permitted in the novitiate. In referring to one another, the novice should prefix the title "carissime" to the last name.

Novices spend ten minutes in preparing for the weekly confession. A five minute thanksgiving should follow the confession.

Novices may not cross their feet or legs in any manner. The posture should always manifest a calm composure and proper conduct becoming a religious.

Should Rev. Father Rector enter or leave the refectory during the reading, the reader should stop until the Superior has seated himself or has left the refectory.

The library is not to be used as a reading room.

It is strictly forbidden to enter the cubicle of another novice. Any necessary talking must be done at the entrance.

Novices may write home every two weeks, and on special occasions, like birthdays and so forth. Letters of a purely social measure are simply not permitted.

It is quite improper for young ladies to visit novices. An exceptionally weighty reason alone could justify this.

The discipline is taken on Monday and Friday. The chain is worn on Wednesday and Saturday. If one feels that he can profit by a more frequent use of the chain and discipline, he should consult Father Master about the matter.

The cassock is to be worn at all times unless the contrary is explicitly stated. . . . It is our ordinary form of attire and helps much to remind us of what we are by profession, namely, men consecrated and dedicated to Christ's special service.

Even before the candidate reached the novitiate, he was prepared for life there by a set of directives which contained such instructions as the following:

From the very beginning of the novitiate, every novice should convince himself of the fact that he is learning to practice poverty according to the mind of the Society. . . . Shaving lotions, hair tonic, hair oil, face creams, and so forth, are not permitted for use in the novitiate. . . . Generally speaking, the less we use of anything, the better will true Jesuit poverty be practiced. . . . We are in religion to strive after perfection; therefore our standard must be that of the Cross, not that of the world.

1967

The novitiate directives of 1967 still have most of the traditional approach. The tone is that of a father talking to a young boy. Directions are spelled out in detail. Every contingency is anticipated and carefully prepared for in advance.

There is still a fixed rising time, cassocks are worn, and mail is inspected. Visits to the Blessed Sacrament are made at regular times.

1968

The 1968 novitiate directives have a different tone. They are more like guidelines than specific detailed instructions. However, except for a page on "outside apostolic work", the substance of the directives is much the same. All lights are to be out by 11:00 P.M., and the rising time for all novices is 6:00 A.M.

The novices have access to newspapers and to television for newscasts. Other programs are available only with special permission ("T.V. permissions should not be presumed"). But mail is now sent out sealed; that is, it is no longer inspected.

The directions regarding visitors are cut by one half, and the exhortation regarding work assignments is reduced to the simple reminder, "Personal responsibility requires that during visits replacements for work assignments be obtained in advance."

1969

The novitiate directives of 1969 move further in the same directions. Now they decree, "No one should stay up in the evening beyond midnight; on Friday night, however, those who wish may stay up until 1:30." Rising time is still 6:00 A.M. except on Saturday and Sunday, when the novices may sleep until 8:00. Advice but not specific directions is offered for watching television. The use of the cassock is now required only of those who are serving in liturgical functions in the main chapel. However, "novice clerics" (black trousers, black tie, white shirt) are suggested for Mass, dinner and visits to town.

1972

Novitiate directives of 1972 continue to simplify, with less explanation and fewer exhortations. "Each individual has the opportunity for eating out or entertainment one evening a month." There are no prescriptions regarding dress. Each novice is allowed to make a five-day home visit during the second-year novitiate. The only restriction on watching television is "after noon and before 11:00 P.M.". Regarding retiring time, the directives merely say, "It is recommended that no one stay up past midnight on class days."

1973

In 1973, the directives still specify rising time at 6:00 A.M. except on Saturday and Sunday. The "monthly entertainment budget for each novice" is specified as limited by a maximum of $5.00. The possibility of a novice having smoking permission is recognized. "All visits, except those from local people, should be approved by Father Socius." The exception is another significant change.

APPENDIX 4

JOSEPH O'ROURKE:
QUINTESSENTIAL SIXTIES REBEL

Joseph F. O'Rourke embodied most of the distinguishing characteristics of the 1960s. Since he exhibited these characteristics in
their most developed forms, he cannot be considered typical in
the sense of average; but principles come clearest in strong cases,
and his history illustrates effectively what made the young Jesuit
of the 1960s different. In him the lines of the times were written
large: the independence that felt free, even obliged, to question
nearly everything; a suspicion of authority and a rejection of its
attempts to bind life within rules; the celebration of life leading to
its enjoyment in any form that did not injure others; a strong
desire for warm, personal relationships with both men and women;
an active concern for the poor and the powerless, shown in a
constant activity of protest against existing institutions, the unfail-
ing mark of the early stages of a revolution.

Joseph O'Rourke was the only child of a widowed mother,
being born two days after his father's death.[1] When he entered
the Society of Jesus in 1958, he was nineteen years old, energetic,
and a natural leader. He had been class president six times. He was
the beadle at Shrub Oak. O'Rourke described the position: "I held
the top house job, which was like president of the student body —

---

[1] The account of his early years is taken from a short autobiographical
sketch, written while he was still a Jesuit and included in a collection entitled
These Priests Stay: The American Catholic Clergy in Crisis (Wilkes 1973). All
subsequent page numbers in this appendix refer to the same source.

really it was more a combination union steward and prison trusty —
and I'd have to go in every morning at nine-thirty and ask
permission for various things for the student body. Totally useless.
Ask for this, no; ask for that, no. Anyway, we finally got smart
and started to use leverage on him [the rector] by proposing
things that looked pretty simple and irrefutable on the surface but
which had larger ramifications. Besides, when things were turned
down we began to go ahead and do them anyway" (pp. 174–75).
During regency he was chosen by his community, over any of the
priests, to represent it at a province assembly.[2] During theology
he was actively supported by his fellow Jesuits on several crucial
occasions, and when he was eventually dismissed, his Jesuit community in New York filed a formal appeal against the dismissal.
He was definitely a leader, and he could always count on some
community recognition and support.

For his novitiate, he was sent to Plattsburgh and, given his
temperament, was fortunate to have as his novice director Andrew
Brady, whom O'Rourke called "kind of a breakthrough liberal"
(p. 172). For his philosophy, he was sent to Shrub Oak. He was
there during its most disturbed days and did his part to loosen the
traditional restrictions. He narrates how on one occasion he and
another scholastic "borrowed" the house truck and drove into
town where they visited with a woman from whom they were
taking a lifesaving course and also with a Maryknoll friend: "So
we went over, had a few drinks with the woman, went to a free
Maryknoll movie, and then came back to the salt mine, feeling all
the better for our little escapade" (p. 177).

The escapade had an unexpected ending: "We had electric
garage doors, so I hopped out in the dark and pressed the button
as Dex was driving this van slowly forward with the lights off. He
went in too quickly and hit the door with the top of the truck and
tore hell out of it." He describes the penance that was imposed but

---

[2] A magazine article describing the Jesuits in New York City after their
move from Woodstock (Wills 1972) finds space for three pictures of O'Rourke;
no one else is accorded this much attention.

concludes, "Robin Hood couldn't take all that too seriously, but we could go along with some of the things that made superiors happy" (p. 177).

His regency years began at Canisius College (Buffalo, New York): "And there I really launched into community action work, which would lead up to the first of three times that the Jesuits tried to launch me out of the Society. I developed a whole bunch of community action programs that eventually had 10 percent of the campus working in something" (p. 178). This was in addition to his work as teacher: "I still loved teaching, getting into the heads of these kids, talking about Sartre or Frantz Fanon and giving them some sense of self-worth and freedom so that, no matter what Sister Perpetual Menopause told them back when, they knew they did count and had to make their life decisions seriously" (pp. 178–79).

Normally he would have been advanced to theology after three years of regency, but superiors were uncertain of his vocation and assigned him to a fourth year of teaching. He remarks, "When my peers heard about it, there was a whole flurry of letter writing" (p. 179). But the decision held, and he did a fourth year of teaching at a high school. While at the high school, he persuaded the rector of the school (not rector of the community) to run for the Democratic National Convention in 1968. The trustees of the school, however, had the rector in for a meeting and persuaded him to withdraw. At the end of his fourth year of teaching (1968), O'Rourke was approved for theology.

From the beginning it was clear that study and social action would be in conflict: "By the time I hit Woodstock, Maryland, for my years of theology, seminary was a less important thing to me, and action, doing something, was primary. . . . I picked up old friendships with guys that felt the same way" (p. 181). True to 1960s values, these friendships were of predominant importance:

> With the eruptions in the church and society going on outside and this senseless life still perpetuated inside, it really drove us together. There was a big heavy interpersonal thing going on,

men feeling themselves out in terms of deeper human emotions, getting in touch with each other now that the system had lost its power. It's really incredible that all good religious don't turn homosexual as they explore the real meaning of interpersonal community with each other (p. 176).

In March 1967, the "D.C. Nine" was born. O'Rourke and eight other people (seven men, two women) walked into Dow Chemical, the napalm maker, and threw the company's files out of the windows: "We were tossed into jail for eight days and a lot of my peers came to visit" (p. 182). His peers also called a public meeting at the theologate to support him when he was threatened with punitive action by his superiors.

During his final year at Woodstock preparing for ordination, he did very little studying: "We didn't really want to go back to school at Woodstock; we wanted to get out on the road and organize. I made some sounds about my studies, took an exam or two, but for the most part I avoided the whole scene and spent a lot of the next six months with Phil Berrigan" (p. 183). (Philip Berrigan was still a member of his religious order, the Josephites, at that time.) Despite his weak academic preparation, he was approved for ordination: "Some friendly priests were part of an examining board, and we more or less rapped for a few hours and they passed me" (p. 184).

O'Rourke had a long and colorful history of relations with women. His editor recalls, "He feels to this day that it was no mean accomplishment to have three women (his mother was not one) weep when he decided to go into the seminary" (pp. 169–70). O'Rourke had difficulties with both the principle and practice of celibacy. Just two days before ordination he was grilled by his superior regarding some statements made the day previous to a group of scholastics.

Everything he quoted back to me was substantially what I believe. Being for optional celibacy notionally is not enough, for even the discussion of celibacy and its alternatives couldn't go on until each priest said to himself and said in public, Yes, I'm sexual; I'm doing it; I'm relating sexually, and these are the real religious problems I'm experiencing. . . . I told him I had no problems about religious men having sexual relations before ordination and I wouldn't have them after (p. 185).

O'Rourke reports, "That seemed to satisfy him so he didn't stop the ordination" (ibid.).

Ordination, in 1971, was the occasion of another action. O'Rourke and Anthony Meyer, after giving assurances that they would cause no disturbance, felt obliged in conscience, nevertheless, to use the occasion to make a protest against war. "At the time when we were supposed to give the cardinal [Terrence Cooke, the ordaining prelate] the kiss of peace, Tony [Meyer] went right over to the microphone and said he was not going to do it until Cooke resigned his military vicariate, stopped his investments in military contractors and his whole complicity with the government in this immoral war." O'Rourke then joined Meyer in the protest (p. 186).

After ordination, his priestly life consisted mainly of various public actions, protests against existing institutions. He summarized his view:

What basically I have to do this year as a priest within this institution called the church is create collision in the ruling class—a good Marxist view—to get the establishment institutions hassling one another, to create some relief from power for the poor. . . . I think an accurate reading of the Gospel would make Jesus a nonviolent revolutionist and we have to train people in that image (p. 192).

On three different occasions during his years of formation, superiors had raised the possibility of dismissal. As O'Rourke continued his life of actions, some of them involving the breaking of Church laws—for instance, officiating at a marriage for which the bishop had refused permission—superiors finally took the threatened step and dismissed him. O'Rourke thereupon (in 1974) appealed to Rome.

His appeal was long, carefully crafted, persuasive. Its mood was quiet, respectful. It sought chiefly to establish that he had followed all prescribed rules regarding consultation with superiors and had not directly violated a command of obedience. It attacked no one and asked only that he be told where he had erred so that he could correct the error. It differed so much from the autobiography (footnote 1) that the curious reader is inclined to say: "Will the real Joseph O'Rourke please stand up?"

His local community, headed by Frederic O'Connor, filled a formal statement supporting his appeal, but the appeal was nevertheless denied. O'Rourke established a new life: he married, fathered a child, and became an active supporter of the pro-choice movement.

APPENDIX 5

JESUITS WHO LEFT THE ORDER

The following are names of Jesuits who appear in this history and who later left the order. The numbers after the names indicate the page or pages on which each name appears.

Albertson, James S., 24, 70
Ambrogi, Thomas E., 127–28
Bourg, Carroll J., 70, 209n
Braun, Richard C., 70, 209n, 221n, 373
Brubaker, John, 88n
Callahan, William R., 80n
Cardegna, Felix F., 70, 88, 172, 237, 373
Carter, Robert, 88n *of NY catalogue*
Cooke, Bernard J., 70, 74–75, 158–59, 289
Cummings, Robert, 88n
Curran, Thomas M., 80n, 81–84
DeVault, Joseph J., 70, 104n
Dolan, James, 88n
Faase, Thomas Philip, 97n
Fallon, Timothy, 321
Fargione, Michael R., 356
Fledderman, Harry T., 70, 327, 335
Healy, John, 88n
Hilsdale, Paul, 89–90
Johann, Robert O., 288–89, 300
Jonsen, Albert, 24
L'Heureux, John, 146, 179–80, 182, 303

COLLOPY, BARTHOLOMEW, J. 133n

APPENDIX 6

STAGES OF TRADITIONAL
JESUIT FORMATION

The course of formation described here is the course followed in
the United States during the period preceding Vatican II. Exceptions to this course could be, and were, made, but they were
relatively few in the traditional period. The course consisted of
the following six stages:

1. Novitiate

A two-year period consisting of the "canonical year" established
by canon law plus an additional year voluntarily added by Jesuits
and by many other religious orders. At the end of the second year,
the novice pronounced his perpetual vows of poverty, chastity,
and obedience and moved on to the next stage.

2. Juniorate

A two-year period of studies in language and literature—chiefly
in Latin, Greek, and English—along with a course or two in
ancient (Roman or Greek) history. Entirely separate from the
novices in studies and living quarters, the juniors were on the
same campus and with the novices made up a single community.

3. Philosophate

A three-year period devoted chiefly to philosophy but including some courses in mathematics and science. The philosophers were entirely separate from the novitiate/juniorate complex.

4. Regency

A period of teaching, usually in high schools and usually for three years. For the first time, the class was not together but was scattered among the Jesuit schools. The class reassembled, however, during the summers for the group vacations and the group retreat.

5. Theologate

This was a four-year period during which the now not-so-young Jesuit studied theology and practiced the skills of the priestly ministry. Of these two activities, the first occupied about nine-tenths of the Jesuit's time. The theologate was a completely separate institution, usually rural in location. The student was ordained after the third year but continued to reside and study at the theologate for a fourth year.

6. Tertianship

This was a one-year return to the life of the novitiate, with its emphasis on prayer, penance, and spiritual ministry. The tertianship was usually a completely separate institution.

If the young man entered from high school, as most did, at about eighteen years of age, he would be about thirty-three years of age when his Jesuit formation was completed.

REFERENCES

Abbott, Walter M., S.J., ed. 1966. *Documents of Vatican II.* New York: New Century Publishers, Inc.

Arrupe, Pedro, S.J. 1970. Father General's first allocution, Congregation of Procurators. Rome. Mimeo.

Ascetical Institute. 1960. Problems in Jesuit asceticism. In *Proceedings of the Ascetical Institute,* vol. 1. Ed. M. J. Buckley and B. L. Maloney. Los Gatos, Calif.: Alma College.

———. 1962. Institute on Jesuit maturity. In *Proceedings of Ascetical Institute on Jesuit maturity,* vol. 3. Los Gatos, Calif.: Alma College.

Becker, Joseph M., S.J. 1977. Changes in U.S. Jesuit membership, 1958–1975: A symposium. In *Studies in the spirituality of Jesuits,* vol. 11, nos. 1 and 2. St. Louis: American Assistancy Seminar.

Biever, Bruce F., S.J., and Thomas M. Gannon, S.J., eds. 1969. *General survey of the Society of Jesus, North American Assistancy.* 5 vols. Chicago: Argus Press.

Calvez, Jean-Yves, S.J. 1975–76. A critical appraisal of the preparation for the Jesuits' Thirty-Second General Congregation. *Review for Religious* 34:936–48.

Campion, Donald, ed. 1975. *G.C. Bulletin,* no. 9 (January 7).

Chicago Province Planning Office. 1970. The better choice and promotion of ministries. In *Phase VI: Task force proposals on spiritual renewal.* Chicago: Chicago Province of the Society of Jesus.

Clancy, Thomas H., S.J. 1976. *An introduction to Jesuit Life: The Constitutions and history through 435 years.* St. Louis: Institute of Jesuit Sources.

Committee for the Evaluation of Weston School of Theology. 1971. Report on evaluation of Weston School of Theology. Weston, Mass.

Committee of Spiritual Review (C.S.R.). 1964–68. Minutes of the Committee of Spiritual Review. Mimeo.

Committee on Theologates. 1965. Minutes of Committee on Theologates meeting, April 18–20.

The Critic. 1975. See "Just before the council, mother."

Curia of the Society of Jesus. 1931. *Epitome Instituti Societatis Iesu* 2nd ed. Rome.

———. 1969. *Acta Romana Societatis Iesu.* vol. 15. Rome.

De Guibert, Joseph, S.J. 1964. *The Jesuits: Their spiritual doctrine and practice.* Trans. William J. Young, S.J.; ed. George E. Ganss, S.J. Chicago: Loyola University Press.

De Lubac, Henri, S.J. 1987. *Paradoxes of Faith.* San Francisco: Ignatius Press.

Documents of the Thirty-First and Thirty-Second General Congregations of the Society of Jesus. 1977. St. Louis: Institute of Jesuit Sources.

Duffner, Andrew J., S.J. 1972. Dean outlines new curriculum. *The Berkeley Jesuit* 3 (no. 2, Spring): 23–24.

Eastern Inter-Province Committee on Formation. 1970. Minutes of the Eastern Inter-Province Committee on Formation, January 22. Mimeo.

Edwards, John, S.J. 1969. Foreword. In *Studies in the spirituality of Jesuits,* vol. 1, no. 1. St. Louis: American Assistancy Seminar.

The English novitiate in 1806. 1956. In *Woodstock Letters,* vol. 85. Woodstock, Md.: Woodstock College Press.

Esenther, Keith J., S.J. 1977. *A report on the Chicago Province Planning, the congresses and assemblies, 1968–1976.* Chicago: Chicago Province of the Society of Jesus.

Faase, Thomas Philip, S.J. 1976. Making the Jesuits more modern. Ph.D. diss., Cornell University.

Fitzgerald, Paul. 1984. *The governance of Jesuit colleges in the United States, 1920–1970.* Notre Dame: University of Notre Dame Press.

Flaherty, Daniel L., S.J. 1978. Reflections on a golden jubilee. Letter from provincial to Chicago Province Jesuits upon 50th anniversary of Chicago province. Chicago Province Archives. Mimeo.

Flaherty, Daniel, S.J., Vincent O'Keefe, S.J., and Gerald Sheahan, S.J. 1991. The final days of Fr. Arrupe. *National Jesuit News,* March, Supplement: 7.

Flannery, Austin, O.P., ed. 1975. *Vatican Council II: The conciliar and post-conciliar documents.* Collegeville, Minn.: Liturgical Press.

Galbraith, Kenneth J., S.J. 1972. Toward discerning the Spirit among us. State of the province. Letter from provincial to Oregon Jesuits. Mimeo.

Ganss, George E., S.J. 1966. The central issue in the decree on the tertianship. In *Woodstock Letters,* vol. 95. Woodstock, Md.: Woodstock College.

——, trans. 1970. *Constitutions of the Society of Jesus.* St. Louis: Institute of Jesuit Sources.

——, ed. 1976. *Conferences on the chief decrees of the Jesuit General Congregation XXXII.* St. Louis: Institute of Jesuit Sources.

Garraghan, Gilbert J., S.J. 1983–84 [1938]. *The Jesuits of the middle United States.* 3 vols. Chicago: Loyola University Press.

G.C. 31 and G.C. 32. See *Documents of the Thirty-First and Thirty-Second General Congregations of the Society of Jesus.*

Hebblethwaite, Peter. 1984. *Pope John XXIII: Shepherd of the modern world.* Garden City, N.Y.: Image Books.

Herberg, Will. 1974. Getting back to Vatican II. *National Review* 366–68.

Hitchcock, James. 1984. *The Pope and the Jesuits.* New York: National Committee of Catholic Laymen.

Hyer, Marjorie. 1983. How our war-blessing Catholic bishops got religion on nukes. *Washington Post* (May 1): B–1, B–4.

Institute on Jesuit Asceticism. 1961. Problems in Jesuit asceticism. *Proceedings of the Institute on Jesuit asceticism.* St. Mary's, Kans.: St. Mary's College.

Institute on the Jesuit Theologate. 1964. *Proceedings of the Institute on the Jesuit Theologate.* Weston, Mass.: Weston College.

Inter-Faculty Program Inquiry. 1966. Rockhurst report. In *Woodstock Letters,* vol. 95. Woodstock, Md.: Woodstock College Press.

Jurich, James P., S.J., ed. 1966a. The 31st General Congregation: The first session. In *Woodstock Letters,* vol. 95. Woodstock, Md.: Woodstock College.

——, ed. 1966b. The 31st General Congregation: Between the sessions. In *Woodstock Letters,* vol. 95. Woodstock, Md.: Woodstock College.

——, ed. 1967a. The 31st General Congregation: Letters from the first session. In *Woodstock Letters,* vol. 96. Woodstock, Md.: Woodstock College.

——, ed. 1967b. The 31st General Congregation: Letters from the first session, part 2. In *Woodstock letters,* vol. 96. Woodstock, Md.: Woodstock College.

——, ed. 1969. The 31st General Congregation: Letters from the second session. In *Woodstock letters,* vol. 98. Woodstock, Md.: Woodstock College.

Just before the council, mother! 1975. *The Critic* 34:6–24.

Kelly, Justin S., S.J. 1966. Toward a new theology. *Woodstock Letters,* vol. 95. Woodstock, Md.: Woodstock College.

———. 1968. The Santa Clara Conference: Reflection and reminiscence. In *Woodstock Letters,* vol. 97. Woodstock, Md.: Woodstock College.

Kennedy, Eugene C., M.M., and Victor J. Heckler. 1972. *The Catholic priest in the United States: Psychological investigations.* Washington, D.C.: United States Catholic Conference.

Klausner, Samuel S. 1976. A review of "The Catholic priest in the United States: Psychological investigations". *Journal for the Scientific Study of Religion* 15.

Lee, James Michael, and Louis J. Putz, C.S.C., eds. 1965. *Seminary education in a time of change.* Notre Dame, Ind.: Fides Publishers, Inc.

L'Heureux, John. 1967. *Picnic in Babylon: A Jesuit priest's journal,* 1963–1966. New York: Macmillan Company.

Lombardi, Riccardo, S.J. N.d. *Communitarian dimensions of Ignatius.* Silver Spring: Movement for a Better World.

Marty, Martin. 1975. What went wrong. *The Critic* 34 (Fall): 49–53.

McLeod, Frederick, S.J. 1970. Letter to New England province. Boston, Mass. Mimeo.

———. 1973. A new twist of the kaleidoscope. *SJNEws* (March): 12–13.

McNaspy, C. J., S.J. 1967. Tomorrow's Jesuits. *America* (September 2): 222–24.

———. 1968. *Change not changes.* New York: Paulist Press.

McSweeney, William. 1980. *Roman Catholicism: The search for relevance.* New York: St. Martin's Press, Inc.

Murray, Robert E., S.J. 1969. Report of the president of Bellarmine School of Theology to province consultors.

New Orleans province. 1956–73. Novitiate directives. New Orleans.

O'Malley, John W., S.J. 1971. Reform, historical consciousness, and Vatican II's *aggiornamento*. *Theological Studies* 32:573–601.

———. 1983a. Developments, reforms, and two great reformations: Towards a historical assessment of Vatican II. *Theological Studies* 44.

———. 1983b. The Jesuits' Congregation: A historical view. *America* (November 19): 308.

Padberg, John W., S.J. 1974. The general congregations of the Society of Jesus: A brief survey of their history. In *Studies in the spirituality of Jesuits,* vol. 6, nos. 1 and 2. St. Louis: American Assistancy Seminar.

———. 1983. The Society true to itself: A brief history of the 32nd General Congregation of the Society of Jesus. In *Studies in the spirituality of Jesuits,* vol. 15, nos. 3 and 4. St. Louis: American Assistancy Seminar.

Pennington, M. Basil, O.C.S.O. 1987. *Thomas Merton, brother monk: The quest for true freedom.* San Francisco: Harper & Row.

Preparatory Commission for the General Congregation 1972. Document 5. Rome: Curia of the Society of Jesus.

———. 1973. Document 12. Rome: Curia of the Society of Jesus.

Reese, Thomas J. 1984. The selection of bishops. *America* (August 25): 65–72.

Roccasalvo, Joseph F., S.J. 1965. Harlem diary. In *Woodstock Letters,* vol. 94. Woodstock, Md.: Woodstock College.

Rock, Leo, S.J. 1973. The California province novitiate: What we do and why. Typescript report to California Jesuits.

Rynne, Xavier [peud.]. 1968. *Vatican Council II.* New York: Farrar, Straus, and Giroux.

Sanks, T. Howland, S.J. 1984. Education for ministry since Vatican II. *Theological Review* 45:481–500.

Santa Clara Conference. 1967. *Proceedings of the Conference on the Total Development of the Jesuit Priest.* 6 vols. Santa Clara, Calif.: University of Santa Clara.

S.C.C. 1967. See Santa Clara Conference.

Schillebeeckx, Edward H., O.P. 1963. *The layman in the Church and other essays.* Staten Island, N.Y.: Alba House.

———. 1967. *The real achievement of Vatican II.* New York: Sheed & Ward, Ltd.

Students at Woodstock College. 1967. Report on student difficulties. Woodstock, Md. Typescript.

Tavard, George H. 1965. *The Church tomorrow.* New York: Herder and Herder.

Toner, Jules J., S.J. 1974. The deliberation that started the Jesuits. In *Studies in the spirituality of Jesuits,* vol. 6. St. Louis: American Assistancy Seminar.

Wagoner, Walter D. 1966. *The Seminary—Protestant and Catholic.* New York: Sheed & Ward.

Weston College Self-Study Committee. Report. 1965. Weston, Mass. Mimeo.

Weston Self-Study Committee. 1965. Report on Weston School of Theology. Mimeo.

Wilkes, Paul, ed. 1973. *These priests stay: The American clergy in crisis.* New York: Simon and Schuster.

Wills, Gary. 1971. The new Jesuits vs. the unheavenly city. New York.

Wynn, Wilton, 1988. *Keepers of the keys: John XXIII, Paul VI, and John Paul II — Three who changed the Church.* New York: Random House.

Yzermans, Vincent A., Msgr., ed. 1967. *American participation in the Second Vatican Council.* New York: Sheed & Ward.

NAME INDEX

SUBJECT INDEX

Academics, 31–35, 40–41; in
new collegiate program,
275–91; in new novitiate,
199–216, 231–35; in new
theologate, 103–5, 110–11,
143–61; in traditional
collegiate program, 261–
68; in traditional novitiate,
194–99; in traditional
philosophate, 197; in traditional theologate, 101–2, 110,
139–42
Aggiornamento, 36, 41, 79; as
objective of Vatican II, 19–
20, 23, 91, 353
Alma College formation
house, 86–87, 255;
academic changes at, 151,
160; Alma Community
Council, 180–81, 185,
191; as generator of
change, 23–30; institutes
at, 25–31, 112–13, 189;
lifestyle changes at, 172,
177–82, 184–87, 189–91;
relocation of, 107–8, 114–15,
124; student participation in
governance at, 105n, 151,
202, 326–28

America, 83, 91n
American Assistancy Seminar
on Jesuit Spirituality, 78
American Association of
Theology Schools, 121, 148
Apostolic activities, 40–41, 74,
195; in collegiate program,
265, 279; field work as, 115,
140, 144, 149; in novitiate,
235–37; in theologate, 171;
theological institute on,
30–35
Arthur D. Little, Inc., 63,
129n
Ascetical Institute (1960), 25–
28, 189
Ascetical Institute (1962), 28–
30
Asceticism, 25–26, 86, 112,
212, *see also* Lifestyle
Auriesville formation house,
343–44
Austin formation house, 348
Authority, 45–46, 53, *see also*
Governance; in collegiate
programs, 300–301; in
new novitiate, 203–4;
in new theologate, 32–35,
158, 171–73, 184–89; in

Sacred Congregation for Religious, 41, 228n

St. Andrew's-on-the-Hudson formation house, 203, 205, 207, *see also* Poughkeepsie formation house; academic changes at, 233–34; relocation of, 224; unrest at, 210

St. Bonifacius formation house, academic changes at, 233–34; relocation of, 220–21, 268–74

St. Louis formation house, 197n; academic changes at, 285; consolidation of, 132–38, 315; relocation of, 268–74

St. Louis University formation house, 139n; academic changes at, 280; and relocation, 107, 109–10, 123–24, 268–74, 315; in traditional system, 264n

St. Mary's College formation house, 326–29; academic changes at, 104–5, 139n, 158–59; as generator of change, 30–31; *Institute on Jesuit Renewal,* 68; lifestyle changes at, 145, 151, 186, 191; and relocation, 107, 109–10, 223n, 315

St. Paul formation house, 220–22

St. Stanislaus formation house,

199, 202, 332–33, *see also* Florissant formation house

St. Thomas College formation house, 222

San Francisco, University of, 124

Santa Barbara formation house, 219–21, 233–34

Santa Clara Conference (1967), 54, 61, 111, 202, 350; and academic changes, 148, 158, 235; on collegiate programs, 266–67, 272; Conference on the Total Development of the Jesuit Priest, 69–77, 169, 275; as generator of change, 69–77, 214; and lifestyle changes, 30, 182, 217, 246n; on novitiates, 208–9, 226, 327; on regency, 327; "Scholastics' Statement on the Attitudes, Ideals, and Expectations of Younger Jesuits", 72–73; on tertianship, 335; on theologates, 106n, 109n, 148, 158, 182, 357; and Third Way, 372–73; and Vatican II, 70, 73

Seattle formation house, 343, 345n

Secular world, 93, 118, 171, 226n, *see also* Outside contacts; field work in, 115, 140, 144, 149; and new collegiate program, 272, 277–79, 281,